"This text more than meets the enduring difficulty of English for theology—namely, the interdisciplinary challenge of navigating both theology and language instruction. The author guides students through the intricacies of both dogmatics and discourse in ways that enable each discipline to reinforce the other. Students will benefit from scaffolded engagement with a range of carefully organized doctrinal loci and will be pushed to bring these doctrines to bear on practical ministry situations. Along the way, students will not only grow in their theological English proficiency, but also come to understand that language is profoundly theological and theology is profoundly communicative. This book both helps to pioneer a field where few resources currently exist and sets a very high standard for other future efforts."

> —**Will Bankston**, coauthor, *Exploring Parables in Luke: Integrated Skills for ESL/EFL Students of Theology*; editor, *Thinking Theologically about Language Teaching*

"Most theological seminaries seek to train students in the use of theological language, particularly in writing academic papers and in their preaching and teaching in the church. Pierce Hibbs has led the program at Westminster Seminary to help those students who have special needs in this area. In his book *Theological English*, he deals not only with the details of English speech and writing, but also with the theological foundations of language itself. He shows how we are able to speak and communicate with each other, because God himself is a speaking being, communicating among his three persons: Father, Son, and Holy Spirit. From this theological perspective, the book moves seamlessly to the details of 'good' speech and writing. In his development of this teaching, Hibbs makes good use of Christian linguists and theologians such as Kenneth Pike and Vern Poythress. I have enjoyed my own communication with him over the years, for his friendship and his clear-eyed perspective on theological issues. This book is much needed, not only for students whose second language is English, but for all who seek to understand language itself as the wonderful divine gift that it is."

> —**John M. Frame**, Professor of Systematic Theology and Philosophy Emeritus, Reformed Theological Seminary, Orlando

"A most welcome one-of-a-kind volume, *Theological English* offers a compelling introduction to theology, while effectively building the reader's mastery of the English language. Though the book is marvelously useful for non-native English speakers, any budding student of theology will profit significantly from the language skills absorbed along this reverent theological pilgrimage. *Tolle lege.*"

> —**David B. Garner**, Associate Professor of Systematic Theology, Vice President for Advancement, Westminster Theological Seminary

"Students of theology around the world will benefit from access to *Theological English: An Advanced Text for ESL Students of Theology*. This volume brings language and content together in ways that help students navigate the linguistic challenges of theological works and provides an introduction to a range of topics such as apologetics, biblical studies, and church history."

> —**Cheri Pierson**, Associate Professor of TESOL, Intercultural Studies, Wheaton College Graduate School

AN ADVANCED ESL TEXT
FOR STUDENTS OF THEOLOGY

THEOLOGICAL
ENGLISH

PIERCE TAYLOR HIBBS *with* **MEGAN REILEY**

PUBLISHING
P.O. BOX 817 • PHILLIPSBURG • NEW JERSEY 08865-0817

Marginal definitions in the reading section of each lesson are taken from *Webster's Third New International Dictionary, Unabridged*, accessed March 2015, http://unabridged.merriam-webster.com.

Unless otherwise indicated, Scripture quotations are from The Holy Bible, English Standard Version®, copyright © 2001 by Crossway, a publishing ministry of Good News Publishers. Used by permission. All rights reserved. ESV Text Edition: 2007.

Scripture quotations marked (NIV) are taken from the Holy Bible, New International Version®, NIV®. Copyright © 1973, 1978, 1984, 2011 by Biblica, Inc.™ Used by permission of Zondervan. All rights reserved worldwide. www.zondervan.com. The "NIV" and "New International Version" are trademarks registered in the United States Patent and Trademark Office by Biblica, Inc.™

Special thanks are due to Megan Reiley, who added reading instructions to this book and provided extensive feedback. Thanks also to Leslie Altena, for her constant support and encouragement, and to the many students whose comments helped to improve the book over several years of classroom use.

ISBN: 978-1-62995-602-2 (casebound)

Printed in the United States of America

For all of the international students at
Westminster Theological Seminary,
past, present, and future.

Contents

Introduction   ix

Unit 1: Who Are We? (Apologetics)

1. Theological English   3
2. The Creator-Creature Distinction   11
3. The Role of Revelation   21

Unit 2: What Is Truth? (Apologetics)

4. Thinking as a Creature   35
5. Thy Word Is Truth   44
6. The Spirit's Testimony   53

Unit 3: What Is Wrong? (Apologetics)

7. Why Details Matter   63
8. The World Awry   73
9. The Mind Awry   81

Unit 4: How Is It Made Right? (Biblical Studies)

10. The Story of Redemption   95
11. Sacrifice and Cleansing   104
12. All Promises Fulfilled   111

Unit 5: Who Is Jesus? (Biblical Studies)

13. The Most Important Question   125
14. The One Who Rose from the Dead   134
15. The One Who Intercedes   142

Unit 6: Do We Still Need the Old Testament? (Biblical Studies)

16. The Place of the Old Testament   153
17. Idols versus the True God   162
18. Christ, the Second Adam   171

Unit 7: Where Have We Been? (Church History)

19. Looking Back   183
20. Looking Further Back   197
21. Looking Forward   206

Unit 8: How Are We Saved? (Systematic Theology)

22. Union with Christ   219
23. Justification   225
24. Sanctification   233

Unit 9: Where Does the Church Fit? (Systematic Theology)

25. The Church and Salvation   251
26. Unity and Division   259
27. The End of the Church   266

Unit 10: How Then Shall We Live? (Practical Theology)

28. Connecting Scripture to Life   279
29. As for the Lord   292
30. Godly Counsel   302

Answer Key   313

Appendix 1: Theological Chart for TE Units   355
Appendix 2: Punctuation   357
Appendix 3: Introductory Theological Texts   361
Index of Subjects and Names   363

Introduction

About the Textbook

In one sense, this textbook is not so special. While it is the product of years of teaching and research in the context of an intensive English program (IEP),[1] it simply attempts to implement the current practices of language learning pedagogy and to use theology as a context for teaching key language skills. The goal of this book, like other EAP (English for Academic Purposes) or ESP (English for Specific Purposes) textbooks,[2] is to teach English effectively and efficiently within a particular setting and for particular students.

However, in another sense, this textbook is quite special for several reasons. First, it is distinctly rooted in the Reformed theological tradition. Thus, the theology you will learn from this text as you improve your English is not a vague or generic form of Christian theology. It aligns with Reformed orthodoxy, as specifically expressed in the Westminster heritage.

Second, this text is written with a few special areas of focus for non-native speakers of English who are interested in theology. Perhaps the most noteworthy areas are an extended focus on advanced grammar for theological purposes and an introduction to, as well as practice within, specific theological genres: apologetics, biblical studies, church history, systematic theology, and practical theology. By practicing grammatical accuracy and precision, students are better equipped to communicate the truth of Scripture to a world desperately in need of the gospel. By studying traits and features of English within the above-mentioned genres, students are more prepared to read, write, listen, and speak theology effectively. Thus, this textbook uniquely serves students by helping them to grow in their expression *and* reception of theological English.

Third, in the "Tasks" in this textbook, we focus on helping students to use theological English to communicate gospel truths.[3] The tasks are meant to give students the opportunity to use the English skills they have acquired in ways that more easily transfer to real-life situations. Real-life situations for theology students, however, are unique. They might require writing an email to a head pastor or a congregant, discussing the gospel with a non-believer, or leading a weekly Bible study. The tasks in this book are thus meant to give theology students practice in the everyday tasks that they will encounter in ministry or teaching settings.

Fourth, the authors of this text have made a conscious decision to build upon principles of language that are informed by Scripture. In other words, we have certain assumptions about what language is and how it functions, and these assumptions affect the way in which we present English. All of these assumptions can be traced back to Scripture directly or indirectly, especially our assumptions that language is Trinitarian. Language can be and has been used to express the truth clearly and powerfully throughout history. The former assumption warrants some explanation.

---

1. For details on the Mastering Theological English (MTE) program, see https://www.wts.edu/programs.

2. For example, Ken Paterson and Roberta Wedge's *Oxford Grammar for EAP: English Grammar and Practice for Academic Purposes* (New York: Oxford University Press, 2013), or the particularly rich resource by Cheri L. Pierson, Lonna J. Dickerson, and Florence R. Scott, *Exploring Theological English: Reading, Vocabulary, and Grammar for ESL/EFL* (Carlisle, Great Britain: Piquant, 2010).

3. In this sense, we are following current practices of CLT (Communicative Language Teaching) and TBLT (Task Based Language Teaching), which are articulated in various ESL pedagogical texts.

Trinitarian Roots of Language

Language is Trinitarian in two senses.[4] First, in a broader sense, we believe that language originates with the Trinitarian, self-communing God of the Bible. From all eternity, the persons of the Godhead have "spoken" to each other in the sense that the Father, Son, and Holy Spirit eternally express love and glory toward one another. The Father loves the Son and shows him all that he does (John 5:20). The Son loves the Father by obeying his commands perfectly, just as he instructs his followers to do (John 14:15, 21, 23). And the Holy Spirit is the bond of personal love between the Father and the Son. In fact, "The Love-life whereby these Three mutually love each other is the Eternal Being Himself. . . . The entire Scripture teaches that nothing is more precious and glorious than the Love of the Father for the Son, and of the Son for the Father, and of the Holy Spirit for both."[5] The same is the case with glory. In John 17:5, Jesus says, "Glorify me in your own presence with the glory that I had with you before the world existed." In the preceding chapter, he proclaimed that the Spirit also glorifies him (John 16:14). Yet, Jesus longs for the Father to glorify him so that he can glorify the Father (John 17:1). And the reason the Son is glorified is that he gives life to all men who are dead in sins and trespasses (Rom. 6:11). While our life is in Christ, this life is none other than "the Spirit of life" (Rom. 8:2, 6), who is the Spirit of Christ (Rom. 8:9). Therefore, we can say that the Spirit shares in the glory of the Son as life-giver.[6]

The divine, perpetual exchange of love and glory is the highest form of communication—the highest form of speech, of language. In short, because "there is—and has been from all eternity—talk, sharing and communication in the innermost life of God,"[7] we need to affirm that language, strictly speaking, is not a human invention; it is a divine gift.[8]

Second, language is Trinitarian in a more specific sense. Language comprises three interlocking subsystems: grammar, phonology, and reference.[9] Many students are familiar with **grammar**, but **phonology** (how words and sentences are spoken) and **reference** (the relationship between words and what they stand for) are also critical. These subsystems are equally important and intersect in a manner analogous to the way in which the persons of the Godhead interlock or "coinhere" with one another.[10] We can associate each of these subsystems in language with a person of the Trinity:

Human purposes using the referential subsystem imitate God's purposes, and more specifically the purposes of God the Father. Human speaking with sound imitates God's utterances, which he utters

---

4. In our assumptions about the Trinitarian nature of language, we are indebted to the work of Vern S. Poythress, especially his *In the Beginning Was the Word: Language—A God-Centered Approach* (Wheaton, IL: Crossway, 2009). But the Trinitarian nature of language has also been recognized by several theologians throughout church history. Another contemporary theologian who draws attention to this is Kevin J. Vanhoozer as seen in his *Is There a Meaning in This Text? The Bible, the Reader, and the Morality of Literary Knowledge* (Grand Rapids, MI: Zondervan, 1998), 455–57. I (Pierce) have also written about this in other places: Pierce Taylor Hibbs, "Closing the Gaps: Perichoresis and the Nature of Language," *Westminster Theological Journal* 78 (2016): 299–322; "Words for Communion," *Modern Reformation* 25, no. 4 (August 2016): 5–8.

5. Abraham Kuyper, *The Work of the Holy Spirit*, trans. Henry De Vries (Chattanooga, TN: AMG, 1995), 542.

6. For details, see Hibbs, "Closing the Gaps: Perichoresis and the Nature of Language."

7. Douglas Kelly, *Systematic Theology: Grounded in Holy Scripture and Understood in Light of the Church*, vol. 1, *The God Who Is: The Holy Trinity* (Ross-shire, Scotland: Mentor, 2008), 487.

8. Poythress, *In the Beginning Was the Word*, 9. See also John M. Frame, *The Doctrine of the Word of God*, A Theology of Lordship (Phillipsburg, NJ: P&R, 2010), 48.

9. The three interlocking subsystems as being reflective of the Trinity goes back to the language theory of Kenneth L. Pike, of whom Poythress was a student. See Kenneth L. Pike, *Linguistic Concepts: An Introduction to Tagmemics* (Lincoln, NE: University of Nebraska Press, 1982), 13–15; and Poythress, *In the Beginning Was the Word*, 259–69. See also Pierce Taylor Hibbs, "Where Person Meets Word Part 1: Personalism in the Language Theory of Kenneth L. Pike," *Westminster Theological Journal* 77, no. 2 (Fall 2015): 355–77; "Where Person Meets Word Part 2: The Convergence of Personalism and Scripture in the Language Theory of Kenneth L. Pike," *Westminster Theological Journal* 78, no. 1 (Spring 2016): 117–34.

10. The "interlocking" of divine persons is called *perichoresis* or "coinherence" by theologians. For a few ancient and contemporary expressions of this concept, see Augustine, *De Trinitate* 6.10; John of Damascus, *Writings*, The Fathers of the Church 37, trans. Frederic H. Chase (Washington, DC: The Catholic University of America Press, 1958), 182–85; John M. Frame, *Systematic Theology: An Introduction to Christian Belief* (Phillipsburg, NJ: P&R, 2013), 479–81; and Robert Letham, *The Holy Trinity: In Scripture, History, Theology, and Worship* (Phillipsburg, NJ: P&R, 2004), 365–66.

through the power and "breath" of the Holy Spirit. Human speaking uses a language system, in imitation of God who uses the systematic wisdom of God the Son.[11]

So, what we say (referential content) and the manner in which we say it (grammar and phonology) are equally important.

Now, what does any of this mean to the theology student who simply wants to improve his or her English? It means that we would encourage you throughout this textbook to consider the ways in which grammar and phonology affect your message with regard to clarity, emphasis, and tone. At various places throughout the text, we will draw your attention to the way in which the interaction of these three subsystems of language affects a particular author's sentence. Whenever you see the symbol on the right (G = grammar; P = phonology; R = reference), that means we are directing you to this Trinitarian feature of language. In light of this, do not cast aside grammar as relatively unimportant to getting your message across, as if to say to your readers, "They'll understand what I mean anyway." You cannot afford to neglect the development of the broad and deep knowledge of words, nor can you assume that if your grammar is accurate and your vocabulary adequate, then you can communicate clearly in speech. You need to improve in all three areas. Keeping this in mind has the potential to help you make more robust improvements in your understanding and use of English.

The Approach and Layout of the Textbook

The layout of this text is explained in more detail in Lesson 1. Each lesson includes a list of "Lesson Goals." There is usually a goal in each of the following areas:

- Theology
- Reading
- Vocabulary
- Grammar

This text offers passive vocabulary development through exposure to a range of theological readings of different eras, with key terms glossed in the margins. Explicit vocabulary learning is encouraged through the collocation exercises in each lesson. This serves the larger end of developing grammar and reading skills in the context of theology.

Each lesson begins with an introduction and a few discussion questions. Then comes instruction on reading skills (one skill is taught per unit) before a passage of theology. Students then answer main idea and detail questions. These questions are often followed by an "Understanding the Reading" activity, a vocabulary exercise using collocations from the reading, and grammar exercises.

Twice in each unit, there are real-life tasks that will give you the opportunity to practice what you have learned in a concrete situation. Pay special attention to these tasks since they indicate how well you have understood and can apply what you are learning. If you are comfortable completing these tasks by the end of the textbook, that means you are in a better position to transfer what you have learned about theological English to your actual use of English in a theological setting.

Lastly, readers should know that this textbook is made for a classroom setting, and that is primarily how we use it. Some of the activities and exercises thus require group or pair-work. If you decide to use this text to study independently, note that the exercises requiring this work can be adapted for an individual student. Nevertheless, it is always good to learn language in community!

We hope that this textbook is of great help to you in your acquisition of theological English, and that our work serves as a small testimony to the greatness of the Trinitarian God who is redeeming all things in the person of his Son by the power of the Holy Spirit.

---

11. Poythress, *In the Beginning Was the Word*, 267.

UNIT 1

WHO ARE WE?
(APOLOGETICS)

1

Theological English

*"We can appreciate language more deeply, and use it more wisely, if we come
to know God and understand the relation of God to the language we use."*
—Vern S. Poythress, *In the Beginning Was the Word*

What Is Theological English (TE)?

Why put the adjective "theological" before the noun "English"? Isn't English just English? What is distinct about theological English (TE), and why treat it differently from academic English? It is important to address these questions in advance so that we have a sense of where we are headed.

The simple answer to the first question is that English takes on distinct qualities and features depending on the context in which it is used. These qualities and features are not limited to different vocabulary; they also include sentence structures, patterns of organization, assumptions about clarity and effectiveness, etc. For example, in a mechanic's shop, you might hear the sentence, "You gotta' use a wrench." But in a theological text, you would probably never read, "You gotta' use Scripture." Why not?

First of all, there is a big difference between spoken and written English. Spoken English is more informal and conversational, while written English is more formal. On the one hand, the mechanic can communicate clearly with a co-worker using language that, when taken out of context, seems vague or even inadequate. The theological writer, on the other hand, needs to explain precisely what he or she means by "use" (e.g., exegete, meditate on, apply,

analyze). The organization of the theological writer's explanation would also differ from that of the mechanic if the latter were to explain what he meant by "use." The sentence structures, as well, would differ. Short, single-clause sentences might suffice for a mechanic in this situation, but more complex structures and clauses are often needed to communicate a theological concept clearly and effectively.

This leads us to an answer regarding the second and third questions: What is distinct about TE, and why treat it differently from academic English? If you are reading this book, you are interested not in mechanics or in academics more broadly, but in *theology*, and so you need to be aware of the features, qualities, assumptions, practices, and expectations that come with the English language in this discipline, as seen in the various genres it encompasses. These features and qualities make TE *distinct* from English as used in other contexts. If you are not aware of these features and qualities or are uncomfortable using English in a theological setting, you will likely miss out on the rich truths communicated to you in theological writings and lectures, and you might be restricted in how effectively you communicate these truths to others in your own writing and teaching. That, in short, is why TE needs to be treated separately from academic English in general.[1]

---

1. Another answer to this "why" question is that a Christian does everything *as a Christian*. "Because all of God's human creatures are covenantally qualified creatures . . . what we are, do, and become takes place *coram deo*; it takes place in the presence of, and in the con-

3

But we still have not said what TE really is, specifically. Broadly speaking, we might say that **theological English** is English used to communicate biblical and theological truths carefully, precisely, and effectively within theological genres.[2] This approach to English in theological contexts should, of course, spill into your use of language in everyday life, but we will keep this definition in mind as we move forward in learning TE.

An Example of Theological English

Now that we know that TE incorporates certain features and qualities that help us express theological truths carefully, precisely, and effectively, we can introduce an example. What are some of the differences you notice among the following sentences?

Notice how the meaning changes in each sentence, moving from conversational to abstract to more precise.

| God loves people. |
| God is love. |
| God is covenantally faithful. |

In fact, there is quite a bit of theology packed into the third sentence, and it is still a relatively simple sentence. Consider just how complex theological sentences can be. For instance, Carl Trueman writes, "God's relationship with Adam is expressed via the medium of language."[3] Then, he follows that relatively simple sentence with these two sentences:

> [Language] is how God defines the nature and limits of the relationship, and, after the Fall, it is how God confronts Adam and Eve with their sin. The same pattern is repeated throughout the whole Bible in both testaments: whether it is command or promise, the two basic aspects of the divine-human relationship, God speaks using words to define his relationship with men and women, to limit it, to move it forward: he speaks to Noah, to Abraham, to Samuel, to David and so on.[4]

You may not be fully able to comprehend sentences at this level of complexity yet, let alone write them, but this textbook is designed to help you read this kind of English and, when necessary, to write it or speak it.

How Are We Going to Study TE?

What follows is an outline of how we are going to study TE.

TE Units and Questions. Each "Unit" of this textbook focuses on a particular theological "Question,"

Unit	Theological Question	Genre
Unit 1	Who are we?	Apologetics
Unit 2	What is truth?	Apologetics
Unit 3	What is wrong?	Apologetics
Unit 4	How is it made right?	Biblical Studies

---

text of, responsibility to God himself." K. Scott Oliphint, "Covenant Faith," in *Justified in Christ: God's Plan for Us in Justification*, ed. K. Scott Oliphint (Ross-shire, Scotland: Mentor, 2007), 153. In other words, you understand and use language based on your beliefs in the God who has revealed himself in Scripture—a God who has communicated his truth in language throughout history, and who has done so with care, precision, and utter effectiveness (cf. Isa. 55:11). It is before *this* God that you are undertaking the task of learning theological English.

2. The writing exercises and tasks in this textbook are meant to help you write clearly, cogently, and profoundly. See John M. Frame, *The Doctrine of the Knowledge of God*, A Theology of Lordship (Phillipsburg, NJ: P&R, 1987), 369–74.

3. Carl R. Trueman, "The Undoing of the Reformation?," in *The Wages of Spin: Critical Writings on Historic & Contemporary Evangelicalism* (Ross-shire, Scotland: Mentor, 2004), 46.

4. Ibid.

Unit	Theological Question	Genre
Unit 5	Who is Jesus?	Biblical Studies
Unit 6	Do we still need the Old Testament?	Biblical Studies
Unit 7	Where have we been?	Church History
Unit 8	How are we saved?	Systematic Theology
Unit 9	Where does the church fit?	Systematic Theology
Unit 10	How then shall we live?	Practical Theology

and these questions fit into theological genres. We will study traits of these genres throughout the book so that you will be better equipped to read and write in each area.

Each unit contains three "Lessons" and two "Tasks" pertaining to the theological question for that unit. The "Lessons" draw on popular and important readings from the Reformed theological tradition. As you work through them, you should acquire reading skills, identify and practice using grammatical structures, learn context-specific vocabulary, recognize genre-specific rhetorical patterns, and develop other advanced writing skills. A summary of the reading and grammar skills you will learn is provided below.

Reading Skills

Unit	Lesson	Skill
1	2	Identifying the topic and main idea
2	5	Understanding vocabulary in context
3	9	Tracing the line of an argument
4	10	Identifying pronoun referents
5	14	Making inferences
6	18	Recognizing the author's purpose
7	20	Understanding stance
8	24	Summarizing
9	27	Outlining
10	29	Understanding logical arguments

Grammar Skills

Lesson	Grammatical Topic
1	NONE
The Structure of Complex Sentences in Theological English	
2	*There is/there are*
3	Adjective forms
4	Passive voice
5	Comparative structures
6	Relative clauses and appositives
7	Multiple tenses within a paragraph
8	Articles
Precise Word Form	
9	Pronouns
10	Suffixes
11	Word families
The Author's Perspective and the Verb Phrase	
12	Modal verbs
13	Principled use of verb tense
14	Prepositions following verbs
Adding Information and Expressing Relations	
15	Complete subjects
16	Infinitives
17	Adverbs
18	Noun clauses
19	Noun phrases
20	Describing and modifying nouns
21	Adjective forms

Lesson	Grammatical Topic
22	Preposition Patterns
23	Definite and indefinite articles
Editing for Structure and Word Choice	
24	Participles
25	*That* clauses
26	Matching subject and predicate
27	Verb/noun + preposition patterns
28	Forming questions
29	Multi-clause sentences (embedded clauses)
30	Effective use of adjectives

Lessons. Each "Lesson" begins with an introduction and discussion questions or Scripture readings to help you begin thinking about the theological topic. While the discussion questions work best in a classroom setting, you can certainly reflect on them if you are studying independently. After the discussion questions, you may have some instruction in reading skills that will help you to work through the theological text that follows. Once you have read that text, there will be a post-reading question, main idea and detail questions, vocabulary activities, and a grammar focus.

Tasks. Twice in each unit you will be asked to carry out a theological task in which you will put to use what you have learned in terms of theological content as well as English vocabulary, grammar, and rhetoric. Each task is a real-life activity, designed to help you authentically use the skills and language features you are learning.

Genre Studies. We will also go through "Genre Studies" for each of the theological genres: apologetics, biblical studies, church history, systematic theology, and practical theology. The purpose of these genre studies is to alert you to specific features within a genre. Recognizing these features in your readings as well as practicing them in your writing will help

you more effectively receive and communicate meaning within each genre.

Scripture and Language: Getting Started

We begin our study of TE where we begin our study of everything else: God's Word. Because the instruction in this textbook is based on biblical truths about language, it would be a good idea to begin thinking about these truths yourself.

Either on your own or with a partner, use a Bible to form a short list of verses that relate to language. If you are not sure where to start, you can search for the key words "words," "told," "said," "listen," and "hear." Once you have formed your list and read over the verses, come up with two or three biblical principles regarding language (e.g., how we should use it, why it is important, etc.). State each principle in a complete sentence below. On the following page, there are some Reformed biblical principles for understanding and using language.

Biblical Principles for Understanding and Using Language

At the top of the next page are some biblical principles for understanding and using language. How do your principles relate to those listed below?

Biblical Passages	Principle	Explanation
Gen. 1:26; Matt. 6:9–13; Mark 14:36; Luke 12:12; John 1:1-2; 5:30; 12:49–50; 17:5; Rom. 8:26; and many others!	*God speaks both to himself in three persons and to us, so language is Trinitarian and part of the* imago Dei.	Throughout Scripture, we encounter a God who speaks.[5] He speaks to himself, but he also speaks *to us*, personally, in Scripture.[6] God has spoken, speaks, and will continue to speak to us through his Word, and because we are made in his image, we speak.
Pss. 15:2; 33:4; 43:3; 119:160; Prov. 30:5; Zech. 8:16; Matt. 22:16; John 8:45; 14:6 (in light of 1:1); 17:17; Jas. 1:18	*Language is apologetic.*	Because language is a means of conveying God's truth, we use it in a way that assumes what God has done in history. Non-Christians might care little for the truth, but we care a great deal about it. Our use of words (in speaking and writing) can be an apology, or a defense, of God's existence. How you understand and use words is a testament to your faith in our speaking God. People will notice.
John 3:33–36; Col. 1:15; Heb. 1:3	*Meaning and purpose in language are rooted in the Trinity.*[7]	"As the Word expresses the Father, so a sentence that God utters expresses the truth that the sentence formulates."[8] Analogically, humans express meaningful thoughts in language. Yet, language is meaningful not just because a person can clearly communicate ideas or experiences to someone else, but because all ideas and experiences only have meaning in God's covenantal plan for humanity.[9] Everything we say or write has meaning because it is either advancing God's purposes or vainly attempting to thwart them.

Preview of Paragraph Unity, Coherence, and Development (UCD)

Later in this textbook, you will learn about paragraph *unity*, *coherence*, and *development*. Every paragraph, in other words, is about one thing, discusses that one thing with logically related sentences, and develops the discussion with different rhetorical tools (logical reasoning, exemplification, description, narration, compare and contrast, analysis, etc.). Paragraph **unity** is often marked with a **topic sentence**, and

5. J. I. Packer, *Knowing God* (Downers Grove, IL: InterVarsity, 1975), 109; Vern S. Poythress, "God and Language," in *Did God Really Say? Affirming the Truthfulness and Trustworthiness of Scripture*, ed. David B. Garner (Phillipsburg, NJ: P&R, 2012), 93. "The New Testament indicates that the persons of the Trinity speak to one another. This speaking on the part of God is significant for our thinking about language. Not only is God a member of a language community that includes human beings, but the persons of the Trinity function as members of a language community among themselves. Language does not have as its sole purpose human-human communication, or even divine-human communication, but also divine-divine communication." Vern S. Poythress, *In the Beginning Was the Word: Language—A God-Centered Approach* (Wheaton, IL: Crossway, 2009), 18.

6. John M. Frame, *The Doctrine of the Word of God*, A Theology of Lordship (Phillipsburg, NJ: P&R, 2010), 3.

7. Poythress, *In the Beginning Was the Word*, 251–58.

8. Ibid., 253.

9. "Every fact and experience is what it is by virtue of the covenantal, all-controlling plan and purpose of God." K. Scott Oliphint, *Covenantal Apologetics: Principles and Practice in Defense of Our Faith* (Wheaton, IL: Crossway, 2013), 53.

this sentence usually occurs toward the beginning of the paragraph. Paragraph **coherence** is expressed by the *order of the sentences* and the *signaled relationships* between them. Paragraph **development** may be more difficult to identify at first, but you can understand how an author is developing his or her ideas by asking, "What is the author doing in order to convince me of the truth or relevance of the topic sentence?" For instance, is the author using logical reasoning (which may be signaled with words or phrases such as "thus," "therefore," "so," "and so")? Is the author offering examples?

In order to help you do the following task, observe how these concepts appear in the example below. As you read the paragraph, note how the unity, coherence, and development of the paragraph clearly and effectively communicate the author's idea.

"PU" = paragraph unity; "PC" = paragraph coherence; and "PD" = paragraph development

PU: Topic Sentence ➤ <u>Different worldviews lead to different conceptions of freedom.</u> If there were no God, freedom might mean freedom to create our own purposes. It might mean freedom from all constraint, which implies, in the end, freedom from the constraints of personal relationships. The ideal freedom would be to live in isolation. **On the other hand**, if God exists and is personal, freedom means not isolation but joy in appreciating both other human beings and God the infinite person. God's moral order is designed by God to guide us into personal fellowship and satisfaction. It is for our good. It is for our freedom, we might say, in the true sense of "freedom." The person who goes astray from God's wise guidance burdens himself with sorrows and frustrations. In fact, he ends up being a slave to his own desires.[10]

PC: Use of pronouns ("it") helps bind sentences together.

PC: **Bolded** phrase signals a change in direction.

PU: Repetition of a key word ("freedom") improves unity.

PD: Logical Development

PD: Continuing Logical Development

The Importance of Words (AP Task 1)

Imagine that you are an associate pastor at a church with approximately 200 members. Recently, your congregation has been encountering problems with gossip and slander. Some members of the church have been deeply hurt, and a few have even left the congregation. Your senior pastor asks you to prepare a Bible study on our use of words. He wants you to focus on the book of Proverbs and asks that you contact him through email with one idea about what Proverbs says concerning our use and abuse of words.

Below we have provided a few verses from Proverbs that you can focus on for this task. Read the verses with a partner and discuss what each one seems to be communicating. Then think of how what the author says here is fulfilled by Christ. Working with your partner, come up with one principle about our use or abuse of language based on these verses and the work of Christ. Then **write a one-paragraph email to your pastor introducing one idea for this Bible study**. Your email should be no more than 300 words. Before writing your email, please read the instructions on "Composing an Email."

Passages from Proverbs

10:21	"The lips of the righteous feed many, but fools die for lack of sense."
10:31–32	"The mouth of the righteous brings forth wisdom, but the perverse tongue will be cut off. The lips of the righteous know what is acceptable, but the mouth of the wicked, what is perverse."
16:24	"Gracious words are like a honeycomb, sweetness to the soul and health to the body."

10. Vern S. Poythress, *Inerrancy and Worldview: Answering Modern Challenges to the Bible* (Wheaton, IL: Crossway, 2012), 24.

Composing an Email

An email message, while often informal and conversational, should still be appropriate and respectful, especially if it is addressed to your senior pastor. In light of this, your email should not be an academic essay, but neither should it address your pastor with "Hey." Follow the basic structure of offering a salutation, message, concluding remark, and a signature.

| Salutation | Pastor Kim, |

Message — I'm writing to let you know that I have been gathering some thoughts for the Bible study on _____.

Conclusion — Please let me know what your thoughts are on _____. Thank you for your time.

Signature — Sincerely,

2

The Creator-Creature Distinction

"Man can never in any sense outgrow his creaturehood."
—Cornelius Van Til, *Christian Apologetics*

Lesson Goals

Theology—To define and understand the importance of the Creator-creature distinction

Reading—To identify the topic, main ideas, and details

Vocabulary—To learn and use collocations from the reading passage

Grammar—To use the *there is /there are* structure

Introduction

We begin our first lesson with the question, "Who are we?" That's a big question, and we can have many answers. But for our purposes, we will focus on the key word *creatures*. We are creatures created by the Triune God, and we are and always will be in covenantal relationship with him.[1]

As creatures, we are part of creation and are in relationship with our Creator. We were meant to grow in that relationship throughout our lives, acquiring more knowledge about and love for God and his world in the process. Our growth in love for and knowledge of God and his world was always meant to be "in service to God, with love for God (Deut. 6:5) and in communion with God. This communion includes faithful reception and reliance on the verbal communication that God gives to human beings."[2] In other words, God has given his creatures revelation—he has spoken to us—so that we might live faithfully *as creatures*. Of course, we know that sin has corrupted all things. And we often try to act as if we can transcend our position as creatures, as if we could be God and have ultimate control over our lives and over the world in which we live.

But this can never really happen. As Cornelius Van Til noted, we cannot outgrow our "creaturehood." God will always be God, and we will always be his image-bearing creatures (Gen. 1:26), who are called to live in submission and obedience to him. To describe this relationship, Van Til coined the phrase "Creator-creature distinction."

---

1. "Man (male and female) as image of God is in covenant with the Triune God for eternity." K. Scott Oliphint, *Covenantal Apologetics: Principles and Practice in Defense of Our Faith* (Wheaton, IL: Crossway, 2013), 50.

2. Vern S. Poythress, *Redeeming Philosophy: A God-Centered Approach to the Big Questions* (Wheaton, IL: Crossway, 2014), 46.

Discussion Questions

(1) What do you think the Creator-creature distinction involves?

(2) Why might this distinction be important to maintain?

Background for the Reading

As the introduction suggests, central to sound theology is an awareness of this Creator-creature distinction. God is completely independent, free, all-knowing, and all-powerful. As his creatures, we are dependent, bound, ignorant, and weak. When we fail to recognize the difference between God's being and our own, we make dangerous errors.

For example, Arius, a priest of the early church, wanted to make Christianity "intellectually respectable to his contemporaries."[3] To do this, he had to make God accessible and acceptable to human thought, which at the time was based on Plato's concept that God was eternal and unknowable. Since Jesus was knowable—he was a real person who existed in time and space and whose words and deeds were recorded in the Gospels—he could not be God.[4] So Arius asserted that Jesus was not God, and thus was born the heresy of Arianism.

Notice that Arius failed to acknowledge the Creator-creature distinction by assuming that God (the Creator) must be fully comprehensible to human reason. He tried to make the Creator fit the intellectual capacities of the creature. But God far exceeds the boundaries of the human intellect. And if God is independent, free, all-knowing, and all-powerful, then he has the ability to make himself known, even through his Son, Jesus Christ, regardless of whether such revelation fits with our concept of human reason.

Reading Skill: Identifying the Topic and Main Idea

Before we get into a theological passage dealing with the Creator-creature distinction, we need to lay out some important reading skills. Learning to identify the topic and main idea of a reading passage quickly is central to your ability to do theological studies. You will likely read hundreds of pages of theology in the future, and, as we said earlier, you need to be able to understand what you read in order to grow in love for and knowledge of God and his world. The reading lesson that follows reviews

How to Identify the Topic

- Read the title of the book or article. The title often contains the topic.
- Look for repeated words.
- Ask yourself, "What is this reading about?"
- Check that your answer is not too specific or too general.
- Note: A topic that is too specific or too general will slow down your ability to identify the main idea correctly.

what the terms "topic" and "main idea" mean and then gives you strategies for finding them in your reading.

The **topic** is the subject of a text, or what the text (a sentence, paragraph, or article) is about. It is usually stated directly and is expressed as a word or phrase.

The **main idea** is the central *focus* of any unit of discourse. In this sense, a sentence, paragraph, or section of a paper, lecture, or conversation can have a main idea. The main idea in the text may be directly stated, or you may have to infer it, but it is usually expressed as a complete sentence (unlike the topic, which can be expressed with a phrase).

A more specialized term that we use to refer to the central *claim* of an article, chapter, book, or lecture is the thesis. The **thesis** shows that the author or speaker has taken a position on a debatable topic and will defend this position with evidence and reasons. If the author or speaker happens to state the thesis explicitly in a single sentence (which is very common in academic writing), this sentence is called the **thesis statement**. The thesis (or thesis statement) will

---

3. Diarmaid MacCulloch, *Christianity: The First Three Thousand Years* (New York: Viking, 2009), 213.
4. Ibid.

How to Identify the Main Idea

- Read the title and any subtitles, subheadings, or captions in the text.

- Look for topic sentences or a thesis statement.

- In many academic texts, the author clearly states his or her main idea in a sentence. At the paragraph-level, this can frequently be found in the first sentence of a body paragraph, also known as the *topic sentence*.

- At the essay, chapter, or article level, this can frequently be found at the end of the introduction, also known as the *thesis statement*.

- Look for repeated words.

- Ask yourself, "What is the author's most important idea on this subject?"

- Check that your answer is not too specific or too general.

- A main idea that is too specific is usually a detail rather than the main idea.

- Check your understanding by skimming the passage and asking, "Is the entire text (paragraph, subsection, article, etc.) about this idea?" If not, you likely have the wrong main idea.

- A main idea that is too general is not helpful because it is not about the idea expressed in this text.

- Check your understanding by skimming the passage and asking, "Is this what the text is primarily about?"

- Remember that the topic or main idea of a smaller passage (i.e., paragraph or subsection) may not be the same as the topic or main idea of the larger text as a whole.

Often a paragraph has the same topic as the text as a whole but its main idea is more specific than the main idea of the larger text.

always contain the main idea of the article, chapter, book, or lecture.

Not every unit of discourse will have a thesis, but every unit of discourse should have a main idea. If an article or lecture has a thesis, then the thesis and the main idea of the whole article or lecture are the same. Below are some steps you might follow to identify the main idea in a text.

In order to help you locate the main idea of a passage, you can pay attention to the main idea of each paragraph. As you read, write a single sentence next to each paragraph, expressing what you think the main idea of the paragraph is. Do your best to put this in your own words (do NOT just quote a sentence from the paragraph).

Pre-Reading

In discussions about the Creator-creature relationship, you may hear the expression, "We think God's thoughts after him." This means that we think God's thoughts only on a creaturely level. Keeping this expression in mind, take only 45 seconds to skim the following passage by John Frame. Then predict (make an educated guess about) what you think he will say concerning the relationship between God and his creatures. Write your prediction below.

Reading

In the passage that follows, John Frame clarifies the distinction between the Creator and the creature.

[¶1] The biblical metaphysic . . . makes a clear distinction[a] between the Creator and the world, his "creaturely other." God is the Lord; the universe serves him. God is entitled[b] by nature to be Lord; we are not. His lordship extends[c] to everything that he has made. So there is no continuum[d] between God and creation. There are no degrees of divinity: God is divine, and we are not. There are no degrees of reality, either. God is real, and we are real.

[¶2] There are, of course, two very different *levels*[e] of reality, the Creator's and the creature's. Cornelius Van Til often drew two circles on the blackboard: a larger one above, and a smaller one below. The upper circle represented God; the lower circle represented the creation. Van Til emphasized[f] that these are distinct, not on a continuum. Often he cited the Chalcedon Declaration of 451 to show that even in the person of Christ, where there is the most intimate[g] communion imaginable between deity and humanity, there is no "confusion" or "change" of the two. Even in the person of Christ, the Creator-creature distinction holds.[h] The two circles, in Van Til's view, emphasize the most important feature[i] of the biblical worldview. Nonbiblical thought, he taught, is always "one-circle" thinking, putting the Creator and the creature on the same level. Neoplatonism was one of Van Til's main examples of one-circle thinking.

[¶3] As there are two different kinds of reality, so there are different kinds of goodness, justice, wisdom, and knowledge: those of God and those of creatures. God's knowledge, for example, is not only more extensive[j] than ours, but also different in character.[k] God's knowledge is essentially self-knowledge, based on his intentions[l] and actions, which control all things. Our knowledge must have a reference point[m] beyond ourselves, namely God's authoritative revelation in nature and Scripture. God's knowledge is the knowledge of the Creator, knowledge that creates the things it knows. It is the knowledge of the Lord, who controls the objects of his knowledge, interprets[n] them with supreme[o] authority, and is always present with them to act in accord[p] with that interpretation. Our knowledge is the knowledge of creatures, which receives the reality and interpretation of its objects from God. There is no continuum between God's knowledge and ours. There is no midpoint, no ladder to heaven for us to ascend[q] to gain a knowledge that is increasingly divine.

[¶4] It is true, of course, that God knows more things than we do, so we cannot rule out[r] entirely the language of degree, or, to that extent, continuum. God's ways are higher than ours (Isa. 55:9), and his might is greater than our powers. But to say that is not to indicate[s] the deepest level of difference between our powers and his. Similarly, we can certainly say that God is far more merciful, gracious, just, and good than we are, using the language of continuum. But is God more good than, say, unfallen Adam or the glorified saints? . . . even their goodness is different from God's, for God's goodness is the supreme standard[t] and example for ours—a perspective[u] . . . on his infinite being. God's goodness is the goodness of the Creator, the Lord. Ours, at its very best, even perfected by grace, is the goodness of creatures.[5]

a. Distinction (n.): something that differentiates one thing from another
b. Entitle (v.): to qualify someone for something
c. Extend (v.): to stretch out (as in distance, space, or time)
d. Continuum (n.): a continuous portion of a spectrum
e. Level (n.): a degree of artistic, intellectual, or spiritual meaning
f. Emphasize (v.): to stress or draw attention to
g. Intimate (adj.): marked by a very close association, connection, or contact
h. Hold (v.): to maintain, to remain
i. Feature (n.): an element or part of something
j. Extensive (adj.): widely extended in scope; broad in range
k. Character (n.): main or essential nature, often distinguishing

l. Intention (n.): the act of having the mind or will concentrated on some end or goal
m. Reference point (n. phrase): a fact forming the basis of an evaluation or assessment
n. Interpret (v.): to explain or tell the meaning of
o. Supreme (adj.): not exceeded by any other in degree, quality, or intensity
p. Accord (n.): agreement
q. Ascend (v.): to move upward upon
r. Rule out (v. phrase): to exclude or eliminate
s. Indicate (v.): to point out or point to or toward with more or less exactness
t. Standard (n.): something that is established as a model or example to be followed
u. Perspective (n.): view

Post-Reading

In your own words, try to summarize Frame's main idea in a single sentence.

1. What is the topic of the following sentence? If you were to speak it, which word(s) would you stress (emphasize) the most? "Ours, at its very best, even perfected by grace, is the goodness of creatures."

2. There are four words in this sentence that would receive stress: "**Ours**, at its very **best**, even perfected by **grace**, is the goodness of **creatures**." The word "creatures" would likely receive the most stress because it is the final word in this *thought group* (we will learn more about thought groups in Lesson 21) and carries the core meaning of the author (drawing our attention to the Creator-creature distinction). So, you would likely stress the noun "creatures" (phonology)—the object of the preposition "of" (grammar)—and stressing this word would draw the hearer's attention to the contrast between the Creator and his creatures (reference).

Main Idea Practice

Put a check (√) by the best topic or main idea, a **G** by an idea that is **too general**, or an **S** by an idea that is **too specific**.

Example: What is the topic of this passage?

   G   a. God   This is too general to say anything about this text.
   S   b. levels of reality This is a detail that is not what the passage is about.
   √   c.   The Creator-creature distinction

5. John M. Frame, *The Doctrine of God, A Theology of Lordship* (Phillipsburg, NJ: P&R, 2002), 217–18.

What is the main idea of this passage?

_____ a. Our knowledge is different from God's knowledge.

_____ b. There is a distinction between God and his created world.

_____ c. The Creator-creature distinction is central to our understanding of reality.

What is the topic of <u>paragraph 1</u>?

_____ a. God as Creator

_____ b. the distinction between God and his created world

_____ c. God's lordship extends to everything that he has made.

What is the topic of paragraph 2?

_____ a. Cornelius Van Til

_____ b. the Creator-creature distinction

_____ c. levels of reality between the Creator and his creation

What is the main idea of paragraph 3?

_____ a. God possesses one kind of characteristics while his creatures possess another kind.

_____ b. God's reality is at a different level than our reality.

_____ c. Our knowledge must have a reference point beyond ourselves.

What is the main idea of paragraph 4?

_____ a. God and humans are not alike.

_____ b. While related, God's attributes and ours are on different levels.

_____ c. God's goodness is different than Adam's since God sets the standard.

Locating the main idea in a passage will require that you notice its **hierarchical structure**, both within each paragraph and throughout the entire passage. You can think of this structure as the organization of a piece of writing (whether a paragraph, a section, or an article), an organization that reveals what is most important to the author.

Here is an example paragraph from the reading (paragraph 1).

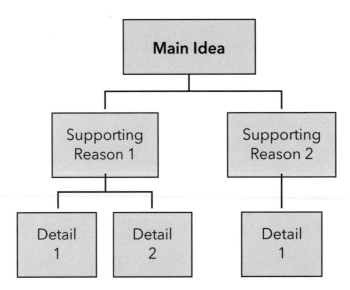

Fig. 2.1. Hierarchical Structure of a Paragraph

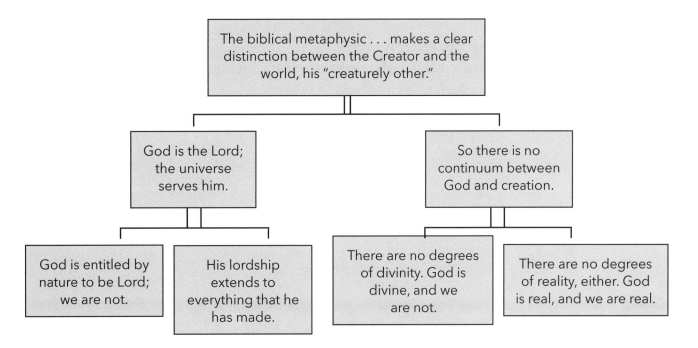

Fig. 2.2. Example of Hierarchical Structure

Throughout this textbook, we will draw attention to this concept of hierarchical structure, showing how it can help you locate the main idea of a passage.

Main Ideas and Details

(1) Which of the following is the main idea of the passage?
   a. God and his creation are on opposite sides of the same spectrum.
   b. God knows much more than his creatures know.
   c. The Creator-creature distinction is central to our understanding of reality.
   d. The Creator-creature distinction applies even to the divine and human natures of Christ.

(2) In paragraph 1, the author writes, "There are no degrees of reality, either. God is real, and we are real." Why does he write this?
   a. Because he wants to affirm that God and his creatures both truly exist.
   b. Because he thinks that many philosophers have argued that humans are imaginary.
   c. Because he thinks the Creator-creature distinction suggests that creatures are imaginary.
   d. Because he thinks that the word "divine" can be confusing when applied to God and his creation.

(3) In paragraph 2, the author uses the word "even" because _____.
   a. Jesus is never confused and never changes.
   b. The Chalcedon Declaration of 451 shows us many biblical truths.
   c. In the person of Christ there is intimate communion of humanity and divinity.
   d. Readers might think that the Creator-creature distinction does not apply to Christ.

(4) In paragraph 3, Frame says that "our knowledge must have a reference point beyond ourselves." What is that reference point? (Be precise!)

(5) What is the referent of the pronoun "its," at the end of paragraph 4?

Understanding the Reading

Label the statements below as either "True" or "False," based on the reading.

_____ 1. God is at one end of a continuum or spectrum, and his creatures are at the other end.

_____ 2. Van Til is critical of "one-circle thinking."

_____ 3. The glorified saints are good in the same way that God is good.

_____ 4. The reference point for God's knowledge is creation.

_____ 5. Our knowledge as creatures is rooted in God's revelation.

_____ 6. Even though there is no continuum, Scripture sometimes uses the "language" of continuum.

Collocations

What exactly is collocation? Collocation simply refers to "the way in which particular words tend to occur or belong together."[6]

Collocations are "words that work naturally with each other and which are used together frequently."[7]

For example, in English we would say that there is *heavy traffic*, but we would not say that there is *strong traffic*. There are four types of collocation commonly recognized, as shown below.[8]

Type of Collocation	Examples
Adjective + Noun	*important* distinction; *wise* decision; *false* assumption
Noun + *Adjective*	His argument was *underdeveloped*.
Verb + Noun	He developed his argument over several chapters.
Adverb + *Adjective*	Fully *developed*; widely *recognized*; sufficiently *persuasive*

Knowing which words collocate or occur with other words is part of vocabulary development. When you learn a word, try to learn what other words can go with it.

In the paragraph that follows, circle the most appropriate collocation from the words in parentheses. Sometimes you may need to look at what comes *after* the choices in order to make your decision. Each of these collocations is taken directly from the theological reading in this lesson.

Theologians in the Reformed tradition make a clear (*point/value/distinction*) between the Creator and his creatures. This Creator-creature distinction assumes that there are two different (*positions/levels/standings*) of being: that of the independent Triune God and that of the dependent creature. In that sense, there are two (*strange/unique/different*) kinds of being. Yet, while these kinds of being are (*opposed/different/diverse*) in character, they are still related, because God's creatures are made in his image (Gen. 1:26). In all areas of theology, this Creator-creature distinction is an important (*feature/character/nature*) of orthodox Christian belief.

Grammar Focus: There Is/There Are

We begin our study of grammar by looking at the structure of complex sentences in TE. But we start in this lesson with a rather simple structure. You probably already know that every sentence contains a subject

---

6. *Oxford Learner's Dictionary of Academic English* (Oxford: Oxford University Press, 2014), R23. Another great resource specifically for collocations is the *Oxford Collocations Dictionary for Students of English*, 2nd ed. (New York: Oxford University Press, 2009).

7. Ken Paterson and Roberta Wedge, *Oxford Grammar for EAP: English Grammar and Practice for Academic Purposes* (Oxford: Oxford University Press, 2013), 166.

8. *Oxford Learner's Dictionary of Academic English*, R23.

and a predicate, but these take different shapes within a passage. In the passage you just read, for example, you have the following subjects and predicates in paragraph 3.

Subject Position	Predicate
There	are
God's knowledge	is
Our knowledge	must have
It	is
There	is

What fills the subject position and the predicate at the beginning and the end of this table may seem odd. "God's knowledge" and "our knowledge" can "be" or "exist," so that makes sense. But the subject "there" cannot perform the action of "being" or "existing," can it? In these sentences, "there" is what we call a **dummy subject**: "there" stands in for the true subject in the sentence. "As there are two different kinds of reality" can be re-written with the true subject in the subject position: "Two different kinds of reality are (exist)." (We would likely say "exist" rather than "are.")

This *there is*/*there are* structure allows us to put longer noun phrases and clauses after the verb *to be*. And this accounts for some of the complex sentences you find in theological prose. Note the use of *there is*/*there are* in the following paragraph. Pay close attention to the structure that follows the linking verb "to be."

As **there are** two different kinds of reality, so **there are** different kinds of goodness, justice, wisdom, and knowledge: those of God and those of creatures. . . . **There is** no continuum between God's knowledge and ours. **There is** no midpoint, no ladder to heaven for us to ascend to gain a knowledge that is increasingly divine.

Activity 1

In English, we often use the structure *there is* or *there are* to express that something exists or is true. Working with a partner, take turns asking and answering questions using the following phrases. The response to each question should begin with either "there is" or "there are." An example is provided for you. Be careful to match the verb to the subject in number. (Remember: "there" is not the subject; it is a placeholder for the subject.)

Example: A heresy known as Arianism
Question: Is there a heresy known as Arianism?
Answer: <u>There is</u> a heresy known as Arianism.

1. levels of reality
2. continuum between God's knowledge and ours
3. a standard that guides a creature's knowledge
4. two different kinds of goodness, justice, wisdom, and knowledge
5. circles in Van Til's diagram of the Creator-creature distinction

Activity 2

For each partial sentence below, write either "are" or "is" in the blank. Remember to look at the noun phrase that follows the verb to determine its number.

1. There _____ many reasons why the Creator-creature distinction is important to remember.

2. There _____ only one place to begin our study of theology: God's revealed Word.
3. There _____ a lot of research that has been done on Cornelius Van Til's apologetic.
4. There _____ much work yet to be done in applying Van Til's work to other areas of theology.
5. There _____ several ways in which we see Scripture confirming the Creator-creature distinction.
6. There _____ two senses in which we can understand God's goodness.
7. There _____ no excuse for those who claim not to know God (Rom. 1).

3

The Role of Revelation

*"It is the truth of God's revelation, together with the work of the Holy Spirit,
that brings about a covenantal change from one who is in Adam to one who is in Christ."*
—K. Scott Oliphint, *Covenantal Apologetics*

Lesson Goals

Theology—To understand the purpose and nature of God's revelation

Reading—To identify the topic, main ideas, and details

Vocabulary—To learn collocations from the reading passage

Grammar—To use adjectives and adjective phrases to describe revelation

---

Introduction

We have seen thus far how important the Creator-creature distinction is. Our next questions might be, "If there is so great a gap between God and his creatures, how can he relate to them? How can we know anything about him?" The answer to these questions can be summarized in the word *revelation*. Simply put, "If we are to know God at all, it is necessary that he reveal himself to us."[1]

Indeed, the Triune God has graciously and richly revealed himself to us! He has done so in the world around us, in our own conscience and being, and in his inerrant Word, Scripture. Scripture is treated uniquely as revelation that leads us to salvation by faith, and is thus called *special revelation*. "The knowledge of God's existence, character, and moral law, which comes through creation to all humanity, is often called '*general revelation*' (because it comes to all people generally). General revelation comes through observing nature, through seeing God's directing influence in history, and through an inner sense of God's existence and his laws that he has placed inside every person."[2] General revelation is of great value to us. It gives us knowledge of God; in fact, it surrounds us with it! As John Calvin said, "No matter which way you turn your eyes, there is no part of the world so small that at least some spark of His glory does not shine there."[3] But that knowledge does not save us; it convicts us. In other words, it makes us responsible as image-bearing covenant breakers.

---

1. Wayne Grudem, *Systematic Theology: An Introduction to Biblical Doctrine* (Grand Rapids, MI: Zondervan, 2000), 149. "If it is true that man can have knowledge of God then this fact presupposes that God on His part voluntarily chose to make Himself known to man in some way or other." Herman Bavinck, *Our Reasonable Faith*, trans. Henry Zylstra (Grand Rapids, MI: Eerdmans, 1956), 32.

2. Grudem, *Systematic Theology*, 123.

3. John Calvin, *Institutes of the Christian Religion: 1541 French Edition*, trans. Elsie Anne McKee (Grand Rapids, MI: Eerdmans, 2009), 30.

As Herman Bavinck wrote, "General revelation . . . is insufficient for human beings as sinners; it knows nothing of grace and forgiveness."[4] In other words, while general revelation reveals God, it does not reveal Christ and the work of the Holy Spirit, and faith-wrought union with the person of Christ is the only way we can once again have communion with God.

 Looking at the sentence that ends the paragraph above, we can rearrange the final phrase as follows: "we can have communion with God once again." Grammar gives us options here, and it may help us to move a key phrase to a natural place of emphasis—the end of the sentence (phonology). However, the reference—what we are trying to say—would essentially remain the same.

Discussion Questions

(1) What is your favorite passage of Scripture and why?
(2) Does your favorite passage tell us something about God's revelation?

Background for the Reading

In light of what we have discussed, we now know that revelation necessarily follows from the Creator-creature distinction. If God is utterly holy, then the only way we could have true knowledge of him (and of ourselves) would be if he condescended to our level and revealed himself. This is precisely what God has done, as the Westminster Confession states:

The distance between God and the creature is so great, that although reasonable creatures do owe obedience unto him as their Creator, yet they could never have any fruition of him as their blessedness and reward, but by some voluntary condescension on God's part, which he hath been pleased to express by way of covenant.[5]

Oliphint reminds us that even "in creating man, God voluntarily determined, at the same time, to establish a relationship with him. That relationship is properly designated a *covenant* . . . . [This covenant] comes to man by virtue of God's revelation, both in the world . . . and in his spoken word."[6] However, the *covenant of works* that was established at creation was broken when man sinned, and instead of ending his relationship with humanity, the Trinitarian God instituted the *covenant of grace*. We will learn more about this later.

The history of these covenants between God and his people is recorded for us in the Bible. The story of the covenants is the story of how God has redeemed his people from their sin; it is a story of redemption that has come through revelation, which climaxes in the revelation of God's own Son. Given the centrality of revelation for the Christian, it is important that we learn more about what this revelation, both general and special, is like. That is where our reading passage will help.

Pre-Reading

Based on your knowledge of the Bible, what are two things you can say about revelation (e.g., its purpose, something that describes it, etc.)?

Reading

In the following passage, J. van Genderen and W. H. Velema discuss five elements of revelation.

[¶1] On the basis[a] of Scripture, we can say the following about the origin,[b] content,[c] manner,[d] progression,[e] and aim of God's revelation:

4. Herman Bavinck, *Reformed Dogmatics*, vol. 1, *Prologeomena*, ed. John Bolt, trans. John Vriend (Grand Rapids: Baker Academic: 2003), 313. Hereafter *RD*.

5. WCF 7.1.

6. K. Scott Oliphint, *Covenantal Apologetics: Principles and Practice in Defense of Our Faith* (Wheaton, IL: Crossway, 2013), 41.

[¶2] *Revelation originates with God.* It is an act of God, which depends on nothing and no one. . . . The Old Testament already indicates with great clarity[f] that God's revelation is theocentric: he acts for the sake of the glorification of his holy name (Ezek. 36:22–23). It is not otherwise in the New Testament. The praise for the revelation of the mystery that was kept secret since the world began, but now is made manifest[g] in Christ, will be accorded[h] to God to all eternity (cf. Rom. 16:25–27).

[¶3] *God reveals himself.* He mentions his name when he appears to Abram, Isaac, Jacob, and Moses. Revelation is God communicating himself. . . . God enunciates[i] his Word, he makes known his ways, he reveals his counsel to his servants (Amos 3:7).

[¶4] *God reveals himself in his words and actions.* As a means[j] of revelation *the word* "corresponds[k] the most with the spirit of the entire revealed religion of the Old Testament, which emphasizes both the fellowship and distance between God and man; it is therefore no wonder that it occupies a most central place in intercourse[l] between God and man in the Old Testament" (Vriezen, *Hoofdlijnen* = main perspectives, 242). That God makes himself known to people by means of his word is no less prominent[m] in the New Testament. His word cannot be compared with human communication. It is full of dynamics[n] and power and is effectual.[o] "God's word is an act and his activity is speech" (Bavinck, *RD*, 1:336). The revelation of salvation that comes to us through words and the redeeming acts of God in history can be distinguished, but at the same time form a unity. . . . God makes himself known and at the same time he asserts[p] himself. Wherever he is present in word/deed, he presents[q] himself as both speaking and acting, and his people may meet him in this way. The main idea is that we rely on his Word and obey his Word.

[¶5] *There is a history of revelation.* Since God has not said and done everything at once, revelation progresses[r] through history in phases.[s] A sequence[t] of revelations was given to the patriarchs, to Moses, and to the people of Israel. During the days of the prophets there was a progression in revelation. Holy Scripture itself refers already to a history of revelation, and this expression is therefore biblically sound[u] (see Heb. 1:1). Revelation in the person and work of Christ is the absolute zenith.[v] In him the revelation of God is *perfect and* definitive,[w] for God has fully expressed himself in him.

Remember?
At the beginning of paragraph 5, you will find an example of the *there is* structure.

[¶6] *The purpose of God's revelation is that we shall know him.* The key[x] idea is knowledge of God in the full biblical sense of the word, as expressed in the words of Jesus: "And this is life eternal, that they might know thee the only true God, and Jesus Christ, whom thou hast sent" (John 17:3). This knowledge of God is the same as life in communion with God. Knowing God means acknowledging[y] God; acknowledging and serving him; serving and glorifying him. Revelation is *communicative.* By revealing himself to human beings, God desires to establish and maintain communion with us and to make this communion between him and us steadily[z] richer.[7]

a. Basis (n.): the foundation or main support
b. Origin (n.): beginning
c. Content (n.): essential meaning or significance
d. Manner (n.): the way something is done
e. Progression (n.): movement forward or development
f. Clarity (n.): precision of expression
g. Manifest (adj.): not hidden or concealed
h. Accord (v.): to render as due
i. Enunciate (v.): to announce, proclaim, or declare
j. Means (n.): something used to attain a desired end
k. Correspond (v.): to be in conformity or agreement
l. Intercourse (n.): dealings between persons
m. Prominent (adj.): noticeable
n. Dynamic (n.): a driving physical, moral, or intellectual force

o. Effectual (adj.): adequate to produce an intended effect
p. Assert oneself (v. phrase): to speak or act in a manner that compels recognition
q. Present (v.): to introduce or make present
r. Progress (v.): to move forward or advance
s. Phase (n.): a stage or interval in a development or cycle
t. Sequence (n.): a continuous or connected series
u. Sound (adj.): free from error or fallacy
v. Zenith (n.): the greatest height
w. Definitive (adj.): most authoritative, reliable, and complete
x. Key (adj.): leading, prominent, or critical
y. Acknowledge (v.): to recognize as genuine
z. Steadily (adv.): in a regular and continuous manner

Helpful Reading Terms

- Before you answer the main idea and detail questions below, it might help to review a few terms you will encounter there.

- Infer: to draw a logical conclusion based on facts. Good readers observe the facts (what is written) in a text and use them to draw logical conclusions (what is unstated). In Lesson 14, we will go into more depth about how to make inferences, but for now, think about the details of a text and what they might suggest or assume—that is making an inference!

- Purpose: the result or effect the author wants to have; the author's goal. Writers choose their words and structure their arguments with the goal of explaining information clearly and persuading their readers that they have a valid argument. In Lesson 18, we will study more closely how to determine an author's purpose, but for now, think about what the writer's goal is in using a particular word or organizing his or her argument in a particular way.

Main Ideas and Details

(1) Which of the following is the authors' *purpose* in this passage?
   a. They want to defend the idea of revelation.
   b. They want to confirm that God reveals Himself.
   c. They want to show us the progression of revelation.
   d. They want to identify and describe elements of revelation.

(2) At the bottom of paragraph 2, we learn that God will be "accorded" _____ for all of eternity.
   a. glory
   b. praise
   c. mystery
   d. revelation

7. J. van Genderen and W. H. Velema, *Concise Reformed Dogmatics*, trans. Gerrit Bilkes and Ed M. van der Maas (Phillipsburg, NJ: P&R, 2008), 24–26.

(3) What is the main idea of paragraph 4?
   a. God primarily uses the word to reveal himself.
   b. God uses words and actions in unity to reveal himself.
   c. God's revelation shows both a fellowship with and a distance from us.
   d. God's words and actions cannot be compared to human words and actions.

(4) In paragraph 4, the author uses the phrase "no less" because he wants to show which of the following?
   a. God reveals himself throughout all of Scripture.
   b. God's revelation is clearer in the New Testament.
   c. God reveals himself impersonally in the Old Testament.
   d. The revelation of God in the Old Testament is difficult to understand.

(5) What is the main idea of paragraph 5?
   a. God has revealed himself.
   b. God has fully expressed himself in Christ.
   c. God's revelation came progressively throughout history.
   d. There was a progression in revelation to the people of Israel.

(6) Based on the highlighted sentence in paragraph 6, which of the following can we infer?
   a. Knowledge of God cannot be purely intellectual.
   b. Knowledge of God requires personal relationship.
   c. Knowing God should draw us into communion with him.
   d. All of the above

Understanding the Reading

(1) Based on the reading, why would it be problematic to say that revelation simply provides us with "information" about God?

(2) What do you think the authors might say to someone who asserted that revelation is unnecessary in order to know God?

Collocations from the Passage

As you did in the previous lesson, circle the appropriate word in parentheses. All of the collocations in this exercise are taken directly from the reading passage.

There was nothing that compelled God to reveal himself. His love and glory could have been kept a (*mystery/secret/puzzle*). But he chose to reveal himself in what could only ever be a pure (*act/doing/statute*) of God. And once God chose to reveal himself, this revelation took a (*big/sovereign/central*) place in the Creator-creature relationship, for at the same (*time/minute/stretch*) that God revealed himself, he bound us in covenant with himself. That is why covenant is a key (*idea/thinking/plan*) in Scripture, from Genesis to Revelation.

Grammar Focus: Adjectives

Thus far, we have seen that complex sentences in TE may use a dummy subject to stand in for the true subject. This allows us to follow the linking verb with a complex noun phrase. Adjectives can play an important role in these phrases, and making sure that they are in the correct form helps the reader to recognize the noun phrase as a unit. Consider some of the noun phrases we encountered in the reading from Lesson 2.

As there are two **different** kinds of reality, so there are **different** kinds of goodness, justice, wisdom, and knowledge.

The adjective "different" modifies the noun "kinds," which is then modified by the prepositional phrase "of reality." The whole phrase goes together as a unit, helping us better understand the head noun, "kinds."[8] If we replace "different" with "differences"

---

8. A head noun is the "head element" or central thing in the phrase and is usually preceded and/or followed by other modifiers: "two different **kinds** of reality." Ron Cowan, *The Teacher's Grammar of English: A Course Book and Reference Guide* (New York: Cambridge University Press, 2008), 14.

("differences of reality"), the phrase is fundamentally changed because we have a different head noun: we would then not be focused on "kinds" but on "differences." Making sure your adjectives have the correct endings ensures that readers can recognize your phrases quickly and understand your meaning.

Note the adjectives used in the following excerpt (indicated in bold). Not all of them are part of a noun phrase, but some of them are. Underline which adjectives are *not* part of a noun phrase.

God reveals himself in his words and actions. As a means of revelation *the word* "corresponds the most with the spirit of the **entire revealed** religion of the Old Testament, which emphasizes both the fellowship and distance between God and man; it is therefore no wonder that it occupies a most **central** place in intercourse between God and man in the Old Testament" (Vriezen, *Hoofdlijnen* = **main** perspectives, 242). That God makes himself **known** to people by means of his word is no less **prominent** in the New Testament. His word cannot be compared with **human** communication. It is full of dynamics and power and is **effectual**. "God's word is an act and his activity is speech" (Bavinck, *RD*, 1:336). The revelation of salvation that comes to us through words and the **redeeming** acts of God in history can be distinguished, but at the same time form a unity.

The adjectives that are not part of a noun phrase are used with verbs.

God makes himself known

It is . . . **effectual**

As you can see from the examples, adjectives have various endings. Some adjectives are participle forms, ending in -ed or -ing. Other adjectives, such as "main" and "human," do not take one of these common endings and instead must be memorized and interpreted in context. "Human," for example, can be an adjective, but it is also a common noun. However, when it is a noun, it must either be made plural or be preceded with an article.

Ending	Example
-ive	redempt*ive*
-ic	histor*ic*
-al	effectu*al*
-ent	promin*ent*
Past Participle (often "-ed")	reveal*ed*, know*n*
Present Participle ("-ing")	redeem*ing*

Activity 1

Each blank in the paragraph below is followed by a noun form. Write the adjective form in the blank. Check your answers by referencing paragraph 2 of the theological text for this lesson. (Note: Sometimes an adjective form and a noun form can be identical.)

Revelation originates with God. It is an act of God, which depends on nothing and no one. . . . The Old Testament already indicates with _____ (*greatness*) clarity that God's revelation is _____ (combine *theo-* with *centrality*): he acts for the sake of the glorification of his _____ (*holiness*) name (Ezek. 36:22–23). It is not otherwise in the New Testament. The praise for the revelation of the mystery that was kept a secret since the world began, but now is made _____ (*knowledge*) in Christ, will be accorded to God to all eternity (cf. Rom. 16:25–27).

Below, list any additional adjectival endings you have found in doing this activity. Also list adjectives that may not have a common ending and simply must be memorized.

Activity 2

Imagine that a close relative of yours asks you what you have been studying in seminary. You reply, "We have been studying God's revelation." Your relative asks, "What have you learned so far?" In three to four sentences, describe revelation to your relative as best as you can. Once you have finished writing your sentences, go through them and underline the adjectives you used.

Introduction to Paraphrasing

A paraphrase is "a restatement of a text, passage, or work giving the meaning *in another form*" (emphasis added).[9] Turabian notes that "you paraphrase appropriately when you represent an idea in your own words more clearly or pointedly than the source does. But readers will think that you cross the line from fair paraphrase to plagiarism if they can match your words and phrasing with those of your source."[10] In other words, readers should be able to recognize the source's *idea* in your paraphrase, but not the source's explicit language. You can, however, use the key words of the source, without fear of plagiarism. We need to use certain key words if we are trying to communicate the same idea. Here is an example.

> **Original**: "With regard to the Old Testament, Paul links divine inspiration with words, not just prophets. God's inspiration—his "breathing out" the Scriptures—affects not only the human instrument but also the human product. Writings are inspired, not just people."[11]

> **Key words**: *Old Testament, words, inspiration* (and *inspired*), *Scriptures, people*

> **Paraphrase**: According to John Piper, when Paul reflects on the inspiration of the Old Testament documents, he connects inspiration not merely with people, but with words. It is not just people who are inspired, but what they have written.[12]

Notice how the author can use the key words without fear of plagiarizing, and the idea expressed is clearly Piper's idea, but it is put in the author's own words, using new vocabulary and different grammatical structures. A safe way of doing this is to read the original from the source, close the book, and then try to re-express it in your own language.

---

9. *Webster's Third New International Dictionary, Unabridged*, s.v. "paraphrase," accessed April 19, 2016, http://unabridged.merriam-webster.com.

10. Kate L. Turabian, *A Manual for Writers of Research Papers, Theses, and Dissertations*, 8th ed., rev. Wayne C. Booth et al. (Chicago: University of Chicago Press, 2013), 80.

11. John Piper, *A Peculiar Glory: How the Christian Scriptures Reveal Their Complete Truthfulness* (Wheaton, IL: Crossway, 2016), 73.

12. Ibid.

One of the ways in which students try to paraphrase from a source is to copy the passage from the source and then change a few words. Do **NOT** do this. If you do, you risk plagiarizing the author's sentence structures. The example below illustrates an incorrect paraphrase. Note which words the author has left out or substituted from the original.

> Incorrect Paraphrase: With regard to the Old Testament, Paul connects divine inspiration with to words, not just prophets. God's inspiration—his "breathing out" the Scriptures—affects not only the human instrument but also the human product. Writings are inspired, not just people.

Notice how the author has changed one of the main verbs, deleted a phrase, and taken out one of the adjectives. But the basic sentence structure has been copied from Piper. This is too close to the original to be considered a paraphrase. Copying the author's sentence structures is not permissible. To write an accurate paraphrase, you must put the author's ideas into your own words—using your own sentence structure and phrases.

Activity

Paraphrase each of the concepts above in your own words. First go through each one and underline key words that you can use without fear of plagiarism. Then try to restate the meaning of each sentence in your own words. Check your paraphrase with that of a partner.

> Language reflects the Trinitarian God in his eternal self-communion and in his communication to his creatures. Our use of words can serve as an apologetic for others. All meaning in language is rooted in God and his plan of redemption.

> We are creatures made in the image of God. As creatures, we are wholly different from God, and yet he condescended to commune with us by means of covenantal revelation.

> God's revelation has come to us through history and is the sole result of God condescending to the level of his creatures. In God's revelation, we come to know him (both through nature and through Scripture), and that knowledge attaches to our lives certain covenantal obligations.

1.

2.

3.

The Creator and the Creature (AP Task 2)

Introduction

In this task, you will be preparing to engage with a non-Christian who thinks that God is irrelevant. What follows may help you in forming a response.

Cornelius Van Til (1895–1987), who taught apologetics at Westminster Theological Seminary from 1929–72, often emphasized what he called the Creator-creature distinction. He used the following diagram to explain it:

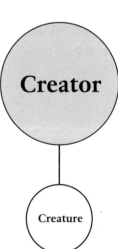

Fig. 3.1. Van Til's Creator-creature Diagram

The larger circle represents God, the Creator, while the smaller circle represents us as his creatures. The diagram is meant to show that God is wholly separate from and above his creatures. In fact, if God did not choose to reveal himself (represented by the line connecting the two circles), we would not know anything about him (WCF 7.1). But he *has* revealed himself, and he has done so in such a way that the Creator-creature distinction still holds.

Vocabulary

Note the vocabulary words below before listening to the lecture clip that follows.

> *Triune*—"being three in one"[13]
>
> *Self-Sufficient*—"able to maintain oneself or itself without outside aid"[14]
>
> *Independently*—"without dependence on another"[15]
>
> *Penetrate*—"to discover the inner contents or meaning of"[16]
>
> *Derivative*—"made up of or marked by elements or qualities [taken from] something else"[17]
>
> *Scale*—"a graduated or ordered series of degrees, stages, or classes"[18]
>
> *Centrally*—in a basic, essential, or dominant manner[19]

Lecture Clip

Without looking at the transcript below, listen to the lecture clip by Van Til.[20] Then, listen to the lecture clip again, this time following along with the transcript. Underline ideas that seem important.

> Now, then, what does the Bible teach? Well, the Bible, first of all, teaches that there is the Triune God, Father, Son, and Holy Ghost, eternally self-sufficient; that this Triune

God exists apart from the world, prior to the world, independently of the world; and that we therefore have to think of the Father, the Son, and the Spirit. We certainly cannot penetrate intellectually the mystery of the Trinity, but neither can we penetrate anything else intellectually because all other things depend on the mystery of the Trinity, and therefore all other things have exactly as much mystery in them as does the Trinity. Now, we say that this God created the world. Now, that means the world is the creation, and that he created man in his own image. Now, there's plenty of difficulty as to what we mean by the image of God in man, but in a general way we mean, of course, that man is like God in that he knows God—that is to say, he knows in dependence upon God; therefore, his knowledge is a dependent knowledge, a derivative knowledge, and what he says that he knows is a repetition on a created scale of what he has received by way of the revelation of God in the world, in himself, and directly, supernaturally, communication—communicated to him in the beginning of time, throughout all history, and centrally in Christ.

Listening/Reading Comprehension

Based on what you have heard in the lecture (and read in the transcript), answer the following questions.

1. According to Van Til, what is the difference between God's knowledge and our knowledge?

---

13. Donald K. McKim, *Westminster Dictionary of Theological Terms* (Louisville, KY: Westminster John Knox, 1996), 288.

14. *Webster's Third New International Dictionary, Unabridged*, s.v. "self-sufficient," accessed May 30, 2014, http://unabridged.merriam-webster.com.

15. Ibid., s.v. "independently."

16. Ibid., s.v. "penetrate."

17. Ibid., s.v. "derivative."

18. Ibid., s.v. "scale."

19. Ibid., s.v. "central."

20. Cornelius Van Til, "Christ and Human Thought: Modern Theology, Part 1," accessed May 30, 2014, http://media1.wts.edu/media/audio/vt612a_copyright.mp3 (lecture, Westminster Theological Seminary, Glenside, PA, no date), 2:32–4:07.

2. How do we know God?

Task

Now we are prepared to engage in some apologetics. Imagine that as you are eating lunch, you overhear two people having a discussion about God.

John: I think, as a society, we're moving closer to the place where God is no longer necessary. Nearly all of the mysteries that used to be attributed to God have now been explained by science. Take creation, for example. Darwin's theory of evolution is much more believable than the Genesis account.

Michael: I guess so. I'm not sure what I think about evolution. But I don't think God is unnecessary.

John: Why not?

Michael: I don't know . . . I guess I just think that God knows a lot more than we know, no matter how much progress we've made as a society.

John: But if one of God's traits is omniscience, then what happens when we get to the point where we know the same things that God knows?

Michael: I don't know. Do you think that's possible?

Part I: Discussion

Directions: With a partner, take ten minutes to discuss the following questions:

- What does John believe?
- How would you respond to John? Try to think of at least one point that you could make regarding John's beliefs.
- What might John say in response?

Part II: Role-Play

Directions: One of you will be John and the other will be a seminary student. Using the ideas that you have discussed in Part I, continue the conversation below. You should each speak at least three times beyond what has already been started for you.

Seminary student: Excuse me, I was sitting here and couldn't help but overhear your conversation. I'm interested in philosophy and religion and wondered if I could join your discussion.

John: Sure, that would be okay.

Seminary student: So, what do you think: Will we ever get to the point where we know the same things that God knows?

John: Yeah, I think it's possible. Someday scientists will have such a thorough understanding of evolution, DNA, the universe, and everything else, that we will know as much as God—whoever he is. Why, what do you think?

Seminary student: Well, I think…

Independent Study Adaptation

If you are studying independently, take a few notes on what you might say—but do not write down everything; just make a simple outline. Then, articulate your response to John and Michael out loud. Start your reply by restating John's position and asking him if you have understood him correctly. Then move on to explain what the problems are with his view. Your response should be less than two minutes in length. For extra practice, record your response and then listen to it. Write down the sentences you have spoken and then read over them for grammatical accuracy. Do the subjects and verbs agree? Does each of your sentences have at least one independent clause?

Also consider your pronunciation. Are you pronouncing the ends of words? Are you stressing the right syllables for key words? You can check the pronunciation of most English words with an online dictionary.

Learning the Genre: Apologetics

Theological Genres

We mentioned in the Introduction to this textbook that theology has several genres or types of writing. A **genre** is "a type of discourse that occurs in a particular setting, that has distinctive and recognizable patterns and norms of organization and structure, and that has particular and distinctive communicative functions."[21] We will focus our attention on five theological genres: *apologetics (AP)*, *biblical studies (BS)*, *church history (CH)*, *systematic theology (ST)*, and *practical theology (PT)*.

But why study these five genres? What makes them important? Well, if a genre has "distinctive and recognizable patterns and norms of organization," and if each genre has certain "communicative functions," then we need to be aware of these patterns and functions if we want to communicate effectively with others. Note the following paragraph, for example.

Anyone who determines to base his life on something other than the lordship of Christ and all that his lordship entails will discover that whatever foundation he thinks is holding him up is actually, even if sometimes slowly or imperceptibly, crumbling to dust beneath him. . . . The supposed basic foundation chosen cannot bear the weight of real life in God's world . . . . It is utterly impotent and so cannot begin to accomplish the task it has been assigned.[22]

- What is Oliphint's *communicative goal* in this paragraph? What does he want to express?
- Does he want to give his readers confidence?
- Is he making a general claim about Christ's lordship?
- Is he telling readers that all non-Christians are impotent?

Does he want his readers to look down on those who reject Christ?

If we do not know something about the genre, we may not know how to answer this question. This passage is taken from Oliphint's book, *Covenantal Apologetics: Principles and Practice in Defense of Our Faith*. Because apologetics has the joint aims of critiquing non-Christian thought and defending biblical truth, we know that Oliphint is not trying merely to make a claim or to insult non-Christians. Neither does he want his readers to feel prideful and superior to those who reject Christ's lordship—since the faith they have is a gift of the Spirit (cf. 1 Cor. 4:7). Given the joint aim of apologetics, the first option seems most probable: he wants readers to have confidence in the solid foundation of Christ's lordship. Those who live apart from Christ stand on a faulty foundation, no matter what foundation that may be. So Christians can take heart and confront unbelief with confidence, knowing that their foundation is sure and immovable.

The above conclusion would be difficult to arrive at if we did not know anything about the genre of apologetics. In this sense, knowing something about a theological genre will not only help you to *write* more effectively; it will also help you to *read* more effectively.

Genre Traits and Tools

Each theological genre has what we might call **genre traits**, that is, features distinct to a kind of writing. These traits are often not exclusive to any one genre, but they may be more predominant in one than in another. In apologetics, for example, one of the genre traits is **logical coherence**. By this we mean that the ideas are presented so as to build an argument with connected reasons. Logical coherence has both an *internal* and an *external* element. Internally, the author orders ideas and connects them based on a certain pattern or method of argumentation. Externally, the author provides the reader with *signal phrases* that point to that internal pattern. Note the following passage by Oliphint.

---

21. Jack C. Richards and Richard Schmidt, *Longman Dictionary of Language Teaching and Applied Linguistics*, 3rd ed. (New York: Longman, 2002), 224.

22. K. Scott Oliphint, *Covenantal Apologetics: Principles and Practice in Defense of Our Faith* (Wheaton, IL: Crossway, 2013), 75.

There is an absolute, covenantal antithesis between Christian theism and any other, opposing position. **Thus**, Christianity is true and anything opposing it is false. This should be obvious to any Christian, but it is oftentimes not as prominent in our thinking as it ought to be. When we claim to be Christians, we are doing more than just listing a biographical detail. We are claiming that the truth set forth in God's revelation describes the way things *really and truly* are in the world. **That is**, we are saying that what God says about the world is the way the world *really* is.

> "Thus" signals the logical effect or result of the preceding cause.

> "That is" signals a restatement of the previous point.

> "Therefore" signals a logical conclusion; "this means that" signals an explanation of the point just made.

> "Not only so" tells us he is about to add support for the argument.

Any view or position that opposes what God has said is **therefore** by definition, false and does not "fit" with the way the real world is. **This means that** the views of any who remain in unbelief are, in reality, illusions. They do not and cannot make sense of the world as it really is. **Not only so**, but, we should notice, there are at bottom only two options available to us. Either we bow the knee to Christ and affirm the truth of what God says, or we oppose him and thus attempt to "create" a world of our own making. No matter what kind of opposition there is to Christianity, before we even know the details of that opposition, we know that it cannot make sense of the real world. We know that it is self-destructive.[23]

The internal structure of Oliphint's argument (the order of ideas) is as follows:

Point 1: There is an absolute antithesis between Christianity and every other belief system.

Point 2: Christianity sees the world as it truly is.

Point 3: Every other system of belief does *not* see the world as it truly is.

Point 4: Christian apologists should assume that all opposing positions are self-destructive.

Activity

In two to three sentences, identify the internal structure (order of ideas) in the paragraph below. Then underline a few signal phrases that highlight this structure.

The Word perceived that corruption could not be got rid of otherwise than through death; yet He Himself, as the Word, being immortal and the Father's Son, was such as could not die. For this reason, therefore, He assumed a body capable of death, in order that it, through belonging to the Word Who is above all, might become in dying a sufficient exchange for all, and, itself remaining incorruptible through His indwelling, might thereafter put an end to corruption for all others as well, by the grace of the resurrection.[24]

---

23. Ibid., 51–52.

24. Athanasius, "The Incarnation of the Word of God," in *Christian Apologetics Past & Present: A Primary Source Reader*, vol. 1, *To 1500*, ed. William Edgar and K. Scott Oliphint (Wheaton, IL: Crossway, 2009), 180–81.

UNIT 2

WHAT IS TRUTH?
(APOLOGETICS)

4

Thinking as a Creature

"We think God's thoughts after Him analogically."
—Cornelius Van Til, *Common Grace and the Gospel*

Lesson Goals

Theology—To define and understand the importance of "analogical thinking"

Reading—To identify the topic, main ideas, and details

Vocabulary—To learn and use collocations from the reading passage

Grammar—To recognize and use the passive voice correctly

Introduction

Thus far, we have learned that there is a Creator-creature distinction and that the Triune God has voluntarily revealed himself to those creatures in a covenantal relationship. Because of God's revelation, we can know much about him and this world. Yet, when we know something about God and his world, how much do we know, and is our knowledge the same as God's knowledge? For example, I can study the structure of a maple leaf, looking at how the veins channel xylem and phloem to other parts of the leaf, and how the composition of the leaf enables it to carry out the process of photosynthesis, among other things. When I learn about all of these details, am I simply getting closer to matching the knowledge that God has of that leaf?

Cornelius Van Til would say, "No." "All of man's thinking must take place in humble subordination to thoughts which God has first and originally thought."[1] In other words, all of the true thoughts that I have, which amount to the real knowledge that I acquire about the leaf, have already been thought by God himself and revealed to me. What's more, God knows the truth about his world in a qualitatively different way than I do. As Greg Bahnsen put it, "God's knowledge is different from man's with respect to the subject (the knower) and the act of knowing."[2] As the one doing the knowing, God knows the leaf exhaustively, in a way that creatures can never fathom. He knows not only every detail about the leaf, but how every one of those details is related to every other detail of the cosmos he has created. In light of the Creator-creature distinction, our knowledge can only ever correspond to God's knowledge on a finite scale.

---

1. Greg L. Bahnsen, *Van Til's Apologetic* (Phillipsburg, NJ: P&R, 1998), 230. See also John M. Frame, *The Doctrine of the Knowledge of God*, A Theology of Lordship (Phillipsburg, NJ: P&R, 1987), 36–37.

2. Bahnsen, *Van Til's Apologetic*, 231–32.

So, we know God and his world truly, but we do not know them exhaustively.[3] In other words, we think *as creatures*. Van Til came to call this kind of thinking *analogical thinking*, and he contrasted it with non-Christian *univocal thinking*, that is, thinking that rejects the Creator-creature distinction.[4]

Discussion Questions

(1) Some people have charged Christians with being fideists, people who blindly and unreasonably believe in something. How would you respond to that charge?

(2) What do you think are the potential dangers of "univocal" thinking?

Background for the Reading

In our time, non-believers might feel as if science and reason have no bounds, that everything that exists is capable of being exhaustively explained and understood, and if we cannot do so with God—if we cannot know him conclusively and exhaustively—then he must not exist. However, this position fundamentally misunderstands who we are. Who we are restricts what we can do. Since we are *creatures*, we cannot comprehend God exhaustively, nor can we comprehend *anything* else exhaustively. As Van Til says, because everything that exists depends upon the mystery of the Trinity, "all other things have exactly as much mystery in them as does the Trinity."[5] This does not mean that we cannot know things truly. We think *analogically* (following God's thoughts on a creaturely level), not *equivocally* (as if we could not know anything truly) or *univocally* (as if we could think exactly as God thinks).

Pre-Reading

If Van Til says that we must think analogically, what are the tendencies that he might be arguing against? In other words, what are some of the conflicts we might have with those who think equivocally or univocally?

The word "conflict" can be a noun or a verb depending how it is pronounced (grammar and phonology). If we stress the first syllable, CONflict, then we are using the noun form. If we stress the second syllable, conFLICT, we are using the verb form. Each of these would then be referencing something different (reference), either a thing or an action.

Reading

In the following passage, Greg Bahnsen, a Van Til scholar, defines and explains Van Til's notion of analogical thinking.

[¶1] Against all unbelieving worldviews and their conceptions[a] of knowing, Van Til presented the epistemological alternative[b] of picturing man as thinking God's thoughts after Him.

[¶2] . . . Van Til speaks of human knowledge as being "analogical" of God's knowledge. This may not be a familiar[c] way of speaking, but by it Van Til stressed the "agreement, correspondence, resemblance,[d] or similarity" (the analogous relation) between God's knowledge and man's knowledge, while recognizing at the same time the elements of discontinuity[e] or difference between God's knowing and

Remember?
Find two adjectives in paragraph 1 and underline their endings.

3. Cornelius Van Til, *Introduction to Systematic Theology: Prolegomena and the Doctrines of Revelation, Scripture, and God*, ed. William Edgar, 2nd ed. (Phillipsburg, NJ: P&R, 2007), 61.

4. Ibid., 31, 177–78.

5. Cornelius Van Til, "Christ and Human Thought: Modern Theology, Part 1" (lecture, Westminster Theological Seminary, Glenside, PA, n.d.).

man's knowing. The fact that God is the transcendent Creator and sovereign controller of all things, and the fact that He (and thus His knowledge) is incomprehensible to man, must not lead anyone to think that He cannot be known or apprehended[f] by man. Much less should these facts suggest theological skepticism, according to Van Til. Just the opposite is the case when we think analogously to God's thinking. "When on the created level of existence man thinks God's thoughts after him, that is, when man thinks in self-conscious[g] submission to the voluntary revelation of the self-sufficient[h] God, he has therewith the only possible ground of certainty for his knowledge."[6] Van Til called the relationship between God's knowledge and man's knowledge "analogical" in order to express and guard the truthfulness and reliability of what man knows. "Since the human mind is created by God and is therefore in itself naturally revelational of God, the mind may be sure that its system is true and corresponds on a finite scale to the system of God. That is what we mean by saying that it is analogical to God's system."[7]

[¶3] In knowing anything, according to Van Til, man thinks what God Himself thinks: there is continuity between God's knowledge and man's knowledge, and thus a theoretical[i] basis for the certainty of human knowledge. At the same time, of course, when man knows something, it is man doing the thinking and not God—which introduces a discontinuity between the two *acts* of knowing, a discontinuity that is greater and more profound[j] than the discontinuity between one person's act of knowing something and another person's act of knowing it.

[¶4] Man cannot do what God does, except by way of finite imitation[k] or reflection. This applies to the act of knowing things. Because the word "analogy" refers to (and indeed stresses) the element of agreement or identity between two things that are different, it seemed an appropriate[l] word to describe the relationship between God's knowing and man's knowing.

[¶5] What man knows is literally[m] the truth (not an analogy of the truth)—the *same truth* known by God, accepted or verified[n] by the *same standard* or "point of reference" for both man and God (namely, God's own mind). Yet there is, to use Van Til's way of putting it, an important "qualitative[o] difference" between God's knowing and man's knowing.[8]

---

a. Conception (n.): a product of abstract or reflective thinking
b. Alternative (n.): an option or choice
c. Familiar (adj.): being well-acquainted with something
d. Resemblance (n.): the quality or state of being similar in appearance or quality
e. Discontinuity (n.): lack of cohesion; disunion of parts
f. Apprehend (v.): to come to know or learn
g. Self-conscious (adj. phrase): aware of oneself as an individual that experiences, desires, and acts

h. Self-sufficient (adj. phrase): able to maintain oneself without outside aid
i. Theoretical (adj.): of or relating to abstract knowledge
j. Profound (adj.): having intellectual depth
k. Imitation (n.): the act of mimicking the form of something
l. Appropriate (adj.): fit or proper
m. Literally (adv.): without metaphor or exaggeration
n. Verify (v.): to establish the truth of
o. Qualitative (adj.): of or relating to the essence or nature of something

---

6. Cornelius Van Til, "Nature and Scripture," in *The Infallible Word: A Symposium by the Members of the Faculty of Westminster Theological Seminary*, ed. N. B. Stonehouse and Paul Woolley (Philadelphia: Presbyterian and Reformed, 1946), 278.

7. Van Til, *An Introduction to Systematic Theology: Prolegomena and the Doctrines of Revelation, Scripture, and God*, 2nd ed., ed. William Edgar (Phillipsburg, NJ: P&R, 2007), 292.

8. Bahnsen, *Van Til's Apologetic*, 224–29.

Post-Reading

Summarize Van Til's understanding of human knowledge in your own words.

Main Ideas and Details

(1) Which pair of statements best captures the main idea of the reading?

    a. "Man cannot do what God does, except by way of finite imitation or reflection"; "What man knows is literally the truth."

    b. "The human mind is created by God"; "God is the transcendent Creator and sovereign controller of all things."

    c. "Man thinks what God Himself thinks"; "There is continuity between God's knowledge and man's knowledge."

    d. "When man knows something, it is man doing the thinking and not God"; "[There is] a discontinuity that is greater and more profound than the discontinuity between one person's act of knowing something and another person's act of knowing it."

(2) Which of the following best represents the purpose of the highlighted sentence in paragraph 2?

    a. Its purpose is to show that Van Til's terminology has been easily understood.

    b. Its purpose is to show that Van Til was trying to avoid two different secular views.

    c. Its purpose is to show that Van Til's terminology is not familiar to many readers.

    d. Its purpose is to show that there is utter discontinuity between man's knowledge and God's knowledge.

(3) In paragraph 2, what does the author mean when he says that the human mind is "naturally revelational" of God?

(4) Why does the writer use the phrase "at the same time" in paragraph 3?

    a. To clarify a temporal relation.

    b. To show that two events occur simultaneously.

    c. To show that the previous statement must be paired with the following one.

    d. To suggest that there is complete continuity between man's thoughts and God's thoughts.

(5) Which of the following can we infer based on paragraph 4?

    a. Man can do all that God does by reflecting Him.

    b. Our knowledge is a finite reflection of God's knowledge.

    c. There is no relationship between God's knowing and man's knowing.

    d. No word can describe the relationship between our knowledge and God's knowledge.

Understanding the Reading

(1) Identify one object in your immediate surroundings and make a list of the things you know about that object.

(2) Given that our knowledge is analogical of God's knowledge, in what ways do you think God's knowledge of that object differs from and agrees with our own? Write your list below.

"Object" is like the word "conflict," in that how we pronounce it determines its grammatical form. OBject is the noun form; obJECT is the verb form. To obJECT to something is to "oppose" it.

Collocations from the Passage

Circle the most appropriate word in parentheses. All of the collocations in this exercise are taken directly from the reading. When you have finished, you can check your answers there. (Note: In one of the sets of parentheses, all three of the choices are appropriate collocations!)

Van Til was always conscious of the Creator-creature distinction when it came to (*person/human/mankind*) knowledge. While there might be many ways to describe his understanding of our knowledge, perhaps the most (*appropriate/necessary/positive*) word is *analogical*, which is the word Van Til himself adopted. For him, there was an important (*divergence/disagreement/difference*) between knowing the (*reason/truth/validity*) in a limited but true sense, and knowing the truth exhaustively. It seemed (*appropriate/fitting/suitable*) to him to explain this difference with the terms analogical, equivocal, and univocal.

Grammar Focus: Passive Voice

Continuing our discussion of complex sentences in TE, we now come to the passive voice. We have seen how adjectives are used to modify head nouns in noun phrases, and how they can follow certain verbs. Verbs also serve an important function in relation to nouns, since verbs can be used to bring a central idea (sometimes a noun or noun phrase) into the reader's focus. Consider the difference between the following sentences.

God created the human mind.
The human mind *was created* by God.

The meaning of these sentences is the same, so why would we use the second one (illustrating the passive voice)? If we are writing a paragraph about the human mind as reflective of God, then we would want the reader to focus on "the human mind." So, it would make sense to use the second sentence because the passive verb ("was created") allows us to keep the noun phrase "the human mind" in focus as the subject of the sentence. Notice as well that a preposition follows the passive form: "by." This preposition marks the *agent* of the action, the one who did the creating.

In the excerpt below, note the use of the passive voice and how it places a certain noun or pronoun in a position of focus. Also note the preposition that follows each passive verb.

The fact that God is the transcendent Creator and sovereign controller of all things, and the fact that He (and thus His knowledge) is incomprehensible to man, must not lead anyone to think that He cannot **be known** or **apprehended** by man. . . . Van Til called the relationship between God's knowledge and man's knowledge "analogical" in order to express and guard the truthfulness and reliability of what man knows. "Since the human mind **is created** by God and is therefore in itself naturally revelational of God, the mind may be sure that its system is true and corresponds on a finite scale to the system of God. That is what we mean by saying that it is analogical to God's system."

We form the passive voice by using "tenses of the auxiliary *be* followed by the past participle."[9] Here are some examples:

Active Voice	Passive Voice
apprehend	*be apprehended*
know	*is known*
create	*is created*
bring	*is brought*
reveal	*has been revealed*
study	*is being studied*

The passive voice can be used with the infinitive as well: *to find* (active) versus *to be found* (passive).[10]

---

9. Michael Swan, *Practical English Usage*, 4th ed. (Oxford: Oxford University Press, 2016), entry 57.

10. As an example of how grammar is rooted in the Trinity, Poythress makes the following observation: "Each language on earth has its own distinct expressions, not entirely identical with other languages. And within English, the two expressions with 'the Father' as subject and 'the Son' as subject are distinct. The possibility of two distinct foci in English reflects human ability to have multiple foci. And this ability reflects—ectypally, derivatively, analogically—the archetypal distinctions within the Trinity. The archetypal distinction in the Trinity is reflected in English in the difference between an 'active' sentence ('The Father loves the Son') and a 'passive' sentence ('The Son is loved

Activity 1

Underline the examples of the passive voice that you find in the paragraph below.

Van Til realized that the epistemological disagreements between believers and unbelievers could not be resolved in a neutral fashion, as though the issue of God's existence and character (and man's relationship to Him) could be treated as secondary—and thus temporarily set aside without any commitment one way or another—while abstract philosophical issues were debated and settled. It is often, but vainly, imagined that once we come to agreement on our epistemology, we can apply those epistemological standards to the questions of whether God exists, whether miracles occur, whether the Bible is true, etc. By contrast, Van Til taught that abstract epistemological neutrality is an illusion and that, given the kind of God revealed in the Bible, imagined neutrality is actually prejudicial against God.[11]

Activity 2

The following sentences use the active voice. Rewrite them so that the passive voice is used.

Active	Passive
Man knows God through his revelation.	
God's thought transcends human thought.	
Van Til presented the idea of analogical thinking.	
Mankind imitates God on a creaturely level.	
Creatures follow their Creator.	

Activity 3

In three to four sentences, identify and explain one way in which God's revelation can *be used* in our search to know more about God and his world. Try to use the passive voice at least twice.

---

by the Father'). Built into English grammar is a reflection of the Trinity." Vern S. Poythress, *In the Beginning Was the Word: Language—A God-Centered Approach* (Wheaton, IL: Crossway, 2009), 254.

11. Bahnsen, *Van Til's Apologetic*, 145–46.

Activity 4

Speaking Focus: With a partner, refer to the reading as you discuss the following questions. Try to use the passive voice when appropriate. One way to make sure you use the passive is to start your answer by restating the question in a sentence form.

(1) How can the idea of analogical thinking be explained to a non-Christian?

(2) How is our knowledge related to the fact that we are created by God?

Collocations

Fill in the missing collocations in the table below. While these collocations have been taken directly from Lessons 2–4, more than one answer may be correct. For example, "true" could go in the first blank: We can have "true knowledge," even though "true" is not the word used in the earlier reading. The important thing is to identify correct collocations that you can memorize and use in your own writing. Try to complete the table below without looking at the reading. See what collocations you can remember.

	knowledge
appropriate	
	difference
know	
seem	
an act	
	a secret
central	
the same	
main	
key	
	distinction
	levels
different	
an important	

Additional Writing Practice

For additional practice, answer the following question in a unified, coherent, and developed paragraph. To help you develop your answer, you might contrast *analogical* with *univocal* knowledge (the idea that we know exactly what God knows) and *equivocal* knowledge (the idea that we cannot know anything for certain).

Why is "analogical knowledge" an important concept theologically? In other words, what theological truths does it communicate?

The Truth Matters (AP Task 3)

Introduction

For this task, you will be reflecting on an encounter you had with two non-Christians. To help you prepare for this, begin by reading John 17:1–19 and 18:33–38.

Vocabulary

The reading below will also help prepare you to respond, but we need to note some key vocabulary words first.

Affirm—"to validate or confirm"[12]
Practical—"given or disposed to action as opposed to speculation"[13]
Finite—"the limitation of objects or persons, their inability to transcend the boundaries of existence"[14]
Entirety—"the sum total or whole"[15]

Reading

The following excerpt may help us to respond to non-Christians who question the existence of truth.

Christ does not say that this Word is a witness to the truth. He does not affirm that it is a pointer thereto or a record of revelation. Rather, it is this Word itself, the message which has come from God and which Christ has given to the disciples, that is truth, and this truth is given to men for a practical purpose. That which is the Word of God, therefore, is truth, and by means thereof men may be sanctified.

God, who is infinite in wisdom and knowledge, has . . . revealed His truth to man in human words, words which man's finite mind cannot fully comprehend, but which man can understand. What then is the Word of God? For us today the Word of God is that which He has spoken. It is, we believe, the Bible in its entirety; the Bible is truth. God is the Author of every word thereof and, hence, we may rightly speak of it as truth.[16]

---

12. *Webster's Third New International Dictionary, Unabridged*, s.v. "affirm," accessed May 30, 2014, http://unabridged.merriam-webster.com.
13. Ibid., s.v. "practical."
14. Donald K. McKim, *The Westminster Dictionary of Theological Terms* (Louisville, KY: Westminster John Knox, 1996), 105.
15. *Webster's Third New International Dictionary, Unabridged*, s.v. "entirety," accessed May 30, 2014, http://unabridged.merriam-webster.com.
16. Edward J. Young, *Thy Word Is Truth: Some Thoughts on the Biblical Doctrine of Inspiration* (Grand Rapids, MI: Eerdmans, 1957), 268–69.

Keeping in mind what Young is saying, write an extended definition of "truth."

Task

As you are walking across the seminary's campus, you encounter two non-Christians taking a walk. They are discussing a recent political debate in which each of the candidates made false statements about the other. In her frustration, one of them says, "John Smith said that the governor spent far more than the state budget allowed, but we all know that isn't the whole truth! The budget was exceeded because of that state-wide emergency in the winter, and so the governor only did what he had to. I don't understand why Smith didn't just tell the whole truth." Her walking partner says, "That's just what people do in politics: they make claims to advance their own agenda. The truth doesn't matter anymore."

In your journal for the day, write a paragraph-long response to this conversation, expressing what the truth is and why it matters (paragraph unity). Support your position with two or three reasons or examples (paragraph development) and clearly state how they connect to your main idea (paragraph coherence).

5

Thy Word Is Truth

"Doubtless it is true that this side of the fall 'to err is human'; that does not mean that to be human is necessarily to err on every occasion and in every utterance. That the sovereign, transcendent God has graciously accommodated himself to human speech is a wonderful truth. But it is this accommodated speech which is then described as the word or words of God that are 'flawless' (Ps. 12:6)."
—D. A. Carson, *Collected Writings on Scripture*

Lesson Goals

Theology—To understand that God instills language with truth
Reading—To understand vocabulary in context; to identify main ideas and details
Vocabulary—To learn and use collocations from the reading passage
Grammar—To use comparative structures to describe differences

---

Introduction

"Truth" is a simple word, but it represents one of the most fundamental questions of human history, especially philosophy.[1] What is truth, and how do we know when we have acquired it? Perhaps these questions were in Pilate's mind when the Son of God stood before him and he asked, "What is truth?" (John 18:38).

We have so far discussed the nature of the Creator-creature distinction, the role of revelation, and analogical thinking, but central to all of these topics is the notion of truth. What is truth?

It might be better to ask a different question, based on what Scripture has revealed to us. Rather than ask "*What* is truth?" we should begin by asking

"*Who* is truth?" Truth, John 14:6 tells us, is ultimately a *person*. Jesus, the Son of God, is truth. The Son of God is not simply true, meaning that he lives and thinks in a manner that is true; rather, he is the truth himself! The truth of God "is manifest in the Word, who is the truth in the absolute sense (John 14:6). To know truth is to know truth from the One who is the truth, from the Son, and in knowing truth from the Son, we know the image of the truth in the mind of the Father."[2]

This understanding of truth may be quite radical when compared to our assumptions. But this is what Scripture reveals. In D. A. Carson's words, "Jesus is the truth, because he embodies the supreme

---

1 See Frame's discussion and references to "truth" in metaphysics, epistemology, and value theory in John M. Frame, *A History of Western Philosophy and Theology* (Phillipsburg, NJ: P&R, 2015), 8–19.

2 Vern S. Poythress, *Redeeming Philosophy: A God-Centered Approach to the Big Questions* (Wheaton, IL: Crossway, 2014), 82.

revelation of God—he himself 'narrates' God (1:18), says and does exclusively what the Father gives him to say and do (5:19ff; 8:29). . . . He is God's gracious self-disclosure, his 'Word,' made flesh (1:14)."[3] And while Jesus, the eternal Word, is truth himself, God has also given us the words of Scripture, which are just as trustworthy and true as the Son.[4]

Discussion Questions

(1) What do you think of when you hear the word "truth"?

(2) What do you think non-believers think of when they hear the word "truth"?

(3) Why do you think it is difficult for people to believe that God's Word is the truth?

Background for the Reading

Given what we have just said about truth, it is critical to affirm that the truth of God can be expressed in language. And if God is omnipotent (all-powerful), then he has the ability to condescend to his creatures' level and reveal himself in any manner he sees fit. He has the ability to speak life and light into death and darkness. This is precisely what God has done: he has spoken to us in his living and active word (Heb. 4:12), and we can trust that what God says is true because he is the author of truth; he *is* the truth (John 14:6).

Reading Skill: Understanding Vocabulary in Context

Let us now consider some important reading skills that will be of use to us in understanding the theological passage that follows.

A good reader knows how to read without looking up every word in the dictionary. Frequently stopping to look words up in the dictionary will mean that you take too long in trying to access the main ideas of a reading and that you will likely forget what the author's points are because you are too focused on understanding a particular word or sentence. This means that you do not have to learn every word in English before you can be a good reader. Good readers have learned strategies to use when they come upon unknown words.

When you use the strategies described below, your definition of a word may not be as precise as if you looked up the word in a dictionary. However, your definition will likely be accurate in context and provide enough understanding for you to continue reading with good comprehension.

Strategy #1: Skip the word.

Often there is enough context for you to know what the basic meaning of a sentence is without knowing what every word in that sentence means. This strategy works best when the word is not a key word (i.e., when it is only used once or twice in the passage) and the context (the words surrounding it) makes the meaning clear.

Example: What does "aspire" mean in this context? "On the one hand, non-Christians secretly *aspire* to be gods. They want to be the ultimate masters of meaning."

1. Read the sentence. Think about the unknown word's part of speech. *aspire = verb*

2. Look for clues in the context that help point to the word's meaning. *"aspire to be gods"* = *"want to be the ultimate masters of meaning"*

3. Check your answer. "non-Christians '**want**' to be gods"

Strategy #2: Look for context clues.

Writers often repeat an idea in several different ways. Learning to recognize the ways in which an author discusses an idea can help give you enough context to understand a word.

When reading, the following may help you to guess a word's meaning accurately.

---

3. D. A. Carson, *The Gospel according to John*, Pillar New Testament Commentary (Grand Rapids, MI: Eerdmans, 1991), 491.

4. Vern S. Poythress, "God and Language," in *Did God Really Say? Affirming the Truthfulness and Trustworthiness of Scripture*, ed. David B. Garner (Phillipsburg, NJ: P&R, 2012), 94–98. On the relation of the incarnate Word to the words of Scripture, see Richard B. Gaffin Jr., *God's Word in Servant Form: Abraham Kuyper and Herman Bavinck on the Doctrine of Scripture* (Jackson, MS: Reformed Academic, 2008), 101.

- Synonyms: words that have the same or similar meanings
  - » May be introduced with these phrases: "like," "or X," "that is"
  - » **Example**: "But we do not understand *comprehensively*, that is, in the way that only God can understand."
  - » *comprehensively = in the way that only God can understand*
- Antonyms: words that have opposite meanings
  - » May be introduced with these phrases: "unlike," "not," "no"
  - » **Example**: "And sentences may be reinterpreted *indefinitely*, with no visible boundaries."
  - » *indefinitely = no boundaries*
- Definitions: The author may provide a definition.
  - » May be introduced with "means," "is," "—X—," "(X)"[5]
  - » **Example**: ". . . uses a form of speech that expresses the meaning of the Tetragrammaton (the 'I am' of Ex. 3:14)."
  - » *Tetragrammaton = "I am"*
- Examples: Sometimes an author provides one or more examples of an idea.
  - » May be introduced by "for example," "such as," "including"
  - » **Example**: "And the context of the whole of the canon can enable us to appreciate relationships between analogous meanings, such as the relation between Exodus and John 8:12."
  - » *analogous = related in some way, like Exodus and John 8:12 are related*

Strategy #3: Identify key words and look them up in a dictionary.

Key words are words that are important to know in order to understand the main idea of the passage. These are words that you should look up in a dictionary because you need to have precise and accurate definitions of them in your mind to understand what you are reading.

Key words include: words in the title or subtitles, words in an abstract or chapter summary, words repeated frequently throughout the text, words in bold or italics.

Examples from this article: mastery, ambiguity, analogy, context.

Pre-Reading

One of the protests of non-believers is that words can have various meanings, and so we cannot be sure what, exactly, God has told us in Scripture. The words are somewhat ambiguous, and so the meaning of what God has said in his Word is not stable. Why do you think the words of Scripture have a stable meaning? Make a prediction.

Reading

In the following passage, Vern Poythress makes an argument for the stability of words.

[¶1] A non-Christian worldview may . . . create difficulties with respect to stability[a] of meaning. On the one hand, non-Christians secretly aspire[b] to be gods. They want to be the ultimate masters of meaning. So any flexibility[c] in the range of meaning of a word or sentence threatens to overthrow their mastery. They do not merely want stability, such as is guaranteed by the faithfulness of God to his own meanings, but godlike mastery. So they may overreach[d] in claims about their understanding of this or that text of Scripture.

Remember?
Here, "guarantee" is used in the passive voice.

5. In these examples, "X" stands for the definition. Here is an example: "The faith that we are defending must begin with, and necessarily include, the triune God—Father, Son, and Holy Spirit—who, as God, condescends to create and to redeem." K. Scott Oliphint, *Covenantal Apologetics: Principles and Practice in Defense of Our Faith* (Wheaton, IL: Crossway, 2013), 48. The author may also place the definition in parentheses.

[¶2] But in the cultures of the West today, people have reacted to this rationalistic extreme by going into postmodern irrationalism. A non-Christian worldview of this type admits that it falls short of absolute mastery. It then goes to the opposite extreme of ambiguity.[e] Words, it might be claimed, may mean almost anything. And sentences may be reinterpreted indefinitely,[f] with no visible boundaries for the endeavor.[g] What do we say in response?

[¶3] We need to avoid merely answering a non-Christian on his own terms. We must think biblically. To begin with, God's standards give us obligations.[h] We have moral responsibility, which includes a responsibility to respect meanings from people made in the image of God. Above all, we respect meanings coming from God's own mouth, that is, the meanings in Scripture. The moral standards of God, which are absolute, give us reason for rejecting manipulative[i] or fanciful interpretations, whereas an unbeliever, who cannot admit to absolutes, may feel free to multiply interpretations without limit.

[¶4] God also provides contexts that eliminate[j] many "theoretical ambiguities." The contexts—including the larger literary context of a biblical book, the context of the full canon of Scripture, the context of the human author, his purposes, his situation in history, and so on—all come to bear and enable us to discern[k] that a word or a sentence is used in one way rather than another that would theoretically be possible in other circumstances. We trust God who controls all contexts, and enables us to receive his word with understanding.

[¶5] We may take a particular example. Exodus 13:21 says, "The Lord went before them by day in a pillar of cloud to lead them along the way, and by night in a pillar of fire to give them *light*, that they might travel by day and by night." What is the meaning of the word *light*? The context of guidance through the wilderness indicates that a physical light is in view, coming from the supernatural phenomenon of the pillar of fire.

[¶6] Now compare this use of *light* in Exodus to John 8:12. Jesus says, "I am the *light* of the world." The context,[l] in which Jesus is talking about himself, and the larger context of the Gospel of John, where "light" is a repeated theme,[m] indicate that the verse is talking about Jesus' role as revealer of God the Father, and by implication[n] his role as guide to redemption and to eternal life. We can also see that the passage in Exodus and the passage in John 8:12 are related by analogy. In Exodus God used the physical light for physical guidance, intending it as a symbol for the larger role that he had in guiding the people spiritually and morally. The word *light* when viewed apart from any context whatsoever has the capability of designating[o] physical light, moral light, spiritual light of revelation, blinding light, and so on. The contexts enable us to appreciate what meaning belongs to a particular occurrence. And the context of the whole of the canon can enable us to appreciate relationships between analogous meanings, such as the relation between Exodus and John 8:12.

[¶7] We do understand. We understand truly. But we do not understand *comprehensively*,[p] that is, in the way that only God can understand. When Jesus says that he is the light of the world, he makes a stupendous claim that we do not fathom completely. His statement is, among other things, one of the "I am" sayings in John. He also says, "I am the bread of life" (John 6:35); "I am the good shepherd" (John 10:11); "I am the resurrection and the life" (John 11:25); "I am the true vine" (John 15:1). We suspect that all these statements resonate[q] with the "I am" in John 8:58, where Jesus claims to be eternally existent and uses a form of speech that expresses the meaning of the Tetragrammaton (the "I am" of Ex. 3:14).

[¶8] God is light (1 John 1:5). The ultimate anchorage[r] for the word *light* is in God himself, who is light. God by his own character and faithfulness gives ultimate stability to meaning in this world. He shows himself to us in speech, including speech about light. He makes definite claims. Only God knows himself perfectly and exhaustively.[s] But we do not need to be God in order to know him truly by receiving his speech in the Son through the power of the Holy Spirit.[6]

a. Stability (n.): the quality or state of being firmly established
b. Aspire (v.): to seek to attain or accomplish something
c. Flexibility (n.): the state of being capable of change or variability
d. Overreach (v.): to defeat oneself by seeking to do or gain too much
e. Ambiguity (n.): mystery arising especially from a vague knowledge or understanding
f. Indefinitely (adv.): without end
g. Endeavor (n.): a serious, determined effort
h. Obligation (n.): something someone is bound to do
i. Manipulative (adj.): tending to negotiate, control, or influence deviously
j. Eliminate (v.): to remove or expel

k. Discern (v.): to come to know or recognize
l. Context (n.): the part or parts of a written or spoken passage preceding or following a particular word or group of words
m. Theme (n.): subject or topic
n. Implication (n.): the act of implying by logical inference, association, or necessary consequence
o. Designate (v.): to serve as a name of; stand for; denote
p. Comprehensively (adv.): in a complete or exhaustive manner
q. Resonate (v.): to echo repeatedly
r. Anchorage (n.): means of security or grounds of trust
s. Exhaustively (adv.): completely

Post-Reading

In a single sentence, summarize what you have learned from Poythress' argument.

Use the chart below to name and briefly describe the two kinds of people Poythress contrasts in the first two paragraphs.

Name:	Name:
Description:	Description:

Main Ideas and Details

(1) Which of the following sentences best expresses the main idea of the reading?

a. There are many different contexts in which words can be used.
b. Though words can be true, they can also be used manipulatively and thus are confusing.

6. Vern S. Poythress, "God and Language" in *Did God Really Say? Affirming the Truthfulness and Trustworthiness of Scripture*, ed. David B. Garner (Phillipsburg, NJ: P&R, 2012), 102–4.

c. Jesus is the true meaning of the word "light" because he reveals his heavenly Father and guides us to eternal life.

d. Though we cannot understand words exhaustively, we understand them truly in their contexts, which are controlled by God.

(2) Without looking back at the text or looking in a dictionary, use the context of the sentence to choose the best meaning of the missing word. "To begin with, God's standards give us _____. We have moral responsibility, which includes a responsibility to respect meanings from people made in the image of God."

a. Meaning

b. Responsibilities

c. The image of God

d. Lack of responsibility

(3) Which of the sentences below best expresses the essential information of the highlighted sentence in paragraph 3?

a. God has absolute moral standards.

b. Unbelievers multiply potential meanings without limit.

c. God's absolute moral standards protect us from false interpretations.

d. Manipulative or fanciful interpretations result from a desire to have godlike mastery.

(4) In paragraph 4, the phrase "come to bear" means _____.

a. Show

b. Withhold

c. Struggle with

d. Contribute to

(5) Which of the following can we infer from paragraph 7?

a. Comprehensive knowledge of meaning is a biblical goal.

b. God is the only one who can understand anything exhaustively.

c. Our understanding of a word's meaning in a specific context can be exhaustive.

(6) Without looking back at the text or looking in a dictionary, use the context of the sentence to choose the best meaning of the missing word.

"The ultimate _____ for the word *light* is in God himself, who is light. God by his own character and faithfulness gives ultimate stability to meaning in this world."

a. Ability

b. Change

c. Stability

d. Variation

Understanding the Reading

In the opening paragraphs of the reading, the author compares two non-Christian approaches to language: a *rationalist* approach and an *irrationalist* approach. After critiquing these, he introduces the *biblical* approach. Based on your understanding of these approaches, label the following statements as either rationalist (R), irrationalist (I), or biblical (B).

_____ 1. The word "light" has so many meanings that we cannot be sure how to interpret it in John 8:12.

_____ 2. Whenever the word "light" is used in Scripture, it always refers primarily to spiritual light, and only secondarily to physical light.

_____ 3. In John 10:11, when Jesus is described as the "Good Shepherd," the author is likely using a metaphor to show how Jesus guides and cares for his people.

_____ 4. Metaphorical language in Scripture creates confusion as to what the primary meaning of a word should be.

_____ 5. The use of "Word" in the prologue of John's Gospel causes much debate because we cannot identify what background the writer is drawing upon.

Collocations from the Passage

Circle the most appropriate word in parentheses. When you have finished, you can check your answers in the reading passage.

Though it is true that all words have a(n) (*area/ scope/range*) of meaning, it does not follow that words have no stable meaning. In fact, words have ultimately stable meaning because God is stable and immovable. In light of this, we (*own/possess/have*) a responsibility to respect the stable meanings of the words people speak. If we do not, we violate the moral (*standards/criteria/measures*) that God has set in place by his creation of human language.

Using some of the collocations above, write a sentence stating how we know what "light" means in John 8:12.

Grammar Focus: Comparative Structures

So far, we have learned that complex sentences in TE can use the *there is/there are* structure to follow a linking verb with a longer noun phrase. Those noun phrases may include adjectives that modify the head noun in the phrase. We can also place a noun or noun phrase in the subject position of the sentence using a passive verb, helping the reader to focus on a central idea.

Another important function of complex sentences in TE is comparing and contrasting ideas to each other, and we use certain structures to do so. These *comparative structures* help us to show similarities and differences between two things. Examine the structures in the following chart.[7] Pay special attention to the form of the central word in each phrase.

Word Form	Comparison	Negative Comparison	Intensified Comparison	Comparison of Equality
Adjective	More important than More biblical than	Less important than Less biblical than	Much more important than Much more biblical than	As important as As biblical as
Adverb	More effectively than More precisely than	Less effectively than Less precisely than	Much more effectively than Much more precisely than	As effectively as As precisely as
Noun	More thought than More evidence than	Less thought than Less evidence than	Much more thought than Much more evidence than	As much thought as As much evidence as
Verb	Focuses more on X than on Y Occurs more frequently than	Focuses less on X than on Y Occurs less frequently than	Focuses much more on X than on Y Occurs much more frequently than	Focuses as much on X as on Y Occurs as frequently as

7. The basis of this chart comes from Susan Earle-Carlin, *Q: Skills for Success 5: Listening and Speaking* (New York: Oxford University Press, 2011), 66. Her colloquial examples have been exchanged for theological ones.

Activity 1

For each of the word forms below, write a complete sentence using the specified structure. Make sure the word form provided is at the center of your structure. An example has been provided for you. Reference the table above for help.

1. *Theological*—Negative Comparison
    His writing is less theological than Grudem's.
2. *Research* (n.)—Intensified Comparison

3. *Faith* (n.)—Comparison of Equality

4. *Emphasize*—Comparison

5. *Disciplined*—Intensified Comparison

6. *Consistent*—Comparison

7. *Reasonable*—Negative Comparison

8. *Recent*—Comparison

Activity 2

Part 1. In the boxes provided below, make a list of observations about how *water* is used in each passage. (You do not need to use complete sentences for your list.)

Exodus 17:6	John 4:10

Part 2. Based on your list, write a short paragraph (at least three sentences) comparing the use of water in Ex. 17:6 to its use in John 4:10. Try to use at least one of the comparative structures from the table in Activity 1.

 How we pronounce a sentence affects the meaning of that sentence. Note the following sentence and the different words we could stress. Each version potentially changes the meaning of the speaker.

Sentence	Potential Meaning
"**You** must be born again" (John 3:7).	*You*—not someone else, but you!
"You **must** be born again" (John 3:7).	It is *vital* that you be born again.
"You must **be born** again" (John 3:7).	This must happen *to* you; it is God's work.
"You must be born **again**" (John 3:7).	You need to be born *a second time*.

Speaking Activity

Part I: Practice reading the sentences from the chart and stressing the appropriate word(s) in each sentence. Then read one of the above sentences to a partner. Your partner should listen carefully and try to identify which sentence you read. Switch roles so you both have a chance to read at least two sentences and hear at least two sentences.

Part II: First, read the sentences below and discuss what potential meaning each sentence has. Then choose one of the sentences from each group to read aloud and have your partner identify which sentence you read.

   a.   "**Blessed** are the meek, for they shall inherit the earth" (Matt. 5:5).

   b.   "Blessed are the **meek**, for they shall inherit the earth" (Matt. 5:5).

   c.   "Blessed are the meek, for they **shall inherit** the earth" (Matt. 5:5).

   d.   "**I am** the Lord your God" (Ex. 20:2a).

   e.   "I am the **Lord** your God" (Ex. 20:2a).

   f.   "I am the Lord **your** God" (Ex. 20:2a).

> ### Note
>
> These exercises have you practice stressing different words for emphasis. Typically, the words that receive the most stress are the *nouns* or *verbs* at the end of a thought group (a phrase or clause). The sentences below show you which words in these sentences would typically receive stress in spoken English.

   1.   "You must be born **again**" (John 3:7).

   2.   Blessed are the **meek**, for they shall inherit the **earth**" (Matt. 5:5).

   3.   "I am the **Lord** your **God**" (Ex. 20:2a).

6

The Spirit's Testimony

"One of the most exciting things about the Spirit's testimony is that it is an intimate, even 'direct,' relation between ourselves and God. Listening to Scripture is not merely a transaction between ourselves and a book, even a very extraordinary book; rather, in Scripture we meet God himself."
—John M. Frame, *The Doctrine of the Word of God*

Lesson Goals

Theology—To understand that the Spirit works in us to prove the truth of Scripture

Reading—To use context to understand unknown words; to identify main ideas and details

Vocabulary—To learn and use collocations from the reading passage

Grammar—To use relative clauses and appositive structures to further identify a noun

---

Introduction

Now we know that the Triune God's Word is true and stable because *he* is true and stable. But having this knowledge does not in itself convince us of the truth of Scripture. After all, we are creatures who have a history of rebelling against what we know to be true (Rom. 1). Reasons and arguments, no matter how strong they are, will not ultimately be enough to convince us. "'Assurance of Scripture's infallible truth and divine authority' comes only from the 'inward work of the Holy Spirit.'"[1] Thus, "We need the Holy Spirit to change our hearts if we are going to be willing to come to God and hear his word submissively."[2] And when the Spirit has changed your heart, you will begin to understand that nothing is more sure and true than God's Word.[3]

Discussion Questions

(1) How does the world know that someone is telling the truth?

(2) How do we know that God is telling the truth?

---

1. Peter A. Lillback, "'The Infallible Rule of Interpretation of Scripture': The Hermeneutical Crisis and the Westminster Standards," in *Thy Word Is Still Truth: Essential Writings on the Doctrine of Scripture from the Reformation to Today*, ed. Peter A. Lillback and Richard B. Gaffin Jr. (Philadelphia: Westminster Seminary Press, 2013), 1307. See also WCF 1.5.

2. Vern S. Poythress, *Inerrancy and Worldview: Answering Modern Challenges to the Bible* (Wheaton, IL: Crossway, 2012), 70.

3. Kevin DeYoung, *Taking God at His Word: Why the Bible is Knowable, Necessary, and Enough, and What That Means for You and Me* (Wheaton, IL: Crossway, 2014), 40–42.

Background for the Reading

Perhaps Isaiah put it most poetically: "The grass withers, the flower fades, but the word of our God will stand forever" (Isa. 40:8). Yet what reason do we have to believe it will? Some biblical scholars have asserted that there are hundreds of prophecies in Scripture that have all come true, but skeptics reply that anyone could fabricate prophecies for historical events that we know have occurred. Why, then, should we take God at his word?

Reading Skill: Using Context to Understand Unknown Words

You have already begun to use context to understand words with which you are unfamiliar. Here are the strategies you have encountered so far: skip the word, look for context clues, and look up key words in a dictionary. The second strategy should be very useful for you and is worth practicing a bit more.

Underline the context clues within the sentence(s) below for each bolded word. Then, choose the best definition for each word. These sentences have been taken directly from the theological reading you are about to encounter.

1. Conjectures: "We ought to seek our conviction in a higher place than human reasons, judgments, or **conjectures**."
   a. Causes.
   b. Effects.
   c. Conclusions.

2. Foolishly: ". . . in order not to believe anything **foolishly** or lightly . . . ."
   a. Unwisely.
   b. Carefully.
   c. With great caution.

3. Genuineness: "We seek no proofs, no marks of **genuineness** upon which our judgment may lean . . . ."
   a. The quality of being true or valid.
   b. The quality of having the power to judge.
   c. The quality of having mistakes or imperfect copies.

Pre-Reading

Why might it be to our spiritual benefit only to have the truth of Scripture ultimately confirmed by the Holy Spirit?

Reading

In the following passage, John Calvin tells us about the Holy Spirit's work in convicting us of the truth of God's word.

[¶1] The highest proof[a] of Scripture derives[b] in general from the fact that God in person speaks in it. The prophets and apostles do not boast either of their keenness[c] or of anything that obtains credit for them as they speak; nor do they dwell upon rational proofs. Rather, they bring forward God's holy name, that by it the whole world may be brought into obedience to him. . . . If we desire to provide in the best way for our consciences . . . we ought to seek our conviction in a higher place than human reasons, judgments, or conjectures,[d] that is, in the secret testimony of the Spirit.

[¶2] They who strive[e] to build up firm faith in Scripture through disputation[f] are doing things backwards. . . . Even if anyone clears God's Sacred Word from man's evil speaking, he will not at once imprint[g] upon their hearts that certainty which piety requires. Since for

Remember? Can you find the comparative structure Calvin uses in this paragraph?

unbelieving men religion seems to stand by opinion alone, they, in order not to believe anything foolishly or lightly, both wish and demand rational proof that Moses and the prophets spoke divinely. But I reply: the testimony of the Spirit is more excellent than all reason. For as God alone is a fit witness of himself in his Word, so also the Word will not find acceptance in men's hearts before it is sealed[h] by the inward testimony of the Spirit. The same Spirit, therefore, who has spoken through the mouths of the prophets must penetrate[i] into our hearts to persuade us that they faithfully proclaimed what had been divinely commanded. Isaiah very aptly[j] expresses this connection in these words: "My Spirit which is in you, and the words that I have put in your mouth, and the mouths of your offspring, shall never fail" (Isa. 59:21).

[¶3] Let this point therefore stand: that those whom the Holy Spirit has inwardly taught truly rest upon Scripture, and that Scripture indeed is self-authenticated;[k] hence, it is not right to subject it to proof and reasoning. And the certainty it deserves with us, it attains[l] by the testimony of the Spirit. For even if it wins reverence[m] for itself by its own majesty, it seriously affects[n] us only when it is sealed upon our hearts through the Spirit. Therefore, illumined[o] by his power, we believe neither by our own nor by anyone else's judgment that Scripture is from God; but above human judgment we affirm with utter certainty (just as if we were gazing upon the majesty of God himself) that it has flowed to us from the very mouth of God by the ministry of men. We seek no proofs, no marks of genuineness[p] upon which our judgment may lean; but we subject our judgment and wit to it as to a thing far beyond any guesswork! This we do, not as persons accustomed to seize upon some unknown thing, which, under closer scrutiny,[q] displeases them, but fully conscious that we hold the unassailable truth! Nor do we do this as those miserable men who habitually bind over their minds to the thralldom[r] of superstition;[s] but we feel that the undoubted power of his divine majesty lives and breathes there. By this power we are drawn and inflamed, knowingly and willingly, to obey him, yet also more vitally and more effectively than by mere human willing or knowing.[4]

a. Proof (n.): something that induces certainty or establishes validity
b. Derive (v.): to have or take origin
c. Keenness (n.): the quality of being sharp or penetrating
d. Conjecture (n.): an inference or conclusion based on guesswork
e. Strive (v.): to try hard or earnestly
f. Disputation (n.): the act of debating or arguing
g. Imprint (v.): to fix permanently
h. Seal (v.): to confirm or make secure
i. Penetrate (v.): to pierce into or through something
j. Aptly (adv.): appropriately

k. Self-authenticated (adj.): given authority by oneself or itself
l. Attain (v.): to gain, achieve, or accomplish
m. Reverence (n.): honor or respect
n. Affect (v.): to produce an effect upon
o. Illumine (v.): to make bright or to enlighten
p. Genuineness (n.): the quality or state of being authentic
q. Scrutiny (n.): close inspection
r. Thralldom (n.): slavery or bondage
s. Superstition (n.): a belief or practice resulting from ignorance, unreasoning fear of the unknown; trust in magic or chance, or a false conception of causation

4. Calvin, Instit. 1.7.4–5, cited in *Thy Word Is Still Truth: Essential Writings on the Doctrine of Scripture from the Reformation to Today*, ed. Peter A. Lillback and Richard B. Gaffin Jr. (Philadelphia: Westminster Seminary Press, 2013), 81–82.

Post-Reading

What do you think Calvin might say about why we should take God at his word?

Main Ideas and Details

(1) Which of the following best expresses the main idea of the reading?
   a. There is a lot of proof for the truth of Scripture.
   b. Only the Spirit can confirm the truth of God's word for us.
   c. Nonbelievers are fully conscious of the fact that the Bible is God's word.
   d. Rational proofs are sometimes required to convince us that God's word is true.

(2) The highlighted sentence in paragraph 1 has which of the following purposes?
   a. To show that rational proofs have no value.
   b. To show that rational proofs are inadequate as testifiers to God's word.
   c. To show that keenness of insight can help one to prove the truth of Scripture.
   d. To show that the prophets and apostles were holy men because they did not boast.

(3) In paragraph 2, the word "clears" is closest in meaning to _____.
   a. Accepts and believes.
   b. Cleans up a mess.
   c. Upholds and defends.
   d. Uses to convict or accuse.

(4) Which of the following can we infer based on paragraph 2?
   a. Reason is worthless when it comes to the Christian religion.
   b. Only God's elect can be persuaded of the truth of his word.
   c. Those who use disputation to build up faith in Scripture are evil.
   d. Faith in the truth of Scripture is more than an intellectual matter.

(5) What is the referent of the highlighted pronoun in paragraph 3?

(6) In paragraph 3, the writer says that Scripture "seriously affects us only when it is sealed upon our hearts through the Spirit." He says this because _____
   a. Scripture has its own majesty.
   b. Scripture seriously affects the hearts of unbelievers.
   c. We can think highly of Scripture without letting it affect our lives.
   d. The act of "sealing" can be linked to the Spirit's work in the book of Revelation.

Understanding the Reading

Some of the following statements about the reading are true, and others are false. Place a "T" next to the statements that are true, and an "F" next to statements containing an error. Then revise each erroneous statement so that it is true.

_____ 1. Only the Spirit's testimony can convict us of the truth of God's word.

_____ 2. We submit our judgment to Scripture because it is completely trustworthy.

_____ 3. They who try to build up faith in Scripture through disputation are doing things biblically.

_____ 4. The Spirit who has spoken through the prophets must penetrate into our minds to persuade us that God's word is true.

_____ 5. We should not seek our conviction of the truth of Scripture in a higher place than human reason and judgment.

_____ 6. The prophets proclaimed God's holy name, that by it all people would be brought to understand God.

Collocations from the Passage

Match the words on the left to the most appropriate collocation on the right. These collocations have all been taken directly from the reading passage. (Each word on the left should have only one match on the right.)

firm	judgment
faithfully	faith
rational	proclaim
human	proof
divinely	commanded

Using some of the collocations above, write a sentence about the Holy Spirit's role in our reception of God's word.

Grammar Focus: Relative Clauses and Appositives

The complexity of sentences in TE often comes from the use of relative clauses and appositives, both of which help us to further describe or identify a noun phrase. But relative clauses and appositives differ in their form. A **relative clause** has a *subject* and a *finite verb*. Finite verbs are conjugated for tense, for example, ending with an -s (for the present) or an -ed (for the past).[5] Nonfinite verbs include -ing participles, -ed participles, and infinitives. Notice how the first example below is not a grammatically correct relative clause, because the verb it contains is a nonfinite verb ("rising").

INCORRECT: Machen refuted liberalism, which rising in popularity during his time.

CORRECT: Machen refuted liberalism, which <u>rose</u> in popularity during his time.

In the example sentence, "which" stands in for the subject ("liberalism"), and so we have a complete relative clause, with a subject and a finite verb ("rose").

Sometimes in English it is possible to leave out the relative pronoun and linking verb or to replace them with a participle, as the following examples illustrate. When this happens, we have a **reduced relative clause**.

The Spirit is the only one who is capable of turning our hearts toward God.

There are Christians who are convinced that they must prove the truth of Scripture.

Anyone who is attempting to prove the truth of Scripture will encounter difficulty.

An **appositive** is "a noun phrase that defines the noun phrase that it follows. . . . Appositives always have commas around them."[6] Note here that an appositive is a *phrase*, not a clause. It does not have a finite verb. Here are some examples.

Van Til, *an advocate of Calvin's theology*, carried on the Reformed tradition.

Calvin's understanding of the Spirit, *the third person of the Trinity*, is still widely accepted.

In short, both relative clauses and appositives help us to identify and further describe noun phrases, but they differ in their form (clause vs. phrase).

Activity 1

Underline the relative clauses in the following paragraph. *Advanced option*: Also underline any reduced relative clauses.

Let this point therefore stand: that those whom the Holy Spirit has inwardly taught truly rest upon Scripture, and that Scripture indeed is self-authenticated; hence, it is not right to subject it to proof and reasoning. And the certainty it deserves with us, it attains by the testimony of the Spirit. . . . We seek no proofs, no marks of genuineness upon which our judgment may lean; but we subject our judgment and wit to it as to a thing far beyond any guesswork! This we do, not as persons accustomed to seize upon some unknown thing, which, under closer scrutiny, displeases them, but fully conscious that we hold the unassailable truth!

5. Randolph Quirk et al., *A Comprehensive Grammar of the English Language* (New York: Longman, 1985), 96.
6. Ron Cowan, *The Teacher's Grammar of English: A Course Book and Reference Guide* (New York: Cambridge University Press, 2008), 19.

Activity 2

Read the sample sentences below. Based on what you have learned from the reading, use a relative clause to add information to each sentence.

Example: Revelation is all around us.

Revelation, through which God discloses himself to us, is all around us.

(1) Scripture is not subject to proof or reasoning.

(2) The Spirit must persuade us that the prophets spoke what God commanded.

(3) We subject our judgment to Scripture.

(4) Many Christians may think that they have to prove the truth of Scripture.

(5) We trust God's Word because we trust God himself.

Activity 3

For the list of nouns on the left, provide a possible appositive phrase in the column on the right. An example is provided for you in the first row.

Noun/Noun Phrase	Appositive Phrase
the Son	*the Word of the Father*
the Holy Spirit	
Scripture	
Isaiah	
language	

Activity 4

On your own, come up with a list of five famous biblical figures. Then, working with a partner, have the other person ask identifying questions to figure out who each character is. For example, if the character you have in mind is Philemon, your partner could ask, "Is the character from the Old Testament or the New Testament? Is the character a servant of Paul?" Let your partner continue asking questions until he or she guesses the figure you have in mind. Then switch roles.

Once you have each done this for a biblical character, use the information that helped your partner identify that character to write sentences that contain relative clauses or appositions. Write one sentence about each biblical figure.

Example: Philemon, a servant of Paul, had fled from his master.

Summary of Theological Concepts for Unit 2

- As God's creatures, we think his thoughts after him; we think "analogically."
- God's Word is the truth on which we stand. Scripture's words have stable meanings because God is the one behind them, and he is unchanging.
- We are convinced of the truth of God's revelation by the internal work of the Holy Spirit.

Activity

Paraphrase each of the concepts above in your own words.

(1)

(2)

(3)

Foolishness to the World (AP Task 4)

Introduction

In this task, your pastor has asked you to meditate on 1 Cor. 2:1–14 and write a summary paragraph that will help get church members excited about a new sermon series. The paragraph will be posted on the church's website.

To begin thinking about this task, read 1 Cor. 2:1–14 and make observations about Paul's reasoning. In what sense is the gospel foolishness to the world?

Task

Using your notes on 1 Cor. 2:1–14, compose a short paragraph for your church's website, explaining why the gospel seems foolish to the world. Your goal in this paragraph is to get members excited about a new sermon series, so while you should stay focused on the biblical text, you may bring in illustrations, examples, or references to culture when helpful.

UNIT 3

WHAT IS WRONG?
(APOLOGETICS)

7

Why Details Matter

"We need to be aware of the difference between the biblical worldview and the worldview presupposed in the assumptions of the historical-critical approach."
—Vern S. Poythress, *Inerrancy and Worldview*

Lesson Goals

Theology–To understand nuances in a theologian's doctrine of Scripture

Reading–To identify main ideas and details, and to draw inferences

Vocabulary–To skim a passage and identify key words; to learn and use additional collocations

Grammar–To practice using multiple tenses within a paragraph

Introduction

There is a saying in English, "The end justifies the means." "Means" refers to "something by the use or help of which a desired end is attained."[1] Essentially, this saying suggests that if your goal is worthy or noble, then it does not matter how you accomplish it. This is criticized, of course, because you can have a noble goal and yet accomplish it in a wicked or sinful way. Serving the poor is a noble goal, but robbing the rich to do so undercuts the nobility of the goal. The end does not justify the means; rather, the nobility of the means must match the nobility of the end. There must be consistency.

While this is true in an ethical sense, it is also true in a theoretical sense, especially when it comes to defending Scripture. We have noted already that we come to believe in the truth of Scripture by the internal work of the Holy Spirit. The Spirit, in fact, convinces us of what God has already said in his Word, namely, that it is true and trustworthy (Num. 23:19; 2 Sam. 22:31; Ps. 33:4; Prov. 30:5; Isa. 40:8; 45:19; John 1:1; 14:6; Titus 1:2). So, when we are asked about the truthfulness and trustworthiness of Scripture, we have the *goal* of defending God's Word. But what should our *means* of defense be?

We could, at first glance, try to look at historical evidence that would confirm the validity of the biblical documents. But we noted already that no amount of evidence, no argument, will convince others of the truth of Scripture. We cannot appeal primarily to either reason or history in defending the truth of Scripture, though these are certainly helpful.

---

1. *Webster's Third New International Dictionary, Unabridged*, s.v. "mean," accessed January 29, 2016, http://unabridged.merriam-webster.com.

To what can we appeal, then? What is our means of achieving the goal of a cogent defense of Scripture?

The Reformed tradition has largely held that Scripture is its own defense. We do not look to history or science to confirm our knowledge of Scripture. We look to Scripture as our highest authority, so whatever Scripture says about itself is what we should believe. What does Scripture say about itself?[2] Many things, certainly, but we can at least say that it testifies to its own truthfulness and inerrancy.[3] And so we believe in the truth of Scripture ultimately because God, in Scripture, tells us that his words are true and trustworthy. This may seem like circular reasoning, but, as John Frame has noted,

Arguments are always circular when they seek to validate an ultimate principle of thought. To show that reason is ultimate, one must appeal to reason. To show that sense experience is ultimate, one must show that this view is warranted by sense experience itself. Similarly with history, feeling, experience, and so on. Christians should not fear charges of circularity when they are proving God's Word by God's own principles of rationality. All alternative systems of thought are in the same boat. And . . . reasoning in accord with God's Word is the only kind of reasoning that doesn't dissolve into meaninglessness.[4]

Scripture is its own testimony. God's Word is true because it tells us that it is true. *This* is what the Spirit has convinced us of, and we must be consistent in showing that the truth of God's Word is established primarily by God's Word itself.

Warm-up

Read Gen. 3:1–13 out loud. Reading the text aloud (phonology) will help you to distinguish individual words (grammar) and may help you notice details in the narrative (reference) that you otherwise might miss.

Discussion Questions

(1) How does the serpent begin his temptation of Eve?

(2) What does his question reveal about his view of God's words?

Background for the Reading

Rather than making bold claims against God, the serpent tempts Eve with a question: "Did God really say . . . ?" After asking Eve this question, the serpent introduces a subtle change to God's words: "Did God actually say, 'You shall not eat of *any* tree in the garden'?" (Gen. 3:1). This subtle change introduces error by distorting and misrepresenting God's original message.[5] Eve followed the serpent's interpretation of God's speech rather than taking God at his word.

Even evangelicals with whom we often agree on many issues can introduce error into the church by failing to take God at his word. One example of this would be N. T. Wright's view of Scripture, which we will examine below. In contrast to such a view, the Reformed tradition has been known for its adherence to the biblical doctrine of Scripture as expressed in the Westminster Confession of Faith. As we said earlier, Scripture attests to its own authority; it is "self-authenticating." The Bible is true not because our human reason approves of it, but because God says it is true. We take God at his word.

However, over the last few centuries, this doctrine has come under serious attack not only from those

---

2. For a clear answer to this question, see Sinclair B. Ferguson, "How Does the Bible Look at Itself?," in *Inerrancy and Hermeneutic: A Tradition, a Challenge, a Debate*, ed. Harvie M. Conn (Grand Rapids, MI: Baker, 1988), 47–66.

3. John Frame suggests that "when we say that the Bible is inerrant, we mean that the Bible makes good on its claims." John M. Frame, *Doctrine of the Word of God*, A Theology of Lordship (Phillipsburg, NJ: P&R, 2010), 174. In other words, whatever Scripture claims to be true is, in fact, true. Scripture also testifies to its own authority, clarity, necessity, and sufficiency. For a discussion of these attributes, see Cornelius Van Til, "Nature and Scripture," in *The Infallible Word: A Symposium by the Members of the Faculty of Westminster Theological Seminary* (Philadelphia: Presbyterian and Reformed, 1946), 263–301. See also Wayne Grudem, *Systematic Theology: An Introduction to Biblical Doctrine* (Grand Rapids, MI: Zondervan, 2000), 73–138; and Frame, *The Doctrine of the Word of God*, 201–38.

4. Frame, *The Doctrine of the Word of God*, 24–25. See also Cornelius Van Til, *The Defense of the Faith*, ed. K. Scott Oliphint, 4th ed. (Phillipsburg, NJ: P&R, 2008), 122–24.

5. See the excellent expositions on this portion of Scripture by Geerhardus Vos, *Biblical Theology: Old and New Testaments* (1948; repr., Carlisle, PA: Banner of Truth, 2014), 34–36; and G. K. Beale, *The Temple and the Church's Mission: A Biblical Theology of the Dwelling Place of God*, New Studies in Biblical Theology 17 (Downers Grove, IL: InterVarsity, 2004), 396.

outside of the church but also from those within it. One of these attacks comes from the practice of *historical criticism*—the idea that we can "achieve only probable judgments about the past," that events in history must match the patterns we see in our immediate environment.[6] Some have tried to place historical criticism *above* the Bible's own self-testimony when trying to prove the Bible's truthfulness.

Reading Skills

Skim this reading to identify 3–5 key words that you think are necessary to know in order to understand the passage. Write the words down and compare the words you chose as key with the words your partner chose. Then look up the words in a dictionary. Try to read the rest of the passage without looking at the glosses (definitions to the right).

Pre-Reading

What do you think the problem might be with practicing historical criticism as the primary means of establishing the truth of Scripture?

Reading

In the excerpt below, John Frame critiques N. T. Wright's view of inerrancy and use of historical criticism.

[¶1] Since Wright prefers not to speak in traditional terms of Scripture's infallibility and inerrancy, one asks how he does evaluate[a] its statements, particularly in historical matters. I focus on history here because of its intrinsic[b] importance, because Wright is a biblical historian more than anything else, and because biblical history is, after all, the narrative[c] Wright considers so central in his theology of Scripture. He says that the historicity[d] of Scripture is important to him: although he challenges biblical literalists to rethink their assurances,[e] he says, this "does not mean that I am indifferent to the question of whether the events written about in the gospels actually took place. Far from it."

[¶2] I mentioned earlier that Wright is more conservative than many biblical scholars in his evaluation of biblical history. As we have seen, Wright opposes the rationalist approach of the Enlightenment, which led to "the muddled debates of modern biblical scholarship." He is himself vitally concerned with "the question of whether the events written about in the gospels actually took place." And for the most part his judgments are that these events did take place. But why does he come to this evaluation?

[¶3] The main reason he mentions is the evidence brought by biblical scholars, of whom he is, of course, a leading representative. In *Simply Christian* he summarizes his scholarly conclusions on the reliability[f] of the four Gospels and on the truth of Jesus' resurrection. In *The Last Word* he says that the way to combat[g] "modernist" views of Scripture influenced by Enlightenment rationalism is to go further into serious historical work than modernism

Remember?
"Wright considers so central . . ." is a relative clause, but the relative pronoun "that" can be left out (because it is the object of the verb "consider").

6. Vern S. Poythress, *Inerrancy and Worldview: Answering Modern Challenges to the Bible* (Wheaton, IL: Crossway, 2012), 47.

(for its own reasons) was prepared to do. When we do this, we discover again and again that many of the problems or "contradictions" discovered by modernist critical study were the result of projecting[h] alien worldviews onto the text.

Today, he says, biblical scholars have better resources than the old modernists had: lexicons, ancient texts, archeological and numismatic[i] discoveries. So, Wright continues,

> We should gratefully use all these historical resources. When we do so . . . we will discover that quite a bit of the old "modernist" consensus[j] is challenged on the grounds to which it originally appealed—namely, serious historical reconstruction.
>
> Christianity should be ready to give an answer about what really happened within history and how, within the historian's own proper discipline,[k] we can know that with the kind of "knowledge" appropriate to, and available within, historical research.

Note also that he says,

> Assessing [the Gospels'] historical worth can be done, if at all, only by the kind of painstaking historical work which I and others have attempted at some length.

So it appears that the scholar is the final arbiter[l] of historical truth. Of course, according to Wright, we should not carry on this work the way the old modernists did. We can do so much better than they.

[¶4] But there's something wrong with this. Wright is saying that historical scholars came up with conclusions radically contrary[m] to Scripture until, say, 1980, but now we can turn their ideas completely around with the resources we have today. But who is to say that a hundred years from now the modernists—or some new movement in the modernist tradition—might not gain the upper hand?[n] History is a human science, and it constantly changes in its methods and conclusions. Is Wright really so sure that his own methods and conclusions will endure forever?

[¶5] It is interesting that in this discussion Wright mentions that one of the problems with modernism was its tendency[o] toward "projecting alien worldviews onto the text." Does Wright think that scholars, even conservative scholars, can entirely avoid doing this today? . . . Clearly he disapproves of the modernists' use of their worldview, but he says nothing about the role of worldview, or what I would call presuppositions, in the work of historical scholarship.

[¶6] I doubt myself whether anyone can read Scripture, or any other book, without any presuppositions at all. . . . And, to make a long story short, it seems obvious[p] to me that Christian scholars should do their work out of a Christian worldview. So it is not just a matter of scholarship, and it is not just a matter of going and looking at the facts. It is a matter of looking at the facts in the right way.[7]

---

7. John M. Frame, "N. T. Wright and the Authority of Scripture," in *Did God Really Say? Affirming the Truthfulness and Trustworthiness of Scripture*, ed. David B. Garner (Phillipsburg, NJ: P&R, 2012), 123–26.

a. Evaluate (v.): to judge the worth of
b. Intrinsic (adj.): essential or inherent
c. Narrative (n.): story
d. Historicity (n.): the quality or state of being part of history
e. Assurance (n.): something that inspires confidence or certainty
f. Reliability (n.): the quality of being worthy of trust or dependence
g. Combat (v.): to struggle against or oppose
h. Project (v.): to put or set forth

i. Numismatic (adj.): of or relating to the study of money and currency
j. Consensus (n.): general agreement or collective opinion
k. Discipline (n.): a field of study
l. Arbiter (n.): judge
m. Contrary (adj.): opposed
n. Upper hand (n. phrase): control or advantage
o. Tendency (n.): proneness to a particular kind of thought or action
p. Obvious (adj.): easily perceived or noticed

Post-Reading

Summarize Frame's main critique of Wright.

Main Ideas and Details

(1) In your own words, state the main idea of the passage.

(2) Below are a few of the main ideas from selected paragraphs in the reading, as well as several supporting details. Write MI on the line next to each statement if it is a main idea in its respective paragraph. Write D on the line if it is a supporting reason or detail. Remember to note the context of each sentence in its paragraph (hierarchical structure) before marking your answers.

_____ 1. I doubt myself whether anyone can read Scripture, or any other book, without any presuppositions at all. (Paragraph 6)

_____ 2. Wright is saying that historical scholars came up with conclusions radically contrary to Scripture until, say, 1980, but now we can turn their ideas completely around with the resources we have today. (Paragraph 4)

_____ 3. Wright is more conservative than many biblical scholars in his evaluation of biblical history. (Paragraph 2)

_____ 4. It is a matter of looking at the facts in the right way. (Paragraph 6)

_____ 5. He is himself vitally concerned with "the question of whether the events written about in the gospels actually took place." (Paragraph 2)

_____ 6. There's something wrong with [Wright's method for supporting the truth of Scripture]. (Paragraph 4)

_____ 7. History is a human science, and it constantly changes in its methods and conclusions. (Paragraph 4)

_____ 8. Wright opposes the rationalist approach of the Enlightenment, which led to "the muddled debates of modern biblical scholarship." (Paragraph 2)

(3) The author introduces a question at the end of paragraph 2 because he wants to do which of the following?
   a. Introduce how Wright arrived at his conclusion.
   b. Challenge whether or not biblical events took place.
   c. Suggest that we cannot know what Wright's method was.
   d. Affirm that Wright has sound judgments about the events of Scripture.

(4) In paragraph 3, the verb "appeal" means _____.
   a. To plead.
   b. To challenge someone.
   c. To charge with a crime.
   d. To refer to as an authority.

(5) Which of the following can we infer based on paragraph 4?
   a. Wright might change his conclusions.
   b. Historical investigation is of little value.

    c. Historical scholars always come up with radical conclusions.

    d. Approximately every 100 years a new movement in history gains the upper hand.

(6) In paragraph 5, why does the author use the word "interesting"?

(7) Which of the following can we infer based on paragraph 6?

    a. A true interpretation of history does not have to be factual.

    b. Christians do not always act consistently with their worldview.

    c. An accurate view of history is simply a matter of scholarship.

    d. Christians are the only ones who do not have presuppositions.

Understanding the Reading

What follows is a summary of the reading, but words have been left out. Based on your understanding, fill in the blanks with your own words.

John Frame challenges us to examine our _____ when it comes to supporting the truth of Scripture. While Wright uses _____ to support the historical validity of Christianity, he seems to put too much weight on this, which amounts to trust in _____. In doing so, he also fails to account for the _____ that everyone has in interpreting history. As Christians, we must make sure that our _____ is biblical and not submit the truth of Scripture to _____, even if that standard or tool provides us with helpful information that can support our faith.

Collocations from the Passage

Circle the most appropriate word in parentheses. You can check your answers by returning to the reading passage for this lesson.

When it comes to the truth of Scripture, some theologians might suggest that we should go first to history in order to settle historical (*things*/*matters*/*events*). Rather than take God at his word, we should look for some way to make sure that God is, in fact, telling the truth in Scripture, or at least make sure that God's instruments (the human authors) did not make mistakes in transmitting God's revelation. Indeed, there is a strand of biblical (*knowledge*/*literacy*/*scholarship*) that encourages this approach. But more (*conservative*/*safe*/*old*) scholars take a different approach and uphold the self-authenticating nature of Scripture. This, they claim, is what all Christian (*scholars*/*authorities*/*apprentices*) should do, because it is consistent with their belief in the ultimate authority of God's revelation.

Grammar Focus: Multiple Tenses within a Paragraph

Complex sentences in TE convey a lot of information about noun phrases (describing them, comparing them, further defining them), but they also convey important information about the author's perspective through verbs. One of the ways in which an author expresses his perspective is through his use of verb tense. The tense of a verb communicates how the author views the action. If I write, "I considered the doctrine of revelation to be critical," that would communicate my view on the action of "considering" as occurring in the past. If I write, "I consider the doctrine of revelation to be critical," then I am communicating that this action of "considering" is current: I still (in the present) consider this doctrine to be critical. Verb tense reflects my perspective on the action.

As you write a paragraph, you may find yourself using more than one verb tense. This is perfectly fine as long as the verb tense choices are consistent. If you use two different tenses to refer to the same action, that would be considered an error. (See the following example.)

I studied biblical Greek for a year, during which time I also write *wrote* many sermons.

Note the use of verb tenses in the following excerpt. Is the author using various verb tenses consistently?

I **mentioned** earlier that Wright **is** more conservative than many biblical scholars in his evaluation of biblical history. As we **have seen**, Wright **opposes** the rationalist approach of the Enlightenment, which **led** to "the muddled debates of modern biblical scholarship." He **is** himself vitally concerned with "the question of whether the events written about in the gospels actually **took place**." And for the most part his judgments **are** that these events **did** take place. But why **does** he come to this evaluation?

Note what each of the tensed verbs refers to in this paragraph. Each of the author's choices is made based upon a certain principle.

Verb	Reference and Meaning	Principle
mentioned (simple past)	This refers to John Frame, and he is using the past tense to mean "what I wrote a few paragraphs ago."	Use the simple past tense to refer to action viewed as having already been completed.
is (simple present)	"Is" refers to N. T. Wright. Frame is making a claim/observation.	Use the simple present tense to make a claim or observation, or to analyze or critique another person's position.
have seen (present perfect)	"Have seen" refers to us as readers. The author is treating his written work as something stretched out across time. We have been moving through the article with him in the past and are currently still reading.	Use the present perfect tense to refer to action that was completed in the past but still is affecting the present.
opposes (simple present)	"Opposes" refers to Wright. Frame is making another claim/observation.	Use the simple present tense to make a claim or observation, or to analyze or critique another person's position.
led (simple past)	"Led" refers to the Enlightenment, a historical movement. Frame is noting how something in the past caused other events.	Use the simple past tense to refer to action viewed as having already been completed.
is (simple present)	"Is" refers to Wright. Frame is making another claim/observation.	Use the simple present tense to make a claim or observation, or to analyze or critique another person's position.

Verb	Reference and Meaning	Principle
took place (simple past)	"Took place" refers to "the events written about in the gospels." Since these events have already happened, the author needs to use the past tense to refer to them.	Use the simple past tense to refer to action viewed as having already been completed.
are (simple present)	"Are" refers to Wright's judgments. Frame is making another claim/ observation.	Use the simple present tense to make a claim or observation, or to analyze or critique another person's position.
did (simple past)	"Did" refers to "these events." The events have already happened.	Use the simple past tense to refer to action viewed as having already been completed.
does (simple present)	"Does" refers to Wright. The author is asking a question about Wright's position; he is analyzing or critiquing.	Use the simple present tense to make a claim or observation, or to analyze or critique another person's position.

As you can see, we can use many different tenses in the same paragraph, but this use is always *principled*. In other words, you must have consistent principles in place for the use of a verb tense, rather than switching back and forth between tenses when referencing the same event. For example, the following sentence would be incorrect.

* Frame argues that Scripture is our ultimate authority and critiqued those who suggest otherwise.

The two main verbs, "argues" (simple present) and "critiqued" (simple past), are referring to John Frame. More specifically, they are both making a claim about a person's position. So, both verbs should be in the present tense ("argues" and "critiques").

Activity 1

Insert the correct tense of the verb in parentheses. You can check your answers by revisiting the reading passage.

It is interesting that in this discussion Wright _____ (*mention*) that one of the problems with modernism _____ (*be*) its tendency toward "projecting alien worldviews onto the text." _____ (*do*) Wright think that scholars, even conservative scholars, can entirely avoid doing this today? . . . Clearly he _____ (*disapprove*) of the modernists' use of their worldview, but he _____ (*say*) nothing about the role of worldview, or what I would call presuppositions, in the work of historical scholarship. I _____ (*doubt*) myself whether anyone can read Scripture, or any other book, without any presuppositions at all. . . . And, to make a long story short, it _____ (*seem*) obvious to me that Christian scholars should do their work out of a Christian worldview.

Activity 2

Insert the correct tense of the verb in parentheses.

In Scripture, God's covenant lordship _____ (*have*) three major connotations: (1) God, by his almighty power, _____ (*be*) fully in *control* of the creation. (2) What God _____ (*say*) is ultimately *authoritative*, in the sense we _____ (*discuss*) previously. (3) As covenant Lord, he _____ (*take*) the creation (and parts of the creation, such as Israel, or the church) into special relationships with him, relationships that _____ (*lead*) to blessing or cursing. So he _____ (*be*) always *present* with them. He _____ (*be*) literally present with Israel in the tabernacle and the temple. He _____ (*become*) definitively present to us in the incarnation of Jesus Christ. And his Spirit _____ (*indwell*) NT believers, making them his temple. Truly God _____ (*be*) "God with us," Immanuel.[8]

Activity 3

With a partner, summarize what Frame thinks about Wright's approach to Scripture. Write your summary sentences down and then note how many different verb tenses you used. Did you follow the principles introduced above or did you encounter a new principle?

Activity 4

Fill in the missing collocations in the table below. While these collocations have been taken directly from Lessons 5–7, more than one answer may be correct. Try to fill in the chart without looking at the previous lessons. See what collocations you can remember.

	of meaning		proof
have			matters
	standards		scholarship
	faith	conservative	
faithfully			scholars

8. Frame, *The Doctrine of the Word of God*, 10.

No Good Reason (AP Task 5)

Introduction

In this task, we will be preparing to engage with a non-Christian who thinks that a wholly good and omnipotent God has no reason for allowing certain kinds of evil or suffering in the world. To prepare for this discussion, work with a partner by taking turns reading Rom. 8:12–30 out loud. Write any notes you may have below.

Why do you think Paul wrote this to the Christians in Rome?

When we encounter trouble in our lives, we often ask why. We want to know the purpose of our struggles. Perhaps we think that if we knew the reason, then we could avoid the same struggle in the future, and sometimes this is correct. But most often we cannot isolate a single, direct cause for our suffering. Even when we can find a cause for our suffering, such as some of the Roman Christians could during Paul's day, that does not mean we can alleviate the suffering.

For all Christians, there is hope because we know the fundamental reason for our suffering: we suffer with Christ so that we will be glorified with him (Rom. 8:17). We follow in Christ's path of humiliation leading to glory. So each time we experience suffering, we are conforming more to Christ's image (8:29).

Task

On a bus driving into the city, two men are talking about the tragedy of having to lose a child. The one man lost a son at the age of three months. The other man has no children, but shakes his head in sympathy and says, "There's just no reason that should happen—no reason. It's things like this that make me wonder why people still believe in God. I don't want to believe in a God who tells me that Jesus is my Savior but then makes me bury my own son." After the bus stops, the man who never had children exits, while the man who had to bury his infant son remains seated, staring out the window.

Imagine that you were on this bus and heard the conversation. The next day, you arrive on the campus of the seminary and are still thinking about all of this. A friend notices that you are quiet and asks you what you are thinking about. Summarize for your friend what you heard on the bus. Then, using three to four *connected* and *complete* sentences, relate this event to what you have learned about suffering from Rom. 8:29. You may use the "Sentence Starters" in the chart below to help you, and you may write down notes on what you want to say. Then deliver your response (the summary and the connection to Rom. 8:29) to a partner.

Sentence Starters

Expressions you can use to introduce your summary	*Well, yesterday I was riding the bus and heard . . . .* *I overheard a conversation yesterday about . . . .* *I heard a guy talking about how . . . .*
Expressions you can use to introduce a Christian approach to suffering	*Then I was thinking about Romans 8:29 and . . .* *This man really suffered, and I started to think about how we suffer as Christians . . . .* *I was trying to imagine the purpose of this man's suffering, and I thought . . . .*
Expressions you can use to finish your response	*Even in horrible situations like the loss of a son . . . .* *While I cannot understand this man's suffering, . . .* *In the midst of our suffering, Christians must . . . .*

8

The World Awry

"There is a difference between, say, a rape and a destructive tornado, between a war caused by human avarice and an earthquake that no human being could either start or stop. Yet from another perspective, both kinds of evil, and the suffering caused by both kinds of evil, are the result of sin, of rebellion—and therefore of moral evil."
—D. A. Carson, *How Long, O Lord?*

Lesson Goals

Theology—To understand the place of rebellion in sin
Reading—To identify main ideas and details, and to draw inferences
Vocabulary—To learn and use additional collocations from the reading passage
Grammar—To practice using the definite and indefinite article

---

Introduction

Thus far, while we have touched on sin and read through the biblical account in Gen. 3, we have yet to discuss the issue of sin and its effects more deeply. This is important to discuss now, since it has implications for everything we have encountered so far. Language, as a means for our communion with the Triune God and with each other, is often misused and abused. We hurt others with our words rather than speaking so as to give grace to those who hear what we say (Eph. 4:29). While the Creator-creature distinction is of utmost importance, it is often denied or ignored because of our sinful rebellion. We want to be the lords of our own lives, and so we suppress the truth of God's sovereignty. While God's revelation in nature and in Scripture is clear and true, we misinterpret it or are blind to it. While we should think God's thoughts after

him analogically, we often try to think univocally, as if we could know exactly as God knows, or equivocally, as if true knowledge were not attainable. While we know that Scripture is proved true by the Spirit's testimony, we sometimes seek a source of authority that might stand above revelation. In short, in all that we have discussed so far, we can see the effects of sin. The whole world, we might say, has gone awry—it has become crooked and contorted by rebellion.

This is why the gospel is always so precious—while Calvin said that we cannot look anywhere without seeing some spark of God's glory, we can also say that we cannot look anywhere without seeing something or someone in desperate need of the redemption that only the gospel can bring. That is what makes it such good news: there is no time or place when the gospel is not relevant or applicable in addressing sin and its

73

effects! But that does not make it easy for us to bring the message to a world in need of redemption, for sin has manifested itself and affected life around us in horrible ways. Many diseases and natural disasters, which are most obviously out of our control, are part of these manifestations. As we saw with the previous task, the loss of life can also be a significant barrier for someone in need of the gospel. In these situations, when it seems impossible to deliver the message of the gospel effectively to someone experiencing great pain, it is critical to remember that the works of healing and regeneration are entirely God's doing (Ex. 15:26; Ps. 103:3; Matt. 8:16; John 3; Rom. 8:2). The task of bringing the gospel to a hurting and hostile world does indeed seem impossible, but God is in the business of doing impossible things through those who commit themselves to him in faith (Matt. 19:26).

Taking a step in this direction, we will focus in this lesson on the nature of evil as expressed in our pain and suffering. We will also examine the theological roots of evil as rebellion against the wise, just, and loving rule of a good God.

Discussion Questions

(1) What reason do you think non-believers would offer for the world's pain and suffering?

(2) Why might the Christian reason for the world's suffering be unattractive?

(3) How can the Christian reason for the world's suffering seem insulting?

Background for the Reading

Something has gone horribly wrong with the world. Pain and suffering afflict more than those subjected to others' acts of violence. In December of 2004, a tsunami killed over 250,000 people around the rim of the Indian Ocean. Each year, 7.6 million people suffer and die from cancer,[1] leaving behind countless mourners in their wake. Other people battle a host of diseases that leave them weak and crippled. No matter what form of pain people may struggle with, almost everyone longs to know why.

Pre-Reading

How would you define evil? Come up with a tentative definition and write it below.

Reading

In the following passage, D. A. Carson defines evil and presents a biblical understanding of it.

[¶1] Evil is evil because it is rebellion[a] against God. Evil is the failure to do what God demands or the performance of what God forbids.[b] Not to love God with heart and soul and mind and strength is a great evil, for God has demanded it; not to love our neighbor as ourself is a great evil, for the same reason. To covet[c] someone's house or car or wife is a great evil, for God has forbidden covetousness; to nurture bitterness and self-pity is evil, for a similar reason. The dimensions[d] of evil are thus established by the dimensions of God; the ugliness of evil is established by the beauty of God; the filth of evil is established by the love of God.

[¶2] From this, it follows that in any Christian understanding of God and the world, Kushner's famous title is profoundly misleading. *When Bad Things Happen to Good People* assumes the world is populated largely by "good people." The drift[e] of the Bible's story line

---

1. This figure is taken from "Cancer Prevention and Control," Centers for Disease Control and Prevention, accessed January 24, 2014, http://www.cdc.gov/cancer/dcpc/resources/features/ WorldCancerDay/.

sees things differently: we are all caught up in rebellion, and therefore none of us belongs to the "good people." In any absolute sense, "good people" is an empty set.

[¶3] I am not saying that this resolves[f] the problem of evil and suffering, as if the proper admonition[g] to everyone enmeshed in sorrow is a brutal "Stop complaining. You are only getting what you deserve." In many contexts the Bible speaks in relative[h] ways of the righteous and the unrighteous. None of us is as evil as we might be. Even a Hitler might have kicked his dog one more time. Moreover, we often ask why, within this fallen world, some seem to prosper[i] and have an easy time of it while others who are on any reckoning far better persons suffer enormously. Many other biblical truths need a little unpacking[j] if such a sense of the inequity of things is to be alleviated.[k]

[¶4] Yet Christians undergoing pain and suffering will be well served by contemplating[l] the Bible's story line and meditating on the price of sin. We live in an age where everyone is concerned about their "rights." But there is a profound sense in which our "rights" before God have been sacrificed by our sin. If in fact we believe that our sin properly deserves the wrath of God, then when we experience the sufferings of this world, all of them the consequences of human rebellion, we will be less quick to blame God and a lot quicker to recognize that we have no fundamental right to expect a life of unbroken ease and comfort. From the biblical perspective, it is because of the Lord's mercies that we are not consumed.[m]

Remember?
What two verb tenses is Carson using in paragraph 4?

[¶5] Most emphatically, this does not mean that every bit of suffering is the immediate[n] consequence of a particular sin. That is a hideous piece of heresy, capable of inflicting untold mental anguish.[o] It would mean that the people who suffer most in this world must be those who have sinned the most in this world; and that is demonstrably untrue, both in the Bible and in experience. Some of the possible connections between a specific sin and a particular illness will be worked out in a later chapter. For the moment it is enough to observe that illness *can* be the direct result of a specific sin (as in the case of those described in 1 Cor. 11:27–34; or in the case of the man in John 5:1–15 who was paralyzed for thirty-eight years), but there is no *necessary* connection between a specific sin and a particular spell[p] of suffering (e.g., the man born blind [John 9]).[2]

a. Rebellion (n.): opposition to a person in a position of authority
b. Forbid (v.): to prohibit
c. Covet (v.): to crave the possession or enjoyment of
d. Dimension (n.): the range, extent, or scope
e. Drift (n.): a general underlying design or intent
f. Resolve (v.): to conclude or solve
g. Admonition (n.): warning, reminder, or advice
h. Relative (adj.): not absolute or independent

i. Prosper (v.): to succeed
j. Unpack (v.): to explain
k. Alleviate (v.): to relieve or lessen
l. Contemplate (v.): to consider with thoughtfulness, attention or reflection
m. Consume (v.): to destroy completely
n. Immediate (adj.): direct
o. Anguish (n.): extreme pain of body or mind
p. Spell (n.): a period of time

2. D. A. Carson, *How Long O Lord? Reflections on Suffering and Evil*, 2nd ed. (Grand Rapids, MI: Baker, 2006), 42–44. Excerpt from *How Long O Lord?* by D.A. Carson, copyright © 1990. Used by permission of Baker Academic, a division of Baker Publishing Group.

Post-Reading

Compare your definition of evil to that of D. A. Carson. How are they different or similar?

Explain why people might be tempted to think that a particular instance of suffering is related to a particular sin.

Main Ideas and Details

(1) Claims from the reading are listed below. Place an A next to the claim if it is reproduced accurately. Place an N next to it if is not accurate, and then correct it.

_____A. There is a profound sense in which our "rights" before God have been sacrificed by our sin.

_____B. In any absolute sense, "good people" is almost an empty set.

_____C. Evil is the failure to do what God demands or the performance of what God commands.

_____D. The dimensions of evil are thus established by the dimensions of God; the ugliness of evil is established by the beauty of God.

_____E. In many contexts the Bible speaks in absolute ways of the righteous and the unrighteous.

(2) In paragraph 1, the word "established" is closest in meaning to _____.
   a. Organized.
   b. Considered.
   c. Documented.
   d. Founded upon.

(3) Which of the following is the purpose for the author introducing a book's title in paragraph 2?
   a. He wants to contrast a popular opinion with a biblical truth.
   b. He wants to show that there are some good people in the world.
   c. He wants to link his topic to the author of a well-known publication.
   d. He wants to suggest that popular culture can understand biblical teaching.

(4) Which of the words in this sentence is the closest in meaning to "contemplating"?

"Yet Christians undergoing pain and suffering will be well served by contemplating the Bible's story line and meditating on the price of sin."

   a. Sin.
   b. Suffering.
   c. Meditating.
   d. Undergoing.

(5) Which of the following sentences best expresses the main idea of paragraph 4?
   a. Sin deserves the wrath of God.
   b. All of us experience the consequences of sin.
   c. Thinking of the Bible's view of sin will help us to avoid suffering.
   d. Meditating on Scripture and the price of sin helps us to see that God is merciful.

(6) Which of the following can we infer based on paragraph 5?
   a. Illness cannot be the direct result of someone's sin.
   b. Those who suffer the most in this world are probably the most righteous.
   c. There is never a connection between a specific sin and an experience of suffering.
   d. Not every instance of suffering is the result of a particular sin.

(7) Why does the author italicize the words "can" and "necessary" in paragraph 5?

Understanding the Reading

Though instances of suffering cannot always be tied to particular sins, the Bible many times shows that people suffer consequences as a result of disobeying God's commands. Consider a biblical character who experienced great suffering as a result of disobedience. Then explain something that we learn about sin from this event. An example is provided for you at the top of the next page.

Biblical Character: King Saul	
Suffering Tied to Disobedience: Saul sinned by sparing the king of the Amalekites, along with their best livestock, rather than destroying them (1 Sam. 15:9), as God had commanded. As a result, he suffered rejection from the Lord (15:26).	**What We Learn about Sin:** From Saul's sin, we learn that it is important to follow God's commands exactly, rather than supplementing them when we feel as if we can benefit from doing things differently.

Biblical Character	
Suffering Tied to Disobedience:	**What We Learn about Sin:**

Collocations from the Passage

Match the word on the left to the most appropriate collocation on the right. Each word has only one correct answer. You can check your answers by re-examining the reading.

resolve	world
suffer	enormously
undergo	a problem
fallen	suffering
biblical	truths

Using some of the collocations above, write two sentences about how sin affects our daily lives.

Grammar Focus: Articles

In this section, we end our discussion of the structure of complex sentences in TE, though we will pick up this discussion later in the book. It might seem strange to discuss articles as part of the structure of a sentence. Articles just modify nouns, and English language learners often think that native English speakers use articles arbitrarily. In fact, articles are not used arbitrarily (without following a principle or reason). They are used according to certain principles. We have provided three of these principles below.

1. Articles tell us something about the author's perspective on the reader's knowledge. Just as verb tense conveys the author's perspective on the action, the use of articles conveys the author's perspective on what the reader knows.

A. Authors will often use the definite article (*the*) to convey that the reader knows what he or she is referencing.[3] Here are some examples.

Have you read *the* Bible today? [There is only one Bible.]

3. Michael Swan, *Practical English Usage*, 4th ed. (Oxford: Oxford University Press, 2016), entry 135.

At seminary, *the* professors strive to prepare their students for ministry. [Every seminary has professors.]

Machen wrote *New Testament Greek for Beginners*, the Greek grammar book that is still used today by many seminary students. [The reader knows that "the Greek grammar book" refers to *New Testament Greek for Beginners*.]

B. If the reader does not know what the author is referencing, then the indefinite article (*a* or *an*) or a plural noun (without an article) may be used.

A discourse analysis is used to discover the central point in a biblical passage. [Here, we are assuming that the reader might not know what a discourse analysis is. Because "analysis" is a countable noun, we place an indefinite article before the phrase to tell the reader that he or she may not have prior knowledge of this concept.]

There is *a* book on Scripture that I would like to read. [We do not know which book.]

2. The presence or absence of an article tells us whether a noun is considered general or specific. When referring to things in general, such as concepts or ideas, the author will not usually use an article, conveying that the reader also has knowledge of this general thing. And while the absence of an article can suggest that the noun is considered general, the presence of an article indicates that the noun is more specific. This is especially common when a noun is modified by a prepositional phrase.

Theology is the study of God and his relationship with his creatures. ["Theology" is being defined here as a general discipline.]

The theology of John Calvin has been studied extensively in the Reformed tradition. [The prepositional phrase "of John Calvin" tells us that a more specific kind of theology is being discussed.]

3. The indefinite article can be used to tell the reader "what kind." We often use the indefinite article with the structure, adjective + noun.

J. G. Machen wrote an important book on the virgin birth of Christ. [Here, we are being told what kind of book Machen wrote.]

Augustine's *Confessions* is a clear example of how personal narrative can be theologically useful to others. [We want to express what kind of example Augustine's *Confessions* is.']

Question	Answer
What kind of book did Machen write?	an important one
What kind of example is *Confessions*?	a clear one

Note the use of the definite (*the*) and indefinite (*a, an*) articles in the paragraph provided below. What do they convey about the author's perspective on the reader's knowledge?

Most emphatically, this does not mean that every bit of suffering is **the** immediate consequence of **a** particular sin. That is **a** hideous piece of heresy, capable of inflicting untold mental anguish. It would mean that **the** people who suffer most in this world must be those who have sinned **the** most in this world; and that is demonstrably untrue, both in **the** Bible and in experience. Some of **the** possible connections between **a** specific sin and **a** particular illness will be worked out in **a** later chapter. For **the** moment it is enough to observe that illness *can* be **the** direct result of **a** specific sin (as in **the** case of those described in 1 Cor. 11:27–34; or in **the** case of **the** man in John 5:1–15 who was paralyzed for thirty-eight years), but there is no *necessary* connection between **a** specific sin and **a** particular spell of suffering (e.g., **the** man born blind [John 9]).

Some of the uses of the article are not covered by the principles above. For example, you may encounter the definite article with the **substantive** use of an adjective. For example, Jesus says, "You always have *the poor* with you" (Matt. 26:11). "Poor" is an adjective, but when it is preceded by the definite article, it means "poor people" or "those who are poor." We see this in the passage from this lesson with the adjective "righteous" (paragraph 3). We will revisit these guidelines for using (and not using) articles in Lesson 23.

Activity 1

Insert the correct article in each blank. If no article is needed, write an "X" in the blank. Note that more than one answer might be grammatically acceptable. "Correct" for this exercise means "what the original author used."

Meanwhile, _____ consequences of _____ human sin infest many of our experiences with some measure of pain. Such afflictions may be splashed onto _____ canvas of human history with _____ very broad brush. Thus _____ God says to Jerusalem, "I am against you. I will draw my sword from its sheath and cut off from you both _____ righteous and _____ wicked" (Ezek. 21:3). In one sense, of course, no one is _____ righteous (Rom. 3:10ff); but that is not what _____ prophet means here. He means that when devastation descends on Jerusalem, the people who will suffer will include both those whose immediate sins have brought _____ city to this horrible punishment, and those who have not participated in _____ sins that have brought about _____ destruction of _____ nation.[4]

Activity 2

What follows is a list of titles of theological essays and articles.[5] Some of the titles have had articles either deleted or added. Correct any article errors you find in these titles. If the title is grammatically correct already, place a √ next to it. Note that while the "correct" answers are based on what the original authors wrote, there may be more than one grammatical possibility for each title.

Transfigured Hermeneutics 4—Jesus as God's Glory Face in John's Gospel	The End of Christmas
Buckets and Burning Churches: Luther, Church, and Catholicity	The Fruit of Spirit 5: Patience
Meet New American Dream	Swimming in Glorious Deep Blue Sea
Infant Baptism and Promise of Grace	Baptist Foundations
WHAT IF: Duns Scotus had not been a Theologian?	Halloween: A Distinctively Christian Holiday

(continued on next page)

4. Carson, *How Long O Lord?*, 45.

5. These titles have been taken from articles posted on *Reformation 21*, accessed February 1, 2016, http://www.reformation21.org/.

Conformity to Jesus as Paradigm for Christian Ethics	Defending Substitution
The Incarnation of God	The World in Church: A Distracted World, Distracted Church?
	The Allure of Gentleness

Activity 3

Working with a partner, choose a topic from the list below. Define and discuss the topic in general. One person should write a sentence that summarizes what you have found. The other person should then introduce a particular example of that issue and write it in another sentence. When you have finished, exchange your sentence with your partner's and try to correct any article errors. Then switch roles and choose another topic.

Example: *Faith*

Partner 1: "The Faith is critical to our relationships with others and with the God."

Partner 2: "The faith that a child has in Jesus is commended by him."

(1) Rebellion

(2) Love

(3) Evil

(4) Suffering

(5) Comfort

(6) Righteousness

(7) Sin

9

The Mind Awry

"Sin has affected the mind as much as the rest of our lives."
—K. Scott Oliphint, *Covenantal Apologetics*

Lesson Goals

Theology–To understand one way in which the mind is affected by sin

Reading–To learn how to trace a line of argument

Vocabulary–To learn and use additional collocations from the reading passage

Grammar–To practice using pronouns to improve paragraph coherence

---

Introduction

Sin is certainly pervasive. It is in the world around us, and it is within the heart of every human. We know that sin is something that we are at war with in our souls. But we may not understand that it is something we are at war with in our minds as well. But this is a critically important truth to grasp. Ever since the fall, *all* that we are is affected by sin, and that means the intellect as well as the soul.

One of the most prominent ways in which this comes to the surface can be expressed with the word **autonomy**. Autonomy essentially means "self-governance," not being subject to any authority but oneself. As you might have guessed, the only autonomous being who exists is the Trinitarian God of the Bible. Yet, since the inception of sin at the fall of Adam, humanity has kept autonomy close, for it is the heart of our sinful behavior.

Intellectually, autonomy "is the view that human beings have the right to seek knowledge of God's world without being subject to God's revelation."[1] While this has certainly plagued the church throughout its lifetime, it is even more apparent outside the church. Frame suggests that "the history of non-Christian philosophy is a history of would-be autonomous thought."[2] Non-Christians prize intellectual autonomy so highly that they truly believe "to surrender autonomy is to abandon reason itself."[3]

Christians, on the other hand, suggest that reason is a gift from God and only functions properly and coherently when practiced in submission to God's revelation. In this sense, there is no such thing as "plain reason" or "neutral reason." Reason is always practiced by someone either in covenantal rebellion against or in submission to the self-revealing Triune God.[4]

---

1. John M. Frame, *The Doctrine of the Word of God*, A Theology of Lordship (Phillipsburg, NJ: P&R, 2010), 15–16.

2. John M. Frame, *A History of Western Philosophy and Theology* (Phillipsburg, NJ: P&R, 2015), 23.

3. Ibid., 32.

4. Van Til was famous for his insistence that there is no such thing as neutral reason. Cornelius Van Til, *The Defense of the Faith*, ed. K. Scott Oliphint, 4th ed. (Phillipsburg, NJ: P&R, 2008), 57, 123–24, 143.

Discussion Questions

(1) If our minds are corrupted by sin, what implications do you think this has?

(2) If we cannot think rightly, what might that lead to?

Background for the Reading

As we discussed, it is easy for us to look around and see the effects of sin. Diseases, acts of violence, and even destructive natural phenomena abound. But we seldom think about how sin has affected our thinking. In reading theology, you may encounter the phrase "noetic effects of sin." This refers to the effects of sin on our minds. How exactly do you think sin has corrupted our minds? What is the remedy for this corruption? The first question receives some attention in our theological reading. The second question is essentially answered by 1 Cor. 2:16 and 2 Cor. 10:5. As in the rest of redemption, we look to Christ and the work of the Spirit to sanctify our thinking and use of reason according to God's true and trustworthy revelation.

Reading Skill: Tracing a Line of Argument

So far in our exploration of reading skills, you have been practicing how to identify a topic and main idea. While this is crucial for your reading of theology, correctly identifying the main idea is only the first step to becoming a good theological reader. Understanding theological texts also depends on your ability to trace a *line of argument* in a text. This helps you to understand the author's main idea (or thesis) and the support that he uses. At this point, we will look at how details, supporting ideas, and main ideas work together to construct an argument. Remember that the position an author defends is a *thesis*, and if that position is expressed explicitly in a sentence, that sentence is called a *thesis statement*. While all readings have a main idea, they may not all have a thesis (or thesis statement). That is, authors do not always have to take up a position on a debatable issue and defend that position.

Most academic English writing follows a general pattern:

I. Thesis Statement: a sentence stating the central claim that an author is defending

II. Contributing Argument #1 (main idea): often in the topic sentence of the first body paragraph
   a. Supporting Idea #1 that explains the rationale for the argument
      i. Detail that provides evidence for supporting idea #1
      ii. Additional details that provide evidence for supporting idea #1
   b. Supporting Idea #2 that explains the rationale for the argument
      i. Detail(s) with evidence for supporting idea #2

III. Contributing Argument #2 (main idea) (This pattern of contributing arguments with supporting ideas can continue for as long as the writer chooses.)

IV. Conclusion restating or summarizing the thesis

Note again the **hierarchical structure** here. It is important to be able to recognize and identify the elements in this hierarchical pattern in order to understand what you read. Once you are familiar with the pattern, you can use it to help you understand what type of information the author is likely to provide at each part of the text. In other words, the writer is less likely to include specific details in the introduction or conclusion, but very likely to include them in the body of the text.

- The **thesis** is the central claim being defended in an excerpt, article, chapter, or book. When this claim is explicitly stated in a sentence, it is called the **thesis statement**.
- The **main idea** is the central focus of a unit of discourse (a section, paragraph, etc.). We can think of **contributing arguments** as main ideas that are set in relation to one another, forming an argument.
- **Supporting claims** are claims that are more specific or detailed than main ideas, but more general than details.
- The **details** are specific pieces of evidence that offer proof or support for the contributing arguments or supporting claims.

First, here are the definitions of these terms, some of which are review:

After identifying the thesis or main idea of an entire passage, note the writer's main contributing arguments (the main ideas of sections and paragraphs). You may find these in the topic sentences of paragraphs. These claims should be directly connected to the main idea or thesis of the passage, often using some of the same vocabulary. But note that not every paragraph introduces a new contributing argument. Authors may develop a contributing argument over multiple paragraphs. In these cases, you will see many supporting claims that establish the validity of a single contributing argument (main idea).

To help you more quickly identify an author's line of argument, here are some of the common ways in which authors logically organize their ideas.

- **Building an Argument**: In some argumentative texts, supporting ideas are organized so that each one is followed by its own distinct support. In other texts, they are organized so that the ideas build upon each other. In the latter type of text, the author will use his first supporting idea as a premise for his second supporting idea, and so on. The result is an argument that is built one logical claim at a time. For an example, see the passage by Edmund Clowney in Unit 4, Lesson 12.
- **Following Chronological Order**: Some texts, especially texts that fit into the church history genre, are organized chronologically.

The claims follow the order of historical events or the development of a theological doctrine throughout church history. For an example, see the passage by Diarmaid Mac-Culloch in Unit 7, Lesson 20.

- **Following the Order of a Biblical Text**: In biblical studies, you will often encounter texts that are organized according to the biblical passage that is being exposited or explored. This makes the overall structure of the argument easy to follow, since you can simply observe the writer moving from phrase to phrase, clause to clause, or verse to verse in the biblical passage. For an example, see the passage by Douglas Moo in Unit 5, Lesson 15.
- **Tracing Cause and Effect**: Authors may attempt to trace causes and effects throughout their writing. This is not specific to any single theological genre. You could see this in biblical studies as well as in church history, systematic theology, and apologetics. For an example, see paragraphs 8–10 in the passage from Carl Trueman in Unit 7, Lesson 19.
- **Presenting Comparison and/or Contrast**: You may find that an author organizes his ideas according to comparison, contrast, or both. This can take the shape of a comparative approach in which the author contrasts his own view with that of others, or contrasts a unique approach with a more traditional one, in order to point out strengths and weaknesses. For an example, see the passage by Lane Tipton in Unit 8, Lesson 23.

Details can be facts, opinions, examples, stories, or any other type of specific support. Some paragraphs may include several distinct details. Other paragraphs, particularly in counseling writing, may provide one extended anecdote or example that as a whole offers support for the author's argument. All of the details should offer direct support for the contributing argument expressed in that paragraph or section.

Tip: Most students find it helpful to mark their reading or take notes about it in a way that follows the line of argument. Some students choose to underline main ideas and key pieces of support. Others paraphrase or summarize these ideas in the margin of the text or in a separate document. Many students do a combination of the above. Whatever method you prefer is fine; the key is to interact with the ideas of the text in a visual way to help you understand the structure and content of a text so that you can easily refer to it.

Pre-Reading

Skim the following passage (45 seconds). What do you think the relationship is between autonomy and revelation?

Reading

In the passage below, John Frame defines "autonomy" and discusses its relation to sin.

[¶1] Intellectual autonomy is the view that human beings have the right to seek knowledge of God's world without being subject to God's revelation. It first appears in the history of thought in Genesis 3's narrative of the Fall, in which Adam and Eve make their decision to disobey God's personal word to them. In their decision, they affirm their right to think autonomously, even to the point of contradicting[a] God himself.

Remember?
"Intellectual autonomy" is a general concept, so it does not need an article.

[¶2] The spirit of autonomy underlies[b] every sinful decision of every human being. . . . It is irrational in an important sense. Paul tells us in Romans 1:18–32 that human beings know God clearly from his revelation to them in creation, but that nevertheless they choose to repress[c] this knowledge and exchange it for a lie. How could anyone imagine that contradicting the Master of the universe could be a wise decision? This foolishness mirrors[d] the biblical paradigm of irrationality, the foolishness of Satan himself, who (again in the face of clear knowledge) tries to replace God on the throne of the universe.

[¶3] In this satanic project, man seeks to become his own lord. He denies[e] God's ultimate control, authority, and presence. Either he denies that there is such a Lord or he ascribes[f] lordship to something in creation. If he denies that there is a Lord, he embraces[g] *irrationalism*, the view that there is no ultimate meaning in the universe. If he ascribes lordship to something finite (i.e., idolatry), he embraces *rationalism*, the view that a godlike knowledge can be obtained from creation alone.

[¶4] Of course, Satan and his followers embrace rationalism irrationally, for they have no right to insist[h] that their minds are the ultimate criterion[i] of truth. Similarly, they embrace irrationalism rationistically, assuming the ultimate authority of their own minds. So in unbelieving thought, rationalism and irrationalism are two sides of a single coin, though they actually contradict each other. That irrationality permeates[j] the whole fabric[k] of human knowledge. So we can understand how the assumption of intellectual autonomy destroys knowledge. Of course, as Romans 1 shows, Satan and his disciples do have a clear knowledge of God, which they repress. But they have that clear knowledge of God in spite of, not because of, their commitment to autonomy. If they were consistent[l] with their commitment to autonomy, they could not know anything at all.

[¶5] We can see this spirit of autonomy in all sin. As in Genesis 3, sin assumes[m] autonomy. It assumes that God does not exist, or that he has not given us a personal word. That is true of the sins of individuals, families, and nations. It is true of all types of sin: stealing, adultery, murder, deceit. It is also true of intellectual sin: denying the truth in the face of clear knowledge. Why should anyone imagine that the intellect could be left out of our account of sin? The mind is part of our being. It contributes[n] to sin as much as our wills and feelings, as much as our arms and legs. So the spirit of autonomy appears in the history of human thought.[5]

a. Contradict (v.): to assert the contrary of; deny the truth of
b. Underlie (v.): to be at the basis of or form the foundation of
c. Repress (v.): to keep down or under by self-control
d. Mirror (v.): to represent or serve as a model for
e. Deny (v.): to declare untrue or to refuse to acknowledge
f. Ascribe (v.): to assign or attribute something to someone or something
g. Embrace (v.): to come to believe in, defend, support, or join willingly
h. Insist (v.): to take a firm stand about

i. Criterion (n.): a standard, principle, or rule on which a decision or judgment may be based
j. Permeate (v.): to spread through something
k. Fabric (n.): underlying structure or framework
l. Consistent (adj.): marked by harmony, regularity, and coherence
m. Assume (v.): to take for granted
n. Contribute (v.): to lend assistance or aid to a common purpose

Post-Reading

Having read the passage, how do you think autonomy is related to revelation? (Hint: The word "rebellion" should be part of your answer.)

Main Ideas and Details

(1) In your own words, define the phrase "intellectual autonomy."

(2) Read the sentences below. Write MI next to the statement if it is a main idea from the reading. Write D on the line if it is a supporting reason or detail. Remember to note the context of each sentence in its paragraph (hierarchical structure) before marking your answers.

_____ 1. Either he denies that there is such a Lord or he ascribes lordship to something in creation. (Paragraph 3)

_____ 2. [Autonomy] first appears in the history of thought in Genesis 3's narrative of the Fall, in which Adam and Eve make their decision to disobey God's personal word to them. (Paragraph 1)

_____ 3. Of course, as Romans 1 shows, Satan and his disciples do have a clear knowledge of God, which they repress. (Paragraph 4)

_____ 4. In this Satanic project, man seeks to become his own lord. (Paragraph 3)

_____ 5. Intellectual autonomy is the view that human beings have the right to seek knowledge of God's world without being subject to God's revelation. (Paragraph 1)

5. Frame, *The Doctrine of the Word of God*, 15–17.

_____6. We can see the spirit of autonomy in all sin. (Paragraph 5)

_____7. [Autonomy] is irrational in an important sense. (Paragraph 2)

_____8. [Autonomy] assumes that God does not exist, or that he has not given us a personal word. (Paragraph 5)

(3) Which of the following can we infer based on paragraph 3?

a. Rationalism and irrationalism are the same.

b. Godlike knowledge can be obtained only through faith.

c. Christians and non-Christians ascribe lordship to something infinite.

d. If people attempt to be autonomous, they can only go in one of two directions.

(4) What is the referent of the highlighted pronoun "that" in paragraph 5?

(5) In paragraph 5, the highlighted pronoun "it" refers to _____.

a. Being.

b. The mind.

Word Forms

Fill out the table below by choosing at least two additional words from the reading and listing the forms in which they occur in the passage. List the noun form of the word in the left column, and more complex forms in the right column. An example is provided for you in the first row, and another noun form is given in the second row. Fill in the last two rows on your own.

Noun Form	Other Forms of the Word in the Passage
Intellect	Intellectual
Autonomy	

Collocations from the Passage

Circle the most appropriate collocation from the choices in the parentheses. Check your answers in the theological passage.

In an important (*level/degree/sense*), Adam and Eve's experience in some way parallels our experience in a sinful world. Adam and Eve made a(n) (*option/decision/conclusion*) in the face of God's clear and present revelation, just as we do each day. We repress the (*knowledge/data/information*) we possess as covenantal creatures made in God's image, just as they did. We have the opportunity to make wise (*decisions/challenges/opinions*) according to the (*clear/crystal/transparent*) knowledge we have from God and his Spirit's work in us. The ultimate (*essence/meaning/scheme*) of those decisions is provided by God's plan for redemptive history.

Rhetorical Focus: Paragraph Unity, Coherence, and Development

In this lesson, we pause in our discussion of grammar to review an important issue of **rhetoric**. Rhetoric can mean a few different things, but for our purposes we might say that, more broadly, rhetoric is the "discussion and exchange of ideas" in an organized, strategic way.[6] While grammar deals with our expressions at the sentence level, rhetoric treats our expressions at the paragraph level or at larger levels (essay, chapter, book).

An important part of what we might call basic rhetoric is the form of the paragraph (recall the hierarchical structure to a piece of writing). A paragraph is not just a block of text. It has certain features that help readers identify key information, follow a line of thinking, and understand content. Writing a clear and cogent paragraph is an art involving organization, strategy, and an awareness of your audience. For now, just remember the three key words we introduced in Lesson 1: *unity, coherence,* and *development*. We will revisit each of these features below, and then you will have an opportunity to practice using pronouns to achieve paragraph coherence.

---

6. This definition is different from the classical definitions of rhetoric that go back to the Greek and Roman era. See Richard E. Young, Alton L. Becker, and Kenneth L. Pike, *Rhetoric: Discovery and Change* (New York: Harcourt, Brace, & World, 1970), 1–5, 8–9.

Unity

Every paragraph should focus on a single main idea, normally expressed in a **topic sentence**. A topic sentence states the main idea of the paragraph, the idea that all of the other sentences develop or support. It is important to have a clear topic sentence because this sentence serves as a sort of promise to your readers. With your topic sentence, you make "a commitment to readers," which the remaining sentences of the paragraph fulfill.[7] These sentences should support your topic sentence by expanding on it, developing it, or restating it in different language. Look at the example topic sentence below.

We can see this spirit of autonomy in all sin. As in Genesis 3, sin assumes autonomy. It assumes that God does not exist, or that he has not given us a personal word. That is true of the sins of individuals, families, and nations. It is true of all types of sin: stealing, adultery, murder, deceit. It is also true of intellectual sin: denying the truth in the face of clear knowledge.

Why should anyone imagine that the intellect could be left out of our account of sin? The mind is part of our being. It contributes to sin as much as our wills and feelings, as much as our arms and legs. So the spirit of autonomy appears in the history of human thought.

Notice how all of the supporting sentences develop the claim of the topic sentence: "We can see this spirit of autonomy in all sin." After briefly defining "autonomy," which is the key word from the topic sentence, the author goes on to describe what "all sin" includes: the sins of individuals, families, and nations; all types of sin; and intellectual sin.

Again, remember that there is a sort of *hierarchy* within a paragraph. The topic sentence is at the broadest level, while the next two sentences more specifically define a key word. Then, on a more focused level, the author spells out what "all sin" includes. The author then moves to focus on a particular type of sin: "intellectual sin." He finishes with a conclusion about this type of sin

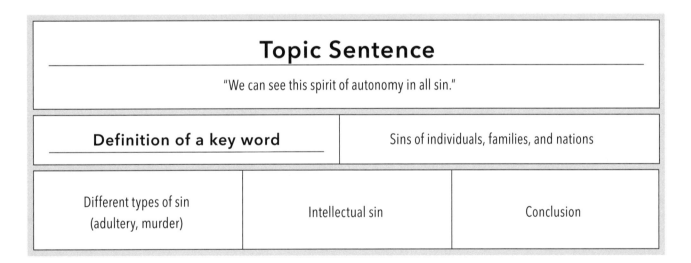

Fig. 9.1. Hierarchy in Frame's Paragraph

To recognize the hierarchy in a paragraph, you must be able to distinguish the topic sentence from the developing sentences. Below, we summarize how the topic sentence usually differs from the developing sentences. When reviewing your paragraphs, check to see that your topic sentences match the criteria in the left column.

---

7. H. Ramsey Fowler and Jane E. Aaron, *The Little, Brown Handbook*, 11th ed. (New York: Longman, 2010), 75. See also Joseph Williams, *Style: Toward Clarity and Grace* (Chicago: University of Chicago Press, 1990).

A topic sentence . . .	Developing sentences . . .
makes a claim, declaration, or assertion;	"explain, elaborate, and support" the topic sentence";[8]
states the main idea of the paragraph clearly, often in general terms;	provide evidence for the claim made in the topic sentence, including examples, definitions, Scripture quotations, descriptions, logical arguments, or explanations;
sets the boundaries for the paragraph.	link to the topic sentence.

Coherence

The word "coherence" comes from the Latin *cohaerentia*, meaning to "adhere or stick together." To say that your paragraphs cohere is to say that your sentences are clearly organized and related to one another, and these relationships are actually signaled in the text. We have already seen some of these in our study of the apologetics genre. See if you can notice the order of the sentences that follow. What signals in the language help you to know that these sentences belong together? Circle them.

We can see this spirit of autonomy in all sin. As in Genesis 3, sin assumes autonomy. It assumes that God does not exist, or that he has not given us a personal word. That is true of the sins of individuals, families, and nations. It is true of all types of sin: stealing, adultery, murder, deceit. It is also true of intellectual sin: denying the truth in the face of clear knowledge. Why should anyone imagine that the intellect could be left out of our account of sin? The mind is part of our being. It contributes to sin as much as our wills and feelings, as much as our arms and legs. So the spirit of autonomy appears in the history of human thought.

Here are some of the ways you can achieve paragraph coherence, in a way similar to that of the paragraph above.[9]

Ways to Achieve Paragraph Coherence

1. Arrange information logically so that the reader can follow your thoughts.
2. Use pronouns to avoid repeating a noun phrase. Also, use *this* or *these* and a single noun to refer to previously mentioned ideas (e.g., *this spirit of autonomy*).
3. Use transitional expressions to signal a shift in perspective (e.g., *again, although, yet, consequently, in spite of, in contrast, still, though, but*).
4. Create a network of similar or repeated key nouns and verbs to refer to the concept under focus (e.g., *sin, assumes, true, mind, intellect, thought*).
5. Maintain a consistent point of view through your use of person. Frame uses the first person (*we, our*) and third person (*it, the mind*) consistently in this paragraph.
6. Use parallelism: repeat the same grammatical structure for comparable ideas to show how the ideas relate (e.g., *It is true . . .*).

8. Janine Carlock et. al, *The ESL Writer's Handbook* (Ann Arbor, MI: University of Michigan Press, 2010), 21.
9. These are adapted from Fowler and Aaron, *The Little, Brown Handbook*, 80.

Development

Paragraph development refers to the substance or completeness of the paragraph. Is there enough detail? Is there enough evidence to argue a claim? Has the writer offered enough logical support? These are the kinds of questions that paragraph development addresses. In the paragraph we have been studying, the author defines a key term (autonomy), provides examples (stealing, adultery, and murder), and uses logical reasoning to develop the topic sentence. So, you are not limited to only one method of development in a paragraph. We often combine methods of paragraph development in support of our main idea. Some other methods of paragraph development are listed below, accompanied by a question that the development answers.[10]

   a. **Narration**: How did it happen?

   b. **Description**: How does it look, etc.?

   c. **Illustration**: What are examples of it? What are other ways to say it?

   d. **Definition**: What is it?

   e. **Division and analysis**: What are its parts?

   f. **Classification**: What groups can it be sorted into?

   g. **Compare and contrast**: How is it similar to or different from other things?

   h. **Analogy**: How can it be compared to something in a different class?

   i. **Cause-and-Effect**: Why did it happen and what are its effects?

   j. **Process**: How does it work?

Using Pronouns to Achieve Paragraph Coherence

Pronouns refer to or take the place of other nouns, and they always agree with those nouns in number. As we have just seen, using pronouns is one of the ways in which we show the reader how our sentences are tied together in the paragraph, i.e., one of the ways we achieve paragraph coherence.

In the paragraph that follows, note how the pronouns agree with the nouns they refer to in number, and notice how each pronoun refers to something that the author has just stated.

The spirit of autonomy underlies every sinful decision of every human being. . . . **It** is irrational in an important sense. Paul tells us in Romans 1:18–32 that human beings know God clearly from **his** revelation to **them** in creation, but that nevertheless **they** choose to repress **this knowledge** and exchange **it** for a lie. How could anyone imagine that contradicting the Master of the universe could be a wise decision? **This foolishness** mirrors the biblical paradigm of irrationality, the foolishness of Satan himself, who (again in the face of clear knowledge) tries to replace God on the throne of the universe.

Activity 1

Insert the correct pronoun in the blank. To check your answers, revisit the theological reading for this lesson.

Of course, Satan and _____ followers embrace rationalism irrationally, for _____ have no right to insist that _____ minds are the ultimate criterion of truth. Similarly, _____ embrace irrationalism rationistically, assuming the ultimate authority of their own minds. So in unbelieving thought, rationalism and irrationalism are two sides of a single coin, though _____ actually contradict each other. _____ irrationality permeates the whole fabric of human knowledge. So we can understand how the assumption of intellectual

10. For further discussion, see Fowler and Aaron, *The Little, Brown Handbook*, 92–101.

autonomy destroys knowledge. Of course, as Romans 1 shows, Satan and _____ disciples do have a clear knowledge of God, which _____ repress. But they have that clear knowledge of God in spite of, not because of, their commitment to autonomy. If _____ were consistent with their commitment to autonomy, they could not know anything at all.

Activity 2

Read Romans 1:21 aloud. Then listen to an excerpt from a lecture by K. Scott Oliphint on the noetic effects of sin (i.e., the effects of sin on our thinking).

Below, we have printed a transcript of Oliphint's lecture. Listen again to the excerpt, reading along and circling all the pronouns. Wherever a pronoun points to a noun that is previously named, draw an arrow to that noun. Can you tell which pronouns refer to the speaker and to the listener?

Alright, so now Paul is into the suppression aspect of what we do with the knowledge that we have. Now again, he's talking about people as they are in Adam. Remember, Paul's going to get to what it means to be in Christ—he's getting to that later. But before you understand that, you need to know what it means to be in Adam; and to be in Adam is to be a covenant breaker—it's to be before the face of God, knowing God, but being disobedient to him and suppressing—trying to hold down—that knowledge that God has given. I've used the illustration before that somebody said to me one time: it's sort of like having a beach ball that you sort of try to hold under water—it's a big beach ball full of air and you're trying—you're pushing it down, pushing it down. But what's it doing? It keeps trying to pop up! And so you're working all the time to keep it under, to keep it under, see, and that's what Paul's saying here—you're trying to keep that down, but it'll bounce up, and then you're trying to keep it down again. You don't want to have God in your thoughts. Like Adam and Eve, you're trying to hide, but there's no place to go, because God's presence is everywhere, and as he makes himself known, you and I continue to know him.[11]

Activity 3

What is Oliphint's main idea in this lecture clip? Take a few minutes to write down or mark in the text his key ideas. Then give a quick, thirty-second oral summary of this lecture. Remember to use pronouns when appropriate, but to use them only when it is clear what the pronoun is referencing.

Activity 4

In three to five sentences, describe an event in your own life or in someone else's life that is a clear example of autonomous thinking. After you have written your paragraph, check to make sure that your pronouns agree with their referents and that each referent is clear. For example, in the following sentence, the referent for the pronoun "its" is *not* clear.

Original
Reading Scripture and worshipping with other believers has an effect on a person's thinking and helps him realize *its* potential. [Does "its" refer to "reading Scripture," "worshipping with other believers," or "a person's thinking"?]

11. K. Scott Oliphint, "AP101: The Doctrine of Man, part 1—Part: 18 of 28" (lecture, Westminster Theological Seminary, Glenside, PA, September 1, 2010), accessed May 29, 2014, http://media2.wts.edu/media/audio/apologetics18-copyright.mp3, 16:14–17:28.

Revision

Reading Scripture and worshipping with other believers has an effect on a person's thinking and helps him realize *his mind's* potential.

Summary of Theological Concepts for Unit 3

- The details of Scripture matter, and small errors introduced into our treatment of the truth of God's Word can be damaging to the church.

- Sin is the root cause of all suffering, though we must be very careful in making a direct correlation between a particular sin and its consequences.

- Our sin corrupts not just our bodies, but also our minds. We cannot think about God rightly apart from his revelation to us. One of the most critical ways in which we sin against God intellectually is by assuming that we are autonomous—either that God does not exist or that his word to us is not necessary for knowledge.

Activity

Paraphrase each of the concepts above in your own words. Check your paraphrase with that of a partner.

(1)

(2)

(3)

Accounting for Counting (AP Task 6)

Introduction

For this task, you will be writing an introductory paragraph to an essay for entry into a local essay competition. The theme for the competition is "the human mind."

It is difficult for us to imagine that Christians think differently from other people. Do not all people *think* the same way? After all, $2 + 2 = 4$ means the same thing for a Christian as it does for a non-Christian, right?

Van Til writes that a result of the fall was that "man tried to interpret everything with which he came into contact without reference to God."[12] Even today, people do this. They think that numbers exist without God.

---

12. Cornelius Van Til, *The Defense of the Faith*, 4th ed., ed. K. Scott Oliphint (Phillipsburg, NJ: P&R, 2008), 70.

Van Til would say that a non-believer could count, but he could not "account for his counting." By this, he meant that the logical order, consistency, and mathematical precision of the universe can only be explained by the existence of the Triune God of Scripture. A non-believer may know that $2 + 2 = 4$, but he cannot explain why numbers fit into a coherent system for measuring and calculating various parts of the created world.

Task

On a community bulletin board, you see an advertisement for a short essay competition. The theme of the competition is "the human mind." The judges for the competition will be looking for an essay that introduces "the most influential event in the history of human thought." Based on what you know of the noetic effects of sin, write the introductory paragraph to an essay arguing for the fall as the most important event in the history of human thought.

UNIT 4

HOW IS IT MADE RIGHT?
(BIBLICAL STUDIES)

10

The Story of Redemption

"Revelation constitutes a part of that great process of the new creation through which the present universe as an organic whole shall be redeemed from the consequences of sin."
—Geerhardus Vos, *Biblical Theology*

Lesson Goals

Theology–To define the phrase "redemptive history"

Reading–To practice finding the referents for pronouns

Vocabulary–To learn and use additional collocations from the reading passage

Grammar–To identify suffixes and learn how they change a word's part of speech

---

Introduction

We have now discussed the horrible effects of sin on both the world around us and upon our own thinking. It is time for good news: before time began, the Father, Son, and Holy Spirit made a pact to save God's people, the *pactum salutis*.

Before the world was even made, God the Father gave a people to his Son, chosen "in him before the foundation of the world" (Eph. 1:4). It was then that "he predestined us for adoption as sons through Jesus Christ, according to the purpose of his will" (v. 5; cf. John 10:29; 17:6).

The Holy Spirit is also a party to this agreement for the Father and the Son (John 15:26; Rom.

1:4) agreed to send the Spirit into the world to bear witness of Christ, to teach the people about him (John 14:26), and to declare to them things to come (John 16:13).[1]

The good news is that the Trinitarian God of the Bible has accounted for your suffering and for mine, and for all of the manifestations of evil in this world. He has done this at great cost to himself, for God's very Son was given as a ransom for us. The Son of God *suffered* on our behalf. And, in Francis Turretin's words, "as the suffering of Christ is the principal part of the ransom paid for us by him and the special foundation of our confidence and consolation, it should also be the primary object of our faith and the theme of meditation."[2]

---

1. John M. Frame, *Systematic Theology: An Introduction to Christian Belief* (Phillipsburg, NJ: P&R, 2013), 59.

2. Francis Turretin, *Institutes of Elenctic Theology*, ed. James T. Dennison Jr., trans. George Musgrave Giger (Phillipsburg, NJ: P&R, 1994), 2:352.

Of course, the coming of Christ did not happen right away. God's eternal plan of salvation *culminated* in Christ's birth, life, death, resurrection, and ascension, but it did not *begin* there. The beginning goes back to the Garden of Eden, and even before that, to the eternal counsel of God himself. God has always been in control. He has always known how and why he would redeem the brokenness of the world: through his Son and Spirit, and because of his great love.

God's great love for his people would unfold in mercy and grace throughout history, "in a long series of successive acts."[3]

Discussion Questions

(1) How might the secular world try to help someone who is suffering from a terminal disease?

(2) What are the strengths of this help? What are the weaknesses?

Background for the Reading

After looking closely at the world around us, we can quickly draw some conclusions. On the one hand, we can find a measure of joy in the activities and relationships of our lives. On the other hand, we cannot deny that the world is often a hideous place. Poverty, crime, disease, and natural disasters take the lives of millions of people each year, and each life is made in the image of God. But, as we noted in Lesson 8, the joy of the gospel is that it announces that God is putting the world back together—all of it. Ultimately, the severity of sin's destruction only serves to accent the glory of God's new creation. Yet, this extended process of restoration, often referred to in Reformed circles as *redemptive history*, does not take place all at once. As Geerhardus Vos, the pioneer of biblical theology, says, this develops over time. God shows grace and favor to his people throughout history, climaxing in the sending of his own Son to die for the sins of his people.

Reading Skill: Finding Pronoun Referents

Before getting to the reading for this lesson, we can pick up where we left off last lesson regarding the use of pronouns. Remember that we said using pronouns is like using rope to tie sentences together. Each pronoun refers to the noun phrase or clause (the referent) that it replaces and helps the reader link the ideas together. In order for this to benefit you as a reader, you must be able to identify the noun, noun phrase, or clause that each pronoun is referring to. This will help you to understand what you are reading and to read more efficiently.

First, we can review what we already know about pronouns. Pronouns can include personal pronouns (e.g., *I*, *he*, *me*, *him*), possessive pronouns (e.g., *my*, *his*), relative pronouns (e.g., *that*, *which*, *who*), demonstrative pronouns (e.g., *this*, *these*), and indefinite pronouns (e.g., *none*, *several*).

Sometimes authors will use general noun phrases like "the trend" or "the situation" to refer to a specific noun that they are describing. In these cases, the noun phrases have referents like pronouns, although the referent is generally a longer noun phrase or clause.

There is one common exception to pronoun references. In sentences such as, "It is difficult to read Geerhardus Vos," the pronoun "it" is acting as a "dummy" or "empty" subject. It does not replace a noun but is used so that the sentence can have an immediate and clear subject. Another way to write this sentence would be, "To read Geerhardus Vos is difficult," replacing the dummy "it" with an infinitive phrase that serves as the subject.

 Restructuring this sentence may serve to communicate a specific message better. "It is difficult to read Geerhardus Vos" places the author's name at the end of the sentence, as the object of the infinitive "to read" (grammar). This might allow a speaker to add emphasis to the end of the sentence (phonology) and communicate to the audience that Vos is in focus (reference). The other way of structuring the sentence moves the infinitive phrase to the subject position (grammar), which might be preferable if the speaker wants to stress (phonology) the ease or difficulty we encounter in reading various authors (reference). So the structure of your sentence has the

---

3. Geerhardus Vos, *Biblical Theology: Old and New Testaments* (1948; repr., Carlisle, PA: Banner of Truth, 2014), 5.

ability to help you more clearly communicate your focus to a listener or reader.

Follow the steps outlined below to find the referent for a pronoun.

Example: God conducts an inquiry of the serpent, the woman, and the man to prepare the terms of <u>his</u> verdict.

What does the pronoun "his" refer to in this sentence from paragraph 1? (a) God? (b) The serpent? (c) The woman? (d) The man?

Answer: With a masculine pronoun, "c" is not an option. Replacing "his" with each of the other choices from the sentence, it is clear that (a), "God," is the only answer that makes sense since it was God who judged Adam, Eve, and the serpent.

Steps to Finding Pronoun Referents

1. *Analyze the pronoun.* Is it singular or plural? Is it the subject of a clause, or an object?
2. *Look for nouns, noun phrases, or clauses that the pronoun may be referencing.* These often come shortly before the pronoun but may come after the pronoun or in an earlier sentence. Use the noun's number and location in the sentence to help you.
3. Read the sentence, substituting the possible noun phrase in place of the pronoun. Ask yourself if the sentence makes sense with the noun phrase replacing the pronoun. If it does, you are finished!
4. If the sentence does not make sense, look for another noun phrase to substitute in place of the pronoun. Continue to do this until you have found a noun phrase that keeps the meaning of the original sentence.

Pre-Reading

Think of one major event in redemptive history. What does that event tell you about the character of God?

Reading

In the following passage, John Frame introduces the beginning of redemptive history.

[¶1] Almost immediately after the first sin comes the beginning of the history of redemption. God conducts[a] an inquiry[b] of the serpent, the woman, and the man to prepare the terms of his verdict.[c] Having conducted his inquiry, he pronounces sentence:[d]

14 The Lord God said to the serpent, "Because you have done this, cursed are you above all livestock and above all beasts of the field; on your belly you shall go, and dust you shall eat all the days of your life.

15 I will put enmity[e] between you and the woman, and between your offspring and her offspring; he shall bruise your head, and you shall bruise his heel."

16 To the woman he said, "I will surely multiply your pain in childbearing; in pain you shall bring forth children. Your desire shall be for your husband, and he shall rule over you."

17 And to Adam he said, "Because you have listened to the voice of your wife and

have eaten of the tree of which I commanded you, 'You shall not eat of it,' cursed is the ground because of you; in pain you shall eat of it all the days of your life;

¹⁸ thorns and thistles it shall bring forth for you; and you shall eat the plants of the field.

¹⁹ By the sweat of your face you shall eat bread, till you return to the ground, for out of it you were taken; for you are dust, and to dust you shall return."

²⁰ The man called his wife's name Eve, because she was the mother of all living.

²¹ And the Lord God made for Adam and for his wife garments^f of skins and clothed them.

²² Then the Lord God said, "Behold, the man has become like one of us in knowing good and evil. Now, lest he reach out his hand and take also of the tree of life and eat, and live forever—"

²³ therefore the Lord God sent him out from the garden of Eden to work the ground from which he was taken. (Gen. 3:14–23 ESV)

As we would expect, God pronounces curses on the three defendants.^g But surprisingly, these curses are mixed with blessings. Among the curses on the Satan-serpent, there is the promise of enmity between his offspring and man's. This is a blessing for man, because it implies that man will not be a passive^h servant of Satan; he will fight back. Further, one of man's offspring will deal to Satan a deadly blow,ⁱ crushing his head, though in the process Satan will bruise his heel. The church has regarded this as the first messianic promise, to be fulfilled^j in Jesus Christ, whose atoning death was the bruise on the heel by which Satan's head was crushed.

[¶2] God curses the woman with pain in childbearing. The blessing, however, is that there will indeed be childbearing. The threat^k "in the day that you eat of it you shall surely die" (Gen. 2:17) is not to be carried out fully or immediately. God is giving time for redemption. And the woman's childbearing is the very means of redemption. Her offspring will crush the head of Satan. God also curses the man in the work of farming: the ground will bear thorns and thistles until the man dies physically. But there is blessing too, for man's work, like the woman's childbearing, is to be successful. He will supply food to his family so that their childbearing can continue. So, as in the cultural mandate (Gen. 1:28), man is to subdue^l the earth (through labor) and to fill the earth (through childbearing).

[¶3] Adam might have named his wife "death," because her decision brought death into the world. But instead Adam called her Eve, "life-giver." Adam believes God's promise that she will bring forth living children and that one of those will bring redemption from death altogether. Similarly, when Eve bears Cain in Gen. 4:1, she says, "I have gotten a man with the help of the Lord." So both Adam and Eve express faith in God's promise. On this basis, we may be confident of their salvation.

[¶4] But there is another curse. God expels Adam and Eve from the garden and forbids them to return. They are sent away from the temple, the area of God's most intimate presence, and they must make their way

Remember?
Note how the author uses pronouns in paragraph 4.

as pilgrims. To these pilgrims, God's cultural mandate still applies: they are to fill the earth and subdue it (cf. Gen. 9:1–7).

[¶5] But in their exile, they take with them faith in God's promise of salvation. They instruct[m] their sons in the need for sacrifice, though one of them fails to bring a proper offering (Gen. 4:1–7). And in the time of their third son, Seth, and his son Enosh, there is a worshipping community: "At that time people began to call upon the name of the Lord" (Gen. 4:26).[4]

a. Conduct (v.): to run, manage, or carry out
b. Inquiry (n.): the act of seeking truth, knowledge, or information
c. Verdict (n.): a decision or judgment
d. Sentence (n.): a decree or judgment to be imposed on someone
e. Enmity (n.): ill-will or hostility
f. Garment (n.): an article of clothing

g. Defendant (n.): a person accused of something in a court of law
h. Passive (adj.): enduring without resistance
i. Blow (n.): a forcible stroke delivered with a part of the body
j. Fulfill (v.): to accomplish or execute
k. Threat (n.): an indication of something impending and usually undesirable
l. Subdue (v.): to bring under control
m. Instruct (v.): to impart knowledge to

Post-Reading

What did you learn about the character of God from Frame's passage?

Main Ideas and Details

(1) In your own words, define "redemptive history."

(2) *Without looking back at the reading*, place a number (1–6) next to each statement to put the statements in the correct order. First, try to find which sentence might be the topic sentence. Then, see which sentence might logically follow that one. Continue to link the sentences together logically until you have written a number next to each sentence. Then, check your answers by looking at paragraph 3 from the reading. (Hint: The beginning of each sentence often contains a clue as to which sentence precedes it.)

_____ On this basis, we may be confident of their salvation.

_____ Adam believes God's promise that she will bring forth living children and that one of those will bring redemption from death altogether.

_____ But instead Adam called her Eve, "life-giver."

_____ Adam might have named his wife "death," because her decision brought death into the world.

_____ Similarly, when Eve bears Cain in Gen. 4:1, she says, "I have gotten a man with the help of the Lord."

_____ So both Adam and Eve express faith in God's promise.

(3) Write the noun or noun phrase that each of the highlighted pronouns below is referencing.

a. "Thorns and thistles it shall bring forth for you." (v. 18 in paragraph 1)

b. "This is a blessing for man…" (paragraph 1)

c. "… he will fight back . . ." (paragraph 1)

d. "… so that their childbearing can continue." (paragraph 2)

e. "On this basis, we may be confident of their salvation." (paragraph 3)

f. "At that time people began to call upon the name of the Lord." (paragraph 5)

4. Frame, *Systematic Theology*, 853–55.

(4) Why does Adam name his wife "Eve"?

Understanding the Reading

(1) List the three blessings that accompanied the curses pronounced in Gen. 3.

(2) In two sentences, describe the repercussions (effects) of the curse discussed in paragraph 4.

Collocations from the Passage

Circle the most appropriate word from the choices provided in parentheses. Check your answers by revisiting the theological passage for this lesson.

At the fall, God certainly pronounced (*order/judgment/conviction*) on the serpent, Adam, and Eve, but he also delivered a promise. In his promise, God told Eve that someone in her line would (*bear/produce/generate*) a child who would crush the head of the serpent. Until that day came, Adam and Eve, along with their offspring, would have to (*instruct/teach/tell*) their children on the necessity of sacrifice.

Grammar Focus: Suffixes

We now return to our discussion of grammar. Since we have explored the structure of complex sentences in TE, we can move on to consider the precise form of words within those sentences. Word form, which you practiced in a brief activity in Lesson 9, usually deals with the multiple forms that are built from a single root. From "intellect," we derive "intellectual" (adj. or n.), and "intellectually" (adv.). We form these words by adding suffixes to the root—different suffixes produce different word forms.[5] There are certain suffixes that occur at the ends of nouns. Note some of these suffixes in the excerpt below, taken from the theological reading for this lesson.

God is giving time for redemp**tion**. And the woman's childbearing is the very means of redemp**tion**. Her offspring will crush the head of Satan. God also curses the man in the work of farming . . . . Adam might have named his wife "death," because her deci**sion** brought death into the world. But instead Adam called her Eve, "life-giv**er**." Adam believes God's promise that she will bring forth living children and that one of those will bring redemp**tion** from death altogether. . . . So both Adam and Eve express faith in God's promise. On this basis, we may be confident of their salva**tion**.

But there is another curse. God expels Adam and Eve from the garden and forbids them to return. They are sent away from the temple, the area of God's most intimate pres**ence**, and they must make their way as pilgrims.

But in their exile, they take with them faith in God's promise of salva**tion**. They instruct their sons in the need for sacrif**ice**, though one of them fails to bring a proper offering (Gen. 4:1–7). And in the time of their third son, Seth, and his son Enosh, there is a worshipping commun**ity**: "At that time people began to call upon the name of the Lord" (Gen. 4:26).

Suffix	Example
-tion	redemp*tion*, salva*tion*
-ion	deci*sion*,
-ence	pres*ence*
-er	life-giv*er*
-ity	commun*ity*
-ice	sacrif*ice*

5. A helpful list of noun suffixes can be found in Michael Swan, *Practical English Usage*, 4th ed. (Oxford: Oxford University Press, 2016), entry 338.

Activity 1

You have just learned some suffixes for nouns, and in Lesson 3 you learned some common endings of adjectives. You have also probably learned that the "-ly" ending usually forms the adverb. Using what you know, fill in the following table with the correct forms of each word.

Verb	Noun	Adjective	Adverb
Create			
	Promise		
Deceive			
	Redemption		
			Willingly
		Rebellious	
Sacrifice			
	Salvation		
Inquire			

Activity 2

For each blank, add the correct suffix to the incomplete word.

One particularly instructive example of Jesus' temptation occurred when he was driven out into the wilder _____ after his bap _____, but before his earthly ministry (Matt. 4; Luke 4). These passages record (in slightly different order) three tempt _____ from Satan: (1) to turn stones into bread, (2) to throw himself down from the temple, testing God's promise of angelic protect _____, and (3) to worship Satan in order to gain all the kingdoms of the world. . . .

We can be thankful that Jesus rejected these tempt _____. He refuted Satan's false applic _____ of Scripture with right uses of it, turning Satan away by the sword of the Spirit. But these are the same tempt _____ that we continue to face each day. Satan continually seeks to make us embrace his lord _____ in place of God's.[6]

6. Frame, *Systematic Theology*, 864.

Activity 3

This activity has two parts.

A. In your own words, define the phrase "redemptive history."

B. We have learned that redemption is something that has occurred throughout history, and it is still in process. Think about where you fit in redemptive history. What redemptive acts of God are behind you, and what still lies ahead?
   1. Take five minutes to think about and write down a few notes on the above questions to help you when you respond orally. Your notes should not be complete sentences, just key words or phrases.
   2. Use a computer, phone or other recording device to record your answer. You should speak for approximately one minute, and no more than 1.5 minutes.
   3. Listen to your response and type or write exactly what you hear. You should not correct the grammar or vocabulary. Just write down exactly what you hear.
   4. When you have finished, look at your transcript and underline any suffixes you used to create nouns. Write in any suffixes you should have used when speaking. Make any other grammar changes that you notice need to be made.
   5. Using your notes and not your transcript, record yourself answering the prompt a second time.
   6. Listen to this recording. Did you use more of the suffixes? Were any other elements of your recording better the second time (e.g., pronunciation, word stress, intonation, fluency, articles, verb tenses)?

Activity 4

As you have done with the previous lessons, fill in the missing collocations in the table below. While these collocations have been taken directly from Lessons 8–10, more than one answer may be correct. Try to fill in the chart without looking at the previous lessons. See what collocations you can remember. Compare your answers with those of a partner to learn other collocations that you might have missed.

resolve			sense
	enormously		decision
undergo		ultimate	
	world		knowledge
biblical		pronounce	
	a decision	bear	
repress		instruct	

Mediation in Redemptive History (BS Task 1)

Introduction

In this task, you will be explaining something from a course lecture to a classmate who does not completely understand it. To prepare for this task, listen to the lecture clip, which is taken from a course on hermeneutics.[7] Then, drawing on what you know from *Theological English* Lesson 10, try to answer your classmate's question.

Task

At the midpoint of the class, your professor gives you a five-minute break. In the hallway, your fellow classmate asks, "Hey, what did you think of the lecture so far? I don't quite understand how the promise of Genesis 3:15 is related to mediation. Did you understand that?"

Based on what you have read in *Theological English* Lesson 10 and what you know from the lecture, try to help your classmate by sharing a brief explanation of how Genesis 3:15 is related to the theme of mediation.

1. Spend ten minutes thinking about the lesson, the lecture, and the prompt. Write down any key ideas to help you when you record your response.
2. Use a computer, phone, or other recording device to record your answer to this prompt. You should speak between 1 and 1.5 minutes.
3. Listen to your recording and type a transcript of your recording in a Word document. You should type exactly what you hear without any corrections. You will need to listen several times to do this.
4. Then, copy the transcript and paste it a few lines below the original. Make any grammatical or vocabulary corrections that are necessary.

---

7. Vern S. Poythress, "Hermeneutics: Redemptive History I" (lecture, Westminster Theological Seminary, Glenside, PA, February 19, 2002), http://media1.wts.edu/media/audio/nt123-5b-copyright.mp3, beginning to 7:03.

11

Sacrifice and Cleansing

"The sacrifice represents life. The bread that is offered represents the crops that the worshiper harvested. The blood shed at the altar represents the animals the worshiper raised. The sacrifice offered symbolizes the owner's life and God's ownership and sovereignty over all."
—Bruce K. Waltke, *An Old Testament Theology*

"The Old Testament blood sacrifices were only shadows; the substance was Christ. For a substitute to be effective, it must be an appropriate equivalent. Animal sacrifices could not atone for human beings, because a human being is 'much more valuable . . . than a sheep,' as Jesus himself said (Matt. 12:12). Only 'the precious blood of Christ' was valuable enough (1 Peter 1:19)."
—John R. W. Stott, *The Cross of Christ*

Lesson Goals

Theology–To understand the role of sacrifice in the Old and New Testaments
Reading–To practice linking claims with their support
Vocabulary–To learn and use additional collocations from the reading passage
Grammar–To recognize and make use of word families

Introduction

Now that we have set the stage for redemptive history, we can begin exploring some of the stages in that history. How did God begin to unfold his plan to redeem his people? One of the important and early stages in redemptive history was the installment of sacrificial and cleanliness regulations. These were critical for the people to follow, because God is utterly holy. In fact, God explicitly told the Israelites, "You shall be holy to me, for I the Lord am holy and have separated you from the peoples, that you should be

mine" (Lev. 20:26). To be God's people is to dwell with him, but to dwell with him, his people needed to be cleansed; they needed their sins to be accounted for if they were to enjoy fellowship with an utterly righteous God.

The laws and regulations concerning sacrifice and cleansing (e.g., Lev. 4–5; 11–15), while newly introduced to the people of Israel at that stage of history, were essentially an extension of the covenantal life in which God's people had always been involved. As such, the laws and regulations were about obedience, and "obedience involves personal sacrifice."[1] Sacrifice, the voluntary submission and loss of something valuable for the sake of another, is a critical theme of the Old Testament, and it foreshadows the ultimate sacrifice of God himself, who, as Augustine prayed, commanded what he desired and gave what he commanded.[2]

Discussion Questions

(1) How do you think sacrifice relates to sin?

(2) Why do you think the sacrificial system was introduced in the Old Testament if it could only be fulfilled by Christ? (Hint: See WCF 7.5 and consider what you learned in Lesson 10 about the story of redemption.)

Background for the Reading

The practice of sacrifice began with the children of Adam and Eve: Cain and Abel (Gen. 4). Their sacrifices were meant to please the Lord, but other sacrifices were offered to appease God's wrath and to atone for sin. The sacrificial system of Leviticus, noted above, is a detailed exposition of the kinds of sacrifices offered for certain sins, along with the cleansing rituals that people had to follow if they wanted to remain a part of God's people. To dwell with God, people must be spotless, pure, and immaculate.

As we can imagine, the sacrifices and rituals were never-ending, for sin was always committed, and the effects of the fall made people continually susceptible to contamination, whether through touching a dead body or certain kinds of animals, or simply by contracting diseases. It would come as no surprise, then, that the sacrificial system was abused as Israel's history progressed, and the motive behind offerings turned from a desire to be holy like God to a desire to be acceptable apart from him. God spoke through the prophets condemning such practices (e.g., Hos. 6:6), but the corruption continued. Drastic measures would be taken to preserve God's people, very drastic measures. Even sending the people into exile did not ultimately help them to turn their hearts toward God.

Pre-Reading

How do you think Christ's sacrifice was different from the sacrifices of the OT? How was it similar to them?

Reading

In what follows, R. T. Beckwith discusses the place of sacrifice in the Old and New Testaments.

[¶1] After the return from the Babylonian exile and the building of the second temple, the Mosaic law of sacrifice was once again put into practice in Jerusalem, and with less interference[a] and fewer distractions, on the whole, than before. In the lifetime of Jesus this observance still continued. He had sacrifice offered for him, or offered it himself, at his presentation in the temple, at his last Passover, and presumably[b] on those other occasions[c] when he went up to Jerusalem for feasts. After his death and resurrection, the apostles continued to frequent[d] the temple, including even Paul, who went up to Jerusalem for the feast of Pentecost, and on that occasion offered the sacrifices, which included sin offerings, for the interruption[e] of Nazirite vows (Acts 18:18; 21:23–26; see Num. 6:9–12).

[¶2] Despite this outward continuity through the NT period, the teaching of the NT

Remember?
Find three suffixes marking nouns in paragraph 1.

---

1. Bruce K. Waltke, *An Old Testament Theology: An Exegetical, Canonical, and Thematic Approach* (Grand Rapids, MI: Zondervan, 2007), 545.
2. Augustine, *Confessions* 10.40.

shows that everything had changed. The sacrifices on which it concentrates attention are not those of the temple but the atoning sacrifice of Christ and the spiritual sacrifices of Christians. In principle,[f] the Mosaic sacrifices were now unnecessary. While the temple stood, Jewish Christians felt some duty to observe its ordinances, but when, in AD 70, the temple was destroyed by the Romans in suppressing the first Jewish revolt,[g] and the offering of sacrifice there came to an end, Christians could see a certain appropriateness in the event. Ever since Jeremiah had announced a new covenant, and had thereby made the covenant of Sinai "old," it had been "obsolete[h] and . . . ready to vanish away" (Heb. 8:13), and now, through the coming and work of Christ, it had actually done so.

[¶3] The fullest NT discussion of the OT sacrifices is found in the epistle to the Hebrews. The writer's teaching on those sacrifices has its positive side (11:4; 17–19, 28), but his great concern is to point out their inadequacy[i] except as types foreshadowing[j] the Christian realities. The fact that they cannot gain human beings entrance into the Holy of Holies proves that they cannot free the conscience from guilt, but are simply fleshly ordinances, imposed[k] until a time of reformation (9:6–10). The rending[l] of the veil[m] came only with the death of Christ (Mark 15:37–38; Heb. 10:20). The inability of the sacrifices to atone is shown also by the fact that mere animals are offered (Heb. 10:4), and by the fact of their repetition (10:1–2). They are not so much remedies[n] for sin as reminders of it (10:3).

[¶4] The sacrifice of Christ is not only foreshadowed in the OT but also prophesied. The NT identifies Jesus with the suffering servant of Isaiah 52–53, who is to be a guilt offering for others (Isa. 53:10), and since the prophecy distinguishes him both from the nation (Isa. 53:8) and from the prophet himself (Isa. 53:2–6), it is difficult to see who the suffering servant can be except an eschatological figure,[o] such as the Messiah. In this prophecy, the ideas of atoning sacrifice and vicarious[p] punishment are combined. In the law of Moses sacrifice and punishment are closely related concepts, as a comparison of Leviticus 16:16 with Numbers 35:33–34 clearly shows, and in Isaiah 52–53 the punishment sinners deserve is accepted by another, the one who offers himself as a guilt offering.

[¶5] Many of the NT references to Christ's sacrifice as a fulfillment of OT types[q] represent him as a lamb, an animal used for various sacrifices (burnt offering, peace offering, and sin or guilt offering). He is represented as the slain lamb of God, whose precious blood takes away the sin of the world (John 1:29, 36; 1 Peter 1:18–19; Rev. 5:6–10; 13:8). In a similarly general way, but again with the emphasis on atonement, the blood of his sacrifice is said to cleanse from sin (Heb. 9:13–14, 21–23; 10:19–22; 12:24; 1 Peter 1:2; 1 John 1:7), and he is said to have been sent by God to be a propitiation for our sins (Rom. 3:25; 1 John 2:2; 4:10). More specifically, he is said to be our sacrificed Passover lamb (*pascha*, 1 Cor. 5:6–8); to have been "made . . . sin" (or a sin offering) for us (2 Cor. 5:21); to have been sent by God as a sin offering (*peri harmartias*, Rom. 8:3, *cf.* LXX Lev. 5:7, 11; 9:2, 3, etc.); and, in Hebrews 9–10, to be the fulfillment of the Day of Atonement offerings in Leviticus 16, of the red heifer[r] sacrifice for corpse-uncleanness in Numbers 19, and of the covenant sacrifice in Exodus 24. His sacrifice has made true atonement; it cleanses the conscience and not just the flesh; and has introduced a new and eternal covenant.[3]

a. Interference (n.): obstruction or inhibition
b. Presumably (adv.): by reasonable assumption
c. Occasion (n.): a particular happening or incident
d. Frequent (v.): to go to often
e. Interruption (n.): the act of halting the continuation of
f. In principle (adv. phrase): in regard to fundamentals
g. Revolt (n.): an uprising against authority
h. Obsolete (adj.): no longer active or in use
i. Inadequacy (n.): the quality of being insufficient
j. Foreshadow (v.): to typify beforehand; prefigure
k. Impose (v.): to make, compulsory, obligatory, or enforceable
l. Rend (v.): to split or tear apart
m. Veil (n.): a curtain protecting a sacred enclosure
n. Remedy (n.): something that relieves or cures a disease
o. Figure (n.): a representative type
p. Vicarious (adj.): performed or suffered as a substitute
q. Type (n.): something that serves as a symbolic representation of something yet to come
r. Heifer (n.): a young cow

Post-Reading

In two to three sentences, state what you feel the author's purpose is. In other words, what was his goal in writing this passage?

Main Ideas and Details

(1) Next to each statement, write MI if the statement is a main idea. Write D if it is a reason or supporting detail. Remember to look at the context of the sentences in their respective paragraphs (i.e., hierarchical structure).

_____ 1. The fullest NT discussion of the OT sacrifices is found in the epistle to the Hebrews. (Paragraph 3)

_____ 2. After the return from the Babylonian exile and the building of the second temple, the Mosaic law of sacrifice was once again put into practice in Jerusalem. (Paragraph 1)

_____ 3. The sacrifice of Christ is not only foreshadowed in the OT but also prophesied. (Paragraph 4)

_____ 4. The inability of the sacrifices to atone is shown also by the fact that mere animals are offered (Heb. 10:4), and by the fact of their repetition (10:1–2). (Paragraph 3)

_____ 5. Despite this outward continuity through the NT period, the teaching of the NT shows that everything had changed. (Paragraph 2)

_____ 6. Many of the NT references to Christ's sacrifice as a fulfillment of OT types represent him as a lamb, an animal used for various sacrifices. (Paragraph 5)

_____ 7. In principle, the Mosaic sacrifices were now unnecessary. (Paragraph 2)

_____ 8. After his death and resurrection, the apostles continued to frequent the temple, including even Paul, who went up to Jerusalem for the feast of Pentecost, and on that occasion offered the sacrifices. (Paragraph 1)

(2) In paragraph 1, to what does the phrase "this observance" refer?
a. The Mosaic law of sacrifice.
b. The return from Babylonian exile.
c. The building of the second temple.

(3) In paragraph 1, why does the author use the word "still"?

(4) Re-read the highlighted sentence in paragraph 2. What does the pronoun "it" refer to there?

---

3. R. T. Beckwith, "Sacrifice," in *New Dictionary of Biblical Theology*, ed. T. Desmond Alexander et al. (Downers Grove, IL: InterVarsity, 2000), 759–60. Used with permission of InterVarsity Press.

(5) Which of the following can we infer based on the highlighted sentence in paragraph 2?
   a. Christ did not support the practice of temple sacrifices.
   b. The atoning sacrifice of Christ devalues the Old Testament witness.
   c. The temple sacrifices served a limited purpose in redemptive history.
   d. We should pay more attention to the New Testament than to the Old Testament.

(6) In paragraph 3, why does the author use the conjunction "but"?
   a. To introduce an exception.
   b. To link two equally important ideas.
   c. To introduce the biblical author's true emphasis.
   d. To show that the previous statement directly contradicts the one that follows.

(7) In paragraph 4, the word "distinguishes" could best be replaced by _____.
   a. Verifies.
   b. Examines.
   c. Discriminates.
   d. Sets him apart.

(8) Which of the following can we infer based on the noun phrase "true atonement" in paragraph 5?
   a. True atonement is ultimately temporary.
   b. Atonement requires more than outward cleansing.
   c. The Old Testament sacrifices provided false atonement.
   d. For any atonement to be true, it must be part of a new covenant.

Grammar Focus: Word Families

Now that we have looked at several word forms (adjectives, nouns, and adverbs) in previous lessons, we have all that we need to understand **word families**. We use the phrase "word families" to refer to groups of words that share a common root. "Discipline," "disciplinary," and "disciplinarian" are part of the same word family. Your knowledge of word families can help you to expand your vocabulary because once you learn one member of the family, you can deduce what the other members are. But we must also be careful to use the right word from the family in a particular context. Below, you have a chance to practice selecting which word from a word family is grammatically necessary for a particular sentence.

Activity 1

Fill in the blanks using the word families provided in the box below. Each word is used only once, so check them off as you go. Some of the blanks have been filled in for you if there was a chance that more than one word from the list was appropriate. (Check these words off as you encounter them.)

glory	important	meaning	reasons	sacrifice
glorify	importance	meaningful	reasonable	sacrificial
history	introduced	necessitates	revealed	sufficient
historical	introduction	necessary	revelation	sufficiency

People might question whether the _____ system of the Old Testament was ___ _necessary___ if God knew that it would be replaced by the perfect _____ of Christ in the New Testament. Yet, here it is _____ to remember that _____ unfolds in _____, and God has his own _____ for doing this. Some of these reasons we might be able to discern, but others we cannot, for they have not been _____ to us.

For example, if we say that God should have "skipped" the Old Testament sacrificial system, we are in danger of downplaying the ____importance____ of history. What, then, is keeping us from saying that God should have sent his Son at the beginning of history? For that matter, what is keeping us from saying that God should have solved the problem of sin before it even started by killing the serpent in the Garden of Eden, thus avoiding the historical problem altogether? Our desire to make history completely _____ can lead us to set up an idol of reason, a standard to which God must submit.

God values history, and our choices within our _____ context are ____meaningful____. We cannot always discern that _____, but we know it exists. The faithfulness of God's revelation _____ that meaning is omnipresent, because God is omnipresent. In this vein, we do not know exactly why the Old Testament sacrificial system was ____introduced____, but we do know that its _____ cannot be detached from the meaning of Jesus' sacrifice. The law delivered at Sinai and the following sacrificial atonement regulations were "part of the program of grace whereby God works to fulfill his promises to Abraham."[4] Those promises were ____sufficient____ at one stage of history and yet fulfilled by Christ in another stage. Their inadequacy from our perspective serves to show the eternal _____ of Christ's death and resurrection. Christ is utterly and exclusively sufficient for our salvation. So, perhaps God instituted the Old Testament sacrificial system with the future _____ of Christ in mind. This would make perfect sense when we read the evangelist's words in John 12:28, "'Father, _____ your name.' Then a voice came from heaven: 'I have glorified it, and I will glorify it again.'" The Father had in mind the glory of the Son even in instituting a sacrificial system that he would fulfill hundreds of years after its installation.

Activity 2

The following paragraph has nine word form errors. Cross out the incorrect word forms and write in the correct forms.

The sacrifices we find offered in the Old Testament (OT) are differently from the sacrifice of Christ in the New Testament (NT) in many ways. First, Christ's sacrifice in the NT was prophesy about by the Bible authors, whereas the OT sacrificed system was delivered by God to Moses at the time it was to be practiced. Second, although both the OT sacrifices and Christ's sacrifice in the NT were meant to atonement for sin, only Christ's sacrifice in the NT definitive atoned for sin, "for it is impossibility for the blood of bulls and goats to take away sins" (Heb. 10:4). Third, a person was never offered as a sacrificial in the OT, but the person of Christ was offered for us in the NT. Thus, the NT sacrifice of Christ has far more valuable to Christians than the OT sacrifices, even though the latter are still important in redemptive history and foreshadow the work of Christ.

4. Graeme Goldsworthy, *Gospel and Kingdom*, in *The Goldsworthy Trilogy* (Colorado Springs, CO: Paternoster, 2000), 74.

Collocations from the Passage

For each number below, select the sentence that correctly uses a collocation from the reading.

1.
    a. The people offered many victims.
    b. The Israelites offered many elements.
    c. The Israelites offered many contributions.
    d. The Israelites offered God many sacrifices.

2.
    a. God had great concern for his people.
    b. The Lord had large concern for the priests.
    c. The covenantal God had lengthy concern for Israel.
    d. God had sizable concern for his people in their wilderness wanderings.

3.
    a. Sacrifice and cleansing are nearly related.
    b. Atonement and cleanliness are closely allied.
    c. The concepts of sacrifice and cleansing are closely related.
    d. The concepts of sacrifice and cleansing are closely realized.

4.
    a. The premium blood of Christ is what saves.
    b. Only the precious blood of Christ can atone.
    c. Some Israelite sacrifices offered the favorite blood of lambs.
    d. The adored blood of Christ was offered to atone for our sin.

Here are a few other words from the reading that have several collocations. Try to memorize them and use them in the exercises ahead. (Note: "Sb" = somebody; "sth" = something.)

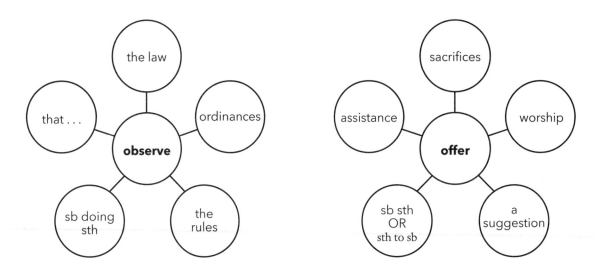

Fig. 11.1. Collocation Diagram 1

12

All Promises Fulfilled

*"God's word of promise will not return empty. His grace will not be frustrated.
His compassion will triumph. The dreadful destruction of His wrath against apostasy
will not be total or final, for God purposes salvation beyond imagining."*
—Edmund P. Clowney, *The Unfolding Mystery*

Lesson Goals

Theology—To see Christ as the fulfillment of God's promises
Reading—To identify main ideas and details, trace pronoun referents, draw inferences
Vocabulary—To learn and use additional collocations from the reading passage
Grammar—To recognize modal verbs and how they affect main verbs

Introduction

We have seen how sacrifices play an important role in Scripture, in both the Old and New Testaments. These sacrifices were a means of sanctifying God's people, of purifying them so that they could dwell with an utterly holy God. Ultimately, God offered his own Son in order to bring about this sanctification. For sinners, communion with God is ever so costly.

But the sacrifices in the Old Testament and even Christ's sacrifice in the New Testament have an important context in redemptive history. These sacrifices were bound up with God's promise to redeem a people for himself (1 Chron. 17:21). That promise, in fact, holds all of history and revelation together. In the words of Edmund Clowney,

Only God's revelation can build a story where the end is anticipated from the beginning, and where the guiding principle is not chance or fate, but promise. Human authors may build fiction around a plot they have devised, but only God can shape history to a real and ultimate purpose. The purpose of God from the beginning centers on his Son: "He is the image of the invisible God, the firstborn over all creation. For by him all things were created: things in heaven and on earth, visible and invisible. . . . All things were created by him and for him" (Col. 1:15–16).[1]

God promised redemption all the way back in Gen. 3:15, and even before that the Father knew that it would be his Son who would fulfill that promise, who would find success where Adam found failure. All of the corruption and destruction brought about by the first Adam's rebellion would be restored and set

1. Edmund P. Clowney, *The Unfolding Mystery: Discovering Christ in the Old Testament*, 25th Anniversary ed. (Phillipsburg, NJ: P&R, 2013), 13.

right by the second Adam. In this sense, all of God's promises in the Old Testament find their fulfillment in the promised person of Christ.

Scripture Reading

The biblical roots of what we have just said about Christ are discussed by Paul in 2 Cor. 1:1–22. Read this passage out loud. What promises do you think Paul has in mind in v. 20?

Background for the Reading

We noted that God's promise to Adam was fulfilled in Christ, but so were all of God's other promises. "The call to share in promise is a call to share in a *heritage* rooted in Scripture."[2] Within that heritage, Paul writes that all of God's promises are "yes" and "amen" in Christ (2 Cor. 1:20). The famous Pauline phrase, "in Christ," is crucial to remember. It is *in him* that the promises find fulfillment. It is in faith-wrought union with him that we are the beneficiaries of those promises.[3]

Pre-Reading

Describe one way in which you see Christ as fulfilling God's promises.

Reading

In the following reading, Edmund Clowney illustrates how Christ is the fulfillment of God's Old Testament promises.

[¶1] Salvation is *in* and *of* the Lord; we may possess[a] it only as we have the Lord as our inheritance, and as we become the inheritance of God, and know as we are known (Ex. 34:9). God must come among us, dwell in our midst, and there reveal the light of His glory and the saving power of His holy Name. In symbol God gave that to Moses. He proclaimed[b] His Name to Moses as the God of sovereign grace (Ex. 33:19; 34:6–7). He did not do what He had threatened to do. He did not cancel the building of the tabernacle in the *midst* of the camp in favor of a tent of meeting *outside* the camp. Rather, God did, in a figure,[c] dwell in the midst of Israel. The tabernacle with its furnishings provided both a screen to contain[d] the holy threat of the Lord's presence and a way of approach by which sinners could come before Him through the shedding of blood and the mediation of the priesthood.

[¶2] The life of Israel was built around that symbol. But what of the reality that was symbolized? The prophet Ezekiel sees a temple that holds[e] the fountain of the water of life, watering a land that becomes a new Eden. Beside the river that flows from the tabernacle, the tree of life again grows, with healing for the nations (Ezek. 47). But what sacrifice shall be offered when God comes? What dwelling will suffice[f] when He comes, not in the symbol of the pillar of cloud, but in the reality of fulfillment?

Remember?
What word family is represented in the first two sentences?

[¶3] And what of the fulfillment of God's covenant? If God comes, how can Israel come

2. Darrell L. Bock, *A Theology of Luke and Acts: God's Promised Program, Realized for All Nations* (Grand Rapids, MI: Zondervan, 2012), 415; emphasis added.

3. See Constantine R. Campbell, *Paul and Union with Christ: An Exegetical and Theological Study* (Grand Rapids, MI: Zondervan, 2012), 73–94.

to meet Him? Who will have clean hands and a pure heart to enter the presence of the Lord (Ps. 24)? God is the Lord of the covenant, but what of the servant of the covenant?

[¶4] God's justice is clear; His requirements[g] cannot be compromised.[h] It will not do for God to come only as Lord, even as Warrior, Shepherd, and Creator. To bring the salvation He has promised He must fulfill the part of the Servant as well as the part of the Lord of the covenant.

[¶5] The tabernacle pictured the way of approach through the altar of sacrifice. But the blood of bulls and goats cannot atone for sin. The final and true sacrifice must be not merely the lamb of the flock, but the son of the bosom.[i] The Passover threat against the first-born must be fulfilled against the representative Seed of the promise, the Isaac God has provided. Abraham's beloved son is the promised seed, but not yet the Son of God. The promise is "Jehovah-Jireh": the Lord Himself must provide the Son who is also the Lamb of God that takes away the sin of the world (Gen. 22).

Note: Capitalization is important to the meaning of the sentences at the end of paragraph 5.

[¶6] When the prophets promise the coming of God, they are brought to see that God's Anointed must come: if God is the Shepherd, so is the Son of David, God's Prince (Ezek. 34:23). When the Servant of the Lord comes, He will fulfill the role of Israel (Isa. 49:3). He will also gather the lost sheep of Israel, restore the remnant of the people, and be a light to the Gentiles, God's salvation to the end of the earth (Isa. 49:6).

[¶7] The name of the Messiah will be, "Wonderful, Counselor, the Mighty God, Everlasting Father, Prince of Peace" (Isa. 9:6). The house of David will indeed be as God, for as the mystery unfolds, God Himself comes in the tabernacle of human flesh. The Lord must come; the Servant must come. Jesus Christ comes, who is Lord and Servant: Immanuel, God with us!

[¶8] The Old Testament, then, in its very structure[j] is formed by God's promise: the promise to Adam and Eve in the garden (Gen. 3:15); the promise to Abraham (Gen. 12:1–3); the promise to Israel (Deut. 30:6); the promise to David (2 Sam. 7:12–16). These are not mere episodes[k] or occasional oracles. They mark the unfolding of God's redemptive plan. The promises of the Seed of the woman and the Seed of Abraham are given in the Pentateuch; they present both the background and the purpose in the calling of Israel. Without them the perspective of blessing to the nations through Israel might be lost from view. Before the call of Abraham in Genesis 12, Israel is to read the table of the nations in Genesis 10. Israel must perceive[l] its own calling in the light of God's purpose for the nations and of God's promise of the Seed to come.

[¶9] For that reason the theme of blessing upon the remnant of the nations with the remnant of Israel (e.g., Isa. 19:19–25) is not a new twist added by more cosmopolitan[m] prophets. It is the reaffirmation of God's original calling of His people, and a vision of the new form of the people of God in the wonder of God's own coming.

[¶10] The focus on Christ in the Old Testament does not spring simply from the fact that Old Testament revelation is given in the framework of a history that does actually lead to Christ. Or, more pointedly, the history that leads to Christ is not a random succession of events. Neither is it simply history under God's providential[n] control, serving His sovereign purpose. It is rather the history of God's own intervention in history, the history of His great work of salvation as He prepares for His own coming in the person of His Son.

[¶11] The epiphany[o] of the Son of God is not a divine afterthought, an *ad hoc*[p] emergency plan developed to meet the unforeseen disaster of the apostasy of the elect nation. It is not the failure of Israel that necessitates the coming of Christ, as though an obedient people would have made a divine and incarnate Savior unnecessary.

[¶12] No, the story of the Old Testament is the story of the Lord: what He has done, and what He has purposed to do. The Old Testament does not provide us with biographies or national history. It is the story of God's work, not men's. It speaks of men in the context of God's covenant with them. Since salvation is of the Lord and not of men, the issue is always faith. The heroes of the Old Testament, as the author of Hebrews plainly tells us, are men and women of faith. They trust in God, believe the promises, and look for the city that has foundations, whose builder and maker is God (Heb. 11:10).[4]

a. Possess (v.): to have or own
b. Proclaim (v.): to declare openly or publicly
c. Figure (n.): the representation of a form
d. Contain (v.): to keep within limits
e. Hold (v.): to have within; contain
f. Suffice (v.): to be enough; to meet or satisfy a requirement
g. Requirement (n.): something that is called for or demanded
h. Compromise (v.): to put in jeopardy; expose to suspicion, discredit, or mischief
i. Bosom (n.): the breast considered as the center of emotions; heart
j. Structure (n.): the way in which the parts of something are put together or organized
k. Episode (n.): a brief unit of action in a dramatic or literary work
l. Perceive (v.): to discern or realize
m. Cosmopolitan (adj.): marked by interest in, familiarity with, or knowledge and appreciation of many parts of the world
n. Providential (adj.): of, relating to, or determined by divine guidance or care
o. Epiphany (n.): an appearance or incarnation of a divine being
p. Ad hoc (adj.): improvised

Post-Reading

Describe in your own words what Clowney says about the "structure" of the Old Testament.

Main Ideas and Details

(1) What two things did the tabernacle provide in Moses' day? (paragraph 1)

(2) To what does the highlighted pronoun "its" in paragraph 1 refer?

    a. God.
    b. Israel.
    c. A figure.
    d. The tabernacle.

(3) What are the questions raised in paragraph 2 focused on?
    a. The importance of sacrifice.
    b. The symbolic nature of prophecy.
    c. The tree of life as healing for the nations.
    d. How God himself will enter human history.

4. Edmund P. Clowney, "Preaching Christ from All the Scriptures," in *Thy Word Is Still Truth: Essential Writings on the Doctrine of Scripture from the Reformation to Today*, ed. Peter A. Lillback and Richard B. Gaffin Jr. (Philadelphia: Westminster Seminary Press, 2013), 1040–41.

(4) What are the questions raised in paragraph 3 focused on?
   a. The presence of the Lord.
   b. The fulfillment of God's promise.
   c. The requirement of God's people in the covenant.
   d. The importance of the Old Testament people of Israel.

(5) Which of the following can we infer based on paragraph 4?
   a. God defeats all of Israel's enemies.
   b. Salvation must be brought about by the work of a shepherd.
   c. God's love in the Old Testament is less clear than his justice.

d. Salvation would be lost if God did not fulfill both sides of the covenant.

(6) In paragraph 5, what is the meaning of the phrase "the Isaac God has provided"?

(7) What does the highlighted pronoun "them" refer to in paragraph 8?

(8) What does the highlighted pronoun "it" refer to in paragraph 9?

(9) Restate the main idea of paragraph 10 in your own words.

(10) Why does the author say that "the Old Testament does not provide us with biographies or national history"?

Understanding the Reading

Choose one of the Old Testament promises referenced in the reading passage (Gen. 3:15; 12:1–3; Deut. 30:6; 2 Sam. 7:12–16) and describe it in your own words. Write your description in the column on the left. Then, in the column on the right, describe what we would miss in our understanding of Christ's work if we were not aware of that Old Testament promise.

Old Testament Promise	What We Would Miss

Collocations from the Passage

Match the words on the left to their collocates on the right.

threaten	for sin
offer	the law
atone	a sacrifice
observe	salvation
possess	to do something

To the right are a few common words from the reading and several words that go with them. Again, try to memorize these and begin using them in the exercises ahead. (Note: "Sb" = somebody; "sth" = something.

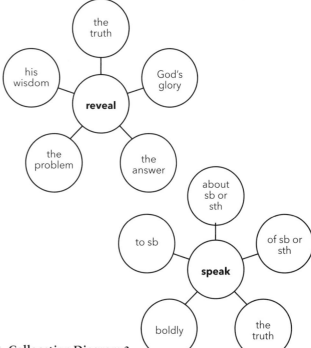

Fig. 12.1. Collocation Diagram 2

We have already discussed how pronunciation can reflect grammar and reference. Consider the verse, "That is why it is through him that we utter our Amen to God for his glory" (2 Cor. 1:20). We could stress (phonology) the prepositional phrase (grammar) "through him" to draw the listener's attention to the instrument (reference) through which (or through whom) we utter our Amen. Or we could stress the prepositional phrase at the end of the verse, "for his glory," to draw the listener's attention to the purpose of our uttering Amen: to bring God glory.

Grammar Focus: Modal Verbs

We have now been exposed to some of the features of complex sentence structures in TE, as well as the precise word forms that we find in them. But another key component of sentences in TE, and of all English sentences, is the verb. The verb is sometimes considered the "engine" of the sentence because it propels the nouns, linking them to the central action. But verbs also tell us something about the author's perspective on the action. We have seen this already with our discussion of verb tense in Lesson 7. In the next three lessons, we will have a more focused discussion on the author's perspective and the verb phrase, starting with modal verbs.

The Author's Perspective

Modal verbs tell us about the author's perspective in two senses: (1) they identify the degree of certainty with which the author wants us to view an action.[5] Is a particular action certain (*must, will*), probable (*should, ought*), improbable (*may, might*), or impossible (*cannot, will not*)? Modal verbs suggest the author's answer. (2) Modal verbs also tell us if an author wants us to view an action as obligatory (necessary) or free. Are we required to do something (*must*), encouraged to do something (*should, might*), willing to do something (*will, shall*), asking permission to do something (*may, could, might*), or able to do something (*can*)? Again, modal verbs suggest the author's answer. Authors

also use modal verbs for what we call "hedging." You will learn more about this in Lesson 20.

Modal Verbs and Main Verbs

Modal verbs affect the form of the main verb they accompany. In the following excerpt, circle the modal verbs. What do you notice about the form of the main verbs that follow them?

God's justice is clear; His requirements cannot be compromised. It will not do for God to come only as Lord, even as Warrior, Shepherd, and Creator. To bring the salvation He has promised He must fulfill the part of the Servant as well as the part of the Lord of the covenant.

Can You See?
What does "cannot" tell us about how the author views the action of "atoning"?

The tabernacle pictured the way of approach through the altar of sacrifice. But the blood of bulls and goats cannot atone for sin. The final and true sacrifice must be not merely the lamb of the flock, but the son of the bosom. The Passover threat against the first-born must be fulfilled against the representative Seed of the promise, the Isaac God has provided. Abraham's beloved son is the promised seed, but not yet the Son of God. The promise is "Jehovah-Jireh": the Lord Himself must provide the Son who is also the Lamb of God that takes away the sin of the world (Gen. 22).

When the Servant of the Lord comes, He will fulfill the role of Israel (Isa. 49:3). He will also gather the lost sheep of Israel, restore the remnant of the people, and be a light to the Gentiles, God's salvation to the end of the earth (Isa. 49:6).

When we use a modal verb, the main verb that accompanies it takes what we call the **bare infinitive form**, the infinitive form of the verb without "to." When writers forget this rule, the following types of errors occur.

---

5. This and the following point concerning what modal verbs reveal have been taken from Michael Swan, *Practical English Usage*, 4th ed. (Oxford: Oxford University Press, 2016), section 7 (on modal verbs).

Every Christian can reads **read** about God's promises in Scripture.

We should to **study** God's Word to see his faithfulness in history.

I do not know how some Christians can denying **deny** Christ's bodily resurrection.

Another difficulty that you may encounter is in choosing which modal verb to use. Below, we provide a simple chart that summarizes the basic uses of each modal verb. Study the examples in the right hand column before doing Activity 1.

Modal Verb	Common Use	Example
Can	Ability	I *can* interpret Scripture accurately.
Could	Possibility	I *could* interpret Scripture if I were taught the original languages.
May/Might	Permission or Possibility	*May* I interpret this text for you? Many people *may* not understand why exegesis is essential to theology.
Shall	Formal promise or command	You *shall* not commit murder.
Should	Prescriptive	All theologians *should* learn biblical languages before doing exegesis.
Will	Future promise (certainty)	I *will* interpret Scripture for my Sunday school students.
Would	Hypothetical	If someone were to teach me how, I *would* interpret Scripture enthusiastically.

Activity 1

Insert the most appropriate modal verb in each blank. There may be more than one correct answer for some of the sentences.

Edmund Clowney notes that "David foreshadows the longsuffering restraint of Christ's humiliation."[6] We _____ confirm this if we reflect on the traumatic stage of David's life when he was fleeing from Saul. As a devout follower of the Lord, David knew that he _____ not raise his hand against the Lord's anointed (1 Sam. 24:6; 26:9). But what happens when the Lord's anointed is seeking to take your life, as Saul was? Here, we _____ think that David would be permitted to make an exception. But he refused to do this; he simply _____ not harm one whom God had put in charge of his people. _____ you do that in David's situation? Could I? Surely, this is one of the ways in which David was longsuffering and restrained himself in obedience to God.

6. Edmund P. Clowney, *The Unfolding Mystery: Discovering Christ in the Old Testament*, 25th Anniversary ed. (Phillipsburg, NJ: P&R, 2013), 173.

Activity 2

Working with a partner, answer the following questions with sentences that each include one or more modal verbs. Provide as many answers as you can.

(1) What if Jesus had not come to fulfill God's Old Testament promises?

(2) Because Jesus has come to fulfill God's promises, what must a person do to be saved?

(3) Because God is faithful, what kinds of things can God do for his people?

Summary of Theological Concepts for Unit 4

- Redemptive history began with a promise of God to restore humanity and destroy the serpent.
- Through a process of sacrifice and cleansing in the OT, we are led to the perfect sacrifice of Christ.
- God fulfills his promise in the person and work of Christ, who restores our communion with him.

Activity

Paraphrase each of the concepts above in your own words.

(1)

(2)

(3)

The Importance of a Promise (BS Task 2)

Introduction

In this task, your goal is to write a letter to an old friend who is going through a time of spiritual numbness (lack of feeling) and is questioning whether or not he has what it takes to hold on to God's promises.

In Lesson 12, we saw how Christ fulfills all of God's promises in the Old Testament. As Clowney states, "Salvation is *in* and *of* the Lord; we may possess it only as we have the Lord as our inheritance, and as we become the inheritance of God, and know as we are known (Ex. 34:9)."[7] If we have Christ, then we have, in him, the security of all of God's promises, no matter

7. Edmund P. Clowney, "Preaching Christ from All the Scriptures," in *Thy Word Is Still Truth: Essential Writings on the Doctrine of Scripture from the Reformation to Today*, ed. Peter A. Lillback and Richard B. Gaffin Jr. (Philadelphia: Westminster Seminary Press, 2013), 1040.

what we experience or how we feel. But sometimes this is difficult to remember during times of trial.

Task

An old friend of yours named Thomas is going through a time of spiritual numbness. He does not feel God working in his life or in the lives of those around him. In fact, he does not *feel* anything. He tells you in a phone conversation, "At first, I was fighting back and trying to keep my faith, but it's been going on for months now, and I don't know what to do."

Based on what you have learned about the fulfillment of God's promises in Christ, and knowing that your friend Thomas is a believer who serves Christ as Lord, write an email to him (approximately 200 words) encouraging him in his faith. Even though this is an email and as such is informal, practice what you have learned about writing unified, coherent, and developed paragraphs. Remember to be careful of your word choice and to be precise. Refer to AP Task 1 in Unit 1 to remind yourself of appropriate email etiquette.

Learning the Genre: Biblical Studies

So far, we have discussed the apologetics genre. Now we will consider the biblical studies genre. But before we do that, we need to know what exactly the purpose of biblical studies is. In other words, according to the definition of genre that we previously considered,[8] how can we summarize the communicative functions of writing in biblical studies?

Biblical Studies

We might say that, while the purpose of apologetics is to defend the Christian faith, the purpose of biblical studies is to define and shape the Christian faith by explaining what the Bible says

and means. It does this defining and shaping by (1) investigating the meaning of the words, sentences, and passages of Scripture; (2) examining the origin of biblical writings and the historical situations of the authors; (3) studying how the books of the Bible fit within the accepted canon; and (4) exploring how revelation unfolds throughout time.[9] This last facet is what Geerhardus Vos properly calls *biblical theology*. Biblical theology can thus be seen as part of the broader genre of biblical studies. Each of these facets of biblical studies helps us better understand what the Bible teaches. That is the purpose, the goal, toward which biblical studies drives us.

Now, what are the *communicative functions* of the writing we encounter in this genre? One function is actually similar to a function we have already examined in the genre of apologetics, that is, building an argument in support of what Scripture teaches. After all, we want to know not only *what* Scripture means, but *why* and *how* it means what we think it means. Yet an argument in the biblical studies genre can be quite different from those we find in apologetics.

If you remember our earlier discussion, we noted that each theological genre has what we might call *genre traits*, that is, features distinct, though not exclusive, to that particular kind of writing.[10] While logical coherence is prominently displayed in apologetics, we might say that **textual awareness** is prominently displayed in biblical studies. By this we mean not only that (1) authors use details from the text to build an argument, but also that (2) they know how to relate one text to another in support of a main idea. We can see these genre traits in the following passage.

The author of the passage below argues that if Adam had not sinned in the Garden of Eden, he would still have received an incorruptible body, different from his earthly body. Note the underlined words and phrases, which mark textual details he uses to build an argument.

8. A genre is "a type of discourse that occurs in a particular setting, that has distinctive and recognizable patterns and norms of organization and structure, and that has particular and distinctive communicative functions." Jack C. Richards and Richard Schmidt, *Longman Dictionary of Language Teaching and Applied Linguistics*, 3rd ed. (New York: Longman, 2002), 224.

9. This description is based on Geerhardus Vos's exposition of "Exegetical Theology." See *Biblical Theology: Old and New Testaments* (Grand Rapids, MI: Eerdmans, 1954), 12–13.

10. Kevin Vanhoozer treats genre traits in more depth within the area of biblical interpretation. He claims that an author "sends signals, in the text itself, that identify its genre." So, we might also call these "genre signals." See *Is There a Meaning in This Text? The Bible, the Reader, and the Morality of Literary Knowledge* (Grand Rapids: MI: Zondervan, 1998), 346.

On the Possible Goal of the Prefall Adam Experiencing Full Security from Death

[¶1] With respect to Adam receiving absolute security from death, there is no explicit reference within Gen. 1–3 or, indeed, anywhere in the OT that Adam's faithfulness would have eventually been rewarded with such a thing. However, 1 Cor. 15:45 is perhaps the preeminent biblical text attesting to such an eschatologically escalated existence as the final goal for the prefall Adam: "So also it is written, 'The first man, Adam, became a living soul.' The last Adam became a life-giving spirit." Here the first Adam in his prefall and sinless condition is contrasted with the last Adam in his glorious resurrected state. Remarkably, Paul draws the contrast not with the first Adam's sinful, corruptible condition but rather with his prefall sinless condition as recorded in Gen. 2:7 ("Adam became a living soul"), and he concludes that even this prefall condition was insufficient for qualification to "inherit the kingdom of God" (1 Cor. 15:50). Verse 45 is a contrast of lesser and greater glorious states. In fact, Paul's argument throughout 1 Cor. 15:39–53 appears to involve contrasts of lesser and greater glories, in addition to contrasts of sinful realities and nonsinful realities or of sinful life and death versus resurrection life. Paul employs illustrative contrasts of different kinds of seeds, animals, and heavenly light sources (sun, moon, and stars), each with differing degrees of glory. These are illustrations also drawn from the prefall description of Gen. 1 to demonstrate the contrast between the "earthly" perishable and corruptible bodies of believers, which have a degree of glory, and their destined "heavenly" imperishable and incorruptible bodies, which have greater glory (15:38–41).

[¶2] Paul then says that "in the same manner" (houtōs) that there are lesser and greater glories observable in the earth and heavens, so also is the resurrection of the dead. "It is sown a perishable [corruptible] body, it is raised an imperishable body; it is sown in dishonor [corruptibility], it is raised in glory; it is sown in weakness, it is raised in power; it is sown a natural body, it is raised a spiritual body. If there is a natural body, there is also a spiritual body" (15:42–44). Since the contrast of relative glories does not involve black-and-white contrasts, "in the same manner also" it is the case with the preconsummate human body and the consummated, resurrected body. Verse 45 says that "in the same manner" Adam's prefall body had a degree of glory (indeed, it was included with all the creation, which God had declared "very good" [Gen. 1:31]).

[¶3] To explain the contrast between the first Adam and the last Adam, Paul refers to the "natural" or "physical" (not sinful) versus the "spiritual" (v. 46), "the first man from the earth, earthy" or "made of dust [choïkos]" versus "the second man . . . from heaven" (vv. 47–48a). Indeed, verses 46–48 continue the contrast in verse 45 of the prefall, sinless Adam with the resurrected last Adam. Verse 47 continues the allusion to Gen. 2:7, this time by alluding to the first part of that verse: "The first man is from the earth, made of dust" (Gen. 2:7: "God formed man of dust from the ground"). Paul concludes by saying that there are also people "made of dust" and bearing "the image of the one made of dust" and people who will become "heavenly" and those also who will "bear the image of the heavenly" (vv. 48b–49). Paul makes the conclusion that "flesh and blood," "the perishable," and "the mortal" cannot "inherit the kingdom of God," but only the "imperishable" and "immortal" will inherit that kingdom (vv. 50–53). Resuming the idea of actual death from verse 36, it appears that in verses 54–57 there comes into Paul's view again the notion that not only is the present body mortal like Adam's prefall body (since neither was qualified to enter the eternal kingdom), but also it will die because of sin; nevertheless, Christ will give his people victory over death.

[¶4] But even if verses 39–44 and verses 49–53 have in view contrasts of postfall sinful, earthly human reality versus sinless resurrected reality, it appears probable, at least, that verses 45–48 go back beyond even Adam's fall to his prefall state and contrast that with resurrected human reality. Paul's understanding, therefore, is that even if Adam had never sinned, his prefall existence still needed to be transformed at some climactic point into an irreversible glorious existence, which Paul identifies as resurrection existence. Accordingly, Paul understood that Adam would have been rewarded with a transformed, incorruptible body if he had remained faithful.[11]

So, how does Beale's writing illustrate the two genre traits we mentioned (using details from the text to build an argument, and relating one text to another in support of a main idea)? It is clear in this passage what question the author wants to answer, and what two texts help him to answer it. He then relates these two texts in order to support his main idea, that is, the answer to the question.

The crux of Beale's argument depends on the allusions in 1 Cor. 15:39–53 to Adam *in his prefall state* (Gen. 1–2). According to Beale, Paul is saying that the first Adam had a body that was not fit to inherit the kingdom of heaven, even before he sinned (paragraphs 1 and 3). We know this because Paul is telling us of our need to inherit a heavenly, imperishable body, a "resurrected body" (paragraph 2). If we need a "heavenly" body, but Adam only had an "earthly" body before he sinned, then it is probable that Adam would have received a new "heavenly" body if he had obeyed God's command and not eaten from the tree of the knowledge of good and evil. Beale relates two passages of Scripture, drawing out their relationships and allusions, in order to support his main idea.

The second genre trait, using details from the text to build an argument, is visible throughout the passage. Note some of the textual details that the author uses to illustrate the contrast between the two kinds of bodies we find in Scripture.

Question	If he had never sinned, would Adam still have received a new body?
Text 1	Genesis 1–2
Text 2	1 Corinthians 15:39–53
Main Idea	Yes, Adam would have received a new body even if he never committed sin.

11. G. K. Beale, *A New Testament Biblical Theology: The Unfolding of the Old Testament in the New* (Grand Rapids, MI: Baker, 2011), 43–45. Excerpt from *A New Testament Biblical Theology* by G.K. Beale, copyright © 2011. Used by permission of Baker Academic, a division of Baker Publishing Group.

Body Type 1	Body Type 2
"the first Adam"	"the last Adam"
"became a living soul"	"inherit[s] the kingdom"
lesser glorious states	greater glorious states
"earthly," "perishable"	"heavenly," "imperishable"
"sown in dishonor"	"raised in glory"
"sown in weakness"	"raised in power"
"sown a natural/ physical body"	"raised a spiritual body"
"very good"	"from heaven"
"made of dust"	"heavenly"
"the image of the one made of dust"	"the image of the heavenly"
"mortal"	"immortal"

The details help the reader to see the stark contrast between the two types of bodies. This contrast helps to build the argument by establishing that there is a significant difference between Adam's prefall body and Christ's resurrected body. Once the author has shown this to the reader, he can draw his conclusion that a greater, heavenly, imperishable body would likely have been given to Adam if he had not committed sin.

Activity

In the passage below, underline the textual details that you find. What passages of Scripture does the author relate in order to support his main idea, and how do the details of the texts help him to build his argument?

In contrast to Dan. 7, which portrays the Son of Man surrounded by an angelic royal host (cf. vv. 9–10) as he approaches the heavenly divine throne to receive a kingdom, Luke 7:34 depicts Jesus as beginning to fulfill the Daniel prophecy in an apparently different way than prophesied. The wording "the Son of Man has come" is sufficient to recognize an allusion to Daniel, and, as with Mark 10:45, it is best to assume that Luke has in view incipient fulfillment rather than a mere analogy to Daniel's Son of Man. Strikingly, those who surround the coming of the son of Man are not angels, as in Dan. 7, but rather Jesus's retinue is tax collectors and sinners. Again, this appears to be part of his incognito victorious coming to receive authority over a kingdom, which begins even before his death and resurrection. Although explicit suffering is not mentioned here, his seeming ignoble appearance receives ridicule and condemnation from the religious leaders. Although a number of scholars have thought that the "wisdom" saying in Luke 7:35 was a floating piece of tradition inserted willy-nilly here, it actually fits well: "Yet wisdom is vindicated by all her children." Jesus is one of God's wise children (he is the "Son"), and God's wisdom of turning the world's values on their head is illustrated with him. The wisdom of the world judged him to be an ignoble figure, but in reality he was a faithful son who persevered through suffering and insults while at the same time inaugurating his own kingdom. God's wise way of ironically introducing the kingdom through Jesus was vindicated at Jesus's resurrection and will be at the end of the age by the resurrection of all the saints who have followed in his ironic footsteps.[12]

12. Ibid, 197–98.

UNIT 5

WHO IS JESUS?
(BIBLICAL STUDIES)

13

The Most Important Question

"The incarnate Son of God remains, even in the incarnation, a divine person."
—Lane G. Tipton, *Resurrection and Eschatology*

Lesson Goals

Theology–To understand the importance of the divine and human natures of Christ
Reading–To identify main ideas and details, and to draw inferences
Vocabulary–To learn and use additional collocations from the reading passage
Grammar–To learn principles for using the present, past, and past perfect tenses

---

Introduction

How we understand the person of Jesus Christ is no small matter. His divine and human natures and his relationship to the Father are particularly important. Indeed, "the issue of the Son's relationship to the Father may appear to be somewhat abstruse but is actually vital to the Christian faith. How one resolves that issue will decisively affect how one understands creation, salvation, and a host of other theological and practical issues."[1]

The early church fathers also spent a great deal of time articulating precisely how and why Jesus possessed both a human and a divine nature and was yet a single person.[2] It was Gregory of Nazianzus who proclaimed of Christ, "that which He has not assumed He has not healed."[3] In other words, if the divine and eternal Son did not truly assume a human nature,

then our human nature has not been redeemed. As you can see, our theological answer to the question, "Who is Jesus?" has profound implications for our own salvation. Looking to Scripture for the answer to this question is critical, and that is where our theological reading for this lesson will take us.

Warm-up

To prepare for the theological reading, read Hebrews 1–2. Write down any notes as needed.

Background for the Reading

While we have discussed how Jesus fulfilled all of God's promises (2 Cor. 1:20), we have yet to address *who* exactly Jesus is. How can we describe his person? As Trueman pointed out in the introduction to this

---

1. Carl R. Trueman, *The Creedal Imperative* (Wheaton, IL: Crossway, 2012), 92.

2. Bengt Hägglund, *History of Theology*, trans. Gene J. Lund, 4th rev. ed. (Saint Louis, MO: Concordia, 2007), 20–21.

3. Gregory of Nazianzus, "To Cledonius the Priest against Apollinarius," New Advent, accessed February 3, 2016, http://www.newadvent.org/fathers/3103a.htm.

lesson, to some people this question seems only to lead to arguments over details. But the history of Christian theology has shown why this is among the most important questions we can ask. The answer to it will shape how we view salvation and how we relate to our Lord and Savior.

Yet within the genre of biblical studies, the way we form our question is different from how we would form it for systematic theology. For systematic theology, we might ask, "How does the Bible as a whole describe Christ?" For biblical studies, we might ask, "What do the details of this particular passage reveal about Christ?" We can start with Hebrews 1–2.

Pre-Reading

Based on your reading of Hebrews 1–2, write an answer to the question, "Who is Jesus Christ?" Remember to be precise and consider details from the biblical text.

Reading

In the passage below, B. B. Warfield highlights Christ's human nature and his divine nature.

[¶1] To the author of Hebrews Our Lord is above all else the Son of God in the most eminent[a] sense of that word; and it is the Divine dignity and majesty belonging to Him from His very nature which forms the fundamental feature of the image of Christ which stands before his mind. And yet it is this author who, perhaps above all others of the New Testament writers, emphasizes the truth of the humanity of Christ, and dwells with most particularity upon the elements of His human nature and experience. . . .

[¶2] The language in which the humiliation of the Son of God is in the first instance described is derived[b] from the context. The establishment of His Divine majesty in chapter 1 had taken the form of an exposition[c] of His infinite exaltation above the angels, the highest of all creatures. His humiliation is described here therefore as being "made a little lower than the angels" (2:9). What is meant is simply that He became man; the phraseology[d] is derived[e] from Ps. 8, from which had just been cited the declaration that God has made man (despite his insignificance) "but a little lower than the angels," thus crowning him with glory and honor. The adoption[f] of the language of the psalm to describe Our Lord's humiliation has the secondary effect, accordingly, of greatly enlarging the reader's sense of the immensity[g] of the humiliation of the Son of God in becoming man: He descended an infinite distance to reach man's highest conceivable exaltation. . . .

Remember?
The phrase "the highest of all creatures" is an appositive for the noun "angels."

[¶3] The proximate[h] end of Our Lord's assumption of humanity is declared to be that He might die; He was "made a little lower than the angels . . . because of the suffering of death" (2:9); He took part in blood and flesh in order "that through death . . ." (2:14). The Son of God as such could not die; to Him belongs by nature an "indissoluble[i] life" (7:16). If he was to die, therefore, He must take to Himself another nature to which the experience of death were not impossible (2:17). Of course it is not meant that death was desired by Him for its own sake. The purpose of our passage is to save its Jewish readers from the offence[j] of the death of Christ. What they are bidden[k] to observe is, therefore, Jesus, who was made a little lower than the angels because of the suffering of death, "crowned with glory and honor, that by the grace of God the bitterness of death which he tasted might redound[l] to the benefit of every man" (2:9), and the argument is immediately pressed home that it was eminently suitable for God Almighty, in bringing many sons into glory, to make the Captain of their salvation perfect (as a Savior) by means of suffering. The meaning is that it was only through suffering that these men, being sinners, could be brought into glory. And therefore in the plainer statement of verse 14 we read that Our Lord took part in flesh and blood in order "that through death he might bring to nought[m] him that has the power of death, that is, the devil; and might deliver all them who through fear of death were all their lifetime subject to bondage." . . . .

[¶4] The completeness of Our Lord's assumption[n] of humanity and of His identification of Himself with it receives strong emphasis in this passage. He took part in the flesh and blood which is the common heritage of men, after the same fashion that other men participate in it (2:14); and, having thus become a man among men, He shared with other men the ordinary circumstances and fortunes of life, "in all things" (2:17). . . .

[¶5] It is not implied, however, that during this human life—"the days of his flesh" (v. 7)—He had ceased to be God, or to have at His disposal[o] the attributes which belonged to Him as God. That is already excluded by the representations of chapter 1. The glory of this dispensation consists precisely in the bringing of its revelations directly by the Divine Son rather than by mere prophets (1:1), and it was as the effulgence[p] of God's glory and the express image of His substance, upholding the universe by the word of His power, that this Son made purification of sins (1:3). Indeed, we are expressly[q] told that even in the days of the flesh, He continued still a Son (v. 8), and that it was precisely in this that the wonder lay: that though He was and remained (imperfect participle) a Son, He yet learned the obedience He had set Himself to (cf. Phil. 2:8) by the things which He suffered. Despite the completeness of His identification with men, He remained, therefore, even in the days of His flesh different from them and above them.[4]

a. Eminent (adj.): prominent or outstanding
b. Derive (v.): to gather or arrive at by reason or observation
c. Exposition (n.): a presentation or interpretation
d. Phraseology (n.): choice of words
e. Derive (v.): to take from a source
f. Adoption (n.): the act of taking up or accepting
g. Immensity (n.): greatness of scope
h. Proximate (adj.): next immediately preceding or following (as in a chain of causes or effects)
i. Indissoluble (adj.): incapable of being decomposed or disintegrated
j. Offence (n.): the state of being displeased, insulted, or morally outraged
k. Bid (v.): to issue an order to either mildly and without especial emphasis or authoritatively
l. Redound (v.): to have an effect for good or ill
m. Nought (n.): nothing
n. Assumption (n.): the act of taking upon oneself
o. Disposal (n.): the power to use something at one's convenience
p. Effulgence (n.): glorious splendor
q. Expressly (adv.): directly

4. B. B. Warfield, *The Person and Work of Christ*, ed. Samuel G. Craig (Philadelphia: Presbyterian and Reformed, 1950), 47–50.

Difficult Sentence Structures

B. B. Warfield's writing is not the easiest for many students to read. Part of this might be due to some of the complex sentence structures he uses. Some of these are illustrated and explained below.

Tip

When reading complex sentences, you might begin by finding the simple subject and predicate (finite verb) of the main clause, or, if the sentence is very complex, of each clause. Then try to figure out how the other parts of the sentence are modifying or adding meaning to the subject and predicate.

"**The language** in which the humiliation of the Son of God is in the first instance described is derived from the context."

"Despite the completeness of His identification with men, **He** remained, therefore, even in the days of His flesh different from them and above them."

- "It is the Divine dignity and majesty belonging to Him from His very nature which forms the fundamental feature of the image of Christ which stands before his mind."

    Explanation: The first clause can be re-written as follows: "The Divine dignity and majesty belonging to Him from His very nature forms the fundamental feature . . . ." In the original, Warfield is using both a dummy "it" and two relative clauses, the second one embedded in the first. The first "which" clause refers to the delayed subject ("The Divine dignity . . ."). The second "which" refers to "the image of Christ."

- "What they are bidden to observe is, therefore, Jesus, who was made a little lower than the angels because of the suffering of death, 'crowned with glory and honor, that by the grace of God the bitterness of death which he tasted might redound to the benefit of every man' (2:9), and the argument is immediately pressed home that it was eminently suitable for God Almighty, in bringing many sons into glory, to make the Captain of their salvation perfect (as a Savior) by means of suffering."

    Explanation: This is tough! But the first main clause is fairly simple: "What they are bidden to observe is . . . Jesus . . . ." In other words, "they" are asked to look at Jesus. What follows the noun "Jesus" are descriptors and modifiers ("who was made . . ."; "crowned with . . ."; "that by the grace . . ."). The second main clause includes a long *that* clause. This clause says "it was eminently suitable for God Almighty . . . to make the Captain of their salvation perfect (as a Savior) by means of suffering." What follows "God Almighty" is a participial phrase.

Post-Reading

Restate one of Warfield's main ideas in your own words.

Main Ideas and Details

(1) In your own words, express the main idea of paragraph 1 in a single sentence.

(2) Mark the following statements as either true (T) or false (F). Correct the false statements based on your understanding of the text.

_____ 1. It was only through suffering that these men, being sinners, could be brought into glory.

_____2. The proximate end of Our Lord's assumption of humanity is declared to be that He might raise from the dead.

_____3. He descended a finite distance to reach man's highest conceivable exaltation.

_____4. He remained . . . even in the days of His flesh different from them and above them.

_____5. The Son of God as such could die because to Him belongs by nature an "indissoluble life" (7:16).

_____6. It is this author who, perhaps above all others of the New Testament writers, emphasizes the truth of the divinity of Christ.

_____7. He shared with other men the ordinary circumstances and fortunes of life, "in all things" (2:17).

_____8. Death was desired by Him for its own sake.

(3) Which of the following can be inferred from paragraph 1?
a. The divinity of Christ is most important to believers.
b. The humanity of Christ is most important to believers.
c. The author of Hebrews treats Christ's divinity and humanity as equally important.
d. The author of Hebrews emphasizes Christ's divinity more than any other biblical writer.

(4) The highlighted pronoun "which" in paragraph 2 refers to _____.
a. Phraseology.
b. The declaration.
c. That he became man.
d. Psalm 8

(5) Based on its immediate context in paragraph 3, the phrase "pressed home" most likely means _____.
a. Forced.
b. Required.
c. Demanded.
d. Emphasized.

(6) Which of the following can we infer based on the highlighted clause in paragraph 3?
a. Our goal is to do what is suitable before God.
b. The Son of God was not perfect until he suffered.
c. God's eminence required that he bring his sons to glory.
d. Suffering is a key feature of Christ's work and our salvation.

(7) Summarize the main idea of paragraph 5 in your own words. (Read the paragraph once more for reference, but do not refer to it as you write your summary.)

Understanding the Reading

Label the following statements as either true of Christ in relation to his human nature **H** or true of Christ in relation to his divine nature **D**. Mark **DH** if the statement applies to both natures.

_____1. He descended an infinite distance to reach man's highest conceivable exaltation.

_____2. He shared with other men the ordinary circumstances and fortunes of life, "in all things" (2:17).

_____3. Our Lord is above all else the Son of God in the most eminent sense of that word.

_____4. The glory of this dispensation consists precisely in the bringing of its revelations directly by the Divine Son rather than by mere prophets.

_____5. He yet learned the obedience He had set Himself to (cf. Phil. 2:8) by the things which He suffered.

_____6. Even in the days of the flesh, He continued still a Son (v. 8).

_____7. Despite the completeness of His identification with men, He remained, therefore, even in the days of His flesh different from them and above them.

Collocations from the Passage

Match the words on the left to their collocates on the right.

subject	different
remain	circumstances
infinite	emphasis
ordinary	distance
strong	to something

Provide collocations from the reading passage for the words in the center bubbles below. These collocations may precede or follow these words. There are enough collocations so that all of the bubbles should be filled.

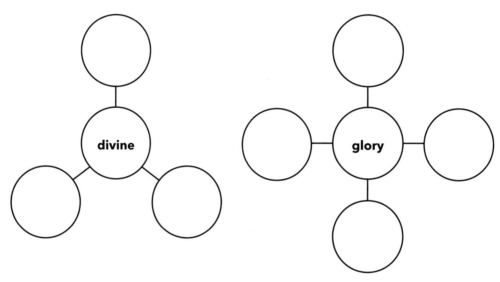

Fig. 13.1. Collocation Diagram 3

Grammar Focus: Principled Use of Verb Tense

In Lesson 12, we began a discussion of the author's perspective and the verb phrase. In that lesson, we explored what modal verbs reveal about the author's perspective and how they change the form of the main verbs that accompany them. In this lesson, we revisit the topic we covered in Lesson 7. In that lesson, we learned that verb tense reveals the author's perspective on the action. As authors, we must be consistent or principled with our use of verb tense. In other words, we must be consistent in how we portray the action occurring in each context.[5] This is

what we mean by "principled use of verb tense." Note the different verb tenses in the following paragraph.

It **is** not implied, however, that during this human life—"the days of his flesh" (v. 7)—He **had ceased** to be God, or to have at His disposal the attributes which **belonged** to Him as God. That **is** already excluded by the representations of chapter 1. The glory of this dispensation **consists** precisely in the bringing of its revelations directly by the Divine Son rather than by mere prophets (1:1), and it **was** as the effulgence of God's

---

5. Remember that "tense in verbs expresses the time that an action occurs in relation to the moment of speaking." Ron Cown, *The Teacher's Grammar of English: A Course Book and Reference Guide* (New York: Cambridge University Press, 2008), 350. Here, we are saying that all of the actions occurring in the same time (context) need to be referenced with the same tense.

glory and the express image of His substance, upholding the universe by the word of His power, that this Son **made** purification of sins (1:3). Indeed, we **are** expressly **told** that even in the days of the flesh, He **continued** still a Son (v. 8), and that it **was** precisely in this that the wonder **lay**: that though He **was** and **remained** (imperfect participle) a Son, He yet **learned** the obedience He **had set** Himself to (cf. Phil. 2:8) by the things which He **suffered**.

Despite the completeness of His identification with men, He **remained**, therefore, even in the days of His flesh different from them and above them.

You should have found three tenses in this paragraph: the simple present, the simple past, and the past perfect. The table below shows how each of these tenses is used in a principled way to refer to action in a particular context.

Tense	Principled Use
Simple Present	Statements of truth; observations; analysis "It <u>is</u> not implied" "The glory of this dispensation <u>consists</u>" "we <u>are expressly told</u>"
Simple Past	References to past action (Jesus' historical life) "the attributes which <u>belonged</u> to Him" [from eternity, but in the incarnation] "it <u>was</u> as the effulgence of God's glory" [again, from eternity, but also in the incarnation] "this Son <u>made</u> purification" "He <u>continued</u> still a Son"
Past Perfect	References to past action that occurred *before* other past action "He <u>had ceased</u> to be God" [The "ceasing" would have occurred *before* "the days of his flesh."] "the obedience He <u>had set</u> Himself to" [He "set Himself" to this obedience before he was tempted and suffered.]

Activity 1

Below is another passage taken from the reading. Identify two different verb tenses in the paragraph and try to state the principle that the author seems to be following in his use of them. Fill in the table with your answers.

The proximate end of Our Lord's assumption of humanity is declared to be that He might die; He was "made a little lower than the angels . . . because of the suffering of death" (2:9); He took part in blood and flesh in order "that through death . . ." (2:14). The Son of God as such could not die; to Him belongs by nature an "indissoluble life" (7:16). If he was to die, therefore, He must take to Himself another nature to which the experience of death were not impossible (2:17). Of course it is not meant that death was desired by Him for its own sake. The purpose of our passage is to save its Jewish readers from the offence of the death of Christ. What they are bidden to observe is, therefore, Jesus, who was made a little lower than the angels because of the suffering of death, "crowned with glory and honor, that by the grace of God the bitterness of death which he tasted might redound to the benefit of every man"

(2:9), and the argument is immediately pressed home that it was eminently suitable for God Almighty, in bringing many sons into glory, to make the Captain of their salvation perfect (as a Savior) by means of suffering. The meaning is that it was only through suffering that these men, being sinners, could be brought into glory. And therefore in the plainer statement of verse 14 we read that Our Lord took part in flesh and blood in order "that through death he might bring to nought him that has the power of death, that is, the devil; and might deliver all them who through fear of death were all their lifetime subject to bondage."

Tense	Principled Use

Activity 2

Imagine that a friend of yours has recently become a Christian. He is curious about whether or not Jesus stopped being divine when he became incarnate. Based on what you know from the reading passage, respond to your friend in a brief paragraph (3–5 sentences). Then go through your sentences to see what tenses you used. Try to identify one principle you may have followed in selecting your verb tenses.

Activity 3

After finishing Activity 2, read your response to a partner. Have your partner identify the tenses you have used and check to see that you have illustrated a principled use of verb tense. Then switch roles and listen to your partner read his or her paragraph.

Activity 4 Collocation

As you have done with the previous lessons, fill in the missing collocations in the table below. While these collocations have been taken directly from Lessons 11–13, more than one answer may be correct. Try to fill in the chart without looking at the previous lessons. See what collocations you can remember. Compare your answers with those of a partner to learn other collocations that you might have missed.

offer		atone	
	concern	subject	
	related	remain	
precious		infinite	
make			emphasis
threaten			circumstances
	sacrifice		

The Nature of Christ (BS Task 3)

In this task, you will write an email to your senior pastor presenting **<u>one main idea</u>** that you notice in Hebrews 1–2. This idea will be used to help you get ready for a future Bible study. To prepare for this task, review your notes from the Warfield excerpt and read over Hebrews 1–2 once more. Then choose <u>one point</u> you notice in the text to present to your pastor, providing reasons and evidence from the text to support it. (Remember to be intentional about the organization of the support for your main idea.)

Task

Your senior pastor has asked you to teach a Bible study to young adults on the book of Hebrews. You will start with Hebrews 1–2, trying to learn from these chapters more about who Jesus is. Your pastor asks you to email him explaining <u>**one**</u> main idea you notice in these chapters. Email your senior pastor, presenting him with your main idea and a brief explanation (i.e., textual support). Your email should consist of one paragraph. After you have drafted your email, check to see that it is unified, coherent, and developed.

14

The One Who Rose from the Dead

"For Paul the resurrection of Jesus is the central event of redemptive history."
—Richard B. Gaffin Jr., *Resurrection and Redemption: A Study in Paul's Soteriology*

Lesson Goals

Theology–To understand the meaning of the word "firstfruits"
Reading–To review and practice making inferences
Vocabulary–To learn and use additional collocations from the reading passage
Grammar–To recognize patterns of preposition use

Introduction

We now know that it is critical for Christ to have both a human and a divine nature. These natures comprise the one *person* of Christ. While the "pre-existent" Son has dwelt in the Godhead from all eternity, the incarnate Son took on flesh and dwelt among us. So we can distinguish between these two natures, but we cannot separate them. As Donald Macleod writes, "The pre-existent Son of Hebrews 1:1 is the very same person who cried to God with strong crying and tears (Heb. 5:7); and in his pre-existent state he is as personal as the God with whom he is compared and the prophets with whom he is contrasted."[1]

While it is critical for us to know about these two natures and their union in the person of Christ, there is still more to know if we are to provide a full answer to the question, "Who is Jesus?" Jesus is also the one who rose from the dead. This cannot be considered an afterthought to our understanding of who Jesus is. We often talk about how the divine Son of God took on flesh and suffered and died on our behalf. *But he rose again on our behalf as well.* In fact, this point is so important to our understanding of Jesus that Paul says, "if Christ has not been raised, then our preaching is in vain and your faith is in vain" (1 Cor. 15:14). To be "vain" is to be "empty, idle, or worthless." Our faith, in other words, is worthless if we do not believe in the resurrection of Christ. Perhaps this is because such a belief is bound up with Jesus' divine identity as the eternal Son. Jesus "was raised because of what he was. He did not become Son by being raised; he was raised because he was Son."[2]

We can turn to 1 Cor. 15 to see an in-depth treatment of the importance of the resurrection for the Apostle Paul.

---

1. Donald Macleod, *The Person of Christ*, Contours of Christian Theology (Downers Grove, IL: InterVarsity, 1998), 54.
2. Ibid., 91.

Warm-up

Read 1 Cor. 15 aloud. Write down any notes as needed.

Background for the Reading

As the author of Hebrews makes clear, Jesus is both fully God and fully man—for our salvation. Only man is responsible for breaking God's law and rebelling against his just and loving rule. And yet the penalty is so great that it could only be paid by God himself. So Jesus did what only we were required to do, and gave what only God could offer. But more needs to be said.

As amazing a gift as Jesus' life and death were, they would not have been sufficient for salvation. Salvation is sealed with Christ's resurrection. That Christ was raised from the dead is what shatters the power of evil, sin, and death. As Paul says, "If Christ has not been raised, your faith is futile and you are still in your sins. Then those also who have fallen asleep in Christ have perished. If in Christ we have hope in this life only, we are of all people most to be pitied" (1 Cor. 15:17–19). Jesus' resurrection, then, is a vital part of who he is. Jesus is the *risen* Lord, the one whom death could not hold, the warrior-king who destroyed the vilest enemy of all time. We are united to Christ, and in that union we enjoy his victory. We are raised from the dead because we are raised *with him*.

Pre-Reading

What do you think the word "firstfruits" means based on your reading of 1 Cor. 15? Write down your definition below.

Reading

Throughout his work, Richard Gaffin emphasizes our union with Christ (this is the referent of "the notion of unity" in the first line of the reading). In the passage below, Gaffin expounds the importance of Christ's resurrection—in which we share because we are united to him—by examining the meaning of the word "firstfruits."

[¶1] The notion of unity is expressed most clearly and graphically[a] in 1 Cor. 15:20, where Christ by virtue of[b] his resurrection is described as "the firstfruits of those who are asleep" (cf. v. 23). The word "firstfruits" in this expression is our particular concern. As Johannes Weis has put it: "This little word contains a thesis." There can be little question that the Septuagint provides the background for its use here. There, with few exceptions, "firstfruits" has a specifically cultic significance. It refers to the "firstfruits" offerings of grain, wine, cattle, and the like, appointed by Moses. The point to these sacrifices is that they are not offered up for their own sake, as it were, but as representative of the total harvest, the entire flock, and so forth. They are a token[c] expression of recognition and thanksgiving that the whole has been given by God. Thus "firstfruits" does not simply have a temporal force. It does bring into view the initial portion of the harvest, but only as it is part of the whole; it focuses on the first of the newborn lambs only as they belong to the entire flock. "Firstfruits" expresses the notion of organic[d] connection and unity, the inseparability of the initial quantity from the whole. It is particularly this aspect which gives these sacrifices their significance.

[¶2] These ideas of representation and organic unity—apart from the specifically cultic

Remember? Does the author use "can" to express possibility or permission?

connotations[e] of the Septuagint usage—find expression in the use of "firstfruits" in 1 Cor. 15:20. The word is not simply an indication of temporal[f] priority. Rather it brings into view Christ's resurrection as the "firstfruits" of the resurrection-harvest, the initial portion of the whole. His resurrection is the representative[g] beginning of the resurrection of believers. In other words, the term seems deliberately chosen to make evident the organic connection between the two resurrections. In the context, Paul's "thesis" over against his opponents is that the resurrection of Jesus has the bodily resurrection of "those who sleep" as its necessary consequence. His resurrection is not simply a guarantee; it is a pledge[h] in the sense that it is the actual beginning of the general event. In fact, on the basis of this verse it can be said that Paul views the two resurrections not so much as two events but as two episodes of the same event. At the same time, however, he clearly maintains a temporal distinction between them. "Then" (v. 23) makes this apparent.[i]

[¶3] The occurrences of "firstfruits" elsewhere in Paul all express the notion of organic connection. In the parallel connection of Romans 11:16, the first clause reasons from the "firstfruits" (of dough) to the whole lump, the second clause from the root to the branches. Since the relation between the first portion of dough and the root is not exactly analogous (the latter unlike the former is productive), yet each is made the basis for postulation,[j] then the specific point of the parallel and so the consideration governing the argument must be the fact of organic union. Similarly, in Romans 16:5 where Epaenetus is called "the firstfruits of Asia in Christ," the thought is not simply that he is the first convert in Ephesus. Rather he stands out in Paul's mind as the beginning of the manifold yield[k] produced by the preaching of the gospel (cf. 1 Cor. 16:15). The broader significance of "the firstfruits of the Spirit" in Romans 8:23 will occupy us below. For the present, however, we can note that, regardless[l] whether the genitive is partitive[m] or appositional,[n] the thought is plainly that the Spirit presently possessed by believers is a token, an initial enjoyment of the adoption (cf. v. 15) which hereafter will be fully and openly received in the resurrection of the body.

[¶4] Returning now to 1 Cor. 15:20, the verses immediately following strengthen our interpretation of "firstfruits." The syntactical ties between them are especially instructive. Verse 21 gives the reason for what has been said in verse 20. This is the force of "for since." Verse 22, in turn, grounds the statement of verse 21. This is the force of "for." In other words, the resurrection of the dead through man (v. 21b) and the making alive of all in Christ (v. 22b) explain the significance of Christ as "firstfruits" (v. 20). Further, verse 22 clearly expresses the idea of solidarity[o] by contrasting Christ with Adam (cf. 45, 47–49); this is a virtual one-sentence summary of the teaching in Romans 5:12ff. where the notions of solidaric relationship play such a dominant[p] role. Hence verse 22b in particular confirms that the ideas of solidarity and organic connection are present in verse 20. Christ is "the firstfruits of those who sleep" because he is raised as the second Adam. At the same time, however, verse 22b does go beyond the idea expressed by "firstfruits" by bringing into view Christ's determinative[q] place in this relationship: it is only as they are "in Christ," united with the second Adam, that "all shall be raised."[3]

a. Graphically (adv.): marked by clear and lively description or striking imaginative power
b. By virtue of (prep. phrase): by reason of; as a result of
c. Token (adj.): serving as a sign or sample of the real thing
d. Organic (adj.): fundamental, inherent, or vital
e. Connotation (n.): something implied or suggested
f. Temporal (adj.): of or relating to time
g. Representative (adj.): serving as a characteristic example, illustrative of a class
h. Pledge (n.): an agreement by which one binds himself to do something
i. Apparent (adj.): easily perceived
j. Postulation (n.): the act of claiming something as true or necessary

k. Yield (n.): something produced or gained
l. Regardless (adv.): without regard or care for
m. Partitive (adj.): a sub-type of the genitive case in Greek, denoting "the whole of which the head noun is a part"[22]
n. Appositional (adj.): a sub-type of the genitive case in Greek, used to state "a specific example that is a part of the larger category named by the head noun"[23]
o. Solidarity (n.): a union of interests and responsibilities [Here, this word refers to our communal identity in Adam or in Christ.]
p. Dominant (adj.): prevailing in number, frequency, or distribution
q. Determinative (adj.): conclusive

Post-Reading

Add to your initial definition of "firstfruits" based on what you have learned here.

Reading Skills: Making Inferences

We noted back in Lesson 3 that an **inference** is a logical conclusion that you can draw from a text. Inferences are not stated directly. Instead, you as the reader must think about what you are reading, what you know about the subject, and what you know about the world. Then you draw a conclusion. Inferences are based on more evidence than a guess, but they require that you "read between the lines" and see what the author is not stating directly.

Example: Re-read the first paragraph. What can we infer about the word "firstfruits"?

a. It has been a significant word for a long time.
b. It has only been studied rather recently by theologians.
c. It was of little importance to the ancient Jews.

Answer "a" is the only correct possibility here. We know "a" is the answer because the paragraph is talking about the importance of the word in the Septuagint. This shows that "a" is the best answer and "b" is incorrect. We know "c" is incorrect since the paragraph describes the firstfruits offerings under Mosaic law.

Practice

1. Skim paragraph 2. Which of the following is a valid inference based on paragraph 2?

How to Make a Good Inference

1. Read carefully and think about what is stated.
2. What is the author suggesting or assuming? An answer to this question is an inference.
3. Test your inference. Does it make sense in the context of this passage? Does it make sense according to your background knowledge or understanding of the world?

3. Richard B. Gaffin Jr., *Resurrection and Redemption: A Study in Paul's Soteriology* (Grand Rapids, MI: Baker, 1978), 34–36.

a. Paul did not choose his words carefully.

b. Paul's opponents did not believe a physical resurrection was necessary.

c. Paul believed the two resurrection events should be considered separately.

2. Skim paragraph 3. Which of the following is a valid inference based on paragraph 3?

a. Epaenetus was primarily significant for being the first Christian in Asia.

b. Epaenetus was important for representing the first of many Christians in Asia.

c. Epaenetus lived in Asia but traveled throughout the Mediterranean world at the time.

Main Ideas and Details

(1) Which of the following best summarizes the main idea of the reading?

a. Christ's resurrection is important for us as his followers.

b. All believers will one day enjoy the blessing of adoption by their heavenly Father.

c. "Firstfruits" in 1 Cor. 15 refers to the beginning of a "resurrection harvest" for those united to Christ.

d. The word "firstfruits" is frequently used in the Septuagint with reference to cultic practices.

(2) In your own words, explain what you think the author means by the phrases "organic unity" and "organic connection" as they relate to Christ's resurrection. (Refer to paragraphs 1 and 2.)

(3) In paragraph 2, the word "thesis" means _____.

a. Complaint.

b. Suspicion.

c. Main idea.

d. Speculation.

(4) In paragraph 2, the author writes, "In fact, on the basis of this verse it can be said that Paul views the two resurrections not so much as two events but as two episodes of the same event." Why does he say this?

a. In order to claim that a resurrection can best be understood as an "event."

b. In order to remind the reader that there are two resurrections being discussed.

c. In order to suggest that the resurrection is a historical fact, not an inspiring metaphor.

d. In order to emphasize the close relationship between Christ's resurrection and our own.

(5) Based on what you understand from paragraph 3, work with a partner to fill out the compare-contrast chart below regarding the analogies introduced in 1 Cor. 15:20 and Rom. 11:16. How are *firstfruits*, *a lump of dough*, and *roots of a tree* similar? (Put your comments in the "Compare" column.) How are they different? (Put your comments in the "Contrast" column.)

(6) What does the author say these analogies have in common?

Compare	Contrast

(7) Why does the author use the expression "initial enjoyment" at the end of paragraph 3?

(8) Underline the sentences in paragraph 4 that summarize the meaning of the "syntactical ties" in 1 Cor. 15:20–22.

(9) Which of the following can we infer based on this reading?

a. Agricultural metaphors are the most helpful in theological contexts.

b. Understanding Christ's resurrection as the "firstfruits" brings us hope.

c. Paul's main idea in 1 Cor. 15:20ff is that Jesus had a bodily resurrection.

d. The "first Adam" can also be described as "firstfruits" of the resurrection.

Applying the Reading

Imagine that you are teaching a Sunday school class and one of the students asks you, "How can I share the hope that I have in the future resurrection?"

With a partner, discuss how you might answer that question. Think about what you learned from this lesson about Christ as the "firstfruits," and how you could communicate this to a lay person. Then, take turns with your partner giving your response.

After both partners have spoken, find a new partner. In each new pair, take turns sharing your response. After you speak, your new partner should provide feedback on the following:

- One good aspect of your response.
- One thing, if any, that was unclear in your response.

Collocations from the Passage

For each of the questions below, select the sentence that correctly uses a collocation from the reading.

1. _____
    a. He spoke the idea precisely.
    b. Gaffin expressed the idea eloquently.
    c. The author produced the idea clearly.
    d. Gaffin expressed the impression clearly.

2. _____
    a. His particular nervousness is that we read the text carefully.
    b. The author's delicate concern is that we not define the term out of context.
    c. His primary desperation is that we do not overlook this word's importance.
    d. His particular concern was that we not misunderstand the meaning of "firstfruits."

3. _____
    a. The sacrifice represented the entire flock.
    b. The exhaustive flock covered the countryside.
    c. The sacrifice was taken from the maximal flock.
    d. The priests selected a bull from the undivided flock.

4. _____
    a. Gaffin notes that there is an organic connection between Christ's resurrection and ours.
    b. The author suggests that there is an organic community between Christ's resurrection and ours.
    c. Paul seems to suggest that there is a resembling connection between Christ's resurrection and ours.
    d. Scholars have written much about the organic intercessor between Christ's resurrection and our own.

5. _____
    a. The specific point that Gaffin is making is quite valuable.
    b. The jagged point that Gaffin is making is exegetically significant.
    c. Gaffin develops a cutting point about the theological meaning of "firstfruits."
    d. The pernicious point that the author is making is that we should put faith in Christ's resurrection.

6. _____
    a. The resurrection of Christ has long significance.
    b. In Paul's message, we find a lesson of tightened significance.
    c. The wider majesty of what Paul is saying can easily be missed.
    d. What Paul says about "firstfruits" has a broader significance than we realize.

Grammar Focus: Prepositions Following Verbs

In this lesson, we will conclude our discussion of the author's perspective and the verb phrase by looking at something that can follow the verb itself: prepositions.[4] For non-native English speakers, prepositions are very tricky to learn, but one of the ways you can learn them more efficiently is by memorizing which verbs take which prepositions. Note some of these verb + preposition pairings in the following excerpt.

---

4. Michael Swan, *Practical English Usage*, 4th ed. (Oxford: Oxford University Press, 2016), entry 213.

The notion of unity is expressed most clearly and graphically in 1 Cor. 15:20, where Christ by virtue of his resurrection is <u>described</u> **as** "the firstfruits of those who are asleep" (cf. v. 23). . . . There can be little question that the Septuagint provides the background for its use here. There, with few exceptions, "firstfruits" has a specifically cultic significance. It <u>refers</u> **to** the "firstfruits" offerings of grain, wine, cattle, and the like, <u>appointed</u> **by** Moses. The point to these sacrifices is that they are not offered up for their own sake, as it were, but as representative of the total harvest, the entire flock, and so forth. They are a token expression of recognition and thanksgiving that the whole has been <u>given</u> **by** God. Thus "firstfruits" does not simply have a temporal force. It does <u>bring</u> **into** view the initial portion of the harvest, but only as it is part of the whole; it <u>focuses</u> **on** the first of the newborn lambs only as they <u>belong</u> **to** the entire flock.

Activity 1

Without looking at the reading from this lesson, fill in the prepositions that you think would fit in the blanks for the paragraph below. (More than one answer may be grammatically correct.) When you have finished, check your answers against the prepositions that occurred in the reading.

Rather he stands out in Paul's mind as the beginning of the manifold yield produced _____ the preaching of the gospel (cf. 1 Cor. 16:15). The broader significance of "the firstfruits of the Spirit" in Romans 8:23 will occupy us below. For the present, however, we can note that, regardless whether the genitive is partitive or appositional, the thought is plainly that the Spirit presently possessed _____ believers is a token, an initial enjoyment of the adoption (cf. v. 15) which hereafter will be fully and openly received _____ the resurrection of the body.

Activity 2

Use the verb + preposition combinations to complete the paragraph below. Each answer is used only once.

governed by	reminded of	atoned for	overcome by	raised from	offered to
belong to	fight against	sealed by	die for	sanctified by	ascended to

While we often praise God for sending Jesus to _____ our sins, we might not as quickly praise God for raising him from the dead. But this is critical! Our world is _____ death and decay. We _____ a realm that is utterly fallen, and we constantly need to be _____ the truth that death has lost its sting (1 Cor. 15:55). Even though we daily _____ the destructive forces of evil and the discouragement of our own sin, we know that Christ has overcome the world (John 16:33) and that our sins—past, present, and future—have been _____ by the blood of Christ (Col. 2:13). But all of this—the loss of death's sting, the restoration of a decayed physical and moral world, the victory we have in Christ over sin—has been _____ the resurrection of Christ. When the tomb opened and our Lord walked in the light of day, everything wicked and ruinous was definitively _____ the God of grace and love. If Christ were not _____ the dead, then, as Paul says, "we are of all people most to be pitied" (1 Cor. 15:19). But he *has* been raised. As new creatures in Christ who are being redeemed and _____ the Spirit every day, we are of all people most to be envied. Our praise should thus be _____ the risen Lamb of God, not just to the crucified Son. We are united with the one who was born, suffered, died, rose, and _____ the right hand of the Father.

Activity 3

A friend of yours is trying to tell one of his co-workers about Christ and wants to make sure he is conveying the full truth about who Jesus is. He asks you how you would describe who Jesus is to someone else. Write your description below, accounting for the elements of Christ's person and work referenced in the final sentence of the previous activity. When you have finished writing your description, underline any verb + preposition combinations.

15

The One Who Intercedes

"Because we offend God every day, we need an advocate to intercede for us every day."
—Francis Turretin, *Institutes of Elenctic Theology*

Lesson Goals

Theology—To understand Christ's work of intercession
Reading—To continue identifying main ideas and details and to draw inferences
Vocabulary—To learn and use additional collocations from the reading passage
Grammar—To practice forming complete subjects

Introduction

We have now learned that Christ is the one who rose from the dead, the "firstfruits" of the resurrection harvest. But his work did not stop with the resurrection, nor did it end with his ascension. *Even now* the Son sits at the right hand of the Father interceding for his people.[1] But what does this intercession entail?

Essentially, Christ's intercessory work is tied to his priestly office.[2] As our great high priest (Heb. 4:14), Christ "has entered, not into holy places made with hands, which are copies of the true things, but into heaven itself, now to appear in the presence of God on our behalf" (Heb. 9:24). This appearing "in the presence of God on our behalf" is what we call *intercession*. More specifically, however, intercession refers to something that Christ does for us, which is

discussed by Paul (Rom. 8:34) and by the author of Hebrews.

Both Paul and the author of Hebrews are saying that Jesus continually lives in the presence of God to make specific requests and to bring specific petitions before God on our behalf. This is a role that Jesus, as God-man, is uniquely qualified to fulfill. . . . In Christ, we have a true man, a perfect man, praying and thereby continually glorifying God through prayer. . . .

Yet in his human nature alone Jesus could not of course be such a great high priest for all his people all over the world. He could not hear the prayers of persons far away, nor could he hear prayers that were only spoken in a person's

---

1. The Spirit also has a sort of intercessory work in that he "helps us in our weakness. For we do not know what to pray for as we ought, but the Spirit himself intercedes for us with groanings too deep for words. And he who searches hearts knows what is the mind of the Spirit, because the Spirit intercedes for the saints according to the will of God" (Rom 8:26–27).

2. For a Reformed exposition of Christ as prophet, priest, and king, see Louis Berkhof, *Systematic Theology*, new ed. (Grand Rapids, MI: Eerdmans, 1996), 356–412.

mind. . . . Therefore, in order to be the perfect high priest who intercedes for us, he must be God as well as man. He must be one who in his divine nature can both know all things and bring them into the presence of the Father.[3]

This is an amazing truth that should bring us great comfort. Louis Berkhof reminds us,

It is a consoling thought that Christ is praying for us, even when we are negligent in our own prayer life; that He is presenting to the Father those spiritual needs which were not present to our minds and which we often neglect to include in our prayers; and that He prays for our protection against the dangers of which we are not even conscious, and against the enemies which threaten us, though we do not notice it.[4]

Warm-up

Read Rom. 8:31–39 aloud. Then read it a second time, taking notes as needed.

Background for the Reading

It can be easy to overlook Christ's work of intercession. We tend to focus on his death and resurrection and may forget that he is still working by interceding for us. Even now, Christ sits at the right hand of the Father; God looks through him to see us; the Father hears requests and petitions on our behalf through the Son. So, Christ's work on our behalf continues.

Yet Christ not only prays for us; he pleads our case. In other words, he continually proclaims our being made righteous and just *in him*. We can never be lost to sin again. Our souls are eternally safe because of Christ. As Francis Schaeffer wrote, "The security of our salvation rests not upon our good works, but upon Christ's work for us at Calvary and upon the work He is still doing for us, pleading our case before God the Father."[5]

Pre-Reading

Come up with two questions you have about Rom. 8:31–39 and write them below. Then fill out the chart on the following page, making at least one detailed observation about each verse.

 "Who shall separate us from the love of Christ?" (Rom. 8:35). Paul's question here is what we call a *rhetorical question*: it is a question to which there is a clearly implied answer— "no one"! Paul is using the form of a question (grammar), but this form is pronounced differently from how we would ordinarily pronounce a question. Questions usually end with rising intonation (phonology). But here, we might place the rising intonation at the beginning, on the word "who," drawing the hearer's attention to the truth that *no one* can separate us from the love of Christ. Paul's aim with this question is not ultimately to elicit an answer but to offer us encouragement (reference). Here, once again, we see how grammar, phonology, and reference are intertwined.

Romans 8	Observation
31	
32	
33	
34	
35	

3. Wayne Grudem, *Systematic Theology: An Introduction to Biblical Doctrine* (Grand Rapids, MI: Zondervan, 2000), 628.
4. Berkhof, *Systematic Theology*, 403.
5. Francis A. Schaeffer, *The Finished Work of Christ* (Wheaton, IL: Crossway, 1998), 229.

Romans 8	Observation
36	
37	
38	
39	

Reading

In the following passage, Douglas Moo comments on Paul's argument concerning the work of Christ, including our justification and Christ's intercession.

The Work of God for Us in Christ (8:31-34)

[¶1] As he has done so often in Romans, Paul launches a new direction with a question: "What, then, shall we say in response to this?" "This" is actually plural in the Greek (*tauta*, "these things"); it refers to many reasons for our confidence that Paul has rehearsed[a] in chapters 5–8. All those reasons can be neatly summed up in one statement: God is "for us." Who, then, Paul rightly asks, can be "against us?" Of course, we know (and Paul recognizes [see 5:3–4; 8:17–18]) that many people and things still oppose us: people who hate Christians, the trials of life, Satan himself. But Paul's point is that with God on our side, none of this opposition ultimately matters. As Chrysostom has written:

> Yet those that be against us, so far are they from thwarting[b] us at all, that even without their will they become to us the causes of crowns, and procurers[c] of countless blessings, so that God's wisdom turneth their plots unto our salvation and glory. See how really no one is against us!

[¶2] Verse 32 is not explicitly connected to verse 31, but it reinforces Paul's point. God's being "for us" is seen climactically in his giving of his beloved Son. If he has done that, we can be certain he will also give us "all things"—or, to put it in the terms of verse 31, nothing can ultimately oppose us. The gift of God in the death of his Son as a basis for our hope harks back[d] to 5:5–8. But the way Paul puts it here suggests a comparison between Christ and Isaac. As Abraham did not spare his beloved son Isaac, so God does not spare his beloved Son (see Gen. 22). The "all things" we are guaranteed as a result of Christ's death for us includes both our final glory and all that God provides to bring us to that glory (see the "good" of Rom. 8:28).

[¶3] The punctuation of verse 33–34 is difficult to sort out. Older Greek manuscripts of the New Testament contain no punctuation at all, so editors of modern Bibles have to decide how to do it. At least six different possibilities exist here. The NIV reflects probably the best of the options, with each verse featuring[e] a question and answer.

[¶4] "Bring [a] charge" (v. 33) is the first of several judicial[f] terms in this context. Again, Paul's point is not that nothing will ever try to prosecute[g] us in the court of God's justice. Satan, "the accuser," will certainly do so, and he will bring our sins as evidence of our guilt. But the prosecution will be unsuccessful, for God has chosen us to be his and has justified us already—pronounced over us the verdict of "innocent" that can never be reversed. Paul alludes[h] at this point to Isaiah 50:8–9a:

> **Remember?** "Alludes to" is a good example of a VERB + PREPOSITION.

> He who vindicates[i] me is near.
> Who then will bring charges against me?
> Let us face each other!
> Who is my accuser?
> Let him confront me!
> It is the sovereign Lord who helps me.
> Who is he that will condemn me?

[¶5] Verse 34 provides more evidence for the same point. No one can successfully condemn us because Christ has died for us and has been raised to life to be our intercessor before the Father. With such a defense attorney, it is no wonder the prosecution loses its case!

The Love of God for Us in Christ (8:35-39)

[¶6] The question at the beginning of verse 35 shifts the focus of the paragraph. It is parallel to the one in verse 31, but sets the tone for verses 35–39 by introducing Christ's love into the picture. Knowing we are declared innocent of all charges against us is a wonderful assurance. But Christ not only defends us; he loves us and enters into relationship with us, and nothing will ever separate us from that love. To make sure we get the point, Paul specifies some threats at the end of verse 35. As a comparison with 2 Corinthians 11:26–27 and 12:10 reveals, Paul himself has gone through most of these. He has learned by experience that they cannot disrupt[j] his relationship with Christ.

[¶7] The quotation of Psalm 44:22 in verse 36 is a bit of a detour[k] in the logic of Paul's argument. But the detour reveals two of his key concerns: to remind us that suffering is a natural and expected part of the Christian life (cf. 5:3–4; 8:17), and to root the experiences of Christians in the experience of God's old covenant people.

[¶8] With verse 37, Paul returns to the main line of his teaching in verse 35. In all the varied difficulties of life, we are "more than conquerors." This felicitous[l] rendering of the Greek verb *hypernikao* (to more than triumph over) goes all the way back to the sixteenth century Geneva Bible. Paul may have chosen this rare intensive form of the verb simply to emphasize the certainty of our triumph. But he may also be suggesting that we more than triumph over adversity; in God's good hand, it even leads to our "good" (v. 28).

[¶9] Paul concludes his celebration of God's love for us in Christ with his own personal testimony: "*I am persuaded . . . .*" The list following is arranged in four pairs, with "powers" thrown in between the third and fourth pair. We can easily "overinterpret" such a list, insisting on a precision of definitions that misses the point of Paul's rhetoric.[m] In general, however, "death" and "life" refer to the two basic states of human existence. "Angels" and "demons" (*archai*, i.e., "rulers," which Paul uses to denote evil spiritual beings [see Eph. 6:12; Col. 2:15]) summarize the entirety of the spiritual world.

[¶10] A few interpreters take[n] "present things" and "coming things" (lit. trans.) as spiritual beings too, but evidence is lacking for these as such titles. Probably Paul chooses to summarize all of history, along with the people and events it contains, in a temporal perspective. It is not clear why Paul disrupts[o] his neat parallelism with the word "powers" at this point, but the word refers again to spiritual beings (1 Cor. 15:24; Eph. 1:21).

[¶11] "Height" and "depth" are the most difficult of the pairs of terms to identify. Since these words were applied to the space above and below the horizon, and since ancient people often invested[p] celestial phenomena with spiritual significance, Paul may be referring to spiritual beings again. Yet Paul uses similar language in Ephesians 3:18 in a simple spatial sense. Thus, perhaps, he chooses yet another way of trying to help us understand that there is nothing in the world—whether we are dead or alive, whether they are things we now face or things we will face in the future, whether they are above us or below us—that can separate us from the "love of God that is in Christ Jesus our Lord." As the chapter began with "no condemnation" (Rom. 8:1), so it ends with the bookends of "no separation" (8:35, 39).[6]

a. Rehearse (v.): to mention one by one or one after another
b. Thwart (v.): to oppose successfully
c. Procurer (n.): someone who brings about or leads to something
d. Hark back (v. phrase): to turn back to an earlier topic or circumstance
e. Feature (v.): to be marked by or have as a characteristic
f. Judicial (adj.): of, relating to, or concerned with the administration of justice
g. Prosecute (v.): to accuse of some crime or breach of law

h. Allude (v.): to make indirect reference
i. Vindicate (v.): to free from any question of error, dishonor, guilt, or negligence
j. Disrupt (v.): to interrupt to the extent of stopping or destroying
k. Detour (n.): a deviation from a direct course
l. Felicitous (adj.): suited to an occasion or purpose
m. Rhetoric (n.): verbal communication; discourse or speech
n. Take (v.): to consider or understand
o. Disrupt (v.): to prevent normal continuance of
p. Invest (v.): to endow with some quality or characteristic

Post-Reading

Did the commentator address the questions you wrote down in the Pre-Reading section? If so, what did he say? If not, how might you go about finding the answers to your questions?

Main Ideas and Details

(1) In paragraph 1, the author introduces a quotation by John Chrysostom. Why does he do this?
   a. To deepen our understanding of the efforts of those who oppose us.

6. Douglas J. Moo, *Romans*, The NIV Application Commentary (Grand Rapids, MI: Zondervan, 2000), 282–84. Used by permission of Zondervan.

b. To show that the enemy of God longs to commit evil against God's people.

c. To introduce the biblical truth that we receive many blessings through Christ.

d. To show that the early church fathers were familiar with the book of Romans.

(2) Which of the following can we infer based on paragraph 2?

a. Verse 32 was most likely written by another author.

b. Paul was definitely referring to Abraham and Isaac in Rom. 8:32.

c. The gift of God's Son assures us that we will have eternal victory over evil.

d. The guarantee that we will receive "all things" applies only to our final glory.

(3) In paragraph 4, the author states that "the prosecution will be unsuccessful." By this he means which of the following?

a. We will not be condemned before the throne of God.

b. The prosecution will attempt to condemn us many times.

c. The devil will always pronounce his verdict that we are guilty.

d. We will not experience suffering at the hands of our adversaries.

(4) In paragraph 6, the author uses the conjunction "but." Why does he use this here?

a. He is opposing a point previously introduced.

b. He is showing that Christ's work extends beyond assurance.

c. Being declared innocent of all charges does not call for rejoicing.

d. He wants to show that assurance is the end of Christ's work for us.

(5) What is an inference we can make based on the author's discussion of Paul's "detour" in paragraph 7?

(6) Why does the author use the word "may" toward the end of paragraph 8?

(7) At the end of paragraph 10, what is the rhetorical purpose of mentioning that something is "not clear"? In other words, why would the author include this?

Understanding the Reading

Go back to your observation chart. What observations does the commentator make that would supplement or challenge your own? Add these to your chart, preceding each one with a "C" (for "Commentator").

Collocations from the Passage

Match the words on the left to the words they occur with on the right.

reinforce	focus
provide	evidence
explicitly	connected
a basis	a passage
allude to	for hope
shift	a point

Using one of the collocations above, write a one-sentence reflection on Rom. 8:31–39.

Grammar Focus: Complete Subjects

We have learned a lot thus far about complex sentences in TE, so be encouraged! We have explored some of the structures that comprise them (comparative structures, relative clauses), noticed how important it is to choose the correct word form in our own writing, and seen how verb tenses and modal verbs reveal the author's perspective on an action. In Lesson 14, we ended our discussion of the verb phrase by studying some verb + preposition combinations. In this lesson, we move on to a new but related topic: adding information and expressing relations.

Sentences in TE can sometimes be intimidating to read (and to write!) because they contain so much information and often address and relate nuanced ideas. But to express your own theological thoughts in English, knowing how to add information and carefully articulate relationships between ideas is vital. In this lesson and the lessons ahead, we will examine some practical ways to do this, starting with an examination of **complete subjects**—simple subjects (such as a single noun) that have had information added to them.

It would be nice if theologians used only simple, one- or two-word subjects all the time, but in reality they can and often need to use longer, complete subjects in order to express nuanced ideas. Examine the complete subjects in the paragraphs below.

Verse 32 is not explicitly connected to verse 31, but it reinforces Paul's point. **God's being "for us"** is seen climactically in his giving of his beloved Son. If he has done that, we can be certain he will also give us "all things"—or, to put it in the terms of verse 31, nothing can ultimately oppose us. **The gift of God in the death of his Son as a basis for our hope** harks back to 5:5–8. But **the way Paul puts it here** suggests a comparison between Christ and Isaac. As Abraham did not spare his beloved son Isaac, so God does not spare his beloved Son (see Gen. 22). **The "all things" we are guaranteed as a result of Christ's death for us** includes both our final glory and all that God provides to bring us to that glory (see the "good" of Rom. 8:28).

The question at the beginning of verse 35 shifts the focus of the paragraph. It is parallel to the one in verse 31, but sets the tone for verses 35–39 by introducing Christ's love into the picture. **Knowing we are declared innocent of all charges against us** is a wonderful assurance. But Christ not only defends us; he loves us and enters into relationship with us, and nothing will ever separate us from that love.

There are a variety of ways you can form a longer, complete subject. You can use a possessive noun and follow it with an object; you can use a noun clause; and you can use a noun phrase followed by a relative clause, among other possible structures. Below are the structures used by the author in the bolded examples above. Notice the verb that goes with each subject.

Structure	Example	Verb
Possessive Noun + Gerund + Prepositional Phrase	*God's being for us*	*is*
Noun Phrase + Prepositional Phrases (5!)	*The gift of God in the death of his Son as a basis for our hope*	*harks back*
Noun Phrase + Relative Clause	*The way Paul puts it here*	*suggests*
Noun Phrase + Relative Clause	*The "all things" we are guaranteed as a result of Christ's death for us*	*includes*
Noun Phrase + Prepositional Phrases (2)	*The question at the beginning of verse 35*	*shifts*
Gerund + Object (*that* clause)	*Knowing we are declared innocent of all charges against us*	*is*

Activity 1

Fill in the verb phrases for the complete subjects in the following sentences (taken from the reading). Check your answers by referencing the reading passage.

1. God's being "for us" _____ climactically in his giving of his beloved Son. (¶2)

2. But the way Paul puts it here _____ a comparison between Christ and Isaac. (¶2)

3. Older Greek manuscripts of the New Testament _____ no punctuation at all, so editors of modern Bibles have to decide how to do it. (¶3)

4. The quotation of Psalm 44:22 in verse 36 _____ a bit of a detour in the logic of Paul's argument. (¶7)

6. This felicitous rendering of the Greek verb *hypernikao* (to more than triumph over) _____ all the way back to the sixteenth century Geneva Bible. (¶8)

Activity 2

Match the complete subject on the left with the predicate it likely goes with on the right.

God's gift of his own Son and our new life in the Spirit	are frequent.
Understanding the atoning work of Christ in Paul's epistle to the Romans	are central themes for Paul.
The cornerstone of every Christian's faith	is critical.
Paul's allusions to other passages in the Old Testament	are sometimes rhetorical.
The questions that Paul asks throughout his epistles	is Christ alone.

Activity 3

Create a complete subject (one that includes more than two words) for each of the verbs provided below, and then finish writing a sentence for each subject and verb combination.

- Is
- Means
- Requires
- Suggests
- Shows

Summary of Theological Concepts from Unit 5

- It is necessary for Christ to be both divine and human because, as divine, he does what only God can do, and, as human, he does what only man was required to do.
- Jesus' resurrection is the "firstfruits" of our own resurrection.
- Jesus continues his work of interceding for us at the right hand of God, and because he is *for us*, no one can successfully oppose us.

Activity

Paraphrase each of the concepts above in your own words.

(1)

(2)

(3)

UNIT 6

DO WE STILL NEED THE OLD TESTAMENT?
(BIBLICAL STUDIES)

16

The Place of the Old Testament

"The Old Testament may be likened to a chamber richly furnished but dimly lighted;
the introduction of light brings into it nothing which was not in it before; but it brings out into
clearer view much of what is in it but was only dimly or even not at all perceived before."
—B. B. Warfield, *Biblical Doctrines*

Lesson Goals

Theology—To understand the role of grace in the Old Testament
Reading—To continue identifying main ideas and details and to draw inferences
Vocabulary—To learn and use additional collocations from the reading passage
Grammar—To recognize and express logical relationships between ideas

---

Introduction

Earlier we considered Christ as the ultimate fulfillment of God's promise of salvation that goes all the way back to Gen. 3:15. We have now learned about Christ's divine and human natures, his resurrection as the "firstfruits," and his continual intercession on our behalf. With such a focus on the person and work of Christ, we might be tempted to belittle the Old Testament. If, for B. B. Warfield, the Old Testament was compared to "a chamber richly furnished but dimly lighted," and if we now have the New Testament and the glorious light of Christ (John 8:12; Eph. 5:14), we might ask, "What good does it do to return to a dimly lit chamber?"

The short answer is, much good, for the light of Christ shines in that chamber! We look at the Old Testament through the gracious, atoning work of Christ. We do this because all that God has accomplished in the past points to what he has done and will do in and through his Son. So our hope in the future is grounded in the surety of God's work in the past, and much of that past is captured in the Old Testament. In this sense, grace is not a New Testament revelation; it is a New Testament consummation: the Old Testament foreshadows the grace and redemption that we see illuminated in the New Testament. Surely, that is a very good reason to revisit the dimly lit chamber of the Old Testament.

And yet, perhaps one of the most important reasons why we should continue to treasure and study the Old Testament is that Christ himself did so (cf. Matt. 5:17–18; 22:29; 23:35; John 10:35). He boldly proclaimed that "it is 'the mouth of God,' by whose every word people are to live."[1] The Old

---

1. Sinclair B. Ferguson, "How Does the Bible Look at Itself?," in *Inerrancy and Hermeneutic: A Tradition, a Challenge, a Debate*, ed. Harvie M. Conn (Grand Rapids, MI: Baker, 1988), 50.

153

Testament, of course, has come to us by the mouth of God. It is inspired, God-breathed revelation (2 Tim. 3:16). And we can pair this with what we have noted above: Christ himself is what the Old Testament was ultimately all about. In a discussion with two travelers on the road to Emmaus, we read that, from Moses and up through the prophets, "he interpreted to them in all the Scriptures the things concerning himself" (Luke 24:27). Indeed, "all the Old Testament Scriptures, not merely a few passages that have been recognized as messianic, point us to Christ."[2]

Warm-up

Read Luke 24:13–27 aloud. Take notes as needed. Then read it a second time silently. Imagine one of the passages that you think Jesus may have discussed with these men. How do you think this passage points to Christ? Explain your answer in a few sentences.

Background for the Reading

In the New Testament, we learn that Christ is the fullness of God (Col. 2:9). Faith in Christ is all that is necessary for salvation and for our reception of every spiritual blessing (Eph. 1:3). The radiance of New Testament revelation helps us to understand how we can read Scripture in a way that will be spiritually satisfying, but sometimes we overlook the "dimly lighted chamber" of the Old Testament. In fact, "for many Christians, the problem is not how to read the Old Testament but *why* it should be read at all."[3] However, many past theologians, such as B. B. Warfield and Geerhardus Vos, and many present theologians, such as Graeme Goldsworthy and G. K. Beale, affirm the importance and necessity of the Old Testament, while drawing our attention to *how* we should read it in light of the New Testament. In the reading passage for this chapter, we will be challenged to re-examine an Old Testament passage in light of the grace of God revealed in the New Testament.

Pre-Reading

Consider the giving of the law on Mount Sinai (Ex. 19). Was the law meant to lead to the Israelites' salvation?

Reading

In what follows, Graeme Goldsworthy argues that the giving of the Law at Mt. Sinai was an act of grace, not an act that establishes a plan of works meriting righteousness.

[¶1] It is not unfair, I think, to say that many Christians . . . [understand that] God gave Israel the law at Sinai as a program[a] of works whose goal is salvation. The history of Israel shows how complete was the inability of Israel to achieve the required standard. God, therefore, in a kind of desperation,[b] scrapped plan A (salvation through works of the law) and instituted[c] as an emergency plan B (the gospel). . . . The Old Testament thus becomes essentially the record of the failure of plan A. Its relationship to the New Testament is almost wholly negative.

[¶2] In order to gain the right perspective on the Sinai law, we must be more careful to examine the treatment[d] of it in both Old Testament and New Testament. We must look at the positive statements about the law in the New Testament and also understand the reason for the many

Remember?
Can you find the complete subject of each clause in the final sentence of paragraph 2?

---

2. Edmund P. Clowney, "Preaching Christ from All the Scriptures," in *Thy Word Is Still Truth: Essential Writings on the Doctrine of Scripture from the Reformation to Today*, ed. Peter A. Lillback and Richard B. Gaffin Jr. (Philadelphia: Westminster Seminary Press, 2013), 1037.

3. Graeme Goldsworthy, *Gospel and Kingdom*, in *The Goldsworthy Trilogy* (Colorado Springs, CO: Paternoster, 2000), 11.

negative statements. If the depreciation[e] of law in the New Testament is seen to apply not to law in itself, but to the perverted[f] use of the law in Israel, the proper understanding and use of law will also be seen in the Old Testament.

[¶3] To begin with, we acknowledge[g] that two major events stand behind Sinai. The one is the Exodus and the other is the covenant with Abraham. If the Exodus means anything, it means freedom from bondage. The continuity[h] of the declared purpose of God requires us to place Sinai in the context of the purposes of God to make a people for himself on the basis of his grace. The call and covenanting of Abraham was an act of grace. The descendants of Abraham were promised the kingdom by grace. The mighty acts of God in Egypt were performed because of the promise to Abraham (Ex. 2:23–25). The Exodus event becomes a model of salvation by grace, its goal being the fulfillment of the promises to Abraham in the promised land. It is utterly inconceivable that God should break off his program of salvation by grace in mid-stream[i] (between Egypt and Canaan) and, despite his promises to Abraham, saddle his people with a frustrating program of salvation by works! . . . The only reasonable assessment of the Sinai law in this context is that it is part of the program of grace whereby God works to fulfill his promises to Abraham.

[¶4] The heart of the law is the Ten Commandments (Ex. 20), which are prefaced by the significant phrase, "I am the Lord your God, who brought you out of the land of Egypt, out of the house of bondage." These words should govern[j] our understanding of the Sinai law. Here we see that God declares that he is the God of this people, that he has already saved them. What follows then cannot be a program aimed to achieve salvation by works since they have already received it by grace. The law is given to the people of God after they become the people of God by grace. Sinai is dependent upon the covenant with Abraham and is an exposition of it. . . . The law explicates[k] further the knowledge of God's character already revealed in his dealing with their forefathers and in his acts in Egypt (Ex. 6:6–8).

[¶5] Given this understanding of the Sinai covenant, the moral prescriptions[l] are easy enough to understand. But what of the ritual details and the many laws concerning what is clean and what unclean (especially with regard to food)? . . . Some laws must deal with the national life of Israel, because that is where they are. Others are ritual requirements which depend on a later fulfillment for their full meaning. A group of apparently meaningless food laws becomes meaningful in the context of the Sinai covenant. They instruct the people in one aspect of the unique[m] relationship they possess as a holy people, separated from all other allegiance[n] and separated to Jehovah. . . .

[¶6] Breaking the law carries heavy penalties, the most severe being death or excommunication. Israel as a nation is expected to be faithful to the law if it is also to enjoy the blessings of God. It is this fact (e.g., see Deut. 28) which may be misinterpreted to imply that the blessings of salvation are the reward for the works of the law. We should note however that the New Testament carries exactly the same conditions. And no New Testament teaching destroys the principle of salvation by grace (e.g., 1 Cor. 6:9–10; 10:6–12; Eph. 4:1; Heb. 12:12–17, James 1:26–27; 1 John 3:14–15). In both the Old and New Testaments the principle operates that the people of God should exhibit° a holiness which is consistent with their calling. The deliberate flouting^p of this principle is clear demonstration that we are not members of God's people. In both Testaments the demand to be holy stems from the prior saving activity of God.[4]

a. Program (n.): a plan of procedure
b. Desperation (n.): a (reckless) seizing of any action that offers hope of success
c. Institute (v.): to set up
d. Treatment (n.): the literary handling of a subject
e. Depreciation (n.): the act or process of lessening in value
f. Perverted (adj.): twisted, corrupt, or vicious
g. Acknowledge (v.): to show by word or act that one has knowledge of and agrees to

h. Continuity (n.): uninterrupted persistence of a particular quality
i. Mid-stream (adv. phrase): in the middle of doing something
j. Govern (v.): to control, direct, or strongly influence
k. Explicate (v.): to unfold the meaning of; to clarify
l. Prescription (n.): an authoritative rule or direction
m. Unique (adj.): being without like or equal
n. Allegiance (n.): devotion or loyalty
o. Exhibit (v.): to present or display
p. Flouting (n.): treating with contempt by disregarding

Post-Reading

According to Goldsworthy, why would the Israelites have practiced the law? Why do we follow Jesus' commands in the New Testament? (Hint: The answer is the same for both questions.)

Main Ideas and Details

(1) In your own words, state the main idea of the reading in a single sentence.

(2) True or False: The author believes that the Old Testament is the record of the failure of God's plan to redeem his people through works of the law.

(3) What does the author imply with the final sentence of paragraph 2?
   a. The OT shows us that we should depreciate the law itself.
   b. There is a proper understanding and use of the law in the OT.
   c. The perverted use of the law in the OT directly indicates the law's value.
   d. The NT shows that the OT law was perverted from the very beginning.

(4) What two events does the author say inform our understanding of the giving of the law at Mount Sinai?

(5) What key word is repeated in the highlighted sentences of paragraph 3? Why do you think the author repeats this key word?

(6) How does the author say we should view the law given at Sinai? (Refer to paragraph 3.)

(7) In paragraph 4, the author argues that the law given at Sinai cannot be viewed as a means of attaining salvation. Why does he say this?
   a. Because God has already saved his people by grace
   b. Because the covenant with Abraham is dependent upon the law at Sinai
   c. Because the heart of the law is the Ten Commandments, which Jesus upholds
   d. Because the law is given to the Israelites before they become the people of God

(8) Which of the following can we infer from the highlighted portion of the sentence in paragraph 5?
   a. Relationships are often based on dietary laws.

---

4. Goldsworthy, *Gospel and Kingdom*, 73–78. Used by permission of Paternoster.

b. When the law was given at Sinai, the Israelites were not yet the people of God.

c. "Apparently meaningless food laws" helped reflect the identity of God's people in the OT.

d. The Sinai covenant implies that the Israelites were religiously similar to other nations.

(9) According to paragraph 6, what might have caused people to think that salvation is a reward for works of the law?

Cause, Effect, and Logical Relationships

Authors show logical relationships between their ideas (such as cause-and-effect) by using certain words and phrases as *markers*. Fill in the missing parts of the sentences below to track how Goldsworthy shows cause-and-effect or other logical relationships in the passage. In the right hand column, write the words or phrases that you think mark the relationship. An example is provided for you in the first row.[5]

Part 1	Part 2	Marker
If the depreciation of law in the New Testament is seen to apply not to law in itself, but to the perverted use of the law in Israel,	the proper understanding and use of law will also be seen in the Old Testament.	*If . . . (then)*
The mighty acts of God in Egypt were performed		
What follows then cannot be a program aimed to achieve salvation by works		
	if it is also to enjoy the blessings of God.	

Collocations from the Passage

Provide collocations from the reading passage for the words in the center bubbles on the top of the next page. These collocations may precede or follow these words. There are enough collocations so that all of the bubbles should be filled, and some of the difficult ones are provided for you. You can check your answers by revisiting the passage.

5. The structure of this exercise is based on a similar exercise provided in Cherie L. Pierson, Lonna J. Dickerson, and Florence R. Scott, *Exploring Theological English: Reading, Vocabulary, and Grammar for ESL/EFL* (Carlisle, UK: Piquant, 2010), 210–11.

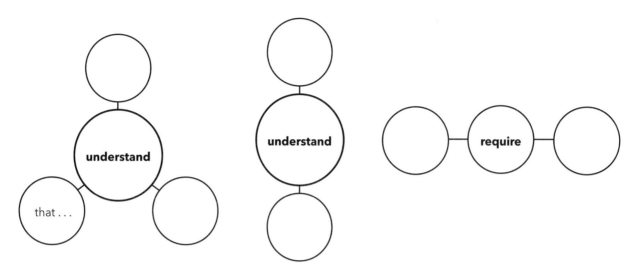

Fig. 16.1. Collocation Diagram 4

Using some of the collocations above, write a sentence about the purpose of the giving of the law on Mount Sinai, according to Goldsworthy.

Grammar Focus: Infinitives

In the previous lesson, we saw how authors can add information to their sentences by using a more complex subject, a complete subject. Another way you can add information to your sentences is to follow an adjective, noun, or verb with an infinitive to express purpose, further specify an adjective or noun, or provide the object for a verb.[6] Have a look at the following examples.

His lecture on heresy in the early church was <u>difficult</u> *to understand.*

Pilate's <u>decision</u> *to hand Jesus over to his accusers* is recorded in Matt. 27:24–26.

Jesus <u>longed</u> *to gather the people of Israel* as a hen gathers her young (Matt. 23:37), but they turned away from him.

In the last example, notice how even more information can be added (in the form of an adverbial clause) to modify the action of "gathering" (from the infinitive).

Examine the infinitives that the author uses in the paragraph below. What parts of speech precede them?

Given this understanding of the Sinai covenant, the moral prescriptions are easy enough **to understand**. . . .

Breaking the law carries heavy penalties, the most severe being death or excommunication. Israel as a nation is expected **to be faithful** to the law if it is also **to enjoy** the blessings of God. It is this fact (e.g., see Deut. 28) which may be misinterpreted **to imply** that the blessings of salvation are the reward for the works of the law. . . . In both Testaments the demand **to be holy** stems from the prior saving activity of God.

In this paragraph, we see infinitives being preceded by three different parts of speech: verbs, adjectives, and nouns.

Part of Speech	Infinitive
Adjective: *easy*	*to understand*
Verb: *is expected*	*to be faithful*
Verb: *is*	*to enjoy*
Verb: *may be misinterpreted*	*to imply*
Noun: *demand*	*to be holy*

---

6. You can also specify (complement) a noun by following it with a prepositional phrase or a clause. See the examples in Michael Swan, *Practical English Usage*, 4th ed. (Oxford: Oxford University Press, 2016), entry 122.

Activity 1

Underline the infinitives in the following passage. Above each infinitive, write the part of speech that precedes it.

Example: It is important <u>to study</u> theology.

The book of Numbers relates the incidents between Sinai and the entry [into the promised land]. In so doing it presents a rather gloomy picture. Israel . . . is shown to be rebellious and ungrateful. . . . After the Sinai encounter the nation asserts its independence of God by refusing the opportunity to take possession of the promised land (Numbers 13–14). The forty years wandering in the wilderness disposes of the generation of adults who came out of Egypt, leaving their children to go in and possess the land.[7]

Activity 2

Follow each of the words below with an infinitive. The first three examples are taken directly from the reading passage. The last three are similar to those in the reading passage.

1. Inability

2. Careful

3. Works (v.)

4. Decides

5. Choice

6. Dangerous

Activity 3

Write three to five sentences in response to the following question: What would be the benefit of interpreting God's giving of the law as an act of grace? After you have written your sentences, underline any infinitives you used and note the parts of speech that preceded them.

7. Goldsworthy, *Gospel and Kingdom*, 78.

Activity 4

As you have done with the previous lessons, fill in the missing collocations in the table below. While these collocations have been taken directly from Lessons 14–16, more than one answer may be correct. Try to fill in the chart without looking at the previous lessons. See what collocations you can remember. Compare your answers with those of a partner to learn other collocations that you might have missed.

express			key	
particular				the reason for
organic			fulfill	
specific				perspective
	significance			understanding
provide				demonstration
explicitly				

The Clean and the Unclean (BS Task 4)

In this task, you will try to explain to a friend that even the Levitical cleanliness laws help us to understand God's grace in the Old and New Testaments. To prepare for this task, read the sections below and consider how Christ cleanses us from all of our sin.

Introduction

The Old Testament plays a vital role in our understanding of the New Testament. We understand the Old Testament more fully when we see that it finds its fulfillment in the New. For example, God's glory is a central focus of the New Testament, but the glory of God in the New Testament builds on his revealed glory in the Old Testament.[8] In this sense, we can understand the events of the Old Testament as foreshadowing the fullness of God's glory in the person and work of Christ. But sometimes this takes some creative thinking. Examine the following passage and take a few notes concerning how the laws for cleanliness in the Old Testament are related to Christ's work in the New Testament.

The laws for cleanness and uncleanness . . . signify and foreshadow the way in which God cleanses sin. They show that a renewed or recreated people are characterized by renewed behavior, behavior conforming to God's order and separating them from sin. A close look at the classification of things into categories of holy, clean, and unclean shows a pattern of order. God, the ultimate Creator of order, is supremely holy. He is the origin of life with its order-producing potential. By contrast, death is associated with sin and disorder. Hence, things associated with death or producing disorder are unclean.[9]

Task: Role-play

You and your partner should skim over the two roles below and each choose a role. Spend a few minutes brainstorming possible answers to the new Christian's dilemma. The person who is the new Christian should

---

8. G. K. Beale, *A New Testament Biblical Theology: The Unfolding of the Old Testament in the New* (Grand Rapids, MI: Baker, 2012), 958.
9. Vern S. Poythress, *The Shadow of Christ in the Law of Moses* (Phillipsburg, NJ: P&R, 1991), 81.

remember to use correct question formation when asking questions. The mentor should remember to explain these ideas clearly to someone who is not familiar with many of the Bible's stories, terms, or concepts.

After brainstorming, you should decide who will begin the conversation. Continue with the role-play until the task is finished. If you have additional time, you can switch roles.

Role: New Christian (Mentoree)

You are a new Christian who is meeting regularly with a mentor. At the beginning of the year, your mentor encouraged you to follow a year-long Bible reading plan. You were excited to start it, but now you are in the middle of Leviticus and are having trouble understanding how the laws and regulations that Moses set before the Israelites are related to your acceptance of Jesus Christ as Lord and Savior. In particular, you do not see how the rules about cleanliness in the OT affect your salvation. Ask your partner to explain this to you. Continue to ask your partner questions about it until he or she gives you a specific and applicable response.

Role: Mentor

You have been mentoring a new Christian since the beginning of the year. You saw this person get very excited about the events in Genesis and the unfolding of redemptive history. However, your mentoree is stuck in the middle of Leviticus and cannot seem to understand how the laws and regulations that Moses set before the Israelites are related to his or her acceptance of Jesus Christ as Lord and Savior. Given what you know about how the Old Testament finds fulfillment in the New, suggest one way in which your mentoree might understand how even something such as the Levitical cleanliness laws are related to his or her relationship with Christ. In your response, try to be specific and provide a way for your mentoree to apply this understanding in his or her life.

17

Idols versus the True God

"What you revere you resemble, either for ruin or restoration."
—G. K. Beale, *We Become What We Worship*

Lesson Goals

Theology—To understand the effects of idolatry

Reading—To continue identifying main ideas and details and to draw inferences; to notice how authors use Scripture to support their claims

Vocabulary—To learn and use additional collocations from the reading passage

Grammar—To practice placing adverbs correctly

Introduction

The Old Testament certainly points to Christ in many ways. For example, there are "Christ-like" figures, such as Moses and David, whose leadership foreshadows elements of Christ's work.[1] But another way in which the Old Testament points forward to Christ is in showing that Christ is the ultimate solution to the problem of sin. And sin has *always* been our problem. "The history of the human race as presented in Scripture is primarily a history of man in a state of sin and rebellion against God and of God's plan of redemption to bring man back to himself."[2] From the standpoint of human history, 1 John 1:7 is more than good news; it is the answer to the problem of sin: "the blood of Jesus [God's] Son cleanses us from all sin." The sinful rebellion we find throughout Scripture is ultimately defeated by the blood of Christ.

Perhaps one of the more obvious manifestations of sin in the Old Testament is idolatry. It does not take long in reading the Old Testament to notice that idol worship is a serious problem. In Gen. 31, we encounter a family confrontation between Laban, Jacob, and Rachel that has to do with the stealing of "household gods" (Gen. 31:19). It was not until a few chapters later that Jacob rightfully demanded that his household put away all foreign gods (Gen. 35:2). But the idols continued to crop up throughout Israel's history, and idol worship was alive and well in the New Testament too.

We might be tempted to think that idolatry is no longer something we struggle with, but this is not

---

1. Edmund P. Clowney, *The Unfolding Mystery: Discovering Christ in the Old Testament*, 25th Anniversary ed. (Phillipsburg, NJ: P&R Publishing, 2013), 118, 158.

2. Wayne Grudem, *Systematic Theology: An Introduction to Biblical Doctrine* (Grand Rapids, MI: Zondervan, 2000), 490.

true. Martin Luther claimed that an idol was that "to which your heart clings and entrusts itself."[3] We may not worship statues as some of the ancient Israelites were tempted to do, but we still struggle with idolatry. We still entrust our hearts to something other than the true and Triune God. And whenever we do, we end up resembling what we trust. As Beale notes above, what we revere we resemble, for restoration or for ruin.

Warm-up

Read Ex. 32:15–29 aloud. Then read it silently, taking notes.

Background for the Reading

One of the ways in which the Old Testament is bound to the New Testament is the continuing problem of idolatry. Even today, we have idols all around us that may deter us from following the true God. Tim Keller writes, "Each culture is dominated by its own set of idols. Each has its priesthoods, its totems and rituals. Each one has its shrines—whether office towers, spas and gyms, studios, or stadiums—where sacrifices must be made in order to procure the blessings of the good life and ward off disaster."[4] Apparently, idols are as much a problem for us as they were for the ancient Israelites. They may appear different, but their effect on us is the same: we begin to resemble what we worship.

As context for the theological passage in this chapter, consider an observation by G. K. Beale. He writes that we all have "organs of spiritual perception," ways of perceiving and responding to spiritual realities. He also calls these "sensory organs." In other words, we are meant to have eyes that see, ears that hear, and hearts that respond to the truth (Isa. 6:10; Jer. 5:21; Ezek. 12:2; 40:4; Matt. 13:15; Acts 28:27; Rom. 11:8). These "sensory organs" are meant to lead us to worship the true God. But sometimes we are deceived; our spiritual sensory organs malfunction, and we can fall into idol worship.[5]

Pre-Reading

Consider the actions of the people in Ex. 32:15–29. In what ways do these people resemble what they worship?

Reading

In the following passage, G. K. Beale interprets Ex. 32, noting how the imagery points to the people acting like what they are worshipping.

[¶1] Exodus 32 illustrates the kind of sensory[a] organ malfunction[b] that is in mind in Deuteronomy 29:4 ("the Lord has not given you a heart to know, nor eyes to see, nor ears to hear"). Though the language of Deuteronomy 29:4 does not occur there, the description of the idolaters in Exodus 32 appears to convey the concept of idolaters becoming like their idols. I will argue that the people became spiritually like the calf they worshiped; the description of their "stiff neck" conveys the picture of a malfunctioning spiritual part of their being. If this is so, then both Exodus 32 and Deuteronomy 29:4 share in common the theme of becoming identified with the idol worshiped. Since both describe Israelite idolaters in the wilderness, the two passages reinforce[c] this idea as it is applied to them. Accordingly, Exodus 32 is one

---

3. *Larger Catechism*, "First Commandment," cited in Bruce K. Waltke, *An Old Testament Theology: An Exegetical, Canonical, and Thematic Approach* (Grand Rapids, MI: Zondervan, 2007), 415.

4. Timothy Keller, *Counterfeit Gods: The Empty Promises of Money, Sex, and Power, and the Only Hope That Matters* (New York: Dutton, 2009), xi–xii.

5. G. K. Beale, *We Become What We Worship: A Biblical Theology of Idolatry* (Downers Grove, IL: InterVarsity, 2008), 41.

of the main episodes of idol worship in the broad purview[d] of Deuteronomy 28–32, where their idol worship is mentioned repeatedly.

[¶2] That the golden calf episode is significantly referred to in this section of Deuteronomy is clear, for example, from Deuteronomy 31:27–29, which explicitly alludes back to[e] the golden calf narration in Deuteronomy 9:6–21 by the following common phrases: (1) "stiff-necked" (Deut. 9:6; 31:27); (2) "you have been rebellious against Yahweh" (Deut. 9:7, 24; 31:27); and (3) Israel "acted corruptly" and "turned aside . . . from the way which I commanded" (Deut. 9:12 [cf. also 9:16] and 31:29, which uses the future tense). In addition, Deut. 31:29 refers to the future idolatry with the words that Israel will "*do evil in the sight of the Lord, provoking[f] him to anger* by the work of their hands," which is a paraphrase of Deut. 9:18: "*provoking the Lord by doing what was evil in the sight of him.*" The point of the comparison between the first generation's idolatry and that of future generations is that the golden calf idolatry was seen to be paradigmatic[g] of Israel's future idolatry, so that the latter was to be patterned after the former. We will see further evidence of this later in the present chapter (see discussion of 2 Kings 17:15; Hos. 4:7; Jer. 2:5, 11). In this respect, Deuteronomy 29:4, in the context of chapters 28–32, is partly, at least, describing a condition of the wilderness generation that is traceable back to the epochal[h] golden calf worship and will be potentially true for future generations.

[¶3] . . . . In this regard Exodus 32 may be instructive, since it shows that when the first generation of Israel worshiped the golden calf, Moses describes them in a manner that sounds like they are being portrayed as wild calves or untrained cows: they became (1) "stiff-necked" (Ex. 32:9; 33:3, 5; 34:9) and would not obey, but (2) they "were let loose" because "Aaron had let them go loose" (Ex. 32:25), (3) so that "they had quickly turned aside from the way," (Ex. 32:8) and they needed to be (4) "gathered together" again "in the gate" (Ex. 32:26), (5) so that Moses could "lead the people where" God had told him to go (Ex. 32:34). The expression in Exodus 32:8, "they quickly turned aside from the way," is placed directly before the phrase "they have made for themselves a molten calf." This is followed by portraying the people as "stiff-necked" in verse 9, so that the three descriptions are inextricably[i] linked.

[¶4] How is their sin of idolatry portrayed in Exodus 32? The description could be taken to be cattle metaphors. Sinful Israel seems to be depicted metaphorically as rebellious cows running wild and needing to be regathered. Is the language just coincidental? The likelihood is that this is a narrative taunt[j] because they are worshiping a cow. This is pointed to by the above-observed three closely juxtaposed[k] phrases "quickly turned aside from the way," "made for themselves a golden *calf*" and "stiff-necked" in Exodus 32:8–9. Hosea 4:16 adds to the picture, which is an echo of the golden calf event: "Since Israel is stubborn like a stubborn heifer, can the Lord now pasture them like a lamb in a large field?" (the expected implied answer is no). Hosea 4:17 then says, "Ephraim is joined to idols; let him alone." The idea in connection with verse 16 is that Israel's stubbornness like a rebellious calf or sheep is idol worship, which in Hosea is often calf worship, and is punished by God through leaving them without a shepherd.

[¶5] Furthermore, the repeated description of Moses' face as having "become horned" in Exodus 34:29–35 echoes the calf idol. The function of the echo was perhaps to mock[l] Israel's trust in the calf as a mediator of divine presence, which they wanted to be near, to be identified with and believed would guarantee their security. The only reality of a calf-like divine presence that they would experience, however, was through Moses, whose horned appearance (perhaps suggesting goring) represented God's wrath against the people. While the people had become as stubborn as their calf idol, Moses' experience in the immediate presence of the true God and his reverence of him resulted in Moses resembling the attribute of this God's wrath against sinful people….

Remember?
The infinitive "to mock" follows the noun "function," joined to it by a linking verb (*was*).

[¶6] Thus the bright horned like appearance of Moses' face suggests a divine mocking of the worshipers of the calf idol, who had come to be described already in Exodus 32 as a calf. The rhetorical[m] point accordingly is: "Oh, you want to worship calf idols, do you? Then not only are you becoming like the calf idol, but in so doing you have become like my idolatrous enemies and are being judged by the only true God, who has the only true glorious power" (symbolized by ox horns flashing on the face of Moses, the mediator of God's wrathful presence). The intention of the parody[n] is to mock the people for mistakenly thinking that true divine glory was possessed by their pathetic calf god instead of by Yahweh. Also pointing to this polemical[o] connection between the golden calf and Moses is the recognition that the glorious "horn" image on Moses' face was an emblem[p] of judgment and presumably would have judged the unspiritual Israelites had Moses not covered his face with a veil. Moses' veiling of his horn-like glory in Exodus 34:29–35 is a response to the golden calf sin and the description of the idolaters as "stiff-necked" (Ex. 32:9, 22; 33:3, 5, which we will see further is stubborn-cow imagery). Thus veiling would appear to be an act of some degree of mercy in the midst of judgment, since the unveiled horn-like glory would apparently have destroyed them if it were not restrained[q] behind the veil.[6]

a. Sensory (adj.): of or relating to sensation or to the senses
b. Malfunction (n.): a failure to operate in the normal or usual manner
c. Reinforce (v.): to make more cogent or convincing
d. Purview (n.): range of sight or knowledge
e. Allude to (v. phrase): to have or make indirect reference to
f. Provoke (v.): to incite to anger
g. Paradigmatic (adj.): exemplary or typical
h. Epochal (adj.): marking the beginning of a new development or era
i. Inextricably (adv.): incapable of being disentangled or untied

j. Taunt (n.): a bitter or sarcastic reproach, insult, or challenge
k. Juxtapose (v.): to place (different things) side by side
l. Mock (v.): to treat with scorn or contempt
m. Rhetorical (adj.): of or relating to the literary effect of speech or discourse
n. Parody (n.): a feeble or ridiculous imitation
o. Polemical (adj.): of or relating to controversy and disputation
p. Emblem (n.): a visible sign of an idea
q. Restrain (v.): to hold back from some action, procedure, or course

6. Beale, *We Become What We Worship*, 76–81. Used with permission of InterVarsity Press.

Post-Reading

In what ways do we resemble the idols of our own day? Identify an idol of contemporary culture and list two ways in which you feel that people who cherish this idol come to resemble it.

Idol	Resemblance

Main Ideas and Details

(1) Summarize the main idea of the reading in a single sentence.

(2) In paragraph 1, the author makes the following qualification: "Though the language of Deuteronomy 29:4 does not occur there . . . ." Why does he say this?

(3) According to paragraph 1, where is idol worship mentioned repeatedly?

(4) In paragraph 2, what kind of evidence does the author use to support his claim that the golden calf incident is referred to in Deuteronomy 28–32?

(5) According to paragraph 2, the author says we should understand the relationship between the golden calf incident and Israel's future idolatry in a certain way. Express this in your own words.

(6) The highlighted pronoun "which" in paragraph 4 refers to _____.
   a. The picture.
   b. The prophet Hosea.
   c. "Stiff-necked."
   d. Exodus 32:8–9.

(7) In paragraph 5, who is performing the action of "guaranteeing" in the phrase "believed would guarantee their security"?
   a. Israel.
   b. Moses.
   c. Yahweh.
   d. The golden calf.

(8) According to paragraph 5, what does Moses' "horned appearance" represent?

(9) According to paragraph 6, what does the author infer about the veil covering the horned-like appearance of Moses' face?

Understanding the Reading

As is common in biblical studies, the author uses scriptural texts to support his claims. Provide either the claim or the corresponding scriptural support in the chart below. For some claims, the support might be an inference based upon details in a particular verse. If so, list the detail upon which the author's inference is based.

Claim	Scriptural Support
The people became spiritually like the calf they worshiped.	
	Deut. 9:6-21; 31:27-29
Moses describes Israel in a manner that sounds like they are being portrayed as wild calves.	
	Hos. 4:16-17

Claim	Scriptural Support
The only reality of a calf-like divine presence that they would experience was through Moses.	
Veiling would appear to be an act of some degree of mercy in the midst of judgment.	

Collocations from the Passage

Match the words on the left to their collocates on the right.

describe	something as
portray	mercy
future	a condition
degree of	generations

Provide collocations from the reading passage for the words in the center bubbles below. These collocations may precede or follow these words. There are enough collocations so that all of the bubbles should be filled. (Hint: The collocates for "appear" are infinitives.)

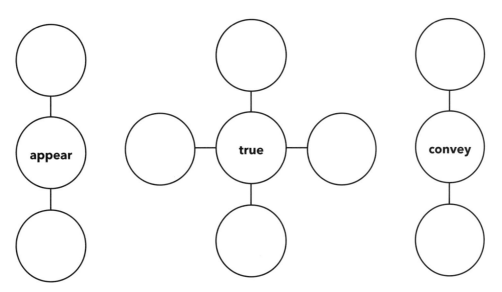

Fig. 17.1. Collocation Diagram 5

Using some of the collocations above, write a sentence about the severity of idolatry.

Grammar Focus: Adverbs

In the last two lessons, we have been discussing how we can add information to sentences. We can put together a complex subject; we can follow an adjective, noun, or verb with an infinitive; and, as we will see in this lesson, we can use adverbs to provide nuance to the action (verb) or descriptions (adjectives) in a sentence. Notice the difference between each pair of sentences below.

> The Israelites *eventually* rebelled against Moses' rule. [They did not rebel immediately.]

> The Israelites *quickly* rebelled against Moses' rule. [Their rebellion did not take very long.]

> The rebellion of the Israelites is related to their lack of faith. [There is some connection between rebellion and faith.]

> The rebellion of the Israelites is *inseparably* related to their lack of faith. [There is a clear and necessary connection between rebellion and faith.]

In addition, since we have already looked at how verb tense and modal verbs reveal the author's perspective, it is important to note that adverbs also reveal something about the author, such as how strongly he feels about an action or description, why he treats the subject in a certain way, and so forth. Adverbs provide interpretive clues for us so that we can correctly understand the author's stance or position (we will discuss stance in Lesson 20).

For adverbs to have their intended effect, they must be placed correctly, and that is where many students have trouble. What position do adverbs take? Do adverbs go immediately before the verb or adjective, or can they follow them? The frustrating but true answer to these questions is that different kinds of adverbs can go in different places in the sentence or clause.[7] Read the passage below and note the placement of the adverbs; we will then explore the guidelines for adverb placement.

> They became (1) "stiff-necked" (Ex. 32:9; 33:3, 5; 34:9) and would not obey, but (2) they "were let loose" because "Aaron had let them go loose"

(Ex. 32:25), (3) so that "they had **quickly** turned aside from the way," (Ex. 32:8) and they needed to be (4) "gathered together" again "in the gate" (Ex. 32:26), (5) so that Moses could "lead the people where" God had told him to go (Ex. 32:34). The expression in Exodus 32:8, "they **quickly** turned aside from the way," is placed **directly** before the phrase "they have made for themselves a molten calf." This is followed by portraying the people as "stiff-necked" in verse 9, so that the three descriptions are **inextricably** linked.

Many adverbs immediately precede verbs or adjectives ("<u>quickly</u> turned aside"); others come after a verb and before another adverb ("placed <u>directly</u> before"), or after a linking verb ("are <u>inextricably</u> linked"). Other adverbs can come at the end of a clause or sentence (e.g., "He interpreted the passage <u>carefully</u>").

In general, adverbs can come in the three positions exemplified in the previous paragraph: *front*, *mid*, and *end*. Knowing which adverbs can go in which position can be difficult. But there are some guidelines you can follow based on the type of adverb you are using. Connecting adverbs, or conjunctive adverbs (e.g., *however, consequently, therefore, moreover, thus*), usually take the front position.[8] Adverbs of frequency and certainty (*always, usually, certainly, definitely*) usually take the mid position. And adverbs of manner (*quickly, briefly, carefully, enthusiastically*) often take the end position.

At the top of the next page is a table with some examples of common types of adverbs in these three positions (we have included the adverbs from Beale's paragraph above). You can use this table to help you practice placing your own adverbs in Activities 2 and 3 below.

* Note that certain types of adverbs (e.g., adverbs of manner) can occur in more than one position.

---

7. Michael Swan, *Practical English Usage*, 4th ed. (Oxford: Oxford University Press, 2016), entry 196.
8. Ibid.

Front Position	Mid Position before one-word verbs, after auxiliary verbs, and after am/are/is/was/were	End Position
Connecting: *then, next, suddenly, however* Comment: *fortunately, regrettably, surprisingly, apparently* Indefinite frequency: *sometimes, usually, always, never* Certainty: *maybe, perhaps* Place: *at the end of Genesis, in the opening verses, on the surface* Time: *today, later, soon, afterwards* Manner: *quickly, suddenly, slowly*	Indefinite frequency: *sometimes, usually, always, never* Certainty: *maybe, perhaps* Completeness: *completely, practically, almost, partly, hardly* Manner: *angrily, suddenly, slowly, quickly, happily, directly, inextricably, gracefully, casually, well*	Manner: *angrily, suddenly, slowly, quickly, happily, gracefully, casually, well* Place: *at the end of Genesis, in the opening verses, on the surface* Definite frequency: *today, every week, afterwards*

Activity 1

Underline the adverbs that you find in the following paragraph, noting their placement.

The first generation of Israelites did not literally become petrified golden calves like the one that they worshiped, but they are depicted as acting like out-of-control and headstrong calves, apparently because they were being mocked as having become like the image that represented a spiritually rebellious and ornery calf that they had worshiped.[9]

Activity 2

Using either some of the adverbs provided in the box below or adverbs of your choice, work with a partner to modify the following sentences. Use at least one adverb in each of the positions you have learned (front, mid, and end).

thoughtlessly	graciously	only	completely	immediately
solely	faithfully	subtly	often	quickly

1. There are many idols today that we worship and serve.

2. Materialism is one idol that steals our attention and suggests that our present comfort is most important.

---

9. G. K. Beale, *A New Testament Biblical Theology: The Unfolding of the Old Testament in the New* (Grand Rapids, MI: Baker, 2011), 368.

3. However, we are never fulfilled by material possessions because they offer momentary satisfaction.

4. True satisfaction is found in Christ, and in Him God has provided for all of our deepest needs.

Activity 3

Using at least three of the adverbs that you have identified in Activities 1 and 2 above, write a short paragraph (three to four sentences) describing a contemporary idol (e.g., money, fame).

18

Christ, the Second Adam

"What is true about Christ historically as the one who follows after Adam does not subvert what is true about Christ eternally as the one who precedes Adam."
—Lane G. Tipton, *Resurrection and Eschatology*

Lesson Goals

Theology—To understand the role of Christ as the last Adam

Reading—To learn how to recognize an author's purpose

Vocabulary—To learn and use additional collocations from the reading passage

Grammar—To practice expressing comparison and contrast

Introduction

We have learned an important lesson from the Old Testament about idolatry: we become like what we worship. And while we continue to struggle with our own idols today, we are in a very different position from that of Old Testament Israel: Christ has come! The sin and destruction, the turmoil and the suffering—all that is wicked and wrong has been definitively defeated by Christ, whom Paul refers to in the New Testament as the "last Adam" (1 Cor. 15:45). While the first Adam of Gen. 3 brought about death and darkness, the last Adam brings life and light (John 14:6; 8:12; cf. Rom. 5:12–21).

It is critical for us to see Christ as the last Adam who has succeeded where the first Adam failed. "Adam's death-bringing sin ultimately necessitated its reversal in another Adam, who would perform a life-giving act."[1] Yet more can be said about what Christ

did in fulfilling the duties that were given to Adam. What, in other words, makes it clear that Christ *is* the second Adam? How does his life and work parallel that of Adam? These questions are explored in the reading passage for this chapter.

Warm-up

Read Rom. 5:12–21 and 1 Cor. 15:35–49. Take notes as needed. Compare your notes with those of a partner.

Background Information

Paul connects Christ to Adam in Rom. 5 and in 1 Cor. 15, among many other places in his writings. One of the many reasons why the Old Testament is still relevant and essential for us today is that throughout it, from Genesis to Malachi, we see how

---

1. G. K. Beale, *A New Testament Biblical Theology: The Unfolding of the Old Testament in the New* (Grand Rapids, MI: Baker Academic, 2011), 440.

the sin of man that entered the stage of redemptive history with Adam is followed by a developing hope of redemption that is fulfilled in the second Adam, Christ. Paul's understanding of Adam and creation in relation to Christ and re-creation is particularly illuminating, as is his discussion of the pre- and post-resurrection body. Both of these topics (Adam and Christ; pre- and post-resurrection bodies) have roots in the Old Testament, giving us two more reasons to affirm that the Old Testament is vital to our Christian faith.

Reading Skill: Understanding the Author's Purpose

Most theological writing has a persuasive element, meaning that the author is trying to persuade his readers that his argument is the best one. A theologian often forms a thesis and then organizes support in such a way as to convince his readers that the thesis is correct as compared to other views on the subject.

Within that broad purpose, writers choose their words and argument structures carefully in order to build the strongest arguments. A good reader can look beyond what the writer is saying to identify the writer's goal or purpose. In other words, good readers ask, "Why did the author choose to structure his argument in this way?"

Tip: Before you can understand the author's purpose, you need to understand the main idea. First, focus on what the author is saying and then you can think about why he or she is saying it in that place and manner.

Pre-Reading

What do you think would have happened to Adam if he had obeyed God's word in the Garden of Eden?

Strategies for Recognizing an Author's Purpose

1. Think about how the author is *developing his argument*. What is the overall structure of the essay, article or chapter? What is the structure of any subsection?
   - The author may clearly describe this structure in a purpose statement (often found near the thesis statement).
   - You may need to infer this structure using transition signals at the beginning of the body paragraphs.
   - Typical patterns of development include:
     » Comparison and contrast;
     » Chronological (time) order;
     » Process;
     » List of items;
     » Cause and effect.
2. Think about how the *support* within the paragraph or between a few paragraphs is organized. What is the relationship between the author's supporting ideas and details?
   - The author may clearly describe this relationship in a topic sentence or concluding sentence.
   - You may need to infer this using transition signals within the sentences.
3. As you read, ask yourself, "What is the author's goal in writing this word/sentence/paragraph/article? How does he think it will help him achieve his goal?"

Reading

In the following passage, G. K. Beale explores Christ's identity as the last Adam.

[¶1] The commission of Gen. 1:26–28 involved[a] the following elements, especially as summarized in verse 28:

1. God blessed them;
2. be fruitful and multiply;
3. fill the earth;
4. subdue the earth;
5. rule over all the earth.

It also appears[b] that God's making of Adam in his "image" and "likeness" is what is to enable Adam to carry out the particular parts of the commission. As an image-bearer, Adam was to reflect the character of God, which included mirroring the divine glory. Together with the prohibition in Gen. 2:16–17, the essence[c] of the commission was that of subduing and ruling over the earth and filling it with God's glory; especially through glorious image-bearing progeny. I explained in more detail in chapter 2 what this commission entailed and what escalated[d] eschatological blessings Adam would have received had he obeyed. The essence of this reward was an irreversible and eternal incorruptibility of physical and spiritual life, which would be lived in an incorruptible[e] cosmos that was free from any evil or sinful threat.

[¶2] Adam, however, failed in the task with which he was commissioned. We also saw in chapter 2 a long list of OT passages indicating that Adam's commission was passed on to other Adam-like figures (e.g., Noah, the patriarchs, Israel), but all of them failed to carry out the commission. Beginning with the patriarchs, however, the repeated Adamic commission was combined with a promise of a "seed" who would "bless" the nations, thus suggesting[f] that the commission would finally be fulfilled at some point by the seed. Failure would continue until there would arise this seed, a "last Adam," who would finally fulfill the commission on behalf of humanity.

Remember?
"Finally" is a mid-position adverb, coming between the modal verb "would" and the main verb "fulfill."

[¶3] The restatements of the Gen. 1 Adamic commission beginning with Abraham are put in terms either of a promise of some positive act that will occur or some command that is to lead to positive obedience. Both the promissory[g] and the imperatival[h] reiterations pertain[i] to the seed's positive "multiplying and increasing," "spreading out," actual conquering and possessing or inheriting. In this light, would it not be odd if the NT never spoke of the last Adam, Jesus, in the same positive terms? Now, it is true that the NT conceives of part of Christ's obedience to the mandate of Adam to be his obedience to death. This is certainly, at the least, what Rom. 5:12–17; Phil. 2:5–11; Heb. 2:6–10 speak about. Jesus did not only what the first Adam should have done but also much more: he even became obedient to death on behalf of his people on the road to his great victory of resurrection and exaltation.

[¶4] It should be admitted that Paul, for example, speaks more about Christ's so-called passive obedience of death than he does his own active obedience in redeeming people. Nevertheless, in addition to the above references to the attribution[j] of Christ's righteousness to saints, there are some places in the NT where Jesus as the last Adam is portrayed without references to his death but instead is viewed as having done what Adam should have done. For example, I analyzed[k] Christ's temptation in the wilderness (Matt. 4:1–11; Luke 4:1–13) in terms of Christ being both a last Adam and a true Israel figure (i.e., corporate Adam) who obeys at just the points where Adam and Israel disobeyed.

[¶5] Likewise, Paul sometimes portrays Christ as the last Adam who has received the victorious position and reward of glorious and incorruptible kingship, apparently as a result of having accomplished all the requirements of obedience that were expected of the first Adam, especially conquering and possessing. . . . In 1 Cor. 15:45 Paul explicitly refers to Christ as the "last Adam," who has achieved the escalated blessing of incorruptibility that the first Adam failed to obtain.

[¶6] Paul views Christ himself as having decisively fulfilled the Adamic commission of Ps. 8; this likely entails Paul's belief, in light of the context of Ps. 8, that Christ himself, individually and flawlessly,[l] ruled, subdued, multiplied spiritual progeny (though this element is missing in Ps. 8), and filled the earth with God's glory, as fully as one human could in one lifetime. This is an inaugurated[m] eschatological idea, since Christ's faithful obedience as the last Adam is the only thing that could have led to the reward of being propelled into the new creation and kingship in that creation. That is, his resurrected body was the literal beginning of the latter-day new creation and his obedient reign in that new creation, which is what was expected of the first Adam but never obtained by him. As believers are identified with Christ's heavenly position of resurrection and kingly exaltation, they also are identified with his reward of exalted kingship in the new creation and the faithful obedience that continues to characterize that new-creational kingship, an obedience that is the climax of his victorious obedience on earth that led up to the heavenly reward. This represents a breaking in of the future new creation into the present. It is not a completed new creation, since believers are not personally on earth perfectly obedient kings, nor have they personally experienced their full reward of consummate[n] resurrection as they will at the very end of the age. Nevertheless, they are identified with Christ as the last Adam, who was completely obedient.

[¶7] This notion of Christ doing what Adam should have done and achieving the glorious blessed position that Adam should have inherited and then having believers identified with this glorious position is close conceptually to and suggestive of the idea of attributing Christ's positive obedience to believers.[2]

2. Beale, *A New Testament Biblical Theology*, 478–80.

a. Involve (v.): to contain or include
b. Appear (v.): to look or seem
c. Essence (n.): the most significant element, attribute, quality, or property of a thing
d. Escalate (v.): to increase the extent, number, volume, amount or scope of
e. Incorruptible (adj.): not subject to decay or dissolution
f. Suggest (v.): to imply or hint at
g. Promissory (adj.): containing a promise or assurance that something will happen

h. Imperatival (adj.): of or relating to a command
i. Pertain (v.): to have a connection with or relation to something
j. Attribution (n.): the process of ascribing something to someone
k. Analyze (v.): t determine the nature, significance, and relationship of the various parts of something
l. Flawlessly (adv.): without flaw or imperfection
m. Inaugurate (v.): to begin or introduce
n. Consummate (adj.): complete or finished

Post-Reading

How is Christ's work as the second Adam related to the "multiplying," "increasing," and "spreading out" of the Abrahamic promise?

Reading Skill Practice

(1) What is the author's purpose in paragraph one?
   a. He is presenting new information about the historical Adam.
   b. He is contrasting the Adamic commission with that of Christ.
   c. He is reviewing Adam's commission to be an "image-bearer."

(2) What is the relationship between paragraphs 1 and 2?
   a. Paragraph 1 describes the Adamic commission, and paragraph 2 focuses on why Adam failed to fulfill it.
   b. Paragraph 1 describes the Adamic commission, and paragraph 2 summarizes how it would ultimately be fulfilled.
   c. Paragraph 1 lists the causes for the commission God gave Adam, and paragraph 2 describes the effects it had on Adam.

(3) The author uses the word "however" in the beginning of paragraph 2 _____
   a. To contrast attaining eschatological blessings with what actually happened.
   b. To introduce exceptions to the list of eschatological blessings given to Adam.
   c. To show that Adam was an exception to the requirements of the commission.

Main Ideas and Details

(1) According to the author in paragraph 1, what is it that enables Adam to carry out the commission of Gen. 1:26–28?

(2) What is the essence of the commission? (Refer to paragraph 1.)

(3) What would "the seed" finally accomplish? (Refer to paragraph 2.)

(4) In paragraph 3, what can we infer from the author's use of the phrase "the promissory and the imperatival reiterations"?
   a. "The seed" will fulfill a promise and obey God's commands.
   b. Christ's human nature carries more weight than his divine nature.
   c. It is imperative that "the seed" offer new promises to God's people.
   d. Reiterations in Scripture do not serve to clarify what was formerly vague.

(5) True or False: We would not expect the New Testament to discuss the Second Adam with the language of the commission. (Refer to paragraph 3.)

(6) Why does the author use a rhetorical question in paragraph 3?
   a. It suggests a negative answer in the readers' minds.
   b. It highlights the fact that Jesus actively obeyed the commission.
   c. It is a question the author wants to know the answer to but does not know.

(7) In paragraph 4, why does the author say, "It should be admitted"?
   a. Paul's discussion of the passive obedience of Christ is not central.
   b. We need to admit that the death of Christ is more important than his life.
   c. The author wants to acknowledge that Paul's focus is different from his own.

(8) What is the relationship between paragraphs 4 and 5?
   a. Paragraph 5 continues the idea of Christ as the last Adam.
   b. Paragraph 5 offers contrasting information about Christ as the last Adam.
   c. Paragraph 5 describes the effects of understanding Christ as the last Adam.

(9) What does 1 Cor. 15:45 reveal that Christ has attained as the "last Adam"? (Refer to paragraph 5.)

(10) What is revealed about Christ according to Paul's reference to Ps. 8? (Refer to paragraph 6.)

(11) Which of the following is NOT the purpose of paragraph 7 in this passage?
   a. It summarizes the author's argument.
   b. It introduces the contrast between Christ and Adam.
   c. It adds information about how believers have positive obedience.

(12) What theological doctrine is the author referring to with the words "the idea of attributing Christ's positive obedience to believers"?

Understanding the Reading

Read 1 Cor. 15:35–49. In the chart below, compare and contrast the "first Adam" with the "last Adam" by writing one quality of the first Adam in the column on the left and a corresponding quality of the last Adam in the column on the right. Add to the chart what you have learned from the reading passage concerning the fulfillment of the commission in Gen. 1:26–28. Then, following the same format, compare and contrast the pre- and post-resurrection bodies that Paul describes.

First Adam	Last Adam
Pre-Resurrection Body	Post-Resurrection Body

Collocations from the Passage

Select the most appropriate word from the choices in the parentheses. All of these examples of collocations have been taken directly from the reading.

In order to (*receive/take/give*) the eschatological (*joys/blessings/ideas*) that were offered to Adam and Eve, they would have had to obey God's word. Adam and Eve, after all, were (*commissioned/nominated/requested*) to rule over and subdue creation. God had given them everything but the fruit of a single tree. But instead of taking God at his word, they took the serpent at his.

Match the words on the left to the words they occur with on the right.

decisively	to obtain
reflect	someone as
redeem	fulfilled
portray	people
fail	the character of
achieve	a position

Grammar Focus: Noun Clauses

As we continue discussing how we can add information and express relations in complex sentences, we come to a more complex structure:

the noun clause.[3] In previous lessons, we reviewed complete subjects, infinitives, and adverbs, each of which adds information to the idea being expressed. Noun clauses not only add information to the sentence; they convey complex relations and processes that cannot be articulated in a word or phrase. For example, note how the author relates Adam's "commission" to the commission of others:

> We also saw in chapter 2 a long list of OT passages indicating that Adam's commission was passed on to other Adam-like figures (e.g., Noah, the patriarchs, Israel), . . .

We cannot express this information in a single word.[4] We need a more complex structure to express it. The noun clause acts like a *noun* (hence the name) in the sense that it can do what most nouns do. For example, it can serve as the object of a verb ("indicating"). But a noun clause is still a *clause* because it has a subject and a finite verb ("Adam's commission was passed on").

Reminder: Key Features of a Clause
Subject + *Finite Verb*

what **this commission** *entailed*
what the **first Adam** *should have done*

So a noun clause is exactly what it sounds like: a clause that functions like a noun or noun phrase. What is critical to remember is what makes these clauses: a subject and finite verb (not an infinitive or -ing form). They can begin with *that* or with an interrogative pronoun (*what, how, whoever*).

Note, however, that a noun clause is not the same as a relative clause, though they look very similar. Students often wonder what the difference is between the clauses in the following two sentences.

The text clearly suggests that God made Adam in his image.

Creation was the gift that God had given to Adam.

The first sentence is an example of a noun clause, whereas the second is an example of a relative clause. What is the difference? In the first sentence, the clause functions as a noun. It is the object of the verb "suggests." In the second sentence, the clause functions as an adjective. It describes the noun "gift." Both types of clause, however, have a subject and a finite verb.

Note the complex relations and process that can be articulated with a noun clause in the following passage. (Be careful not to mistake the relative clauses for noun clauses.)

> It also appears that God's making of Adam in his "image" and "likeness" is . . . what is to enable Adam to carry out the particular parts of the commission. . . . I explained in more detail in chapter 2 what this commission entailed and what escalated eschatological blessings Adam would have received had he obeyed. The essence of this reward was an irreversible and eternal incorruptibility of physical and spiritual life, which would be lived in an incorruptible cosmos that was free from any evil or sinful threat. . . .
>
> . . . . In this light, would it not be odd if the NT never spoke of the last Adam, Jesus, in the same positive terms? Now, it is true that the NT conceives of part of Christ's obedience to the mandate of Adam to be his obedience to death. This is certainly, at the least, what Rom. 5:12–17; Phil. 2:5–11; Heb. 2:6–10 speak about. Jesus did not only what the first Adam should have done but also much more: he even became obedient to death on behalf of his people on the road to his great victory of resurrection and exaltation.

---

3. We will focus on four different types of noun or *nominal* clauses: *that* clauses ("I suggested that he study Calvin's view of the Sabbath"); subordinate interrogative clauses ("What he studied was Calvin's view of the Sabbath"); subordinate exclamative clauses ("It is remarkable how much he knows about Calvin's view of the Sabbath"); and nominal relative clauses ("Whoever reads Calvin's theology extensively must be diligent"). See Randolph Quirk et al., *A Comprehensive Grammar of the English Language* (New York: Longman, 1985), 1048–61.

4. Note that you *can* express this information as a phrase—"the passing on of Adam's commission to other Adam-like figures"—but this would make the sentence more difficult to read. Using a noun clause means we can give the reader another clean subject and action.

Function	Example
As the object of a verb	It also appears that God's making of Adam in his "image" and "likeness" is I explained in more detail in chapter 2 what this commission entailed
As the complement of an adjective	Now, it is true that the NT conceives of part of Christ's obedience to the mandate of Adam to be his obedience to death.
As the subject of the sentence	What Christ did as the last Adam redeems all that the first Adam and his progeny corrupted.

Activity 1

Underline the noun clauses in the following paragraph and note how they function in the sentence.

I argued in an earlier work that in Revelation a "mark" on the forehead and hand identifies one with commitment to the beast, and a different mark also distinguishes the followers of the Lamb (see Rev. 13:16–14:1). These marks connote that the followers of Christ and the followers of the beast are stamped with the image (= character) of their respective leader. Each group also bears the "name" of its respective leader (whether of the beast or of the Lamb and God). We also saw that to bear or reflect the name of someone is to reflect that person's character. I argued that this is likely the conceptual way that Revelation conveys the idea of fallen humans bearing the image of Christ and the Father (see Rev. 14:1). Thus, one resembles what one reveres, either for ruin or for restoration.[5]

What often begins the noun clauses in this paragraph?

Activity 2

Create your own noun clauses using the subjects and verbs provided in the left hand column. Then try to use your noun clauses in sentences. An example is provided for you in the first row.

Subject and Verb	Noun Clause	Sentence
the last Adam; *succeed*	that the last Adam succeeded in obeying God's word . . .	*That the last Adam succeeded in obeying God's word* is clearly implied in 1 Cor. 15.
Christ; *rise (from the dead)*		
the covenant; *entail*		
we; *resemble*		
sin; *defeat*		

5. Beale, *A New Testament Biblical Theology*, 465.

Activity 3

Write a one-paragraph summary about who Christ is as the last Adam. Use at least two noun clauses in your paragraph. Check with a partner to make sure that each of your noun clauses has a subject and a finite verb.

Summary of Theological Concepts for Unit 6

- The Old Testament is vitally important to our faith as it points forward to Christ and shows how God's grace has unfolded in Israel's history.
- Idolatry, one of the famous Old Testament sins, is still with us today, and whatever we revere we come to resemble (G. K. Beale).
- Christ, as the second Adam, succeeded where the first Adam failed, and his resurrection has signaled both a new beginning and a foreseeable end (inaugurated eschatology) for creatures who are bound to him in faith.

Activity 4

Paraphrase each of the concepts above in your own words.

(1)

(2)

(3)

Defending the Old Testament (BS Task 5)

There are many themes in the OT with which popular culture has a problem (e.g., the status of women, divinely sanctioned war, etc.). These are sometimes the parts of the OT that draw the most attention from non-Christians. Christians have a responsibility to proclaim the whole counsel of God (Acts 20:27), not just part of it, so that means the OT needs to be defended consciously by Christians who have been trained to see its continuing relevance and necessity.

Task

As you are browsing the web, you come across a liberal theological blog post on the Old Testament. The author of the post claims that the Old Testament narrative concerning the conquest of Canaan is a perfect example of how Scripture cannot be taken literally. He writes, "God would never prescribe the extermination of entire peoples simply because of their idolatrous practices. We need to understand that human sin has affected Scripture. We need to draw on cultural and intellectual progress in order to get the truth from the Bible. People who take Scripture as God's absolute truth have left their minds behind and taken up fideism, which always leads to bad results."

At the bottom of the blog post, the author says that he welcomes comments. Write a one-paragraph comment in which you defend Joshua's conquest of Canaan as ordained by God. Use the passage below to help get you thinking about the topic, but focus on contributing your own thoughts in response to the author's blog post.

The just kingdom of God rightfully replaces the unjust kingdoms of this world that have usurped his rule over the earth . . . . The wicked cannot stand before a holy army, one that obeys God's commands and trusts in him. . . . God hardened the hearts of the Canaanites to wage battle and be slaughtered (11:20; see Ex. 8:32; 9:34). His longsuffering and patience, which had restrained his moral indignation and righteous anger, now bursts, and he unleashes his righteous judgment on the wicked nations who worshiped fertility deities instead of the sublime God.[6]

6. Bruce K. Waltke, *An Old Testament Theology: An Exegetical, Canonical, and Thematic Approach* (Grand Rapids, MI: Zondervan, 2007), 523.

UNIT 7

WHERE HAVE WE BEEN?
(CHURCH HISTORY)

19

Looking Back

"While there is no such thing as neutrality in the telling of history, there is such a thing as objectivity."
—Carl R. Trueman, *Histories and Fallacies*

Lesson Goals

Theology—To learn about the importance of context in historical investigation
Reading—To continue identifying main ideas and details and to draw inferences
Vocabulary—To learn and use additional collocations from the reading passage
Grammar—To recognize and practice forming noun phrases

Introduction

We have certainly seen why we need the Old Testament: it foreshadows the redemptive work of Christ in important ways and also shows how God has organically revealed himself throughout history (biblical theology). And while biblical revelation came to an end in the early first and second centuries C.E., history in the broader sense has certainly continued.

What can we learn from the history of the church, and how do we go about separating truth from error? We can trust Scripture if we believe it is God's inerrant Word, but what can we learn from the errant men and women of history who have struggled to explain and defend biblical truths and to live out those truths in the face of enmity? Very much! We can learn a great deal about the gospel, about ourselves, and even about our own times simply by investigating the past and the persons we encounter there. Certainly, as Trueman notes, no historian's recounting of history is strictly neutral; there is perspective and selection involved in the writing of history. And it is helpful to remind ourselves that history and Scripture are in different categories; only the latter is ultimately authoritative for faith and life. But we are often aided in our understanding of Scripture and our own times if we study the history of the church. While we must be careful in interpreting the work of church historians, this does not mean that historians do not or cannot bring objective truths to people in contemporary times.

Church history, in fact, is a rich reservoir of truth. It is often concerned with *how* and *why* questions. Take the watershed figure of Martin Luther, for example. A church historian might ask, *How* was Martin Luther's understanding of the end-times influenced by his historical context? *Why* did Luther's work toward the end of his life seem to be anti-Semitic? *How* can we accurately understand some of Luther's claims in light of his developing theology?

As we will see in the reading passage, answering such questions is no small task; we must be careful. All people are complex creatures, rooted in specific times and places, engaging with unique movements and social dynamics that are difficult for us to understand in the twenty-first century. While the historical investigation of a theologian may appear simple, there is much that we must be aware of when trying to draw conclusions.

also must account for particular sections of time in a historical figure's life. You and I are not the same today as we were yesterday, or five years ago, or ten years ago; we change and develop over time. The same is the case with men and women in history. In the reading passage for this chapter, we will see why it is important to account for context before drawing conclusions about the theology of a figure such as Martin Luther.

Background for the Reading

Context is a critical word for church historians. When looking at a particular figure in church history, we find economic, social, political, psychological, and other factors that must be taken into account. We

Pre-Reading

Suppose we chose a section of ten years of Martin Luther's life, and we looked at what he wrote during those ten years. Could we then draw conclusions about his theology as a whole? Why or why not?

Reading

In the following passage, Carl Trueman discusses how we might best understand Martin Luther's work in his historical context.

[¶1] One of the most vexed[a] questions among those who seek to appropriate[b] Luther's theology of the Christian life is the extent to which personal holiness matters. In more popular Christian parlance,[c] does Luther's theology have a place for sanctification? This is a very important question because it touches on precisely what it means, in practical terms, to be a Christian. Should the Christian expect to grow in holiness, and to what extent (if any) should she be able to discern such growth? What constitutes[d] growth in holiness? And how does the law of God play into this? Does it fulfill a purely negative role, reminding us of our unrighteousness before God? Or does it have more positive things to say about the ethical behavior of the Christian? These are not abstract[e] issues but rather points of concern for every Christian.

[¶2] The temptation in addressing these matters is to turn immediately to the works of Luther and to mine[f] them for any statements that might touch on the issue. That has often been the approach to great theologians of the past. In this present age, when such vacuous[g] phenomena as Twitter have persuaded vast tracts[h] of the human race that no idea is so profound as to require more than 140 characters, such a method may have even more appeal than in times past.

[¶3] In this chapter, however, I am going to argue that this kind of proof texting is to be eschewed[i] on an issue such as this. Luther's position is nuanced,[j] complicated, and deeply embedded in his life and times. Thus, we must first address the context before we will be in any position to assess his thinking.

The Reformation: A Work in Progress

[¶4] One of the most striking things about the popular evangelical reception of Luther today is its rather truncated[k] view of his life and works. One might almost say that if Luther had perished of an aneurysm[l] on his wedding night in 1525, not only would he have perished happy, but the way in which his theology is typically understood would be entirely unaffected. The key texts for the popular evangelical understanding of Luther were all in place by then: *The Ninety-Five Theses, The Heidelberg Disputation, The Freedom of the Christian Man,* and *The Bondage of the Will.* . . . They also contain most of the exciting sound bites and Tweetable phrases with which we are familiar: "theologians of glory and of the cross," "the whole of life as repentance," "the hidden God and the revealed God," and so forth. In addition, the 1525 date is also helpful because it avoids our having to address the writings in the Zwingli controversy,[m] which, with their high sacramentalism and their blistering[n] rejection of symbolic views of the Eucharist, are simply embarrassing, extreme, and incomprehensible from the perspective of an incredulous[o] evangelicalism.

[¶5] Yet there is an obvious problem: Luther lived on until 1546; and he also continued to write, teach, and preach as if words were in danger of going out of style. By 1525, he had lived just eight years as a Reformer and had only just arrived at the point where he was introducing vernacular[p] liturgy to Wittenberg. He had another twenty-one years of active theological life before him.

> **Idioms**
> What does the author mean by "going out of style"?

[¶6] This leads to a second point that is rarely noticed: Luther's Reformation theology was a work in progress. When he started moving toward reformation, he changed the nature of the pastoral task and the tools of the pastoral trade. As he did so, his new theology itself generated[q] new questions—pastoral, theological, and social. These new questions caused him to refine, revise, and in some places rethink his theology. To imagine this process somehow stopping or dramatically slowing down in 1525 would be both an arbitrary[r] judgment and inherently implausible.[s]

[¶7] Thus, we need to bear in mind that Luther's declaration of Christian freedom in 1520 was a dramatic break with, indeed an inversion of, previous Christian thinking and also, therefore, would have generated unforeseen consequences for those who received the new teaching. Some of these consequences would most likely have required Luther to reflect upon his 1520 statements at some point and possibly to nuance or change them where necessary. Of course, we may find that he did not do so; but we cannot simply assume that 1520 remains normative[t] in either expression or content for Luther over the next twenty-six years.

> **Remember?**
> "That Luther's declaration" begins a long noun clause. Where does it end?

Knowing the Times

[¶8] Another part of reading Luther correctly is knowing how he himself understood the times in which he was living. We noted in chapter 1 that Luther experienced a violent and extreme change of mind on the matter of the Jews. In 1523, he argued that they should be treated well by Christian neighbors, to open opportunities for the gospel. In 1543, however, he argued that they should be subject to persecution and, where possible, genocide.ᵘ The change in mind is significant, not simply for exemplifying the bitter anger of a man reaching the end of his life but also for illustrating his transformed understanding of the times.

[¶9] The change actually reflects in part Luther's eschatological frustration. He was heir of the late medieval view that the world was coming to an end and that Christ would soon return. In the early years of the Reformation, the spectacular and unlikely successes of the Reformation seemed to indicate that this was indeed happening. When Luther began to be identified with figures in the book of Revelation after the Diet of Worms, the eschatological expectation took on a heightened and concreteᵛ form. Yet by the late 1520s, matters were taking a darker turn: the conflict with the radicals and then with Zwingli had fragmented the Reformation movement. Squabblingʷ and petty rivalries among the Lutherans were weakening the cause. The nobles had shown themselves to be more interested in secular power than in true reform. All of this implied that perhaps the end was not as near as expected and that the Reformation might not be setting the stage for the imminent return of Christ.

[¶10] How does this impinge uponˣ the question before us? It is significant because there is a world of difference between how one preaches when convinced that God is moving with eschatological decisiveness and is bringing history to its close and how one preaches when bracingʸ for the long haul. In 1522, Luther was able to boast from the pulpit that the Reformation succeeded because he, Melanchthon, and Amsdorf sat in the pub drinking beer while the Word of God did all the work. That is the kind of bravuraᶻ statement a man can make who is supremely confident that history is flowing precisely his way. But by 1527–28, the picture looked somewhat different. By then, it was becoming clear to Luther that the preaching of the Word was not in itself enough to achieve all the things he wished to see done. There was need for nuance, organization, and a clarification and even recalibration of certain doctrines and emphases.

[¶11] In summary, we can now see the problem with the "evangelical Luther canon." The texts were all written at a time when Luther was very confident of the Reformation outcome and very confident that the simple preaching of the Word could do it all. Given his altered understanding of the times after 1525, we cannot automatically assume that statements before that date are normative or that they proved unproblematic even within Luther's own lifetime.[1]

---

1. Carl R. Trueman, *Luther on the Christian Life: Cross and Freedom* (Wheaton, IL: Crossway, 2015), 159–62. Taken from *Luther on the Christian Life: Cross and Freedom* by Carl Trueman, © 2015, pp. (insert). Used by permission of Crossway, a publishing ministry of Good News Publishers, Wheaton, IL 60187, www.crossway.org.

a. Vexed (adj.): causing difficulty with regard to finding an answer
b. Appropriate (v.): to make use of
c. Parlance (n.): a manner or way of speaking
d. Constitute (v.): to make up or form
e. Abstract (adj.): considered apart from application; theoretical
f. Mine (v.): to dig out or extract from rock (used metaphorically here)
g. Vacuous (adj.): empty; lacking content
h. Tract (n.): an area or region
i. Eschew (v.): to abstain from; shun
j. Nuanced (adj.): containing subtle aspects and distinctions
k. Truncate (v.): to shorten or cut off (negative connotation)
l. Aneurysm (n.): the abnormal dilatation of a blood vessel, which can lead to death
m. Controversy (n.): the act of disputing or contending

n. Blistering (adj.): severe and intense
o. Incredulous (adj.): not able or willing to believe something
p. Vernacular (n.): using a language native to a region or country
q. Generate (v.): to produce or lead to
r. Arbitrary (adj.): based on random or convenient selection or choice
s. Implausible (adj.): not likely or probable
t. Normative (adj.): prescriptive or authoritative
u. Genocide (n.): the systematic extermination of a people group
v. Concrete (adj.): specific and particular
w. Squabble (v.): to quarrel noisily and to no purpose
x. Impinge upon (verb phrase): to come into relationship with or make an impression upon
y. Brace (v.): to prepare for
z. Bravura (adj.): aggressively confident or commanding

Post-Reading

What is a *how* or *why* question that you think Trueman might be addressing in this passage?

Many clauses can be reordered to emphasize different elements in the clause. Take this clause as an example: "We can now see the problem with the 'evangelical Luther canon.'" We can position the word "now" in a few places. We could write:

a. We can see, **now**, the problem . . .
b. We can see the problem with the 'evangelical Luther canon' **now**.
c. **Now** we can see the problem with . . .
d. We can see the problem, **now**, with the . . .

The different placement of the adverb "now" (grammar) may lead to different emphases in pronunciation (phonology). It also may send slightly different messages to the hearers (reference). Options (a) and (d) interrupt the flow of the clause to add a comment before we are told "what" we can see. This interruption might allow the speaker to stress the word "problem" more easily. Option (b) carries out the full statement before offering the adverb, and may allow the speaker to stress the adverb. Option (c) allows us to stress the adverb at the very beginning of the clause. The grammatical, or syntactic, flexibility we have with the placement of the adverb is related to our pronunciation and our message.

Main Ideas and Details

(1) In your own words, summarize what Trueman means by "the evangelical Luther canon."

(2) True or False: In this passage, the author's main concern is to answer the question, "Does Luther's theology have a place for sanctification?"

(3) Which sentence below best summarizes the main idea(s) of the passage?
a. The progressive nature of the Reformation means that Luther's theology was always developing.
b. There is no "evangelical Luther canon" because scholars disagree on which works belong in that canon.
c. Understanding Luther's eschatology will help us to appreciate his treatment of Jews at the beginning and end of his life.
d. The progressive nature of the Reformation and the complexities of Luther's life demand that we account for context before assessing his theology.

(4) At the end of paragraph 1, the author writes, "These are not abstract issues but rather points of concern for every Christian." Which of the following may he be implying?
a. Many readers are very interested in abstract issues.

b. Many readers will think of "sanctification" as very concrete.

c. Many readers might think that the questions he has listed are impractical.

d. All readers would understand that these questions only apply to some Christians.

(5) In paragraph 2, why does the author mention Twitter?

a. To provide an example of a bad approach to understanding a famous theologian's beliefs.

b. To explain why it is good to use a topical approach to studying a theologian's doctrine.

c. To express his embrace of new technology in making it easier for people to learn about theologians.

(6) In paragraph 3, the author mentions "proof texting." Is this a positive or a negative thing? What does the author mean by this phrase?

(7) Based on the context in paragraph 4, "sound bites" most likely means _____.

a. Words that are spoken loudly.

b. Words that are commonly cited.

c. Words that are theologically sound.

d. Words that can easily be understood.

(8) In paragraph 6, what do the words "pastoral, theological, and social" modify?

(9) In paragraph 7, to what does the word "so" refer?

(10) The author uses the word "heir" in paragraph 9 to mean that _____.

a. Luther inherited a view from the medieval era.

b. Luther considered medieval theologians to be royal.

c. Luther was the next major theologian, following the medieval era.

d. Luther's early success in the Reformation can be attributed to medieval theology.

(11) What is the purpose that paragraph 10 plays in the author's argument?

a. It provides new information about Luther's context and how his context changed over time.

b. It concludes the author's argument by summarizing how Luther's beliefs changed over time.

c. It takes the previous information about Luther's context and applies it to the discussion of why Luther's views changed.

Understanding the Passage

Place an "A" next to the statements with which you think the author would agree, and a "D" next to the statements with which you think he would disagree.

1. _____ Social media such as Twitter have had a positive influence on scholarship.

2. _____ We should be critical of the concept of an "evangelical Luther canon."

3. _____ Popular evangelical approaches to Luther usually account for his entire life.

4. _____ Luther continued revising and refining his theology after 1525.

5. _____ Luther's eschatology significantly shaped his treatment of the Jews.

Collocations

Select the most appropriate word from the choices in the parentheses. All of these examples of collocations have been taken directly from the reading.

When investigating a historical figure, we should consider how that figure's work affects us in practical (*words/terms/sayings*). Does the person's thought shed light on our own ethical (*doings/behavior/acting*), or does it leave our moral development entirely (*unaffected/unused/ignored*)? Do we come away from our study of the figure noticing that we have obvious (*problems/hurts/pains*) with our own approach to a given topic? Does the figure's thought have a positive or negative (*role/act/job*) when it comes to our assessment of contemporary life? These are questions that will help us to benefit practically from a study of history.

Match the words on the left to the words they occur with on the right.

rarely	anger
unforeseen	noticed
bitter	power
secular	consequences
imminent	assume
automatically	return

Grammar Focus: Noun Phrases

In the previous lesson, we looked at noun clauses and how they can convey complex relations and processes that cannot be captured in a word or simple phrase. But phrases themselves can still add much information to your sentences, depending on how complex your phrases are. And while phrases are often less complex than clauses, they are not always easy to form, especially longer ones. The difficulty comes from building up the noun phrase around the head noun. Note the noun phrases in the following paragraph.

The change actually reflects in part Luther's eschatological frustration. He was heir of the late medieval view that the world was coming to an end and that Christ would soon return. In the early years of the Reformation, the spectacular and unlikely successes of the Reformation seemed to indicate that this was indeed happening. When Luther began to be identified with figures in the book of Revelation after the Diet of Worms, the eschatological expectation took on a heightened and concrete form. Yet by the late 1520s, matters were taking a darker turn: the conflict with the radicals and then with Zwingli had fragmented the Reformation movement. Squabbling and petty rivalries among the Lutherans were weakening the cause. The nobles had shown themselves to be more interested in secular power than in true reform. All of this implied that perhaps the end was not as near as expected and that the Reformation might not be setting the stage for the imminent return of Christ.

As we noted in an earlier lesson, noun phrases are units in which words are "built" around a noun, usually called the head noun. Sometimes these words precede the head noun, and other times they follow it, as shown below. What patterns do you notice?

Preceding Words	Head Noun	Following Words
Luther's eschatological	frustration	_____
_____	heir	of the late medieval view
the early	years	of the Reformation
the spectacular and unlikely	successes	of the Reformation
_____	figures	in the book of Revelation
the eschatological	expectation	_____
a heightened and concrete	form	_____
the	conflict	with the radicals
the Reformation	movement	_____

Preceding Words	Head Noun	Following Words
secular	power	_____
true	reform	_____
the imminent	return	of Christ

In the left hand column we find adjectives, and in the right hand column we find prepositional phrases. This is common way of structuring a noun phrase. The head noun falls in the middle of the phrase and is preceded by an adjective, followed by a prepositional phrase, or both. See if these patterns occur again in the following activities. Do you encounter any new patterns?

Activity 1

Underline the noun phrases in the following paragraph. Circle the head noun in each phrase.

Luther's basic position on righteousness is set forth in his 1519 sermon "Two Kinds of Righteousness." There he distinguishes between alien and proper righteousness. *Alien righteousness* is that which the Christian obtains when he receives Christ by faith. This is an infinite righteousness that swallows up all sins and renders the believer perfect before God. There is progression in this righteousness, but it is progression gauged by growth in faith and knowledge of Christ, and thus should not be confused with growth in what we might term actual righteousness. *Proper righteousness* involves the slaying of the flesh and the crucifying of wicked desires, coupled with the performance of good works for our neighbors. This is akin to what we might typically call the work of sanctification, and it has an outward manifestation.[2]

Activity 2

Use the following head nouns to create noun phrases of your own. An example is provided in the first row.

Head Noun	Noun Phrase
Position	Luther's position on eschatology
Righteousness	
Eschatology	
Perspective	
Decision	
Power	

2. Ibid., 162–63.

Activity 3

Using some of the noun phrases you created in Activity 2, summarize (in two to three sentences) why Trueman feels we should be critical of the "evangelical Luther canon." When you have finished your summary, underline the noun phrases and circle the head nouns.

Learning the Genre: Church History

Church History

Thus far, we have examined the genres of apologetics and biblical studies. We now move on to consider church history.[3] As a genre, church history is often concerned to show "how a given event, written work or important individual relates to surrounding historical forces," and so authors in this genre may attempt "to explain why an event, written work, person, movement or doctrine took the particular shape it did."[4] As mentioned in the previous chapter, focus on the words *why* and *how* when trying to remember the aim of church history writing.

What might be some of the "distinctive and recognizable patterns and norms of organization" in this genre? Read the following paragraphs and look for what is unique as compared to writing in the areas of apologetics and biblical studies.

> For Luther, the doctrine of justification is the article by which the Church stands or falls, the acid test of what is truly Christian. His distinctive development of the doctrine is inextricably linked with the troubles of his own soul and his desperate search for a gracious God. The medieval system within which he was nurtured taught that justification involved a process of being made righteous and that the believer only had to do his best and God would save him. The problem of how to decide whether one had done one's best was, of course, lethal for assurance: the subjectivity of the process left conscientious individuals in constant fear that they had not quite done as much as they could and were thus liable to be damned.
>
> According to Luther's own account, his problems focused on the text of Rom. 1:17, which declares that the righteousness of God is revealed in the gospel. The understanding of righteousness which Luther's teachers in the *via moderna* had taught him was the classic Ciceronian definition: righteousness was giving to each person what he deserved. Such a definition became problematic when applied to God. After all, how could such justice be gospel, that is, good news: for someone as conscious of his sin as Luther, being rewarded with what he deserved could only lead to despair. If God's righteousness was truly good news, it could not be understood in the way accepted by the *via moderna*.
>
> The insight came when Luther realized that the righteousness of God was not some objective standard by which God assessed the individual's worthiness of entering heaven, but that by which God made the sinner righteous and saved him.[5]

What did you find? In our genre study of apologetics, we asked what the author's communicative goal was in a paragraph. Let us ask that same question

---

3. Recall our definition of a genre: a genre is "a type of discourse that occurs in a particular setting, that has distinctive and recognizable patterns and norms of organization and structure, and that has particular and distinctive communicative functions." Jack C. Richards and Richard Schmidt, *Longman Dictionary of Language Teaching and Applied Linguistics*, 3rd ed. (New York: Longman, 2002), 224.

4. Center for Theological Writing, "Writing for Church History," Westminster Theological Seminary, accessed January 25, 2016, http://www.wts.edu/resources/westminster_center_for_theolog/paper_ formatshtml/wc_churchhistory.html.

5. Carl R. Trueman, *Luther's Legacy: Salvation and English Reformers, 1525–1556* (New York: Oxford University Press, 1994), 56–57. By permission of Oxford University Press.

for the paragraphs above. What are Trueman's *communicative goals* here? What does he want to express? For starters, we might say the following:

- He wants to disclose *why* the doctrine of justification is so central for Luther.
- He wants to show *how* Luther came to be concerned with a particular understanding of justification.
- He wants to situate his answers in the historical movements of that time.
- He wants to describe the particular context in which we should understand Luther.

Genre Traits and Tools

We have noted that each theological genre has **genre traits**, that is, features distinct to a kind of writing. Given the nature of the communicative goals we have outlined above, the predominant traits on which we might focus for church history are *signals of time and context*. Note some of these signals in Trueman's writing and the purposes they serve.

Signal	Time or Context	Purpose
"the troubles of his own soul and his desperate search for a gracious God"	Context	to show the reader that we are focused on Luther's biographical context
"the medieval system within which he was nurtured"	Time/Context	to situate Luther in the post-medieval era
"according to Luther's own account"	Context	to point the reader to the context of Luther's own writing
"The understanding of righteousness which Luther's teachers in the *via moderna* had taught him was the classic Ciceronian definition."	Time/Context	to situate Luther in his historical setting by pointing out a historical movement (the *via moderna*)
"for someone as conscious of his sin as Luther"	Context	to show the reader that we are focused on Luther's biographical context
"The insight came when Luther realized that the righteousness of God was not some objective standard . . . ."	Time	to point out when, in Luther's life, he developed his view of justification

Even within these "signals" that the author sends, there are key words that focus especially on time, or context, or both.

his own soul—subjective context
medieval—time period
own account—Luther's writing
via moderna—intellectual movement (time and context)

his sin—subjective context
when—time

Certainly, these signals can vary from author to author; there are many different forms of them, and we must be careful not to be too mechanical about finding them. But many of the church historians you will encounter will make it clear that they are concerned with both time and context—historical, economic, political, intellectual, and so forth.

Activity 4

Read the passages below and then answer the questions that follow. In Passage 1, historian Henry Chadwick discusses the influence that Cicero's writing had on Augustine of Hippo. As you read, think about the *how* or *why* question that Chadwick is addressing.

Passage 1

The most potent initial influence guiding the young Augustine in philosophical matters came from Cicero's dialogues. Of the many works of Cicero which Augustine knew intimately, one dialogue called *Hortensius*, vindicating the necessity of philosophical thinking for any critical judgment even for someone engaged in public and political life, exercised an extraordinary, catalytic effect. In the works of his [Augustine's] old age he was still to be quoting phrases from this book which he first read as a nineteen-year-old student at Carthage. Cicero partly adapted for the Roman world an exhortation to study philosophy written by no less than Aristotle himself. Cicero's ideal was personal self-sufficiency and an awareness that happiness, which everyone seeks, is not found in a self-indulgent life of pleasure, which merely destroys both self-respect and true friendships. Contemplating the paradox that everyone sets out to be happy and the majority are thoroughly wretched, Cicero concluded with the pregnant suggestion that man's misery may be a kind of judgment of providence, and our life now may even be an atonement for sins in a prior incarnation. The *Hortensius* also included a warning that the pursuit of bodily pleasure in food, drink, and sex, is distracting for the mind in pursuit of higher things. . . .

The immediate effect of reading *Hortensius* was to make Augustine think seriously about ethical and religious issues. His father had been a pagan, baptized only on his deathbed. He was hot-tempered and not always faithful to his wife; Augustine betrays no sign of having felt close to him. His mother, on the other hand, was devout in Christian faith and practice, daily at prayers in her local church, often guided by dreams and visions. As a skeptical teenager he used occasionally to attend church services with her, but found himself mainly engaged in catching the eye of the girls on the other side of the basilica. At Carthage aged nineteen he found that the seriousness of the questions raised by Cicero, especially about the quest for happiness, moved him to pick up a Latin Bible. He was repelled by the obscurity of its content and the barbarous style of the rather primitive version made by half-educated missionaries in the second century. The Old Latin Bible (the reconstruction of which by modern scholars has been a remarkable critical operation) was not a book to impress a man whose mind was full of elegant Ciceronian diction and Virgilian turns of phrase, and who enjoyed good plays at the theatre. In disgust Augustine turned away from what seemed a naïve myth about Adam and Eve and from the doubtful morality of the Israelite patriarchs.[6]

(1) In your own words, what do you think the "how" or "why" question is that Chadwick is trying to answer?

(2) What signals of time or context did you find? Underline at least three.

(3) Are there other features of this example that you have not yet encountered in the readings thus far? In your own words, try to describe them.

In the next passage, Jaroslav Pelikan discusses the allegorical interpretation of Scripture by the early Christian apologists. Again, as you read, think about the *how* or *why* question that the author is addressing. Then answer the questions that follow.

Passage 2

The reply of the apologists to [the challenge that immortality is not a gift of God] has also continued to affect the development of Christian doctrine both directly and indirectly. It was at least partly in response to pagan criticism of the stories in the Bible that the Christian apologists, like their Jewish predecessors, took over and adapted the methods and even the vocabulary of pagan allegorism. Not even the most shocking of biblical narratives could match the crudity and "blasphemous nonsense" of the Greek myths, in which the gods were depicted as being superhuman not in virtue but in endurance, "not more superior in dominion than in vice." The apologists recited lengthy catalogs of the amorous exploits of the gods, taking care to note that these pornographic details were being quoted from the pagan authors themselves. Those who held to such shameful accounts of the divine had no right to reproach the Christian narrative of "the birth of God in the form of a man. . . . For it is not permissible even to compare our conception of God with those who are wallowing in filth and mud." If the myths were true, they should not be admitted in public; if they were false, they should not be circulated among religious people. A common way out of this difficulty among sophisticated pagans was allegorical exegesis. A sophisticated pagan such as Celsus "claims that his own exegesis of ancient writers is in harmony with their intention

6. Henry Chadwick, *Augustine* (New York: Oxford University Press, 1986), 9–11. By permission of Oxford University Press.

of handing down the truth in veiled form, to be uncovered by philosophical exegesis, while Jewish and Christian exegesis is merely defensive"; Porphyry accused Origen of misapplying Hellenistic allegory to the Jewish Scriptures. In his reply to Celsus, Origen was willing to concede at least some validity to the allegorical exegesis of the Homeric poems. Most Christian writers, however, denounced Stoic and other allegory as "the veneer of sophistic disputes by which not the truth but its image and appearance and shadow are always sought after." At one and the same time the apologists cited the pagan philosophers against pagan religion and denounced them for the artificiality of their efforts to square their teachings with Homer and Hesiod. Seneca was "often in agreement with us"; but Socrates was the most important of all, because he had refrained from allegorizing Homer and had banished him.

The reason for this importance was that Christ had been "known in part even by Socrates." As the apologists came to grips with the defenders of paganism, they were compelled to acknowledge that Christianity and its ancestor, Judaism, did not have a monopoly on either the moral or the doctrinal teachings whose superiority Christian apologetics was seeking to demonstrate. To some extent this acknowledgement was a tacit admission of the presence within Christian thought of doctrines borrowed from Greek philosophy. To account for the presence of such teachings in pagan philosophy, the apologists drew upon several devices. Justin sought to draw a connection between the philosophers and the preexistent Logos. It was the seed of reason in man which enabled pagan thinkers like Socrates to see dimly what came to be clearly seen through the revelation of the Logos in the person of Jesus. As the Logos had been adumbrated in various ways during the history of Israel, so also what paganism had learned about God and about the good life could be traced to the universal functioning of the Logos. The Stoics, the poets, and the historians all "spoke well in proportion to the share [they] had of the seminal Logos." But now that the seminal Logos had come in person, those who had been under his tutelage could find the fuller meaning of their intuitions. For Origen, too, the "Logos who came to dwell in Jesus . . . inspired men before that." The apologists' use of the idea of the Logos in their dispute with classicism certainly helped to establish this title in the Christian vocabulary about Christ, but other factors were no less important.[7]

(1) In your own words, what do you think the "how" or "why" question is that Pelikan is trying to answer? (Hint: keep in mind the key word that is repeated throughout the passage.)

7. Jaroslav Pelikan, *The Christian Tradition: A History of the Development of Doctrine*, vol. 1, *The Emergence of the Catholic Tradition* (100–600) (Chicago: University of Chicago Press, 1971), 30–32. See the original for references to the apologists of the early church and to the classical sources cited in this passage. Republished with permission of University of Chicago Press, from Jaroslav Pelikan, *The Christian Tradition: A History of the Development of Doctrine*, vol. 1, *The Emergence of the Catholic Tradition* (100–600) (Chicago: University of Chicago Press. 1971).

(2) What signals of time or context did you find? Underline at least three.

(3) What does the author hope to convince you of in this passage? In other words, what is his (implied) thesis?

The Relevance of History (CH Task 1)

Introduction

History is full of truth and insight that can be communicated powerfully to people today. It is possible for gifted history teachers "to construct narratives of the past in a way that unlocks that past for an audience in the present."[8] In other words, history is *relevant*—it is important and meaningful for us right now.

In fact, history has a special meaning and relevance for Christians.[9] The person and work of Christ in history is the climax of history itself. What the Father has done through the Son by the power of the Spirit changes us in the present and orients us toward the future. Moreover, we trust that we can know this because we believe that God has communicated with us in Scripture, through history, in a clear and trustworthy manner. We believe what the Bible says about what happened in history and what will happen in eternity. So, for Christians, history could not be more relevant! What God has done in the past, and what the biblical writers have reported in the pages of Scripture, is what our faith stands upon today.

Task

A documentary about how people today view the Bible is on television, and you decide to watch it. At the beginning of the documentary, someone interviews lay people, asking them what they think about biblical history. One man says, "I love history, but only objective history, so I don't think the Bible is really relevant." Respond to this man's comment about objectivity and relevance with a brief paragraph (3–5 sentences). Consider the quotation by Carl Trueman that we provided at the beginning of Lesson 19: "While there is no such thing as neutrality in the telling of history, there is such a thing as objectivity."[10]

8. Carl R. Trueman, *Histories and Fallacies: Problems Faced in the Writing of History* (Wheaton, IL: Crossway, 2010), 15.
9. "All that has happened in the past, all that happens in the present, and all that will happen in the future rests for its presupposition upon the self-sufficient internal activity of the self-predicating and therefore non-delimited being [the Triune God]." Cornelius Van Til, *Introduction to Systematic Theology: Prolegomena and the Doctrines of Revelation, Scripture, and God*, ed. William Edgar, 2nd ed. (Phillipsburg, NJ: P&R Publishing, 2007), 337.
10. Trueman, *Histories and Fallacies*, 21.

20

Looking Further Back

"There are two thousand years' worth of Christian stories to tell . . . ."
—Diarmaid MacCulloch, *Christianity: The First Three Thousand Years*

Lesson Goals

Theology—To recognize the subtle interpretations of church historians
Reading—To learn how to identify an author's stance
Vocabulary—To learn and use additional collocations from the reading passage
Grammar—To practice describing nouns using various structures

---

Introduction

In the previous lesson and the genre study on church history, we noted that church historians are often concerned with *how* and *why* questions, and that context is very important when they go about searching for answers to such questions.

You could probably see from the reading passages that another common feature of church history writing (and of history writing in general) is the reporting of information. Church historians aim to inform their readers about what happened in the past, and so they constantly make statements about people, events, and dates. Look at some of these statements in the following sentences.

Like the saintly Bishop Cyril of Alexandria, Jerome is not a man to whom it is easy to warm, although he certainly had a powerful effect on various pious and wealthy ladies in late-fourth-century Rome. One feels that he was a man with a six-point plan for becoming a saint, taking in the papacy on the way.[1]

Such reporting of information might seem purely impersonal and objective. But when we look a bit closer, the author's interpretation of this information begins to surface. For instance, the author says that Jerome is not easy to "warm to," that is, to like. Can the author support this claim universally, or is he generalizing based on a few written documents and a contemporary view of Jerome's behavior? In the second sentence, he says, "One feels . . . ." This language is more explicitly telling the reader that this is his (the author's) understanding of Jerome, but we should not take this understanding as normative simply because it was given to us by a church historian.[2]

---

1. Diarmaid MacCulloch, *Christianity: The First Three Thousand Years* (New York: Viking, 2009), 300–301.
2. "I . . . argue that all histories are provisional in the sense that no one can offer an exhaustive account of any past action, given the limited state of the evidence and the historian's inevitably limited grasp of context as well as distance from the past. But provisional merely means limited and subject to refinement; it does not make all readings of the evidence equally valid, or equally unreliable." Carl R. Trueman, *Histories and Fallacies: Problems Faced in the Writing of History* (Wheaton, IL: Crossway, 2010), 21.

This leads us to another element of church history writing that is important to discuss: the issue of **stance**, that is, an author's beliefs, opinions, and assumptions. We will explore this in the Reading Skills section below. Stance is not something that is restricted to church history; it is present in all of the genres, but we will focus on it in this lesson because the reading passage provides a particularly good example of it.

Background for the Reading

It is important to keep in mind the quotation from Carl Trueman in the previous task, especially the first part: "there is no such thing as neutrality in the telling of history."[3] The author whom we will read in this section believes that Christianity has many stories to tell. But believing that Christianity has many stories to tell and believing *in* those stories are two very different things. As you read, take note of the assumptions that come through in the author's language. What does the author's language suggest about his view of Christianity?

Reading Skills: Identifying an Author's Stance

Each writer brings his beliefs, opinions, and presuppositions to his writing. These constitute the author's *stance* on a subject. In many texts, particularly in textbooks and newspaper articles, the author attempts to maintain a neutral or unbiased stance. However, in many journal articles, essays, and books, the author wants his readers to know his opinion. Good readers can identify the author's stance and use that to help evaluate the validity of his or her argument.

In some texts, particularly editorials or other opinion pieces, the author clearly states his or her opinion. You can often locate this opinion by looking for first-person pronouns (I, my, etc.) and opinion statements. For example, in the Trueman passage from Lesson 19, we read, "In this chapter, however, I am going to argue that this kind of proof texting is to be eschewed on an issue such as this."[4]

In most texts, however, the author expresses his opinion less directly. MacCulloch, for instance, writes "One feels" (third person) rather than "I feel" (first person). In this section, we will discuss two of these less direct methods, learn how to recognize them, and practice making inferences based on what we know from the text.

Strategies for Identifying an Author's Stance

Word Choice

A word has a definition (the word's denotation) and connotations, that is, feelings or qualities that the word implies. These connotations can be positive or negative. If an author is expressing his support of an idea, he is likely to use words with positive connotations. If an author does not support or agree with what he is describing, he is likely to use words with negative connotations. Below are two examples, the first of words with positive connotations, and the second of words with negative connotations. In both examples, the important words are **bolded**.

The **most potent** initial influence guiding the young Augustine in philosophical matters came from Cicero's dialogues. Of the many works of Cicero which Augustine knew **intimately**, one dialogue called *Hortensius*, **vindicating** the necessity of philosophical thinking for any critical judgment even for someone engaged in public and political life, exercised an **extraordinary**, **catalytic** effect.[5]

When, in later years, Augustine came to discuss the concept of original sin, that **fatal flaw** which in his theology all humans have inherited from the sin of Adam and Eve, he saw it as **inseparable from** the sexual act, which transmits sin from one generation to another. It was a view **momentous** in its consequences for the Western Church's attitude to sexuality.[6]

---

3. Ibid., 21.

4. Carl R. Trueman, *Luther on the Christian Life: Cross and Freedom*, Theologians on the Christian Life (Wheaton, IL: Crossway, 2015), 159–62.

5. Henry Chadwick, *Augustine* (New York: Oxford University Press, 1986), 9–11.

6. Diarmaid MacCulloch, *Christianity: The First Three Thousand Years* (New York: Viking, 2009), 301-3. Excerpt(s) from *Christianity: The First Three Thousand Years* by Diarmaid MacCulloch, copyright © 2010 by Diarmaid MacCulloch. Used by permission of Viking Books, an imprint of Penguin Publishing Group, a division of Penguin Random House LLC. All rights reserved.

Think about the words the authors are using. In the second example, the passage would have a different impact if it was worded this way: "Reflecting back on his life, Augustine came to discuss the concept of original sin which he believed was linked to the sexual act, and this belief has shaped the way the Western Church has viewed sexuality." Simply by calling original sin a "fatal flaw," MacCulloch hints that his opinion differs from Augustine's.

Hedging Language

In addition to a word's connotation, the tentative or strong nature of the verb can indicate an author's stance. If an author feels strongly about a position, he is likely to use modal verbs (*will*, *shall*) and adverbs (*definitely*, *strongly*) that express his stance. Or he may not use any modal verbs, and this can also be a clue that he feels strongly that the position he is writing about is correct.

If an author is unsure about a position or wants to distance himself from it, he will use modal verbs such as *may*, *could*, and *might*. He may also use more tentative adverbs such as *probably* and *possibly*.

As you read, notice the strength of the verbs. Is the author expressing support with certainty? Is the author proposing a conclusion of which he is uncertain? Is he trying to distance himself from the position he is describing?

Practice: Read the paragraph below that comes from the reading in this lesson. Underline each word with negative connotations.

Yet increasingly he was dissatisfied by Manichaean belief, and as he pursued academic success in Rome and Milan he was haunted by doubts and anxieties about the nature of truth, reality and wisdom. As he ceased to find Manichaeism of use, he turned to Neoplatonist belief, but in Milan he also became fascinated by Bishop Ambrose. Here, for the first time, he met a Christian whose self-confident culture he could respect and whose sermons, sonorous and rich in their language, made up for the crudity and vulgarity of the Bible which had distressed the young Augustine. Even though he remained embarrassed by his mother's demonstrative piety (she had followed him to Milan), he now contemplated a faith which united the imperious nobleman in the pulpit with the elderly woman from a provincial backwater. The contradictory influences of career and Christian renunciation came to tear him apart and made him disgusted with his ambitions.[7]

Pre-Reading

As you read, think about what MacCulloch's overall opinion of Augustine is. Where does he express a negative stance? Where does he express a positive stance?

Reading

In the following passage, Diarmaid MacCulloch, a popular church historian, introduces us to Augustine of Hippo.

[¶1] Augustine was a Latin-speaking theologian who had little interest in Greek literature, only came to the Greek language late in life, read virtually[a] nothing of Plato or Aristotle, and had very little influence on the Greek Church, which in fact came to look with profound[b] disapproval on one aspect of his theological legacy, a modification of the Nicene Creed. By contrast, his impact on Western Christian thought can hardly be overstated; only his beloved example, Paul of Tarsus, has been more influential, and Westerners have generally

7. Ibid., 302.

seen Paul through Augustine's eyes. He is one of the few writers from the early Church era some of whose work can still be read for pleasure, particularly his remarkable and perhaps too revealing self-analysis in his *Confessions*, a gigantic prayer-narrative which is a direct conversation—I-Thou—with God. His life was played out[c] against the background of the rise, final splendor and fall of the Christian Western Empire, but apart from these great political traumas,[d] his life's work can be seen as a series of responses to conflicts both internal and external.

[¶2] The first struggle was with himself. Who did he want to be and how would he find a truth which would satisfy him? He was brought up in the 350s and 360s in small-town North Africa. His father, Patricius (of whom he says little), was a non-Christian; his mother, Monica, a deeply pious if not very intellectual member of the Catholic Church. The relationship of mother and son was intense and often conflicted. Augustine reacted against her unsophisticated[e] religion, and after his parents had scrimped and saved to send him to the School of Carthage, he was increasingly drawn by the excitements of university life to the philosophy and literature of Rome. The world was at his feet; he settled down with a mistress and she bore him a son whose name, Adeodatus ('Given by God'), may have been a reflection of the fact that the baby's arrival was evidently[f] unplanned. But even as Augustine began an exceptionally promising career as a teacher of rhetoric (the language study which lay at the heart of Latin culture, a ticket to success and perhaps a political career), he was becoming tormented by anxieties which remained his theological preoccupations[g] all his life.

[¶3] What was the source of evil and suffering in this world? This was the ancient religious question which the gnostics had tried to answer by picturing existence as an eternally dualistic[h] struggle, and it was the gnostic religion of Augustine's day, Manichaeism, which first won his allegiance and held it for nine years. Yet increasingly he was dissatisfied by Manichaean belief, and as he pursued academic success in Rome and Milan he was haunted by doubts and anxieties about the nature of truth, reality and wisdom. As he ceased to find Manichaeism of use, he turned to Neoplatonist belief, but in Milan he also became fascinated by Bishop Ambrose. Here, for the first time, he met a Christian whose self-confident culture he could respect and whose sermons, sonorous[i] and rich in their language, made up for the crudity[j] and vulgarity of the Bible which had distressed the young Augustine. Even though he remained embarrassed by his mother's demonstrative[k] piety (she had followed him to Milan), he now contemplated a faith which united the imperious[l] nobleman in the pulpit with the elderly woman from a provincial[m] backwater. The contradictory influences of career and Christian renunciation[n] came to tear him apart and made him disgusted with his ambitions. To add to his pain, on his mother's urging, in 385 he broke with his mistress in order to make a good marriage. The woman went back to Africa, swearing to remain

Remember?
"One of the few **writers** from the early Church era" is a complex noun phrase.

faithful to him—in the middle of his narrative of worldly renunciation in the *Confessions*, Augustine at least had the grace to record her resolution, even though he could not bring himself to name her. We may wonder what she felt as she slipped out of the life of the man who had been her companion for fifteen years, leaving behind her charming and talented teenage son to her lover's care.

[¶4] In a state bordering on nervous breakdown, and physically unwell, Augustine arrived in 386 at a crisis which was to bring him a new serenity[o] and a new certainty. In his own account, the crucial prompting[p] was the voice of a child overheard in a garden—children seem to have had a good sense of timing in Milan. The repetitive chant sounded to Augustine like *'tolle lege'*—'take it and read.' The book Augustine had to hand was the Epistles of Paul, which he opened at random at the words of Romans 13, from what is now verses 13–14: 'put on the Lord Jesus Christ, and make no provision for the flesh, to gratify its desires . . .' It was enough to bring him back fully to his mother's faith and it meant that his plans for marriage were abandoned for a life of celibacy. Another woman spurned:[q] the fiancée has received no more consideration than the mistress from historians until modern times. On Augustine's announcement of the resolution of his torment, Monica 'was jubilant with triumph and glorified you . . . And you turned her sadness into rejoicing . . . far sweeter and more chaste than any she had hope to find in children begotten of my flesh.' There is more than one way of interpreting this maternal triumph. When, in later years, Augustine came to discuss the concept of original sin, that fatal flaw which in his theology all humans have inherited from the sin of Adam and Eve, he saw it as inseparable from the sexual act, which transmits[r] sin from one generation to another. It was a view momentous[s] in its consequences for the Western Church's attitude to sexuality.

[¶5] Augustine found his conversion a liberation from torment. One element in his crisis had been the impact of meeting a fellow North African who had been thrown into a state of deep self-doubt and worry about his own successful administrative career by an encounter with Athanasius's *Life of Antony*. Now Augustine determined on his own abandonment of ambition, leaving his teaching career to follow Antony's example—after a fashion, for his was to be the life of the desert minus the desert and plus a good library. His plan was to create a celibate religious community with cultivated[t] friends back in his home town: a monastery which would bring the best of the culture of old Rome into a Christian context. This congenial[u] scheme was soon ended by the turbulent[v] Church politics of North Africa. Augustine's Catholic Christian Church was connected with the rest of the Mediterranean Church and with the deep-rooted localism of the Donatists, cherishing grievances[w] now a century old from the Great Persecution of Diocletian and including some of the ablest theologians of the African Church.[8]

8. Ibid., 301–3.

a. Virtually (adv.): almost entirely
b. Profound (adj.): deeply realized or felt
c. Play Out (verb phrase): to unfold
d. Trauma (n.): a psychological or emotional stress or blow that may produce disordered feelings or behavior
e. Unsophisticated (adj.): lacking complexity; plain and simple
f. Evidently (adv.): clearly or obviously
g. Preoccupation (n.): something that engages the attention
h. Dualistic (adj.): characterized by the doctrine that the universe is under the dominion of two opposing principles, one of which is good and the other evil
i. Sonorous (adj.): marked by imposing or impressive effect or style (describing speech)
j. Crudity (n.): the quality or state of lacking refinement or subtlety

k. Demonstrative (adj.): easily seen or demonstrated
l. Imperious (adj.): majestic or stately
m. Provincial (adj.): lacking the refinement of urban society
n. Renunciation (n.): the act of rejecting or giving something up
o. Serenity (n.): peacefulness
p. Prompt (v.): to serve as the cause of thought or action
q. Spurn (v.): to treat with disdain or contempt
r. Transmit (v.): to pass on or spread
s. Momentous (adj.): very important
t. Cultivated (adj.): socially well-trained, cultured, and educated
u. Congenial (adj.): agreeable, pleasant, or attractive
v. Turbulent (adj.): causing great unrest; inciting violence
w. Grievance (n.): anger, annoyance, displeasure

Post-Reading

Now that you have read the passage, how would you describe the author's opinion of Augustine?

Main Ideas and Details

(1) Which of the following expresses the author's goal in this passage?
 a. To support the claim that Augustine was a pious saint.
 b. To describe Augustine's relationship with his mother, Monica.
 c. To show that Augustine is an important figure in church history.
 d. To summarize major events and note important figures in Augustine's life.

(2) The pronoun "which" in paragraph 1 refers to _____.
 a. Greek literature.
 b. The Greek Church.
 c. Plato and Aristotle.
 d. The Greek language.

(3) The author begins paragraphs 2 and 3 with questions. What purpose do these questions serve?
 a. They express the internal conflicts that Augustine was experiencing.
 b. They are questions that Augustine asks and then answers in his *Confessions*.

 c. They are questions that the author wants each reader to ask of his own life.
 d. They act as rhetorical questions that the author assumes the readers can easily answer.

(4) Based on paragraph 4, what can we infer about MacCulloch's view of Augustine?
 a. MacCulloch thinks that Augustine dealt with the women in his life in a loving way.
 b. MacCulloch does not think that Augustine treated the women in his life with respect.
 c. MacCulloch believes that Augustine received a special call from God through the voice of a child.
 d. Augustine cared about the physical and spiritual well-being of all of the people who came into his life.

(5) In paragraph 4, the author writes, "There is more than one way of interpreting this maternal triumph." Based on what follows this sentence, what might the author be implying?
 a. Augustine considered marital sex to be an act of pure love.
 b. Augustine did not consider original sin to be a biblical teaching.
 c. Augustine's decision to be celibate is what his mother had always longed for.
 d. It was Augustine's view of sin, rather than his mother's encouragement, that lead him to be celibate.

(6) What is the referent of the pronoun "it" in paragraph 4?

(7) To what does the highlighted phrase in paragraph 5, "this congenial scheme," refer?

Understanding the Passage

Write an "A" next to the statements with which you think the author would agree. Write a "D" next to the statements with which you think he would disagree.

1. _____ From an early age, Augustine was very familiar with the Greek language and Greek culture.

2. _____ In his *Confessions*, Augustine is formal and modest.

3. _____ Augustine's mother was blessed with profound intellectual insight.

4. _____ Questions about the nature of evil, truth, and reality can have a profound impact on any person.

5. _____ Augustine was especially kind to the women in his life.

6. _____ Augustine's decision to live a life of celibacy was planned and executed thoughtfully.

7. _____ Augustine had a very positive view of human sexuality.

8. _____ Augustine's conversion liberated him from the internal struggles he had faced his whole life.

Collocations

Select the most appropriate word from the choices in the parentheses. All of these examples of collocations have been taken directly from the reading.

Though some people today might have (*little/ few/small*) interest in an early church figure such as Augustine, we can learn much from him. Like all of us, Augustine struggled with his own (*inside/internal*) conflicts: How could he live a truly "good" life? How does Christian faith interact with a person's contemporary culture? While Augustine originally sought a promising (*job/career/life*) as a teacher of rhetoric, he realized that academic (*success/ victory /winning*) would not ultimately fulfill him. The only "good" life that any of us can hope to live is a life that remains (*faithful/trusting/ constant*) to God. All of us, like Augustine, must eventually abandon our (*plans/actions/thoughts*) and surrender to God's will as revealed in Scripture. While in modern (*years/eras/times*) Augustine may seem outdated, studying his life and work can be particularly relevant to us in our own Christian (*setting/context/place*).

Grammar Focus: Describing and Modifying Nouns

We have discussed the use of both noun clauses (Lesson 18) and noun phrases (Lesson 19) as ways to add information to sentences. In this lesson, we will focus even more specifically on how we can describe and modify nouns themselves. Note the structures the author uses to describe or modify nouns in the following paragraph.

The **first** struggle was with himself. Who did he want to be and how would he find a truth which would satisfy him? He was brought up in the 350s and 360s in **small-town** North Africa. His father, Patricius (**of whom he says little**), was **a non-Christian**; his mother, Monica, **a deeply pious if not very intellectual member of the Catholic Church**. The relationship of mother and son was **intense** and **often conflicted**. Augustine reacted against her **unsophisticated** religion, and after his parents had scrimped and saved to send him to the School of Carthage, he was increasingly drawn by the excitements **of university life** to the philosophy and literature **of Rome**. The world was at his feet; he settled down with a mistress and she bore him a son whose name, **Adeodatus ('Given by God')**, may have been a reflection of the fact that the baby's arrival was **evidently unplanned**. But even as Augustine began an **exceptionally promising** career as a teacher **of rhetoric** (the language study **which lay at the**

heart of Latin culture, a ticket to success and perhaps a political career), he was becoming tormented by anxieties **which remained his theological preoccupations all his life**.

MacCulloch uses adjectives, relative clauses, prepositional phrases, and other noun phrases to describe or modify nouns. You have these same options in your own writing as well.

Adjectives/Adjective Phrases	Relative Clauses	Prepositional Phrases	Other Noun Phrases

first
small-town
intense
often conflicted
unsophisticated
evidently unplanned
exceptionally
  promising
	of whom he says
	  little
	which lay at the heart
	  of Latin culture
	which remained
	  his theological
	  preoccupations all
	  his life
		of university
		  life
		of Rome
		of rhetoric
			A deeply pious if not very
			  intellectual member of
			  the Catholic Church
			Adeodatus ('Given by
			  God')
			a ticket to success and
			  perhaps a political
			  career

Activity 1

In the passage below, underline the structures used to describe or modify nouns.

From 387 the Donatists suddenly gained the advantage of political support from a local rebel ruler, Gildo, who established a regime semi-independent of the emperor. In 391 Augustine happened to visit the struggling Catholic congregation in the city of Hippo Regius (now Annaba in Algeria), the most important port of the province after Carthage. The bishop, an idiosyncratic but shrewd old Greek named Valerius, encouraged his flock to bully this brilliant stranger into being ordained priest and soon Augustine was coadjutor (assistant) bishop in the town. From Valerius's death until his own in 430, he remained Bishop of Hippo. All his theological writing was now done against a background of busy pastoral work and preaching for a Church in a world in collapse; much of it was in the form of sermons.[9]

Activity 2

Based on the paragraph above, identify each of the underlined structures below. Refer to the table above for help. An example is provided for you.

1. The advantage <u>of political support</u>—*prepositional phrase.*

2. <u>Local rebel</u> ruler—

3. Gildo, who established a regime semi-independent of the emperor—

4. The <u>struggling Catholic</u> congregation—

9. Ibid., 304

5. Port of the province—

6. An idiosyncratic but shrewd old Greek—

7. A background of busy pastoral work and preaching—

8. A Church in a world in collapse—

Activity 3

Provide your own descriptions for the following nouns. Choose whatever structure you wish. When you have finished, exchange your work with a partner's to see what structures he or she used.

1. Augustine.

2. Church.

3. Culture.

4. Monica (Augustine's mother).

5. Belief.

6. Understanding.

7. Nature.

8. Decision.

Activity 4

While maintaining eye contact with a partner (i.e., do not read from the passage), tell your partner one thing you learned about Augustine from this excerpt. Your partner should identify at least one noun phrase in your response, and, if necessary, help you correct any grammatical problems with it. Then switch roles. If time allows, continue to practice by stating other things that you learned about Augustine from this church historian.

21

Looking Forward

"Not everyone has the opportunity to live for extended periods as a guest in another's culture, but history confronts the student with a different time and a different place, where people think, act, and behave in different ways. In this manner, rather like immigration, we come to understand the forces and influences that shaped the way the world was in the past, and hopefully we become more aware of the way in which forces previously unnoticed and invisible shape and guide the present."
—Carl R. Trueman, *Histories and Fallacies*

Lesson Goals

Theology–To learn in what sense evangelicalism should be offensive
Reading–To continue identifying main ideas and details, and to draw inferences
Vocabulary–To learn and use additional collocations from the passage
Grammar–To revisit the form of adjectives (Lesson 3) and to practice using them

---

Introduction

While we certainly can look back in history and learn much from the words and actions of figures such as Luther and Augustine, we can also use the not-so-distant past to see where we might be heading in the present. As Trueman notes, a study of the past can make us more aware of "the way in which forces previously unnoticed and invisible shape and guide the present."

Perhaps one of the most common words one hears in contemporary theological discussions is the word "evangelical." Donald McKim defines this as "a term used in Europe for 'Protestant.' In America it has come to refer to one who stresses the need for a personal relationship with God in Jesus Christ by

faith."[1] This is certainly a broad definition. What, more precisely, can we say about evangelicalism to help us better understand this movement of history that we seem to be a part of? The reading passage for this chapter will explore an answer to this question.

Background for the Reading

We can learn much about theological movements from the writings that its key theologians produce. We can also learn a great deal about such movements by looking at the written works it values. Calvin's *Institutes*, for example, is regarded highly by modern Reformed theologians. Yet, while we can certainly learn a lot about evangelicalism from examining the works it has produced and the volumes it cherishes,

---

1. Donald K. McKim, *The Westminster Dictionary of Theological Terms*, 2nd ed. (Louisville, KY: Westminster John Knox, 2014), 110.

we can also learn much about it from the songs it sings. In the reading passage for this chapter, church historian Mark Noll aims to examine the heart of evangelicalism by exploring its prized hymns.

Pre-Reading

What is one of your favorite hymns? State one or two beliefs that this hymn teaches you.

Reading

In the following passage, Mark Noll expounds upon the heart of modern evangelicalism, as seen in the historical hymns of the eighteenth and nineteenth centuries. (Warning: Be careful how you understand the word "offense" in this passage.)

[¶1] The history of modern evangelicalism could be written as a chronicle[a] of calculated[b] offense. Those who know even a little evangelical history know how prone[c] evangelicals have been to violate decorum,[d] compromise integrity, upset intellectual balance, and abuse artistic good taste. In specifically theological terms, the evangelical movement, including many of its subcanonical hymns, offers the spectacle of a luxurious expanse of weeds, with multiple varieties of gnosticism, docetism, manichaeism, modalism, and wild eschatological speculation, not to speak of confusion over doctrinal details and manifold outbreaks of unintended Unitarianism, springing up as a threat to the good seed of classic orthodoxy.

Remember?
What two nouns are modified by a prepositional phrase in the first sentence?

[¶2] The great hymns are not like that. They do not meander[e] theologically. Whatever else they may lack, they possess the virtue of clarity. In turn, by focusing on the great hymns of evangelicalism, proponents, opponents, and the merely curious can see clearly the essence of evangelicalism with a minimum of distraction. That essence is the central theme in a vast panoply[f] of classic hymns.

[¶3] Professor Stephen Marini of Wellesley College has twice in recent years tallied the most often reprinted hymns in American Protestant hymnbooks from the colonial era to the decades after the Second World War. Because of the different range of hymnals he sampled for the two surveys, he has identified two different hymns as the most often reprinted in American Protestant history. Because the message of one of those two is so often repeated in so many of the other classic hymns of evangelicalism, its compact,[g] forceful lines are an especially good record of the center of evangelical concern. That hymn appeared in 1776, and I say, with calculated awareness of what else was going on in that year in Philadelphia and in Scotland, when Adam Smith published his *Wealth of Nations*, that of all world-historical occurrences in that year the publication of August Montagu Toplady's hymn may have been the most consequential:

Rock of Ages, cleft[h] for me, Let me hide myself in Thee;
Let the water and the blood, From Thy riven[i] side which flowed,
Be of sin the double cure, Cleanse me from its guilt and power.
Not the labours of my hands, Can fulfill Thy law's demands;

Could my zeal no respite[j] know, Could my tears for ever flow,
All for sin could not atone: Thou must save, and Thou alone.
Nothing in my hand I bring, Simply to Thy Cross I cling;
Naked, come to Thee for dress; Helpless, look to Thee for grace;
Foul, I to the fountain fly;[k] Wash me, Saviour, or I die.

Toplady's theme was never put more succinctly, with more theological acumen,[l] and greater dramatic power than in a hymn Charles Wesley wrote at the very beginning of the evangelical movement:

And can it be that I should gain An interest[m] in the Savior's blood?
Died he for me, who caused his pain? For me? Who him to death pursued?
Amazing love! How can it be That thou, my God, shouldst die for me?
'Tis myst'ry all: th'Immortal dies! Who can explore his strange design?
. . .
Long my imprisoned spirit lay, Fast bound in sin and nature's night.
Thine eye diffused a quick'ning[n] ray; I woke; the dungeon flamed with light.
My chains fell off, my heart was free, I rose, went forth, and followed thee.
No condemnation now I dread, Jesus, and all in him, is mine.
Alive in him, my living head, And clothed in righteousness divine,
Bold I approach th'eternal throne, And claim my crown, through Christ my own.

It is impossible to illustrate quickly the fixation[o] of evangelical hymnody on the saving death of Christ. The theme is prominent even in many songs written specifically for children:

Jesus loves me, this I know, For the Bible tells me so. . . .
Jesus loves me! He who died Heaven's gate to open wide;
He will wash away my sin, Let his little child come in.

It remained a fixture in the memorable, though more sentimental,[p] hymns of the Victorian era, as from Philip P. Bliss:

"Man of Sorrows," what a name for the Son of God, who came
Ruined sinners to reclaim! Hallelujah! what a Savior!
Bearing shame and scoffing rude, in my place condemned he stood;
Sealed my pardon with his blood: Hallelujah! what a Savior!

Or Horatio G. Spafford's "It Is Well with My Soul":

My sin—O, the bliss of this glorious thought, my sin—not in part but the whole,
Is nailed to the cross and I bear it no more:
Praise the Lord, praise the Lord, O my soul!

Even in the much more therapeutic[q] concerns of the modern praise chorus, emphasis upon the redemption won by Christ on the cross is by no means absent.

[¶4] The classical evangelical hymns do not offend on doctrines of the church and the sacraments because they touch on these matters only indirectly, if at all. Neither do they offend by promoting the particular doctrines of a faction.ʳ The Arminian Charles Wesley and the Calvinist A. M. Toplady both wrote hymns excoriatingˢ the theological positions of the other—these hymns died long before their authors, while compositions like "Rock of Ages" and "And Can It Be" are found in the hymnals of almost all Protestants and, since the 1970s, some Roman Catholics as well. While the great hymns everywhere betrayᵗ implicit trust in the Scriptures, they do not offend by insisting on a particular definition of biblical authority. Again, the classic evangelical hymns have virtually no politics. Charles Wesley thought the American Revolution was sinful through and through, but American patriots hardly noticed as they went on reprinting his hymns in edition after edition. I could go on— different evangelicals of different sorts and at different times have tolerated or advocated racism, they have cheered attacks on the intellect, they have indulged unimaginable vulgarityᵘ in the production of religious kitsch,ᵛ they have been callousʷ to the dispossessed, they have confused their political allegiances with divine mandates, they have equated middle-class decorum with sanctification in the Holy Spirit, and they have tried to pass off gratuitousˣ nonsense as if it were gospel truth—as Toplady, for example, did in the essay where he first published "Rock of Ages" by claiming that the average number of sins committed by each individual in his or her lifetime was 2,522,880,000.

[¶5] Such failings, as well as the particular dogmas and practices insisted upon by differ- ent evangelical churches, have been the occasion for oceans of offense. Whether all or some of these offenses are justified is an open question deserving a degree of serious attention.

[¶6] The classic evangelical hymns, by contrast, are virtually innocent of such offenses. Rather, their overridingʸ message and the single offense upon which they insist is compacted into the four words that best summarize their message: *Jesus Christ Saves Sinners*. These hymns, in other words, proclaim a particular redemption of substitutionary atonement through a particular act of God accomplished in the particularities of the birth, life, death, resurrection, ascension, and kingly rule of Jesus Christ.

[¶7] Evangelicalism at its best is an offensive religion. It claims that human beings cannot be reconciled to God, understand the ultimate purposes of the world, or live a truly virtu- ous life unless they confess their sin before the living God and receive new life in Christ through the power of the Holy Spirit. Such particularity has always been offensive, and in the multicultural, postmodern world in which we live it is more offensive than ever. But when evangelicalism is at its best, as it is in its greatest hymns, that declaration of a particular salvation is its one and only offense.²

2. Mark A. Noll, *American Evangelical Christianity: An Introduction* (Malden, MA: Blackwell, 2001), 269–72. Republished with permission of John Wiley and Sons Inc., from Mark A. Noll, *American Evangelical Christianity: An Introduction* (Malden, MA: Blackwell, 2001; permission conveyed through Copyright Clearance Center, Inc.

a. Chronicle (n.): a historical account of facts or events
b. Calculated (adj.): thought out in advance; deliberately planned
c. Prone (adj.): predisposed to something
d. Decorum (n.): propriety and good taste
e. Meander (v.): to wander aimlessly or casually
f. Panoply (n.): a magnificent or impressive array
g. Compact (adj.): brief; pithy
h. Cleave (v.): to pierce or drive a way through
i. Riven (adj.): split or pierced
j. Respite (n.): an interval of rest
k. Fly (v.): to flee from danger
l. Acumen (n.): sharpness of mind
m. Interest (n.): a legal share in something
n. Quickening (adj.): making alive; life-giving
o. Fixation (n.): the act or state of concentrating upon something

p. Sentimental (adj.): appealing to the emotions
q. Therapeutic (adj.): of or relating to the treatment of disease or disorders
r. Faction (n.): a set or class of persons
s. Excoriate (v.): to censure (judge) scathingly (severely)
t. Betray (v.): to show or indicate (something not obvious on the surface)
u. Vulgarity (n.): the quality or state of being crude, indecent, or offensive
v. Kitsch (n.): artistic or literary material held to be of low quality, often produced to appeal to popular taste
w. Callous (adj.): feeling no sympathy for others
x. Gratuitous (adj.): adopted or asserted without good ground
y. Overriding (adj.): dominant or primary

Post-Reading

In your own words, state what the author feels is rightfully offensive about evangelicalism.

One of the ways in which we show readers that parts of our sentences are meant to go together is by the use of **parallelism**. Parallelism refers to the repeated use of the same grammatical structure in order to show relationships between ideas. Take this sentence, for example: "It claims that human beings cannot be reconciled to God, understand the ultimate purposes of the world, or live a truly virtuous life unless they confess their sin before the living God and receive new life in Christ through the power of the Holy Spirit."[3] The first part of the sentence introduces a subject and three verbs, and the second part of the sentence uses essentially the same subject with two verbs.

The use of parallelism helps the reader to see that a conditional relationship exists between the two parts of the sentence. This relationship is signaled by "unless." If spoken, the word "unless" would likely be stressed in order to make it clear that part 1 of the sentence is conditional with regard to part 2. The use of parallelism (grammar) aids in pronunciation (phonology), which then more clearly communicates the content of the author's message (reference).

Main Ideas and Details

(1) Which of the following is the main idea that the author communicates in this passage?
   a. Evangelicalism makes up only a small portion of Christianity.
   b. Evangelicalism is especially opposed to today's American culture.
   c. The best kind of evangelicalism is offensive because of its message about Christ.
   d. Evangelical Christianity is properly

Part 1	Unless	Part 2
Human beings cannot be reconciled (cannot) understand (cannot) live		They confess receive

3. Ibid., 272.

understood only with reference to its most popular hymns.

(2) What opinion does the author convey in paragraph 1?
   a. The evangelical movement is a generally positive one.
   b. The evangelical movement has been incredibly successful.
   c. The evangelical movement has had a lot of problems and is rightly often viewed negatively.
   d. The evangelical movement is viewed negatively by most non-Christians, but there are no grounds for this opinion.

(3) When the author describes the evangelical movement as "a luxurious expanse of weeds," what is he suggesting?
   a. That evangelicalism is full of life.
   b. That evangelicalism has grown very quickly.
   c. That evangelicalism is rooted in good theological soil.
   d. That evangelicalism has produced many theological faults.

(4) What opinion does the author convey in paragraph 2?
   a. Hymns frequently add to the confusion over evangelicalism.
   b. Hymns provide people with a clear way to understand evangelical doctrine.
   c. In an effort to be clear, hymns take away the rich nuances of doctrine.
   d. In an effort to be clear, hymns make evangelical doctrine more confusing.

(5) Based on the context in paragraph 3, the word "tallied" means _____, and the word "range" means _____.
   a. Subtracted; kind.
   b. Counted; variety.
   c. Described; power.
   d. Examined; placement.

(6) Based on the context in paragraph 3, the word "consequential" is closest in meaning to _____.
   a. Offensive.
   b. Influential.
   c. Disturbing.
   d. Disruptive.

(7) What is the main idea of paragraph 4?
   a. The best hymns do not offend anyone based on doctrinal differences.
   b. The best hymns do not offend anyone based on political differences.
   c. The best hymns do not contain material that is doctrinally or politically divisive.
   d. The best hymns have a spiritual depth that touches on doctrine, the sacraments, and biblical authority.

(8) In paragraph 5, what word does "deserving" modify?

(9) In paragraph 6, the word "compacted" is closest in meaning to _____.
   a. Dispersed.
   b. Expanded.
   c. Broken up.
   d. Compressed.

(10) At the end of paragraph 7, why might the author repeat the word "particular"? (Hint: This is related to the main idea of the passage.)

(11) At the end of the passage, the author writes, "But when evangelicalism is at its best, as it is in its greatest hymns, that declaration of a particular salvation is its one and only offense." Based on this statement, which of the following can we infer?
   a. Evangelicalism is not usually at its best.
   b. The "offense" of salvation in Christ is actually a good thing.
   c. Evangelicalism should not be offensive in its doctrine or teaching.
   d. Evangelicals should be punished for the offense that they have committed.

Understanding the Passage

Complete the chart on the top of the next page by writing the main idea of each paragraph in the appropriate box.

Paragraph	Main Idea
1	Modern evangelicalism has often been offensive and theologically confusing.
2	
3	
4	
5	
6	
7	The great evangelical hymns highlight redemption through Christ, and this is evangelicalism's strength.

Collocations

Match the words on the left to their collocates on the right. Make sure you check the reading to support your choices, since some of the words on the left could go with multiple words on the right.

theological	theme
multiple	varieties
classic	terms
central	someone pain
cause	orthodoxy

Provide collocations from the reading passage for the words in the center bubbles below. These collocations may precede or follow these words. There are enough collocations so that all of the bubbles should be filled.

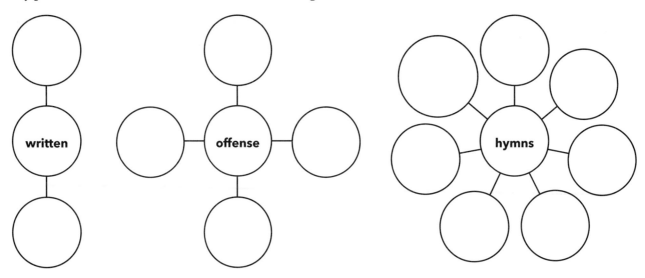

Fig. 21.1. Collocation Diagram 6

Using some of the collocations above, write a sentence about the main "offense" of the evangelical movement.

Grammar Focus: Adjective Forms

In this lesson, we do a bit of review. For several lessons now, we have been discussing how we can add information to our sentences and how we can express relations between ideas. In Lesson 20, we saw several examples of adjectives being used to describe nouns, and so now would be a good time to revisit the forms of adjectives (this was covered in Lesson 3). Once more, note the forms of the adjectives in the following paragraph.

The **classical evangelical** hymns do not offend on doctrines of the church and the sacraments because they touch on these matters only indirectly, if at all. Neither do they offend by promoting the particular doctrines of a faction. The Arminian Charles Wesley and the Calvinist A. M. Toplady both wrote hymns excoriating the **theological** positions of the other—these hymns died long before their authors, while compositions like "Rock of Ages" and "And Can It Be" are found in the hymnals of almost all Protestants and, since the 1970s, some Roman Catholics as well. While the great hymns everywhere betray implicit trust in the Scriptures, they do not offend by insisting on a particular definition of **biblical** authority. Again, the **classic evangelical** hymns have virtually no politics. Charles Wesley thought the **American** Revolution was **sinful** through and through, but **American** patriots hardly noticed as they went on reprinting his hymns in edition after edition. I could go on—**different** evangelicals of **different** sorts and at **different** times have tolerated or advocated racism, they have cheered attacks on the intellect, they have indulged **unimaginable** vulgarity in the production of **religious** kitsch, they have been **callous** to the dispossessed, they have confused their **political** allegiances with divine mandates, they have equated middle-class decorum with sanctification in the Holy Spirit, and they have tried to pass off **gratuitous** nonsense as if it were gospel truth—as Toplady, for example, did in the essay where he first published "Rock of Ages" by claiming that the average number of sins committed by each individual in his or her lifetime was 2,522,880,000.

Based on this paragraph, we can add a few more endings to the adjective chart we presented in Lesson 3.

Ending	Example
-able	unimagin*able*
-al	centr*al*
-an	Americ*an*
-ent	promin*ent*
-ical	class*ical*, theolog*ical*, bibl*ical*

Ending	Example
-ous	relig*ious*, gratuit*ous*
Past Participle (often "-ed")	reveal*ed*, know*n*
Present Participle ("-ing")	redeem*ing*

Activity 1

Provide the correct adjective form for the noun in parentheses.

Evangelicals, in point of _____ (*history*) fact, may have never been factious,[a] fissiparous,[b] and sectarian[c] as is commonly thought. To be sure, leaders of_____(*evangelicalism*) groups have indulged in their fair share of back-stabbing, power-mongering,[d] petty minded polemicizing,[e] _____ (*gratuity*) boundary-marking, and _____ (*schism*) devilment.[f] Although I am convinced that lay evangelicals have done better than their leaders in preserving the unity of the Body of Christ, there is enough fragmentation in the evangelical world to go around for all. I have often heard said in my circles what is no doubt said about _____ (*difference*) issues in other communions as well: the presence of three _____ (*confession*) Presbyterians guarantees at least four potentially schismatic options on the doctrine of predestination.[4]

a. Factious (adj.): broken into factions
b. Fissiparous (adj.): divisive
c. Sectarian (adj.): confined to the limits of one religious group, one school, or one party

d. Mongering (n.): the act of peddling or spreading
e. Polemicizing (n.): the act of engaging in controversy and debate
f. Devilment (n.): devilish conduct; reckless mischief

Activity 2

Choose an adjective of your own to describe the following nouns. Underline each adjective's ending.

1. Hymns.

2. Debates.

3. Message.

4. Requirement.

5. Doctrines.

Activity 3

Write a brief paragraph (three to five sentences) about the "offense" of the gospel in contemporary culture. When you have finished, underline the endings of any adjectives you used.

4. Ibid.

Activity 4

Thought Groups: Speakers usually divide their sentences into "thought groups." A **thought group** is a phrase or clause of words that can be said in one breath. Speakers usually take a very short pause to allow themselves to breathe before and after each thought group. Typically, the last word in the thought group, usually a noun or verb, receives more stress.

Using songs like hymns can help you to practice recognizing thought groups. The music typically pauses between thought groups at the same place a speaker would if he or she were saying the words. However, note that sometimes the poetry of the lyrics (words) or the musical features of the song cause singers to stress words that would not typically be stressed.

(1)   The first verse of "Rock of Ages" has been reprinted below, but with most of the punctuation removed and with some changes to the capitalization. First, mark the end of each thought group with a slash (/). The first line has been done for you.

> Rock of ages / cleft for me / let me hide / myself in thee
> Let the water and the blood from thy riven side which flowed
> Be of sin the double cure cleanse me from its guilt and power
> Not the labours of my hands can fulfill thy law's demands
> Could my zeal no respite know could my tears for ever flow
> All for sin could not atone thou must save and thou alone
> Nothing in my hand I bring simply to thy cross I cling
> Naked come to thee for dress; helpless, look to thee for grace
> Foul I to the fountain fly; wash me saviour or I die

(2)   Then listen to this hymn being sung. (Because this is a popular hymn, you can easily find an audio clip online.) As you listen to the hymn, ask yourself a few questions. Does the singer pause at the same places where you marked the ends of thought groups? Does the singer put stress on the last word in each thought group?

(3)   Finally, read aloud or sing the verse yourself. Think about where you are pausing to breathe and which words you are stressing when you read or sing it.

Summary of Theological Concepts for Unit 7

- We must take account of a theologian's historical context before drawing conclusions about his theology, and before applying his theology to our own lives.
- The stance of a church historian reveals how that theologian views history as a whole, and the orthodox faith in particular.
- The evangelical movement, as expressed through its most cherished hymns, reminds us that the gospel—the good news that Christ saves sinners—is an offense for which we should not apologize.

Activity

Paraphrase each of the concepts above in your own words.

(1)

(2)

(3)

The Offense of the Gospel (CH Task 2)

Introduction

From Mark Noll, we learned that the evangelical movement, at its heart, has embraced the offense of the gospel in its great hymns. The word "offense" is worth exploring. Why might the gospel be offensive to people today? Here are a few thoughts.

- The message that Christ saves sinners means that *every person* is in need of Christ. People are not okay on their own.
- Being told that Christ is the only way to receive salvation is an offense to those who practice other religions (or to atheists).
- The gospel is an offense to sinful reason, which would reject the claim that God would send his Son to die for sinners, raise him from the dead, and then bless with his Spirit those who believe in him.[5]

Task

Imagine that your uncle has never been very interested in the Christian faith. He has said in conversation with you that he hardly ever thinks about the gospel, and when he does, he is offended by it. When you ask him why he is offended, he says, "Because the gospel suggests that we are 'saved' only by faith in Jesus, and there are a lot of people like me who don't have any reason to have faith in God, let alone in God's Son." Respond to your uncle by restating the offense of the gospel and suggesting one reason why he should believe in Jesus. To help you get started, you may draw on the quotation below.

> Every person on the face of the earth is, by virtue of being created in God's image, a God-*knower*. No person operates in a religious vacuum. No person is outside the bounds of God's covenantal relationship. Those who are in Adam are, nevertheless, in a covenant-breaking relationship with the God who made, and who sustains, them.
>
> In our defense of Christianity, therefore, we may be confident in the fact that, even before we begin our defense, God has been there, dynamically and perpetually making himself known through every single fact of the unbeliever's existence. Our apologetic is, then, in a very real sense, a reminder to the unbeliever of what he already knows to be the case.[6]

Present your response to a partner, who will pretend to be your uncle. Then switch roles. Your response should be less than 3 minutes.

---

5. We say "sinful reason" because unbelief is ultimately irrational. See K. Scott Oliphint, "The Irrationality of Unbelief: An Exegetical Study," in *Revelation and Reason: New Essays in Reformed Apologetics*, ed. K. Scott Oliphint and Lane G. Tipton (Phillipsburg, NJ: P&R, 2007), 59–73.
6. Ibid., 72.

UNIT 8

HOW ARE WE SAVED?
(SYSTEMATIC THEOLOGY)

22

Union with Christ

*"The central soteriological reality is union with the exalted Christ by Spirit-created faith.
That is the nub, the essence, of the way or order of salvation for Paul."*
—Richard B. Gaffin Jr., *By Faith, Not by Sight*

Lesson Goals

Theology–To understand the importance of our union with the person of Christ
Reading–To continue identifying main ideas and details, and to draw inferences
Vocabulary–To learn and use additional collocations from the passage
Grammar–To recognize prepositions that occur with certain nouns and verbs

---

Introduction

We have come far in our theological journey at this point. We have covered three genres (apologetics, biblical studies, and church history), and we have learned about the importance of Christ in both the Old and New Testaments. Now we come to the more specific issue of how we, as believers, are related to Christ.

In this chapter, we begin with a few questions. What do you think it means to be united to Christ? And why do you think our salvation is described this way?

While these questions might seem abstract and relatively unimportant, biblical scholars in the Reformed tradition have argued the opposite: "[The union of Christians with Christ] is of paramount importance for Paul, absolutely decisive for what falls within the purview of matters 'of first importance.'"[1] One scholar remarks, "Union with Christ is theological shorthand for the gospel itself."[2] Another claims that our very identity is rooted in this concept: "One of the most important consequences of faith union with Christ is that it defines believers. It gives them an identity in relation to Christ."[3] Even death and eternal life seem to be shaped profoundly by this union: "Our experience of death, burial, and the intermediate state will be in union with Christ. He has gone there before us. We will go there in him."[4] If union with Christ is so central a concern for Reformed theologians, we certainly should examine it carefully.

---

1. Richard B. Gaffin Jr., *By Faith, Not by Sight: Paul and the Order of Salvation*, 2nd ed. (Phillipsburg, NJ: P&R, 2013), 40.
2. J. Todd Billings, *Union with Christ: Reframing Theology and Ministry for the Church* (Grand Rapids, MI: Baker, 2011), 1.
3. Robert A. Peterson, *Salvation Applied by the Spirit: Union with Christ* (Wheaton, IL: Crossway, 2015), 414.
4. Robert Letham, *Union with Christ: In Scripture, History, and Theology* (Phillipsburg, NJ: P&R, 2011), 134.

219

Background for the Reading

It seems natural for us to think of salvation as one simple event. Certainly, in a sense this is correct. As Gaffin notes, we are saved by faith-wrought union with the person of Christ. Still, for centuries theologians have debated the order of certain theological events in the life of the believer that can be subsumed under the word "salvation." Hence, we have John Murray's list from *Redemption Accomplished and Applied*: calling, regeneration, faith and repentance, justification, adoption, sanctification, perseverance, and glorification.[5] Yet Gaffin is quick to precede any order of salvation with the truth that beneath all the salvific benefits we receive is our union with the crucified and resurrected *person* of Christ.

Pre-Reading

Why do you think Richard Gaffin focuses his attention on "union with the person of Christ"?

Reading

In the following passage, Gaffin describes our faith-wrought union with the person of Christ.

The Role of Faith

[¶1] Faith unites[a] to Christ, so that his death and resurrection are mine, in the sense of now being savingly effective[b] in my life. Better, faith is the work of God by his Spirit, effective in "calling" sinners—otherwise "dead in trespasses and sins" (Eph. 2:1, 5) and thus utterly incapable of faith in and of themselves—"into the fellowship of his Son" (1 Cor. 1:9), into union with Christ, who is what he now is as crucified and resurrected. This union with the exalted Christ is such that his death and resurrection in their saving efficacy[c] from sin and all its consequences—that is, basically, from its guilt and power—are mine. Or, put even more elementally[d] and integrally,[e] by union with the exalted Christ, all that he now is and has secured for believers in virtue of having been crucified and raised is mine, whether presently or in the future. . . .

[¶2] This emphasis on the individual and personal is not meant to deny or downplay the broader corporate,[f] even cosmic, dimensions of the salvation revealed in the cross and resurrection and appropriated[g] by faith. The call into fellowship with Christ (1 Cor. 1:9) is also a call into fellowship of his Spirit-baptized body (12:13). The bodies of believers are, individually, temples of the Holy Spirit (1 Cor. 6:19; cf. 1 Thess 4:6, 8), while the church itself, as a whole, is God's temple (1 Cor. 3:16–17). Further, that is so in the context of the entire creation "anxiously longing" for the future "revelation of the sons of God," when it will be "set free from the bondage of corruption" (Rom. 8:19, 21). To polarize[h] personal and corporate, or personal and cosmic, concerns in matters of the gospel is simply foreign[i] to Paul. So is allowing either one to eclipse[j] or negate the other.

Remember? How many different adjective forms can you find in the first paragraph?

5. John Murray, *Redemption Accomplished and Applied*. (Grand Rapids, MI: Eerdmans, 1955).

The Center of Paul's Theology and the Order of Salvation

[¶3] Our reflections tethered[k] to the center of Paul's theology, with an eye to the question of how in Paul salvation is actually applied to and received by the individual sinner, have brought us to this overall conclusion: the central soteriological reality is union with the exalted Christ by Spirit-created faith. That is the nub,[l] the essence, of the way or order of salvation for Paul.

[¶4] The center of Paul's soteriology, then, at the center of his theology as a whole, is neither justification by faith nor sanctification, neither the imputation of Christ's righteousness nor the renewing work of the Spirit. To draw that conclusion, however, is not to decenter[m] justification (or sanctification), as if justification is somehow less important for Paul than it is for the Reformers. Justification is supremely important; it is absolutely crucial in Paul's "gospel of salvation" (cf. Eph. 1:13). If his teaching on justification is denied or distorted,[n] it ceases to be the gospel; there is no longer saving "good news" for guilty sinners. But no matter how close justification is to the heart of Paul's gospel, in our salvation there is an antecedent[o] consideration, a reality that is deeper, more fundamental, more decisive, more crucial: Christ and our union with him, the crucified and resurrected, the exalted, Christ. Union with Christ by faith—that is the essence of Paul's *ordo salutis*.[6]

a. Unite (v.): to become one or as if one
b. Effective (adj.): productive of results
c. Efficacy (n.): the power to produce an effect
d. Elementally (adv.): in an elementary or introductory manner
e. Integrally (adv.): in a way that is organically joined or linked
f. Corporate (adj.): relating to a unified body made up of individuals
g. Appropriate (v.): to claim or use as if by an exclusive or preeminent right
h. Polarize (v.): to produce or bring about a division of something into two opposites
i. Foreign (adj.): alien in character
j. Eclipse (v.): to make insignificant by comparison
k. Tether (v.): to bind
l. Nub (n.): core, crux, gist, kernel, or point
m. Decenter (v.): to cause to lose or shift from an established center or focus
n. Distort (v.): to twist out of the true meaning
o. Antecedent (adj.): prior or preceding

Post-Reading

According to Gaffin, why does union with the person of Christ take precedence over any specific benefit?

Main Ideas and Details

(1) In your own words, what are the main ideas of the passage? (Hint: There are two.)

(2) What is the reason the author provides for our inability, in and of ourselves, to have faith in Christ? (Refer to paragraph 1.)

(3) The highlighted pronoun "its" in paragraph 1 refers to _____.
   a. Sin.
   b. Death.
   c. Consequences.
   d. Saving efficacy.

(4) Which of the following can we infer from paragraph 1?
   a. For nonbelievers, faith in Christ is not the work of the Holy Spirit.
   b. The benefits of Christ's work are applied to the life of each believer.

6. Gaffin, *By Faith, Not by Sight, Paul and the Order of Salvation*, 2nd ed. (Phillipsburg, NJ: P&R, 2013), 47–49.

c. Though believers have union with Christ, they do not currently have peace.

d. The benefits we have from union with Christ are in some sense applied to nonbelievers too.

(5) In paragraph 2, the author implies that different levels of redemption exist. What are those levels?

(6) What is the author's main concern in paragraph 2?

(7) In paragraph 2, the word "downplay" could best be replaced by _____.
   a. Magnify.
   b. Exaggerate.
   c. De-emphasize.
   d. Over-emphasize.

(8) Which of the following can we infer based on the highlighted sentence in paragraph 4?
   a. Sanctification precedes justification.
   b. Justification is not a very important issue for Paul.

c. Neither justification nor sanctification was important for the Reformers.

d. Paul's focus on union with Christ runs deeper than blessings we receive from it.

(9) Which of the following does the highlighted conjunction "but" in paragraph 4 signal?
   a. That justification is the heart of Paul's gospel.
   b. The idea that justification does not matter to Paul.
   c. The introduction of the real essence of Paul's *ordo salutis*.
   d. A following statement that will contradict what came before it.

Understanding the Passage

For Gaffin, union with Christ is the center of Paul's soteriology. From our union with the crucified and resurrected Lord, we are recipients of every spiritual blessing (Eph. 1:3). In the diagram below, match each pair of biblical passages to the particular benefit of union with Christ that they describe.[7] Each word in the box is used only once.

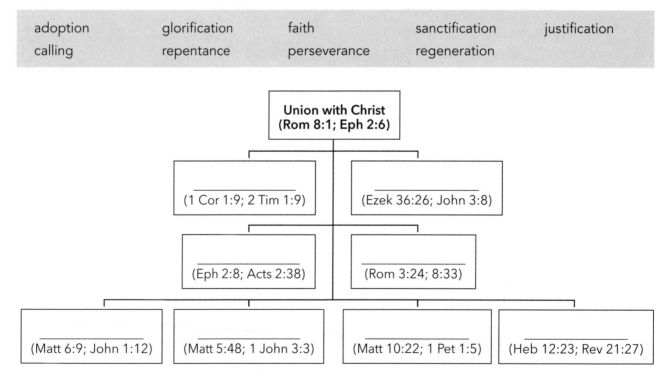

| adoption | glorification | faith | | sanctification | justification |
| calling | repentance | perseverance | | regeneration | |

Fig. 22.1. Benefits of Union with Christ

---

7. These passages are taken from Murray, *Redemption Accomplished and Applied.*

Collocations from the Passage

Match the words on the left to their collocates on the right.

broader	fundamental
overall	dimensions
the center	of something
draw	conclusion
less	important
more	a conclusion

Using some of the collocations above, write a sentence about our union with Christ.

Grammar Focus: Patterns of Preposition Use

Adding information to our sentences, we have seen, can be done in several ways. We can use complex subjects, infinitives, adverbs, noun clauses, and noun phrases. In the previous lesson, we learned of several structures we can use to describe or modify individual nouns. One of those structures was a prepositional phrase. In this lesson, we will focus on patterns of prepositions with nouns.[8] Learning these patterns will enable you to form noun phrases that are grammatically correct, and thus better equip you to add information to your sentences.

In the paragraph below, fill in the prepositions coming before and after the noun. Try to do this first *without* looking at the reading for this lesson (paragraph 4). Once you have tried to fill in all of the prepositions yourself, check your work against the original.

The center _____ Paul's soteriology, then, _____ the center of his theology as a whole, is neither justification _____ faith nor sanctification, neither the imputation _____ Christ's righteousness nor the renewing work _____ the Spirit. To draw that conclusion, however, is not to decenter justification (or sanctification), as if justification is somehow less important _____ Paul than it is for the Reformers. Justification is supremely important; it is absolutely crucial _____ Paul's "gospel of salvation" (cf. Eph. 1:13). If his teaching _____ justification is denied or distorted, it ceases to be the gospel; there is no longer saving "good news" _____ guilty sinners. But no matter how close justification is to the heart _____ Paul's gospel, in our salvation there is an antecedent consideration, a reality that is deeper, more fundamental, more decisive, more crucial: Christ and our union _____ him, the crucified and resurrected, the exalted, Christ. Union with Christ by faith—that is the essence _____ Paul's *ordo salutis*.

Activity 1

Underline the prepositions preceding or following nouns in the passage below.

At the opening of Book 3 of his *Institutes of the Christian Religion* and controlling all that he has to say about "the way" of salvation—that is, its personal, individual appropriation, including what he will eventually say about justification—Calvin writes, "First, we must understand that as long as Christ remains outside of us, and we are separated from him, all that he has suffered and done for the salvation of the human race remains useless and of no value for us." This is eminently faithful to Paul and is quoted here because it captures the essence of his soteriology.[9]

Activity 2

Write the most appropriate preposition in each blank on the top of the next page.

---

8. Again, for helpful lists of prepositions that precede or follow certain words, see Michael Swan, *Practical English Usage*, 4th ed. (Oxford: Oxford University Press, 2016), entries 212–13.

9. Gaffin, *By Faith, Not by Sight*, 50.

Several Reformed theologians have argued that, _____ Paul, union _____ Christ is a central theme. Our union with the person of Christ is _____ the center of our understanding _____ salvation. If we are, in Calvin's words, "separated from him," then what he has done cannot benefit us.[10] To be united with the person _____ Christ, to be _____ Christ, is "all-encompassing, extending in fact from eternity to eternity."[11] And this everlasting union that we have with Christ is both *mystical* and *spiritual*. It is mystical "_____ the sense of involving 'a great mystery' that _____ Paul apparently has its closest analogy in the relationship _____ husband and wife (Eph. 5:32)."[12] It is spiritual "because of the activity and indwelling _____ the Holy Spirit."[13]

Activity 3

In the chart below, write four phrases that Gaffin has used involving prepositions, and then write a sentence of your own using the same phrase. An example is provided for you.

Phrase from the Text	Your Example
center of	The *center of* Reformed theology is Scripture.

Activity 4

Using at least three of the noun + preposition patterns you have learned, provide a definition of "salvation." In your definition, show what you have learned about union with Christ.

Is That It? (ST Task 1)

Imagine that you have just had a conversation with an old friend concerning how you have come to faith in Christ. Your friend, who is not a Christian, listens intently as you describe your thoughts and experience. At the end of your explanation, he asks, "Is that it? You just believed in Jesus as your Savior? That's all there is to salvation?"

Write a paragraph-long email to your friend explaining why union with the person of Christ is "all there is" to salvation, but that this is so very precious. You might include in your response the many spiritual blessings we have because we are united to Christ (e.g., adoption, justification, sanctification, etc.). You may refer to the chart provided in the "Understanding the Passage" exercise for help. If you need to, refer to the instruction on email etiquette in AP Task 1 of Unit 1.

10. Calvin, *Instit.* 3.1.1.
11. Gaffin, *By Faith, Not by Sight*, 41.
12. Ibid., 43.
13. Ibid.

23

Justification

"Believers are justified in Christ by receiving through faith alone the imputed righteousness of the crucified and resurrected Son of God."
—Lane G. Tipton, *Justified in Christ*

Lesson Goals

Theology—To understand justification in relation to union with Christ
Reading—To continue identifying main ideas and details, and to draw inferences
Vocabulary—To learn and use additional collocations from the passage
Grammar—To recognize patterns in definite and indefinite article use

---

Introduction

Mystical and spiritual union with the person of Christ—that, we have learned, is the essence of salvation for Paul. Yet, in Eph. 1:3, Paul also tells us that the Father "has blessed us in Christ with every spiritual blessing in the heavenly places." What "spiritual blessings" does Paul have in mind?

One of these blessings is the blessing of *justification*. Before we get to the reading passage for this lesson, we might ask ourselves a few questions:

(1) What exactly does it mean to be "justified"?

(2) Why is it important to be "justified" before God?

(3) How do you think contemporary cultures (especially your own) would view this idea?

These are important questions to ask ourselves—questions that deepen our understanding of this blessing and show us how the world might see those who have claimed to receive it. The first two questions we will treat below. But the last question deserves some consideration here.

The concept of justification, just as the gospel itself, might be offensive to people today because it assumes two things: (1) that people are sinners, and (2) that there is only one way to have the guilt of and the punishment for sin removed. People might be further offended by our claim that sin cannot be erased or made up for by good works. This, in short, would be the path of legalism: the idea that we somehow work for God's grace. But this is what Sinclair Ferguson calls "a heart distortion of the graciousness of God and of the God of grace."[1] To assume that we can

---

1. Sinclair B. Ferguson, *The Whole Christ: Legalism, Antinomianism, and Gospel Assurance—Why the Marrow Controversy Still Matters* (Wheaton, IL: Crossway, 2016), 88.

absolve ourselves of sin is not only arrogant; it is to assume that God has not given us true grace in his Son and that he is, in essence, not the wise and generous God who has a loving plan for each of us.[2] Points (1) and (2), along with the "heart distortion" that often dwells within non-believers, explain why justification may offend people today.

Background for the Reading

Now we can come back to the first two questions we suggested above: What exactly does it mean to be justified, and why must we be justified before God?

In a strictly legal sense, to be justified means to be *absolved*, to be pronounced "free from guilt or blame."[3] In a theological sense, to be justified is to be regarded as righteous and worthy of salvation. Just

as an accused thief cannot enter the public world as a free man without either paying the penalty for his crime or being declared innocent, so people cannot enter eternal communion with God unless their debt of sin is paid and they are declared righteous before him.

In the Reformed tradition, our justification is attributed to the imputation of Christ's righteousness to us. Adam's sin was imputed to all of his progeny in the Fall, and Christ's righteousness is imputed to us through our Spirit-given, faith-wrought union with him.

Pre-Reading

How do you think union with Christ is related to justification by faith alone?

Reading

In this passage, Lane Tipton examines the Westminster Larger Catechism to see how our union with Christ by faith relates to our justification.

[¶1] Let us move on, then, to consider how Spirit-wrought[a] union with Christ by faith alone relates to justification by faith alone.

[¶2] The Westminster Larger Catechism expands and expounds[b] what union with Christ involves. What, specifically, are the benefits of being united to Christ by faith in effectual calling? Westminster Larger Catechism, Q&A 65 asks, "What special benefits do the members of the invisible church enjoy by Christ?" The answer, "The members of the invisible church by Christ enjoy union and communion with him in grace and glory." Notice that before any particular benefit is discussed in the Westminster Larger Catechism, union and communion with Christ is invoked.[c] This positions[d] union with Christ as the organizing structure in terms of which the Spirit applies to believers several benefits of redemption. In addition—and this is a point I can only note in passing, although it is of importance—notice that union and communion with Christ is set[e] in terms of grace and glory, language that denotes[f] the eschatological "already" and "not yet" of the believer's situation in Christ. Union with Christ is an expansive reality that encompasses[g] both realized and future aspects of eschatology.

[¶3] Question 66 recapitulates[h] and expands what we saw from Q&A 30 of the Westminster

Remember?
"Union with," "by faith," and "application of" are good preposition patterns to memorize.

---

2. Ibid., 82–83.

3. *Webster's Third New International Dictionary, Unabridged*, s.v. "justify," accessed April 15, 2014, http://unabridged.merriam-webster.com.

Shorter Catechism. Question 66, "What is that union which the elect have with Christ?" The answer:

> The union which the elect have with Christ is the work of God's grace, whereby they are spiritually and mystically, yet really and inseparably, joined to Christ as their head and husband; which is done in their effectual calling.

While this is a more elaborate statement than what we found in Westminster Shorter Catechism 30, what remains constant is the central role played by union with Christ in the application of redemption. It is within this basic frame of reference that we need to understand Westminster Larger Catechism 69. The question reads, "What is the communion in grace which the members of the invisible church have with Christ?" The answer is as follows:

> The communion in grace which the members of the invisible church have with Christ, is their partaking of the virtue of his mediation, in their justification, adoption, sanctification, and whatever else, in this life, manifests[i] their union with him.

This language crisply delineates[j] the relationship between union with Christ and justification—between the benefactor to whom we are united and an attendant[k] benefit of that union.

[¶4] Justification is a forensic[l] benefit of union with Christ, and, as such, the benefit of justification manifests Spirit-wrought union with Christ by faith. This needs to be explicit: the believer's justification is never applied apart from or prior to union with Christ by faith alone.

[¶5] Richard B. Gaffin, Jr., summarizes the constellation[m] of these realities tersely when he comments,

> Faith is Spirit-worked, sovereignly and effectively. Union with Christ, then, is forged by the Spirit's working faith in us, a faith that "puts on" Christ (Gal. 3:27), that embraces Christ as he is offered to faith in the gospel.

I should note at this point that the Westminster Standards and Calvin are in fundamental agreement here, a point that Gaffin has expressed quite clearly. The net[n] effect of the teaching contained in the Shorter and Larger Catechisms is that union with Christ occurs by a Spirit-wrought faith in effectual calling.

[¶6] Following closely upon this, and integrally related to it, the divines insist that justification is also by faith alone. Westminster Shorter Catechism 33 asks, "What is justification?" The answer is,

> Justification is an act of God's free grace, wherein he pardoneth all our sins, and accepteth us as righteous in his sight, only for the righteousness of Christ imputed to us, and received by faith alone.

Justification is by faith alone (*sola fide*) and based on the imputed righteousness of Christ alone. Critical to note in this formulation is the location of justification relative to union with Christ, on the one hand, and faith, on the other hand. Spirit-engendered° faith is the sole instrumental^p bond of union with Christ. The faith that unites to Christ is likewise the sole instrumental organ^q that receives the imputed righteousness of Christ. Justification does not precede, either temporally or logically, union with Christ by faith.

[¶7] These twin truths must be kept clear throughout. First, union with Christ is by faith alone in effectual calling. Second, justification in Christ, which manifests the logically prior, Spirit-wrought union with Christ, is likewise by faith alone. These truths, of course, derive from the biblical data with regard to (a) the central structural significance of union with Christ in the application of redemption, and (b) the uniform testimony of Scripture that the believer's justification is by faith alone.

[¶8] Regarding the former, Scripture teaches that believers are effectually called in Christ (1 Cor. 1:9); made alive together with Christ (Eph. 2:5); and die and rise with Christ in the past-historical event of his death and resurrection (Rom. 6:7), in the present personal reality of faith-union (Col. 2:12), and bodily in the age to come (1 Cor. 15:45–49). It is in Christ that believers have every spiritual blessing in the heavenly places (Eph. 1:3). Christ has become for believers "righteousness, holiness and redemption" (1 Cor. 1:30) and the "life-giving Spirit" (1 Cor. 15:45). Believers have been justified in Christ (Rom. 8:1; Gal. 2:17), sanctified in Christ (Rom. 6:10–11; 1 Cor. 6:11), and adopted in Christ (Gal. 3:26). In brief, Paul can say that "Christ in you" is the "hope of glory" (Col. 1:27).

[¶9] Scripture also teaches that justification is by faith alone in Christ alone. The biblical testimony to this truth is clear, but I will cite one particularly relevant text, noted by Murray in *Redemption Accomplished and Applied*—a text that has controlling significance on our understanding of justification by faith. In Gal. 2:16 Paul declares that we have "believed in Jesus Christ, so that we might be justified by faith in Christ and not by works of the law." In commenting on this verse Murray observes, "In a word, faith in Christ is in order to justification and is therefore regarded as antecedent to it (cf. also Romans 4:23, 24)." It is in this context, then, that we are to understand Paul's language that believers are justified by faith (Rom. 3:28), as they receive the free gift of righteousness (Rom. 5:17). There is no justification for believers prior to or apart from Spirit-engendered faith-union with Christ.

[¶10] The Westminster Standards therefore situate the justification of believers within (a) the larger context of union with Christ by faith, and (b) faith as the exclusive receiving instrument of imputed righteousness. There is no context for the justification of believers that occurs prior to union with Christ, whether that priority is understood temporally or logically. Likewise, there is no context for a justification of believers that occurs prior to faith, either temporally or logically.[4]

---

4. Lane G. Tipton, "Biblical Theology and the Westminster Standards Revisited: Union with Christ and Justification *Sola Fide*," *West-minster Theological Journal* 75 (2013): 3–6.

a. Wrought (adj.): created
b. Expound (v.): to set forth, present, or teach
c. Invoke (v.): to introduce
d. Position (v.): to place or situate
e. Set (v.): to cause to assume a specified relation
f. Denote (v.): to serve as the linguistic expression of something; to mean
g. Encompass (v.): to include
h. Recapitulate (v.): to restate briefly; to give a summary of
i. Manifest (v): to make evident or certain by showing or displaying

j. Delineate (v.): to describe in detail especially with sharpness or vividness
k. Attendant (adj.): accompanying; connected with
l. Forensic (adj.): of or relating to legal matters
m. Constellation (n.): a pattern or arrangement
n. Net (adj.): basic or fundamental
o. Engendered (adj.): caused to exist or develop
p. Instrumental (adj.): being an instrument that functions in the promotion of some end or purpose
q. Organ (n.): something exercising some function or accomplishing some end

Post-Reading

According to Tipton, what do union with Christ and justification have in common? Which has logical priority?

Main Ideas and Details

(1) Which of the following is the main idea of this passage?
   a. Justification must precede union with Christ by faith.
   b. Union with Christ by faith precedes justification by faith.
   c. Union with Christ and justification occur at precisely the same time.
   d. We can receive benefits of our union with Christ when we have faith.

(2) Which of the following sentences supports the main idea of the passage?
   a. The Westminster Larger Catechism expands and expounds what union with Christ involves.
   b. Union with Christ is an expansive reality that encompasses both realized and future aspects of eschatology.
   c. Notice that before any particular benefit is discussed in the Westminster Larger Catechism, union and communion with Christ are invoked.
   d. The net effect of the teaching contained in the Shorter and Larger Catechisms is that union with Christ occurs by a Spirit-wrought faith in effectual calling.

(3) Based on the context at the end of paragraph 2, the word "realized" means _____.
   a. Made real.
   b. Concealed.
   c. Overlooked.
   d. Accomplished.

(4) At the end of paragraph 3, the phrase "the benefactor" refers to _____.
   a. Christ.
   b. Oneself.
   c. Justification.
   d. The Holy Spirit.

(5) In paragraph 5, it is implied that the author agrees with what three sources?

(6) In your own words, restate the main idea of paragraph 7.

(7) The phrase "the former" at the beginning of paragraph 8 refers to _____.
   a. "These twin truths" in paragraph 7.
   b. Scripture's testimony that justification is by faith alone.
   c. Union with Christ as central to the application of redemption.

 We can use intonation to show the relationships between our ideas, and this can mirror the grammatical parallelism we have already noted. Consider the final few sentences of the reading passage:

There is no context for the justification of believers that occurs prior to union with Christ, whether that priority is understood <u>temporally or logically</u>. **Likewise**, <u>there is no context for</u> a justification of believers that occurs prior to faith, either <u>temporally or logically</u>.

The sentence structure and words introduced in the first sentence are repeated in the second sentence, and they are joined by the word "Likewise." This word suggests that the intonation (e.g., rising pitch on the word "no") that we use in the first sentence will likely be matched in the pronunciation of the second sentence. So the repeated sentence structures (grammar) align with choices of intonation (phonology) and tell the hearer that there is a clear relationship between the ideas, a relationship of similarity (reference).

Understanding the Passage

Write a "T" next to the statements that are true, and an "F" next to the statements that are false. If a statement is false, revise it to agree with the reading passage.

1. _____ Before union with Christ is discussed in the Westminster Larger Catechism, particular benefits are presented.

2. _____ Union with the person of Christ is logically prior to any specific benefit we receive from such union.

3. _____ Union with Christ is an attendant benefit of justification.

4. _____ On the matter of Spirit-given faith, Calvin, Gaffin, and Tipton are in agreement.

5. _____ By faith we are united to Christ, and by faith we are justified.

6. _____ In reflecting on Gal. 2:16, Murray notes that justification is antecedent to our union with Christ.

Collocations from the Passage

Select the most appropriate word from the choices in the parentheses. All of these examples of collocations have been taken directly from the reading.

Both union with Christ and justification come to us by faith (*only/alone/solely*). It is by Spirit-wrought faith that we are joined to Christ, and it is through that same faith that the benefits of salvation are (*applied/associated/engaged*). While we could be more (*sophisticated/elaborate/simple*) here, we can say concisely that faith plays the (*central/middle/innermost*) role in our redemption. On this point, the creeds of the church, the majority of Reformed theologians, and, most importantly, the biblical (*confirmation/testimony/conjecture*) are in agreement. It is in the larger (*place/climate/context*) of union with Christ that we receive all of the spiritual blessings mentioned in Eph. 1:3.

Using some of the collocations above, answer the following question: How do we understand justification in relation to union with Christ?

Grammar Focus: Revisiting Definite and Indefinite Articles

In this lesson, we will finish our discussion of how we can add information to our sentences. In the remaining lessons, we will focus on editing for structure and word choice.

As we noted in Lesson 8, articles can seem insignificant, and they may simply be irritating for non-native English speakers. But they still play an important role in English grammar. In Lesson 8, we introduced three principles for using articles:

1. Articles tell us something about the author's perspective on the reader's knowledge.

2. The presence or absence of an article tells us whether a noun is considered general or specific.

3. The indefinite article can be used to tell the reader "what kind."

In this lesson, we introduce three more principles, focusing on how articles can affect the meaning of our expressions. In this sense, they belong in a discussion of how to add information to our sentences. For instance, consider the difference between the following expressions.

Union with Christ
Union with *the* Christ of liberal Christianity

Is the referent of the noun "Christ" the same in both phrases? No! "Christ" in the first sentence refers to the one divine and human person faithfully attested to in Scripture. "The Christ of liberal Christianity" refers to a certain type of Christ—perhaps Christ as a mere moral example.

1. Use "the" before a noun or noun phrase to further specify it or to say, "This is a very particular thing."[5]

"What, specifically, are **the** benefits of being united to Christ by faith in effectual calling?"

Explanation: The author has specific benefits in mind (adoption, justification, sanctification). As noted before, we often specify a noun with a prepositional phrase.

2. If you are talking about a concept (e.g., *theology, science*) or an abstract idea (e.g., *truth, wisdom*), then you will generally not use an article.[6]

"This positions **union with Christ** as the organizing structure in terms of which the Spirit applies to believers several benefits of **redemption**."

Explanation: "Union with Christ" and "redemption" are both concepts.

3. For the words "Bible," "gospel," "Christian," and "human" to be recognized as nouns, we must either add an article to them or make them plural.

A Christian should live by faith.
Christians should live by faith. NOT Christian should live by faith.

Some expressions, such as "**the** same as" and "**the** fact that," use the article and must simply be memorized. You will also need to memorize cases in which a historical document's title requires the article (e.g., the Westminster Confession of Faith; the Westminster Standards).

Activity 1

Note the articles in the passage below. Then answer the questions that follow concerning the articles that have a superscript (e.g., the[1]).

> The[1] Standards are also painstaking in their insistence that the[2] justification of believers occurs only within the[3] context of faith-union with Christ, and not in the[4] eternal decree or in the[5] past-historical atonement or resurrection of Jesus Christ. Put with a[6] different focus, the justification of believers does not occur in terms of predestinarian or past-historical union with the[7] Mediator but only in terms of present personal union with Christ by faith.[7]

1. The phrase "the Standards" uses the article because _____.
   a. Christianity has the only true standards.
   b. "The" is part of the title for the document.
   c. We are saying "what kind" of standards we have in mind.

2. The author writes "the justification of believers" because _____.
   a. Justification is an abstract idea.
   b. Justification is something that everyone knows about.
   c. The noun "justification" is being specified by a prepositional phrase.

5. Swan, *Practical English Usage*, section 12.
6. Ibid., entry 134.
7. Tipton, "Biblical Theology and the Westminster Standards Revisited," 6.

3. The author writes "the context of faith union with Christ" because _____.
    a. "Context" is an abstract idea.
    b. "Context" is a non-count noun.
    c. The noun "context" is being specified by a prepositional phrase.

4. Articles 4 and 5 are used because _____.
    a. The author is saying, "you know which one I mean."
    b. The author is telling us "what kind" of degree/atonement.
    c. These expressions always require the article and must be memorized.

5. The author writes, "a different focus" (article 6) because _____.
    a. "Focus" is a non-count noun.
    b. He is telling us "what kind" of focus.
    c. "Focus" always occurs with the article and must be memorized.

6. The author uses article 7 because _____.
    a. The noun "Mediator" always occurs with the article.
    b. There is only one mediator, and we all know who this is.
    c. The noun "Mediator" is specified by a prepositional phrase.

Activity 2

Insert either the definite (*the*) or indefinite (*a, an*) article in the blank as needed. If no article is needed, place an "X" in the blank.

Moving now in _____ positive direction, we need to note first and foremost that no aspect of forensic justification comes to _____ believers (logically or temporally) prior to union with Christ by faith, so that _____ *justification sola fide depends on union with Christ sola fide.* This statement has significant implications that we need to spell out more clearly.

_____ declaration of righteousness depends on and brings into view _____ righteousness of Christ that is imputed *by faith alone* to _____ believer. The declaration of justification brings into the tribunal of God (objective aspect) _____ concrete reality of union with Christ by Spirit-wrought faith, and _____ imputation of his righteousness received by faith alone (subjective aspect), as that reality to which _____ declaration is addressed. It is only when _____ sinner, by faith, is united to Christ in effectual calling, and when _____ sinner receives by faith alone _____ imputed righteousness of Christ, that the sinner is declared righteous before God.[8]

Activity 3

In a single paragraph (three to four sentences), explain why the expression *"sola fide"* is important to use when we are discussing union with Christ and justification. When you have finished, check with a partner to see if you can find at least one of the following in your paragraph:

• No article used with an abstract idea or concept;
• An indefinite article used to say "what kind";
• A definite article used with a noun that is specified by a prepositional phrase.

8. Ibid., 10.

24

Sanctification

*"The benefit of sanctification immediately follows
justification as inseparably connected with it."*
—Francis Turretin, *Institutes of Elenctic Theology*

Lesson Goals

Theology–To understand sanctification and how it differs from justification

Reading–To learn how to summarize a text accurately

Vocabulary–To learn and use additional collocations from the passage

Grammar–To identify and use participles correctly

Introduction

Union with the person of Christ by faith alone, we have learned, is the ground of justification by faith alone. But we also noted that justification is one of many salvific blessings we receive in Christ. *Sanctification* is another one of those blessings. As Herman Bavinck writes, "To understand the benefit of sanctification correctly, we must proceed from the idea that Christ is our holiness in the same sense in which he is our righteousness."[1] What do you think it means to be sanctified?

"Sanctification" is an old word, dating from the fourteenth century. It comes from the Latin verb *sanctificare*, which means "to make holy." So in simple terms, to be sanctified is to be made holy—perfectly holy, in fact. In John Murray's words, after we are delivered from the ultimate power of sin, there is much work to be done in our lives.

This deliverance from the power of sin secured by union with Christ and from the defilement of sin secured by regeneration does not eliminate all sin from the heart and life of the believer. There is still indwelling sin (*cf.* Rom. 6:20; 7:14–15; 1 John 1:8; 2:1). The believer is not yet so conformed to the image of Christ that he is holy, harmless, undefiled, and separate from sinners. Sanctification is concerned precisely with this fact and it has as its aim the elimination of all sin and complete conformation to the image of God's own Son, to be holy as the Lord is holy. If we take the concept of entire sanctification seriously we are shut up to the conclusion that it will not be realized until the body of our humiliation will be transformed into the likeness of the body of Christ's glory, when the corruptible

---

1. Herman Bavinck, *Reformed Dogmatics*, vol. 4, *Holy Spirit, Church, and New Creation*, ed. John Bolt, trans. John Vriend (Grand Rapids, MI: Baker, 2008), 248.

will put on incorruptible and the mortal will put on immortality (Phil. 3:21; 1 Cor. 15:54).[2]

Sanctification involves every part of us—our intellect, our emotions, our will, our spirit, and even our bodies.[3] And it will not be completed until we enter into glory.

Background for the Reading

In light of Murray's words above, sanctification runs deep and is more than simply "becoming a better person"; it is the process by which the Holy Spirit works in us to conform every part of us to Christ's image.[4] Sanctification is "a real and internal renovation of man by which God delivers the man planted in Christ by faith and justified . . . more and more from his native depravity and transforms him into his own image."[5] The image of Christ—that is the goal toward which sanctification is pressing us.

Reading Skill: Summarizing

As you probably know, a summary is a short retelling of the main ideas of a text in your own words. It should include the main ideas and give the audience a clear picture of the most important support in the original. A summary can be as short as one sentence and as long as an entire article or essay. The length of the summary determines the level of detail you can include.

Here are four things to avoid when summarizing a text.

- **Avoid being too general**. You cannot represent the text so broadly that your audience does not know what the author has contributed to the field. In other words, you need to avoid providing general theological information that the reader would know even if he or she had not read the original source. For example, if you summarize Francis Turretin on the Trinity and say that he believes there are three hypostases in one essence, that is too general. Every orthodox theologian would say the same thing. What does Turretin *add* to the discussion? If your reader cannot distinguish your summary from a summary of a similar work by another author, then your summary is too general.

- **Avoid being too specific**. You need to focus on the most important ideas and leave out unnecessary details. For longer summaries, you can include more details, but you should still only include those details that help your audience understand the author's line of argument.

- **Do not express your opinion on the text**. Unless otherwise instructed by a professor, you should not include your opinion with a summary. Focus on representing the author's original thoughts.

- **DO NOT COPY THE AUTHOR'S WORDS!** When you summarize a text, *even when the reader knows that you are doing so,* you must use quotation marks and an acceptable method of citation whenever you use the author's own words. You can use key words from the original without fear of plagiarism, since you need these key words to discuss the topic. But the background vocabulary, phrases, and sentence structures must be accounted for with citation. Failing to do so is considered plagiarism, and you will likely face negative, and often serious, consequences for this, even if you claim you did not intend to plagiarize. Once you understand what plagiarism is, you are responsible for making sure it never occurs in your work.[6]

---

2. John Murray, *Redemption Accomplished and Applied* (Grand Rapids, MI: Eerdmans, 1955), 179–80.

3. Wayne Grudem, *Systematic Theology: An Introduction to Biblical Doctrine* (Grand Rapids, MI: Zondervan, 2000), 756–57.

4. The Spirit "descends into us and confirms [the Father's] promises, while on our part he makes us ascend to God to the execution of our duty." Francis Turretin, *Institutes of Elenctic Theology*, ed. James T. Dennison Jr., trans. George Musgrave Giger (Phillipsburg, NJ: P&R, 1994), 2:692.

5. Ibid., 2:689.

6. For an explanation of plagiarism, with examples, see the web page entitled "Plagiarism," Westminster Theological Seminary, accessed August 9, 2017, https://students.wts.edu/resources/westminster_center_for_theolog/plagiarism.html.

Steps to Writing a Summary

1. Read the passage and take notes, focusing on the main idea(s).
2. Analyze your notes. Decide which points are the most important to express the main idea of the passage. Plan to omit any details or points that do not help express the main idea.

   Tip: Some students find it helpful to take notes by putting the author's thoughts in their own words.

3. Write your summary, remembering to use your own words. Make sure that your summary reflects what is most important to the author.

   Tip: For shorter summaries, you can restate the main idea of the original in your first sentence.

4. Read your summary.
   a. Does it express the main idea and basic argument structure of the original text?
   b. Is the information accurate?
   c. Is it too general or too specific?
   d. Did you use your own words and properly cite the material?

For additional help with summarizing, see the tables on the following pages. We have suggested a template you might use for writing summaries and important connecting words that will help you maintain coherence in your summary.

Template for Summary Writing

You can use the basic organization below when writing a summary of a reading passage. The potential phrases and expressions may help you to convey the relationships between important ideas from the reading. Remember that accuracy and grammar are important elements in an academic summary, so make sure you have accurately represented the ideas of the author.

Organization	Potential Phrases and Expressions
Main Point[7]	Grudem's focus in this passage is the claim that _____. Grudem's main point in this passage is _____. The central idea for this passage is _____. According to Grudem, _____. [*Quote Grudem's main claim.*] Grudem demonstrates that _____. The author reminds us that _____. In this passage, Grudem emphasizes that _____.
Important Details	Grudem first notes that _____. Then he tells us that _____. After noting that _____, the author claims that _____. In support of his main point, the author offers two pieces of evidence: [*List the evidence and then explain each piece.*] Grudem supports his claim by _____.

7. Additional verbs can be used in these structures, and a brief list can be found in Gerald Graff, Cathy Birkenstein, and Russel Durst, *They Say/I Say: The Moves That Matter in Academic Writing* (New York: Norton, 2009), 37. The important thing is to use verbs that precisely

Organization	Potential Phrases and Expressions
Conclusion (Optional)	Thus, for Grudem _____. In sum, the author shows us that _____. In short, Grudem points out that _____.

Other Important Connectors for Maintaining Coherence

The following words and phrases express important relationships between ideas and are sometimes misused, often when explaining important details. Make sure that, when you use the words or phrases below, those words or phrases accurately represent the relationships between the author's ideas.

Meaning	Words/Phrases
Logical conclusions Use these to introduce a conclusion to an explicit or implied argument or to introduce the effect of a cause.	*Therefore* *Thus* *Hence*
Simple Addition Use these to convey that the author is simply adding one element to another.	*Also* *In addition* *Last but not least* [*introducing a final element in a series*]
Advancing an Argument Use these to show that the author is building upon a previous reason or piece of evidence.	*Moreover* *Furthermore* *What's more* *Accordingly*
Comparison and Contrast Use these to show that the author is comparing or contrasting two ideas.	*Yet* *However* *In comparison* *In contrast* *While X does . . . , Y does . . . .* *On the one hand . . . . On the other hand*
Moving from Less Detailed to More Detailed Use these to show movement from general to specific.	*Specifically* *In particular* *To be specific* *To be more precise,*
Summarizing Use these to introduce a summarizing statement at the end of your paragraph.	*In sum* *In short* *All in all* *To sum up* *Thus*

reflect what the author is doing. Is he *explaining, arguing, critiquing,* or *interpreting*?

Meaning	Words/Phrases
Disagreement or Conflict Use these to express a conflict in ideas or a disagreement between ideas or persons.	*Although* *Even though* *On the contrary* [*defending a person or persons from an accusation or attack*] *In fact* [*following the statement of the incorrect position*]
Showing an Exception or Expressing Surprise Use these to introduce an exception or to show that what follows might not be expected.	*Nevertheless* *Still* *Even though* *Although*
Introducing Ideas Use these to begin discussing an idea or argument.	*In the first place* *To begin with* *First,*
Restatement Use these when you are re-expressing the previous idea.	*In other words* *That is to say* *Put differently*

Pre-Reading

Based on what you now know about justification and sanctification, how exactly does sanctification differ from justification?

Can you think of any biblical analogies that describe how we should now live as new creatures in Christ?

Reading

In the following passage, John Murray explores the meaning of sanctification in Paul's Epistles.

[¶1] What is this sanctification? No passage in the New Testament is more instructive than Rom. 6:1–7:6. The teaching here is oriented[a] against the question with which Paul begins: "Shall we continue in sin that grace may abound?," a question provoked by the exordium[b] accorded to grace in the preceding context. "Where sin abounded, grace superabounded, that as sin hath reigned in death, even so might grace reign through righteousness unto eternal life through Jesus Christ our Lord" (Rom. 5:20, 21). If the grace of God, and therefore his glory, are magnified the more according as grace overcomes sin, the inference would seem to be: let us continue to sin in order that God's grace may be the more extolled.[c] It is this inference the apostle rejects with the most emphatic negative at his disposal, properly rendered[d] in the corresponding Hebrew idiom, "God forbid!" The

Remember?
Can you explain why each article is used in paragraph 1?

perversity[e] of the inference he lays bare[f] by asking another question: "How shall we who are such as have died to sin live any longer therein?" (Rom. 6:2). The pivot[g] of the refutation is: "we died to sin." What does Paul mean?

[¶2] He is using the language of that phenomenon with which all are familiar, the event of death. When a person dies, he is no longer active in the sphere or realm or relation in reference to which he has died. His connection with that realm has been dissolved; he has no further communications with those who still live in that realm, nor do they have with him. He is no longer *en rapport*[h] with life here; it is no longer the sphere of life and activity for him.

[¶3] In accord with this analogy, the person who lives in sin, or to sin, lives and acts in the realm of sin—it is the sphere of his life and activity. And the person who died to sin no longer lives in that sphere. His tie with it has been broken, and he has been translated into another realm. . . . This is the decisive cleavage[i] that the apostle has in view; it is the foundation upon which rests his whole conception of a believer's life, and it is a cleavage, a breach,[j] a translation as really and decisively true in the sphere of moral and religious relationship as in the ordinary experience of death. There is a once-for-all definitive and irreversible breach with the realm in which sin reigns in and unto death.

[¶4] When we take into account the sin which still inheres in the believer, and of the fact that he has not yet attained to the goal appointed for him, the condition of the believer in this life is not one of a static *status quo*.[k] There is abundant evidence to show that it is one of progression, a progression both negative and positive in character; it embraces both mortification and sanctification.

[¶5] The progressiveness in its more positive character is set forth in a great variety of ways. Paul prayed that the love of the Philippians might "abound more and more in knowledge and in all discernment" (Phil. 1:9). Peter speaks of believers as growing, by the sincere milk of the Word, unto salvation (1 Peter 2:2), salvation being understood as salvation consummated and ready to be revealed in the last time (cf. 1:5). And he also exhorts his readers to "grow in the grace and the knowledge of our Lord and Savior Jesus Christ" (2 Peter 3:18). . . . The law of growth applies, therefore, in the realm of Christian life. God is pleased to work through process, and to fail to take account of this principle in the sanctification of the people of God is to frustrate[l] both the wisdom and the grace of God. The child who acts as a man is a monstrosity;[m] the man who acts as a child is a tragedy.[n] If this is true in nature, how much more in Christian behavior. There are babes in Christ; there are young men, and there are old men. And what monstrosities and tragedies have marred the witness of the church by failure to take account of the law of growth!

[¶6] This progression has respect, not only to the individual, but also to the church in its unity and solidarity as the body of Christ. In reality the growth of the individual does not take place except in fellowship of the Spirit. Believers have never existed as independent units. In God's eternal counsel they were chosen in Christ (Eph. 1:4); in the accomplishment of their redemption they were in Christ (2 Cor. 5:14, 15; Eph. 1:7); in the application of redemption they are ushered into the fellowship of Christ (1 Cor. 1:9). And sanctification itself is a process that moves to a consummation which will not be realized for the individual until the whole body of Christ is complete and presented in its totality faultless and without blemish.[8]

a. Orient (v.): to direct toward or place in relation to
b. Exordium (n.): the introductory part of a discourse
c. Extol (v.): to praise highly or glorify
d. Render (v.): to translate
e. Perversity (n.): the quality or state of being corrupt or wicked
f. Lay bare (v. phrase): to uncover, reveal, or expose
g. Pivot (n.): a central or indispensable element

h. En rapport (adj.): in harmony
i. Cleavage (n.): the state of being split or divided
j. Breach (n.): the act of breaking into or out of
k. Status quo (n. phrase): the existing state of affairs at the time in question
l. Frustrate (v.): to make ineffectual or bring to nothing
m. Monstrosity (n.): an excessively shocking example
n. Tragedy (n.): a failure or disaster

Post-Reading

In a single sentence, state something you learned from Murray about sanctification.

Main Ideas and Details

(1) Read the following summaries of this article. Decide which summary is best. Be prepared to explain your reasoning.

    a. In this passage from his *Collected Writings*, Murray discusses Paul's understanding of sanctification. He begins with Rom. 6:1–7:6 and summarizes the verses that immediately precede it. Then he suggests that Christians can sin more freely. Murray explains that this is wrong and uses an illustration of spheres. Then he moves on to discuss the progression Christians should have toward increased holiness. Finally, the passage ends by discussing the church.

    b. In this passage from his *Collected Writings*, Murray discusses Paul's understanding of sanctification. He begins with Rom. 6:1–7:6, which addresses the question of whether Christians can sin more, and thus have grace abound more. Paul's response was a strong "no," since we are dead to sin. Murray explains that this means, negatively, that Christians are completely cut off from sin

and are dead to their sinful nature. Positively, the Christian should be moving away from sin and toward sanctification. Several places in the NT (Phil. 1:9; 1 Peter 2:2; 2 Peter 3:18) discuss how sanctification is a process in which people move toward increased maturity. This process is not only individual, but communal (involving the whole body of Christ), and it will not end until the entire church has been sanctified.

    c. In this passage from his *Collected Writings*, Murray discusses Paul's understanding of sanctification. Paul's language implies that Christians are completely cut off from sin and no longer active in that "sphere of life." Their break from it is as final and complete as death itself. He writes, "There is a once-for-all definitive and irreversible breach with the realm in which sin reigns in and unto death." In other words, our old sinful self has been crucified with Christ, so now we are free to live a holy life in him. However, this does not happen all at once.

(2) In paragraph 1, why does the author use the word "seem" in the clause, "the inference would seem to be"?

(3) What is the object of the verb "lays bare" in paragraph 1?

8. John Murray, *Collected Writings of John Murray* (Carlisle, PA: Banner of Truth, 1977), 2:278–79, 295, 298–99.

(4) In your own words, define the purpose of paragraph 2 (that is, explain how it is functioning in this passage).

(5) Referring to the change that has taken place for one who has moved from "life in sin" to "life in Christ," Murray affirms that this change is "really and decisively true" (paragraph 3). Why does he do this?

    a. Because he wants to emphasize this change.

    b. Because people might think that this change is reversible.

    c. Because he is making a point about the nature of Bible translation.

    d. Because people might think that this change is not as real as physical death.

(6) In paragraph 4, the word "one" is referring to

_____.

    a. Believer.

    b. Evidence.

    c. Static *status quo.*

    d. The condition of the believer.

(7) Which of the following can we infer based on paragraph 4?

    a. The "progressiveness" properly refers only to mortification.

    b. The "progressiveness" properly refers only to sanctification.

    c. Only focusing on either mortification or sanctification misrepresents biblical truth.

    d. There is not really abundant evidence to show that this progression is both negative and positive.

(8) Explain what you think Murray means by the following statement: "The child who acts as a man is a monstrosity; the man who acts as a child is a tragedy."

(9) What do the biblical passages referenced at the beginning of paragraph 5 all have in common (i.e., why is the author referencing them)?

(10) In your own words, state the main idea of paragraph 6.

(11) Which of the following could we infer based on paragraph 6?

    a. No one can be sanctified until all are sanctified.

    b. Believers cannot be distinguished from one another.

    c. The progressiveness of sanctification refers only to the body of Christ.

    d. Excluding the communal nature of sanctification is a biblical distortion.

Understanding the Reading

Label the biblical passages below as either supporting the progressiveness of sanctification (P) or its final consummation (F). (Hint: Not all passages will have a single correct answer.)

_____ 1. "Like newborn infants, long for the pure spiritual milk, that by it you may grow up into salvation" (1 Peter 2:2).

_____ 2. "We know that when he appears we shall be like him, because we shall see him as he is" (1 John 3:2).

_____ 3. "And you, who once were alienated and hostile in mind, doing evil deeds, he has now reconciled in his body of flesh by his death, in order to present you holy and blameless and above reproach before him" (Col. 1:21–22).

_____ 4. "Grow in the grace and knowledge of our Lord and Savior Jesus Christ" (2 Peter 3:18).

_____ 5. "Do all things without grumbling or disputing, that you may be blameless and innocent, children of God without blemish in the midst of a crooked and twisted generation" (Phil. 2:14–15).

_____ 6. "But now we are released from the law, having died to that which held us captive, so that we serve in the new way of the Spirit and not in the old way of the written code" (Rom. 7:6).

Speaking about the Reading

There are times in a class when the professor may ask students to summarize an assigned reading for the class or in small groups. Often when this happens, the professor wants the students to be able verbally to identify the main idea of the text and a few key details the author used to present or support his argument. If you know that there will be a group discussion of an article or book, prepare by asking yourself the "wh-" questions.

- Who or what is the passage about? What is the main argument or claim?

- How does the author argue or support his claim?

- What does the author use for support?

- Why is this passage significant? How does this passage relate to other things I have read? How does it relate to church ministry and spiritual life?

Discuss this reading in small groups of three to four by answering these questions.

Collocations from the Passage

Match the words on the left to their collocates on the right.

communicate	behavior
Christian	rendered
decisively	true
properly	with someone
preceding	context

Provide collocations from the reading passage for the words in the center bubbles below. These collocations may precede or follow these words. There are enough collocations so that all of the bubbles should be filled.

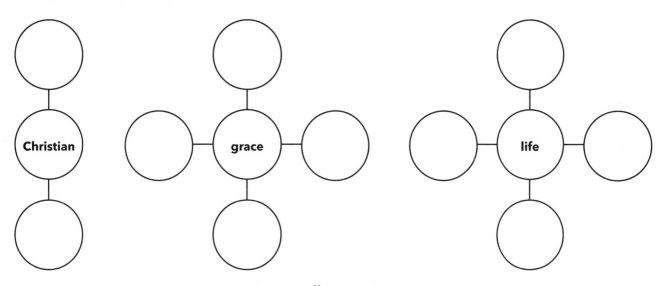

Fig. 24.1. Collocation Diagram 7

Grammar Focus: Participles

Our final grammatical discussion in this textbook will address editing for structure and word choice. Editing is often overlooked, especially by students who are already weighed down with reading and writing assignments. But editing is a critical part of the writing process, and when you edit your writing, you will likely find that you notice errors that you did not notice as you wrote.

One item you can check in your writing is the correct use of participles. Participles are called "non-finite" verbs because they do not have tense and are not conjugated according to person.[9] As you probably know, the past participle often ends in an "-ed," while the present participle ends in "-ing." Participles have a variety of uses, but the main ones are shown below.[10] Note the crossed out form of the participle in each example, which illustrates common errors you might encounter.

9. Infinitives are also non-finite verbs. Finite verbs, on the other hand, do show tense and are conjugated according to person. So we would say, "Jesus rose from the grave," but *not*, "Jesus to rise from the grave."

10. Michael Swan, *Practical English Usage*, 4th ed. (Oxford: Oxford University Press, 2016), entries 96 and 115.

Use	Example
Adjectivally	Jesus' preaching must have been *tired tiring*. *Explanation*: Jesus' activity is being described. We cannot say "tired" because that would mean that Jesus' preaching, like a person, became tired. Instead, we say "tiring," which could mean either that his preaching was an activity that made him tired, or it was an activity that made his listeners tired.
Adverbially	Jesus slept *to face facing* the helm of the boat. *Explanation*: "Facing" tells us how or in what way Jesus slept. "Slept to face" would mean "slept in order to face," but that could mean Jesus could not face the helm of the boat unless he slept.
Clause-like	*Tiring Tired* from the day's activities, the people traveled home. *Explanation*: This means, "Because most of the people were tired from the day's activities . . ." In contrast to the first example, we cannot say "tiring" because that form means "to cause tiresomeness." The "-ed" (past participle) form is passive in meaning, referring to the people.

Notice in the explanations that the past participle can have a passive sense. "Tired from the day's activities" means that the subject of the participle, the people, received the action of being tired; they *were tired*. The present participle can have a more active sense. "Jesus' preaching," the subject of the participle, *causes* either himself or others to become tired. We cannot say that Jesus' actual preaching *was tired*, since it is not possible for an action ("preaching") to become tired. Only people can become tired.

Activity 1

Underline the participles you find in the following passage.

What is this sanctification? No passage in the New Testament is more instructive than Rom. 6:1–7:6. The teaching here is oriented against the question with which Paul begins: "Shall we continue in sin that grace may abound?," a question provoked by the exordium accorded to grace in the preceding context. "Where sin abounded, grace superabounded, that as sin hath reigned in death, even so might grace reign through righteousness unto eternal life through Jesus Christ our Lord" (Rom. 5:20, 21). If the grace of God, and therefore his glory, are magnified the more according as grace overcomes sin, the inference would seem to be: let us continue to sin in order that God's grace may be the more extolled. It is this inference the apostle rejects with the most emphatic negative at his disposal, properly rendered in the corresponding Hebrew idiom, "God forbid!" The perversity of the inference he lays bare by asking another question: "How shall we who are such as have died to sin live any longer therein?" (Rom. 6:2). The pivot of the refutation is: "we died to sin." What does Paul mean?

Activity 2

Insert the correct form of the participle in each blank. The verb is given to you in parentheses behind each blank.

For Murray, sanctification as a "_____ (*mortify*) and _____ (*cleanse*) process is concerned with sin and defilement still adhering to the believer, and it contemplates as its aim the removal of all defilement of flesh and spirit."[11] _____ (*examine*) our own spiritual lives, we find many concrete ways in which we are still "defiled." We awake each morning _____ (*know*) that we will be faced with material temptations as well as opportunities to display our pride. All throughout the day, the devil uses the "principalities and powers" around us (Eph. 6:12), _____ (*encourage*) us to profane God's name. And by the time night comes, we often forget the _____ (*liberate*) truth of the gospel. We may even bring glory to someone other than Christ. But thank God that we are not left to ourselves! The Spirit of the _____ (*live*) God always "works in the interests of glorifying Christ, and of bringing to perfection the goal of the redemptive process."[12] _____ (*shelter*) and _____ (*protect*) by the power of the Spirit, we are progressively refined and purified, _____ (*conform*) more closely each day to the image of Christ.

Activity 3

There are many reasons why Christians should not continue to walk in sin. Some of these reasons were explored in the passage from Murray. Write a paragraph (three to five sentences) explaining one or two of these reasons. (Try to avoid beginning a clause with *because*. Practice using participles instead.) When you have finished, exchange your paragraph with a partner's and check to see if your partner used a participle adjectivally, adverbially, or in a clause-like structure.

Summary of Theological Concepts for Unit 8

- Our union with the person of Christ is the center of Paul's view of salvation. It is only in union with Christ that we can receive other spiritual blessings such as justification, adoption, sanctification, and so forth.
- Justification is our being declared righteous before God. Just as we are united to Christ by faith alone, we are justified in him by faith alone.
- Sanctification is the process by which we are made more holy and conformed more and more to the image of Christ. This process will not be completed until we enter into glory.

Activity 4

Paraphrase each of the concepts above in your own words.

(1)

(2)

(3)

11. Murray, *Collected Writings*, 2:296.
12. Ibid., 2:298.

Justification and Sanctification (ST Task 2)

You have recently begun a ministry for your church in which you choose a prison inmate and correspond with him about the gospel. One day you receive a letter from an inmate who says, "I'm not interested in being accepted by God; what I've done can't be forgiven. I'll always be guilty, and I just keep doing the same things over and over again."

Write this man a one-paragraph letter explaining *either* why God's justification is important for him *or* how God can sanctify us by the power of his Spirit. Because this is a letter, your language might be more conversational.

Learning the Genre: Systematic Theology

We are continuing in our study of genre, moving from church history to systematic theology (ST). It would be helpful at this point to review the genres, some of their communicative goals, and the selected traits we have explored so far.

As we did with biblical studies and church history,

we need to know what systematic theology is as a theological genre before we can understand some of its communicative functions.[13]

Systematic Theology

Geerhardus Vos once wrote, "Biblical Theology draws a *line* of development. Systematic Theology draws a *circle*."[14] What did he mean by this? Essentially, he meant that while biblical theology traces the development of God's plan of redemption throughout history, systematic theology focuses on a particular topic, gathering the teaching of Scripture into one place in order to answer a question or address a theological issue. In other words, "systematic theology is any study that answers the question, 'What does the whole Bible teach us today?' about any given topic."[15]

Using that as a working definition, we can ask what some of the communicative functions of ST writing are. What does writing in this genre seek to do? What are its tasks? Louis Berkhof suggests that systematic theology in the Reformed tradition has a *constructive*,

Genre	Communicative Goals	Selected Traits
Apologetics	critiquing non-Christian thought defending biblical truth	Logical coherence: *internal* organization of ideas signaled *externally* by words and phrases
Biblical Studies	understanding (through explanation and description) what Scripture teaches building an argument in support of what Scripture teaches	Textual awareness: using details from the text to build an argument, and relating one text to another in support of a main idea
Church History	learning from and understanding figures and movements in church history answering a *how* or *why* question	Signals of time and context: pointing out the historical, social, economic, political, and other circumstances surrounding a figure or movement

13. Recall, again, our earlier definition of genre: a genre is "a type of discourse that occurs in a particular setting, that has distinctive and recognizable patterns and norms of organization and structure, and that has particular and distinctive communicative functions." Jack C. Richards and Richard Schmidt, *Longman Dictionary of Language Teaching and Applied Linguistics*, 3rd ed. (New York: Longman, 2002), 224.

14. Geerhardus Vos, *Biblical Theology: Old and New Testaments* (Carlisle, PA: Banner of Truth, 2014), 16.

15. Wayne Grudem, *Systematic Theology: An Introduction to Biblical Doctrine* (Grand Rapids: Zondervan, 2000), 21. Grudem notes that this definition is one he has taken from John Frame during his teaching days at Westminster Theological Seminary. We are, of course, using a simplified definition for systematic theology (also treated as "dogmatics"). There is more to ST than answers to topical questions, but this definition is generally accurate and serves our current needs.

defensive, and *critical* task.[16] Constructively, it gathers and relates the biblical truths confessed by the church into a functional whole. In other words, it fits together all of what we know from Scripture. For example, in the Reformed tradition, consider how the Creator-creature distinction fits well with a Reformed view of revelation (God's condescension) and a Reformed view of grace (God doing what only he, as God, could do to save us). Defensively, systematic theology must show that (1) its conclusions are rooted in Scripture, and (2) attacks against its teaching have biblical responses. Critically, ST critiques other approaches that either are not built upon Scripture or misinterpret some part of what Scripture teaches. In this last sense, systematic theological texts of the Reformed tradition often argue that the Reformed tradition is more biblically faithful than others.

We can summarize Berkhof's three ST tasks and label them as *communicative functions,* since all of these tasks serve communicative purposes. In this sense, the communicative functions of systematic theology are (1) presenting the gathered teachings of Scripture on a particular topic, while being sensitive to the broader range of other biblical truths confessed by the church; (2) showing how abstract claims are actually rooted in Scripture, and using these "roots" to refute unbelievers' attacks on the faith; and (3) showing the biblical contradictions or inconsistencies in other approaches to a specific topic.

What about the specific *traits* of this genre? We do not have the time to explore several of these traits, so here we will examine just three of them, paying special attention to the final one: (1) engaging with other figures in church history, (2) appealing to confessional documents, and, most importantly, (3) gathering Scriptural teaching to address a topical question. Notice how this final trait is distinct from the trait of textual awareness in biblical studies, which seeks to explain or describe a biblical text itself. All of these traits can be described as, in one sense or another, **appeals to authority**.

An example from the ST genre will help us understand these traits more concretely. Consider the following passage. What topical question are the authors trying to answer? How do they go about answering it?

Having defined "sin" as the breaking of the covenant, the main distinction that remains to be made is the question whether sin should be characterized as unbelief or disobedience. . . .

Sin is indeed *unbelief.* Adam did not believe the word of God that came to him in the prohibition as a word of life. He did not consider it to be true, reliable, or forceful. To Calvin this characterizes sin. "Therefore unbelief was the root of apostasy. This in turn led to ambition and pride, coupled with ingratitude, because Adam, more covetous than warranted, despised the great goodness of God with which he had been blessed" (*Institutes,* 2.1.4).

For this reason, Calvin opts for the definition of sin as unbelief and combines this with other characterizations that are its consequences. Earlier he says that Augustine is not incorrect in saying that pride is the beginning of all calamities. Yet Calvin does not end with Augustine.

In this connection it is good to point out that especially the New Testament warns against unbelief (coupled with distrust and doubt; e.g., Matt. 13:58; 17:17; John 20:27; Acts 28:24; Rom. 11:20; 2 Cor. 4:4; Heb. 3:19; Rev. 21:8). *Disobedience* is equivalent to unbelief. It consists in transgressing God's command (Gen. 3:6; Rom. 5:12–21; 2 Cor. 10:6; Heb. 2:2).

It is difficult to choose between these two. Sin is an act of the heart (Prov. 4:23; Matt. 15:18–19; the converse is the beatitude of the pure in heart, Matt. 5:8). He who in his heart chooses against God engages in both unbelief and disobedience. Both are aspects of the same thing. Sinful man rejects the Word of God that calls for faith. He rejects the commandment, which demands obedience.[17]

The authors are trying to answer the question, "Is sin unbelief or disobedience?" Their answer is

---

16. Louis Berkhof, *Systematic Theology,* new ed. (Grand Rapids: Eerdmans, 1996), 58–59.

17. J. van Genderen and W. H. Velema, *Concise Reformed Dogmatics,* trans. Gerrit Bilkes and Ed M. van der Maas (Phillipsburg, NJ: P&R, 2008), 397–98.

"both," and they present this in two ways. First, they engage with figures in church history (Calvin and Augustine), noting how those figures addressed the same question. This is common in systematic theology, since history contains not only all of God's special revelation (Scripture) but also the people who have tried to interpret that revelation. We explored this in our genre study of church history. Second, the authors gather Scriptural teachings on various topics and bring them together. They are not exhaustive in their gathering, but they do draw from a range of passages in order to account for what Scripture has to say about a certain topic such as unbelief.

Topic	Scriptural Teaching
Unbelief	Matt. 13:58; 17:17; John 20:27; Acts 28:24; Rom. 11:20; 2 Cor. 4:4; Heb. 3:19; Rev. 21:8
Disobedience	Gen. 3:6; Rom. 5:12–21; 2 Cor. 10:6; Heb. 2:2
The Heart	Prov. 4:23; Matt. 5:8; 15:18–19

Activity 5

Have a look at another passage and see if you can find the question or topic the author is addressing and how he answers or addresses it.

What is a good work? Reformed theologians have addressed this question in response to the *problem of the virtuous pagan*. Reformed theology teaches that human beings by nature are *totally depraved*. This means not that they are as bad as they can be, but that it is impossible for them to please God in any of their thoughts, words, or deeds (Rom. 8:8). So apart from grace, none of us can do anything good in the sight of God. Yet all around us we see non-Christians who seem, at least, to be doing good works: they love their families, work hard at their jobs, contribute to the needs of the poor, show kindness to their neighbors. It seems that these pagans are virtuous by normal measures.

Reformed theology, however, questions these normal measures. It acknowledges that unbelievers often contribute to the betterment of society. These contributions are called *civic righteousness* and come from God's common grace, which restrains sin. Their civic righteousness does not please God, however, because it is altogether devoid of three characteristics:

> Works done by unregenerate men, although for the matter of them they may be things which God commands; and of good use both to themselves and others: yet, because they proceed not from an heart purified by faith; nor are done in a right manner, according to the Word; nor to a right end, the glory of God, they are therefore sinful, and cannot please God, or make a man meet to receive grace from God: and yet, their neglect of them is more sinful and displeasing unto God. (WCF 16.7)

Note the three necessary ingredients: (1) a heart purified by faith, (2) obedience to God's Word, and (3) the right end, the glory of God.

The first is a plainly biblical emphasis. The confession cites Hebrews 11:4 and some other texts. Romans 14:23b also comes to mind: "For whatever does not proceed from faith is sin." In Jesus' arguments with the Pharisees, too, it is evident that our righteousness must not be merely external (see esp. Matt. 23:25–26). In describing the necessity of an internal motive of good works, Scripture refers not only to faith, but especially to love, as in 1 Corinthians 13:1–3 and many other passages. We learn from these passages that love is not only necessary for good works, but also sufficient: that is, if our act is motivated by a true love of God and neighbor, we have fulfilled the law (Matt. 22:40; Rom. 13:8; Gal. 5:14).

The second element of good works, according to the confession, is obedience to God's Word, to his law. Note the references in the previous section to the importance of obeying God's Word. Certainly, obedience to God's Word is a necessary condition of good works, for disobedience to God's law is the very definition of sin (1 John 3:4). It is also a sufficient condition: for if we have obeyed God perfectly, we have done everything necessary to be good in his sight. Of course, among God's commands are his command to love (see the paragraph above) and to seek his glory (see the next paragraph).

The third element is the right end, the glory of God. Ethical literature has often discussed the *summum bonum*, or "highest good," for human beings. What is it that we are trying to achieve in our ethical actions? Many secular writers have said that this goal is pleasure or human happiness. But Scripture says that in everything we do, we should be seeking the glory of God (1 Cor. 10:31). Certainly, any act must glorify God if it is to be good, so seeking God's glory is a necessary condition of good works. And if the act does glorify God, then it is good; so it is a sufficient condition.

So there are three necessary and sufficient conditions of good works: right motive, right standard, and right goal.[18]

1. What is the question the author is answering? Can you summarize his answer?

2. To what authorities does the author appeal?

In this passage, we see that systematic theologians can appeal not only to other figures in church history, but also to confessional documents. This is especially prevalent in the Reformed tradition, which frequently appeals to the Westminster Confession of Faith (WCF). But notice that Frame does not stop there; he goes on to show that the WCF is built upon Scripture (Heb. 11:4; Rom. 14:23; 1 Cor. 13:1–3; 1 John 3:4; 1 Cor. 10:31). In doing this, he is fulfilling the systematic theological "task" of showing how abstract claims are rooted in Scripture. This, in turn, shows that Frame is also appealing to the gathered teaching of the Bible, which stands behind the statements of the confession.

There are many other traits of the systematic theology genre, but the ones we have seen, particularly the gathering of Scripture to address a topic, are certainly prevalent. Each of the traits we have looked at is a kind of *appeal to authority*. We can now update our chart of theological genres.

Genre	Communicative Goals	Selected Traits
Apologetics	critiquing non-Christian thought defending biblical truth	Logical coherence: *internal* organization of ideas signaled *externally* by words and phrases

18. John M. Frame, *Systematic Theology: An Introduction to Christian Belief* (Phillipsburg, NJ: P&R, 2013), 1102–3.

Genre	Communicative Goals	Selected Traits
Biblical Studies	understanding (through explanation and description) what Scripture teaches building an argument in support of what Scripture teaches	Textual awareness: using details from the text to build an argument, and relating one text to another in support of a main idea
Church History	learning from and understanding figures and movements in church history answering a *how* or *why* question	Signals of time and context: pointing out the historical, social, economic, political, and other circumstances surrounding a figure or movement
Systematic Theology	presenting the gathered teachings of Scripture on a particular topic showing how abstract claims are rooted in Scripture showing the biblical contradictions or inconsistencies in other approaches to a specific topic	Appeals to authority: gathering Scriptural teaching to address a topical question, engaging with other figures in church history, and appealing to confessional documents

UNIT 9

WHERE DOES THE CHURCH FIT?
(SYSTEMATIC THEOLOGY)

25

The Church and Salvation

"Jesus did not just die for individuals; he died for a people, a body, a bride,
consisting of many people, united in the bonds of a larger whole."
—John M. Frame, *Systematic Theology*

Lesson Goals

Theology–To understand various aspects of the church in relation to salvation
Reading–To continue to identify main ideas and details, and to draw inferences
Vocabulary–To learn and use additional collocations from the passage
Grammar–To identify and use *that* clauses

Introduction

Thus far, we have looked at salvation for the individual in terms of union with Christ and its attendant benefits. At places, however, we have seen authors reference the entire church in this process. In this lesson, we turn our attention specifically to the church in the context of salvation.

We might start by asking a few questions:

(1) How would you define the church?

(2) Why would it be detrimental for a Christian not to be part of a church?

These questions get at the heart of how the church relates to our salvation. The church is the body of Christ (Rom. 12:5; 1 Cor. 12:12, 27; Col. 1:18, 24)—one body with many members. So we are not saved merely as individuals, but *as members of the one body of Christ.* Unity within that body "is both a fact and a norm. God has made it one, but he commands us to seek oneness."[1] One of the reasons we are commanded to do so is that the church plays an integral role in our spiritual health and maturity. That is why it is detrimental for a Christian not to be part of a church.

The roots of this truth go back to the Old Testament. In Ecclesiastes, we are reminded that fellowship with the saints is for our betterment:

Two are better than one, because they have a good reward for their toil. For if they fall, one will lift up his fellow. But woe to him who is alone when he falls and has not another to lift him up! Again, if two lie together, they keep warm, but how can one keep warm alone? And though a man might prevail against one who

---

1. John M. Frame, *Systematic Theology: An Introduction to Christian Belief* (Phillipsburg, NJ: P&R, 2013), 1022.

is alone, two will withstand him—a threefold cord is not quickly broken (Eccl. 4:9–12).

Following up on this truth in the light of Christ's work, Paul writes in Eph. 4:2–3 that we are to treat fellow believers "with patience, bearing with one another in love, eager to maintain the unity of the Spirit in the bond of peace." Again, in 1 Thess 5:11, he tells us to "encourage one another and build one another up." Our relationships with other believers are essential to our growth and development in the faith. We isolate ourselves from the body of Christ at our own peril.

Background for the Reading

Western culture tends to be more individualistic rather than communal. As a result, it can be easier for Christians in the West to think of salvation and Christian faith as an individual journey rather than both an individual and corporate one. Indeed, Edmund Clowney reminds us, "We are not only individual points of light in the world, but a city set on a hill."[2] He goes on to say that "only as the church binds together those whom selfishness and hate have cut apart will its message be heard and its ministry of hope to the friendless be received."[3]

In short, we cannot "go it alone." The church is our necessary environment as new creatures in Christ. As Murray tells us, "Believers have never existed as independent units. In God's eternal counsel they were chosen in Christ (Eph. 1:4); in the accomplishment of their redemption they were in Christ (2 Cor. 5:14, 15; Eph. 1:7); in the application of redemption they are ushered into the fellowship of Christ (1 Cor. 1:9)."[4]

Pre-Reading

Describe the church in two to three complete sentences. (Consider its parts or aspects.)

Reading

In the following passage, Louis Berkhof outlines a few distinctions concerning the church.

[¶1] In speaking of the Church several distinctions come into consideration.

[¶2] 1. That of a militant and a triumphant church. The Church in the present dispensation is a militant Church, that is, she is called unto, and is actually engaged in, a holy warfare. This, of course, does not mean that she must spend her strength in self-destroying internecine[a] struggles, but that she is duty bound to carry on an incessant[b] warfare against the hostile world in every form in which it reveals itself, whether in the Church or outside of it, and against all the spiritual forces of darkness. The Church may not spend all her time in prayer and meditation, however necessary and important these may be, nor may she rest on her oars[c] in the peaceful enjoyment of her spiritual heritage. She must be engaged with all her might in the battles of her Lord, fighting in a war that is both offensive and defensive. If the Church on earth is the militant Church, the Church in heaven is the triumphant Church. There the sword is exchanged for the palm of victory, the battle-cries are turned into songs of triumph, and the cross is replaced by the crown. The strife is

Remember?

How is the participle "fighting" functioning here?

---

2. Edmund P. Clowney, *The Church*, Contours of Christian Theology (Downers Grove, IL: InterVarsity, 1995), 15–16.
3. Ibid., 16.
4. John Murray, *Collected Writings of John Murray* (Carlisle, PA: Banner of Truth, 1977), 2:299.

over, the battle is won, and the saints reign with Christ forever and ever. In these two stages of her existence the Church reflects the humiliation and exaltation of her heavenly Lord. . . .

[¶3] 2. That between a visible and an invisible Church. This means that the Church of God is on the one hand visible, and on the other invisible. It is said that Luther was the first to make this distinction, but the other Reformers recognized and also applied it to the Church. This distinction has not always been properly understood. The opponents of the Reformers often accused them of teaching that there are two separate Churches. Luther perhaps gave some occasion[d] for this charge by speaking of an invisible *ecclesiola*[e] within the visible *ecclesia*. But both he and Calvin stress the fact that, when they speak of a visible and an invisible Church, they do not refer to two different Churches, but to two aspects of the one Church of Jesus Christ. The term "invisible" has been variously interpreted as applying (a) to the triumphant Church; (b) to the ideal and completed Church as it will be at the end of the ages; (c) to the Church of all lands and all places, which man cannot possibly see; and (d) to the Church as it goes in hiding in the days of persecution, and is deprived of the Word and the sacraments. Now it is undoubtedly true that the triumphant Church is invisible to those who are on earth, and that Calvin in his *Institutes* also conceives of this as being included in the invisible Church, but the distinction was undoubtedly primarily intended to apply to the militant Church. As a rule it is so applied in Reformed theology. It stresses the fact that the Church as it exists on earth is both visible and invisible. This Church is said to be invisible, because she is essentially spiritual and in her spiritual essence cannot be discerned by the physical eye; and because it is impossible to determine infallibly who do and who do not belong to her. The union of believers with Christ is a mystical[f] union; the Spirit that unites them constitutes an invisible tie; and the blessings of salvation, such as regeneration, genuine conversion, true faith, and spiritual communion with Christ, are all invisible to the natural eye;—and yet these things constitute the real *forma* (ideal character) of the Church. . . .

[¶4] The invisible Church naturally assumes a visible form. Just as the human soul is adapted[g] to a body and expresses itself through the body, so the invisible Church, consisting, not of mere souls but of human beings having souls and bodies, necessarily assumes a visible form in an external organization through which it expresses itself. The Church becomes visible in Christian profession and conduct, in the ministry of the Word and of the sacraments, and in external organization and government. . . . It is very important to bear in mind that, though both the invisible and the visible Church can be considered as universal, the two are not in every respect commensurate.[h] It is possible that some who belong to the invisible Church never become members of the visible organization, as missionary subjects who are converted on their deathbeds, and that others are temporarily excluded from it, as erring[i] believers who are for a time shut out from the communion of the visible Church. On the other hand there may be unregenerated children and adults who, while professing Christ, have no true faith in Him, in the Church as an external institution; and these, as long as they are in that condition, do not belong to the invisible Church. . . .

[¶5] 3. That between the church as an organism[j] and the church as an institution.[k] This distinction should not be identified with the preceding one, as is sometimes done. It is a distinction that applies to the *visible* Church and that directs attention to two different aspects of the Church considered as a visible body. It is a mistake to think that the Church becomes visible only in the offices, in the administration[l] of the Word and the sacraments, and in a certain form of Church government. Even if all these things were absent,[m] the Church would still be visible in the communal life and profession of the believers, and in their joint opposition to the world. But while emphasizing the fact that the distinction under consideration is a distinction within the visible Church, we should not forget that both the Church as an organism and the Church as an institution (also called *apparitio*[n] and *institutio*[o]) have their spiritual background in the invisible Church. . . . The Church as an organism is the *coetus fidelium*,[p] the communion of believers, who are united in the bond of the Spirit, while the Church as an institution is the *mater fidelium*,[q] the mother of believers, a *Heilsanstalt*,[r] a means of salvation, an agency for the conversion of sinners and the perfecting of the saints. . . . The Church as an institution or organization (*mater fidelium*) is a means to an end, and this is found in the Church as an organism, the community of believers (*coetus fidelium*).[5]

Remember?
How is the participle "preceding" functioning here?

a. Internecine (adj.): of, relating to, or involving conflict within a group
b. Incessant (adj.): continuing without interruption
c. Oar (n.): a long wooden pole with a broad flat blade at one end that is used for propelling a boat
d. Occasion (n.): a circumstance or state of affairs that provides ground or reason for something
e. *Ecclesiola* (n.): Latin for "little church"
f. Mystical (adj.): having a spiritual meaning, existence, or reality
g. Adapt (v.): to make suitable or fit (for a purpose or situation)
h. Commensurate (adj.): equal in measure or extent
i. Err (v.): to violate an accepted standard of conduct

j. Organism (n.): something felt to resemble a living plant or animal
k. Institution (n.): a significant element in the life of a culture that centers on a fundamental human need, activity, or value, and is usually maintained and stabilized through social regulatory agencies
l. Administration (n.): a furnishing or tendering according to a prescribed rite or formula
m. Absent (adj.): not present
n. *Apparitio* (n.): Latin for "service"
o. *Institutio* (n.): Latin for "instruction" or "education"
p. *Coetus fidelium* (n. phrase): Latin for "group of the faithful"
q. *Mater fidelium* (n. phrase): Latin for "mother of the faithful"
r. *Heilsanstalt* (n.): German for "institution of salvation"

Post-Reading

Using what you have learned from Berkhof, revise or add to your original description of the church.

Main Ideas and Details

(1) What are the three distinctions the author makes in reference to the church?

(2) Based on the context in paragraph 2, what does the author mean by saying that the church may not "rest on her oars"?

(3) In paragraph 2, which sentence does the author use to signal that he is shifting his focus within the paragraph? (Underline the sentence.)

(4) What were the Reformers accused of doing by their opponents? (Refer to paragraph 3.)

(5) What is the referent for the highlighted pronoun "it" in paragraph 3?

5. Louis Berkhof, *Systematic Theology*, new ed. (Grand Rapids, MI: Eerdmans, 1996), 565–67.

a. The Word.
b. The Church.
c. The Word and the sacraments.
d. None of the above.

(6) Which of the following can we infer based on paragraph 3?
   a. The invisible church is more important that the visible church.
   b. The visible church is more important than the invisible church.
   c. We should not attempt to discern who belongs to the invisible church.
   d. The distinction between the visible and invisible church cannot be understood.

(7) In paragraph 4, the word "assumes" means _____.
   a. To take for granted.
   b. To take upon oneself.
   c. To claim more than is due.
   d. To take up a certain place or position.

(8) Which of the sentences below best expresses the essential information in the highlighted sentence from paragraph 4?
   a. People who err are disassociated from the visible church.
   b. Some members of the visible church are temporarily excluded.
   c. Not all members of the true church are part of the visible church.
   d. Those who are converted on their deathbeds cannot be part of the invisible church.

(9) Which of the following is not an accurate statement concerning the invisible church?
   a. It is spiritual in nature.
   b. It cannot be seen by the physical eye.
   c. It includes the spiritual union of believers to Christ.
   d. Its difference from the visible church has always been understood.

Understanding the Reading

(1) Practice what you have learned about summarizing a text by writing a one paragraph summary of the passage for this lesson. Make sure you have included the main ideas and are appropriately specific (not too vague, but not too thorough).

(2) Without looking at the reading, label the following statements with a "1" (militant/triumphant church), "2" (visible/invisible church), or "3" (church as organism/institution).

_____ The union of believers with Christ is a mystical union; the Spirit that unites them constitutes an invisible tie.

_____ The Church is duty bound to carry on an incessant warfare against the hostile world in every form in which it reveals itself.

_____ The Church reflects the humiliation and exaltation of her heavenly Lord.

_____ This is a distinction that applies to the *visible* Church and that directs attention to two different aspects of the Church considered as a visible body.

_____ This Church is essentially spiritual and in her spiritual essence cannot be discerned by the physical eye.

_____ The Church must be engaged with all her might in the battles of her Lord, fighting in a war that is both offensive and defensive.

_____ There may be unregenerated children and adults who, while professing Christ, have no true faith in Him.

_____ The opponents of the Reformers often accused them of teaching that there are two separate Churches.

Collocations from the Passage

Select the most appropriate word from the choices in the parentheses. All of these examples of collocations have been taken directly from the reading.

The church (*engages in/fights for/combats*) spiritual (*fighting/warfare/quarrels*), and for Berkhof, it is both militant and triumphant. We recognize this (*value/separation/distinction*) because we know that, on the one hand, we are still fighting against the powers of evil, and, on the other hand, Christ is ultimately victorious. While we spend all of our (*seconds/ time/moments*) fighting against the destructive powers of sin, we know that the battle has been (*won/waged/succeeded*). We live in a hostile (*world/planet/place*), but Christ has overcome it (John 16:33).

Using some of the collocations above, write a paragraph (three to five sentences) in which you describe how, as a member of the militant/triumphant church, you are still fighting against sin and are yet victorious over it.

Grammar Focus: *That* Clauses

We are continuing our discussion of editing for structure and word choice. In the last lesson, we learned how participles can be used (and misused) adjectivally, adverbially, and in clause-like structures. You can check your writing to make sure you have used the correct form of the participle by asking whether or not the subject of the participle is receiving (past participle) or producing (present participle) the action.

In this lesson, we focus on another common structure that may be misused or formed incorrectly in your writing: a *that* clause. In Lesson 18, we studied noun clauses. A **that clause** is a noun clause

beginning with the word "that," which is used not as a demonstrative or relative pronoun but as a "connector," showing that what follows is only part of a larger sentence structure.[6] In this sense, a *that* clause is a unit within a sentence and either functions like a noun or completes the meaning of a verb, noun, or adjective. It has the following form:

"that" + subject + predicate (finite verb)

Michael Swan suggests four ways in which *that* clauses are used.[7]

(1) As the **subject** of the sentence.

> That Paul served the church is uncontested.

(2) As a **complement** after the verb "to be."

> What is important is that we study God's word carefully.

(3) As an **object** of the verb.

> Luther knew that it would be difficult to hide from the papacy.

(4) As a complement of a noun or adjective.

> I admire Calvin's point that we should always be humble in approaching theology.

Activity 1

In the paragraph below, underline the *that* clauses.

This means that the Church of God is on the one hand visible, and on the other invisible. It is said that Luther was the first to make this distinction, but the other Reformers recognized and also applied it to the Church. This distinction has not always been properly understood. The opponents of the Reformers often accused them of teaching that there are two separate Churches. Luther perhaps gave some occasion for this charge by speaking of an invisible *ecclesiola* within the visible *ecclesia*. But both he and Calvin stress the fact that, when they speak of a visible and an invisible Church, they do not refer to two different Churches, but to two aspects of the one Church of Jesus Christ. . . . Now it is undoubtedly true that the triumphant Church is invisible to those who are on earth, and that Calvin in his *Institutes* also conceives

6. Michael Swan, *Practical English Usage*, 4th ed. (Oxford: Oxford University Press, 2016), entry 264.
7. Ibid.

of this as included in the invisible Church, but the distinction was undoubtedly primarily intended to apply to the militant Church. As a rule it is so applied in Reformed theology. It stresses the fact that the Church as it exists on earth is both visible and invisible. This Church is said to be invisible, because she is essentially spiritual and in her spiritual essence cannot be discerned by the physical eye; and because it is impossible to determine infallibly who do and who do not belong to her.

Activity 2

In a complete sentence, describe the church using a *that* clause with the structure provided.

(1) Following the verb "suggests."

(2) As the subject of a sentence.

(3) Following the verb "is."

(4) Following an adjective.

Activity 3

In light of the reality that the church is the *militant* church, you likely know of several people who are struggling with some spiritual or physical trauma. One of the important ways in which we encourage and build one another up in the body (1 Thess 5:11) is through prayer. In four to six sentences, write out a prayer for a fellow believer. Try to use the verbs "ask," "pray," and "know" at least once.

Activity 4

Read your prayer out loud by yourself. Think about your word stress. Remember that function words such as articles, prepositions, and pronouns (including "that") are rarely stressed.

The Visible and Invisible Church (ST Task 3)

Introduction

In this task, you will be composing an email to a college student in your church. You have learned that we can look at the church from two perspectives: (1) that of the visible church and (2) that of the invisible church. Edmund Clowney uses the figure below to illustrate this.[8] Use this information when writing your email.

8. Clowney, *The Church*, 109.

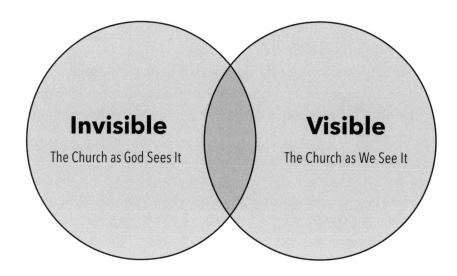

Fig. 25.1. Clowney's Diagram of the Invisible and Visible Church

Task

Phillip, a college student in your church, is being criticized by another student at his school. The other student says, "The church is full of hypocrites, and everyone knows just from looking at what goes on there that people who go to church aren't really 'God's people.'" Based on what you have learned about the visible and invisible church, write an email to Phillip, advising him as to how he might use the visible/invisible church distinction to explain, in part, the hypocrisy that occurs within the church to his non-believing friend.

26

Unity and Division

"I believe that denominationalism is an offense against
God and that it has weakened the church's witness."
—John M. Frame, *Systematic Theology*

Lesson Goals

Theology–To understand the unity of the church amidst denominationalism

Reading–To continue to identify main ideas and details, and to draw inferences

Vocabulary–To learn and use additional collocations from the passage

Grammar–To recognize how subjects match their predicates

Introduction

We have seen how the one body of Christ is essential to the spiritual health of the believer, and that this church can be understood in various aspects (militant vs. triumphant, visible vs. invisible, etc.). In this lesson, we will focus on the unity of the church, which in history has been referred to as the *catholicity* of the church. Here are some questions to consider in this lesson:

(1) What do you think it means when the church is described as catholic?

(2) How do you feel about the fact that there are countless denominations of Christians?

(3) How can we understand the church as still unified in Christ?

Edumund Clowney has a helpful explanation of what the term "catholic" means.

> The Greek term *katholikos* means that which is universal or general, having to do with the whole; it is not used in the New Testament to describe the church. The early church fathers used it to express an important New Testament teaching: that the church as a whole is more than the local church. . . .
>
> Catholicity is not a wide gate opening to a broad road, but that narrow gate to which the Lord of the church calls us. Catholicity means that the church is Christ's. We cannot exclude those whom he welcomes, or welcome those whom he excludes. . . . Love cannot ignore the seriousness of error, but neither can it forget the power of the truth.[1]

---

1. Edmund P. Clowney, *The Church*, Contours of Christian Theology (Downers Grove, IL: InterVarsity, 1995), 91, 97.

For Clowney, the catholicity of the church includes both its selectivity and its breadth, as determined by the teaching of Scripture.

Background for the Reading

In the creeds of the early church, the church is described as *catholic* (The Apostles' Creed: "I believe in . . . the holy catholic church"). As Clowney notes, "catholic" (from the Greek καθ᾽ ὅλης; see Acts 9:31) means "universal," affirming that the church throughout the world is *one* church, but today there are many denominations within Christianity. How are we to make sense of the unity of the church in the midst of this division? In what way can we say the church is one? Herman Bavinck suggests an answer to this question in the reading passage.

Pre-Reading

In what way would you say the church is "one"?

Reading

In the following passage, Herman Bavinck discusses unity and division within the church.

[¶1] The church is . . . not an idea or an ideal,[a] but a reality which is becoming something and will become something because it is already something. Thus it is that the church continues in constant change; it was being gathered from the beginning of the world, and it will be gathered until the end of the world. Daily there depart[b] from it some who have fought the fight, kept the faith, earned the crown of righteousness, and who constitute the church triumphant, the church of the firstborn and the spirits of just men made perfect (Heb. 12:23). And daily new members are added to the church on earth, to the militant church here below.

> **Remember?**
> Find the *that* clause in this paragraph.

[¶2] That the apostles, in ascribing such wonderful characteristics to the church as a whole, do not have an idea or an ideal in mind, but a reality, is indicated most clearly by the fact that they speak in the same way about each local church and even of each individual believer. The local church at Corinth, for example, is, despite[c] its many errors and defects,[d] called the temple of God, the dwelling place of His Spirit and the body of Christ. All of them together, the church in its entirety, each local church, and every individual believer, share the same benefits, partake[e] of the same Christ, are in the possession of the same Spirit, and by that Spirit are led to one and the same Father.

[¶3] If the church is really an organism,[f] a living body, this implies that it comprises many and various members, each of whom receives his own name and place, his own function and calling inside the whole. . . . For as the body is one, so it is for the church.

[¶4] In its rich variegation,[g] therefore, the church of Christ remains a *unity*. That is to say not merely that there has always been but one church and there will always be but one; it means to say also that this church is always and everywhere the same, having the same benefits, privileges, and goods. The unity is not one which accrues[h] to the church from the outside, which is imposed[i] upon it by force, that is called into being by contractual arrangement, or is temporarily organized against a common enemy. It is a unity, rather, which is spiritual in character. It depends upon and has its foundation and example in the unity which exists between the Father and Christ as Mediator (John 17:21–23). It is a unity which comes up out of Christ as the vine who gives rise to all the branches and who nourishes them (John 15:5), as the head in whom the whole body has its growth (Eph. 4:16); and it is brought into being by that one Spirit with whom we are all led to one Father. The love of the Father, the grace of the Son, and the fellowship of the Holy Spirit are the portion[j] of every believer, of every local church, and of the church in its entirety. In this consists its profound and immutable unity.

[¶5] All the same the church by reason of the various backgrounds and customs of the Christians who stemmed from[k] Jews and those who stemmed from the Gentiles encountered a big impediment[l] to this unity; often the two groups stood sharply opposed to each other in the frequently mixed churches, and sometimes, often, in fact, there was outright conflict between the two. Even Peter proved himself weak at a given moment in that conflict at Antioch and brought down Paul's reprimand upon his head (Gal. 2:11–14). But the apostle of the Gentiles who was a Jew to the Jews and became all to all kept the great goal of unity steadily before his eyes and in all the church admonished[m] to love and peace. They were all, he said, one body, they all had one Spirit, one Lord, one baptism, one faith, one God and Father above all and in all (Eph. 4:4–6). Nor did they all have to be precisely alike, for a body assumes difference of members, and each was to serve the whole with his particular abilities (1 Cor. 12:4ff) and they had to honor each other's liberty (Rom. 14). By the death of Christ the middle wall of partition was broken, and those two, the Jews and the Gentiles, were reconciled with each other, and made to be a new man (Eph. 2:14ff).

[¶6] But later the church of Christ was divided by all kinds of heresy and schism in the successive centuries. At the present time its multitudinous denominations and sects present a most lamentable[n] spectacle of disunity. Still, something of the old unity can still be seen, inasmuch as all Christian churches are still separated from the world by one and the same baptism, in the confession of the twelve Articles of Faith still continue in the doctrine of the apostles, and, be it in very different forms, still join in the breaking of bread and in prayers. The church is in its unity an object of faith; even though we cannot see it, or cannot see it as plainly as we should like to see it, it exists now and it will some time be perfected.[2]

a. Ideal (n.): a conception of something in its highest perfection
b. Depart (v.): to go away or leave
c. Despite (prep.): notwithstanding; in spite of
d. Defect (n.): absence of something necessary for completeness, perfection, or adequacy in form or function
e. Partake (v.): to share in something; to participate
f. Organism (n.): something felt to resemble a living plant or animal
g. Variegation (n.): the state of being varied

h. Accrue (v.): to come as a direct result of some state or action
i. Impose (v.): to establish forcibly
j. Portion (n.): an individual's part or share of something
k. Stem from (v. phrase): to grow out of or develop from like a stem
l. Impediment (n.): something that hinders or blocks
m. Admonish (v.): to give reproof, warning, reminder, or advice
n. Lamentable (adj.): to be regretted; deplorable; pitiable

2. Herman Bavinck, *Our Reasonable Faith*, trans. Henry Zylstra (Grand Rapids, MI: Eerdmans, 1956), 521–24.

Post-Reading

How does Bavinck suggest we should understand the unity of the church?

Main Ideas and Details

(1) Which of the following best captures the main idea of the passage?
a. The many denominations within the church testify to its unity.
b. The church is united in the teaching of particular biblical doctrines.
c. Though diverse and constantly changing, the church is spiritually one.
d. Schisms within the church are lamentable.

(2) Three main distinctions in the church were presented in the previous lesson. Which of these is Bavinck highlighting in paragraph 1?

(3) Which of the following is a valid inference based on the information in paragraph 2?
a. The church in its entirety includes most local churches.
b. We can say that the apostles, in describing the church, have an idea or ideal in mind.
c. Individual believers still struggling with sin are nevertheless part of the unified church.
d. Due to its errors and defects, the church at Corinth cannot be called a dwelling place of the Holy Spirit.

(4) In paragraph 2, the author uses the word "reality" to mean _____.
a. Something ideal.
b. A concrete entity.
c. The local church.
d. Something that is not fake.

(5) Why does the author repeat the word "same" at the end of paragraph 2?

(6) In paragraph 3, the phrases "many and various members," "each of whom," and "his own" highlight which of the following?
a. The life of the church.
b. The unity of the church.
c. The diversity of the church.
d. The possessions of the church.

(7) Which of the following expresses the meaning of the highlighted part of the second sentence of paragraph 4?
a. There will not always be one church.
b. There has not always been one church.
c. More needs to be said than that the church is "one."
d. The church does not always have the same benefits and privileges.

(8) In paragraph 4, the author writes that the unity of the church "is not one which accrues to the church from the outside." Why does he say this?
a. Because we might fail to account for Christ's work as the basis of this unity.
b. Because we might be tempted to assume that this unity is something we establish.
c. Because we might be tempted to think that this unity is physical rather than spiritual.
d. All of the above.

(9) What is the referent for the phrase "the two" in paragraph 5?

(10) Which of the following inferences can we not draw based on the information in paragraph 6?
a. Heresy leads to disunity in the church.
b. Though we may not be able to see the unity of the church, we believe in it.
c. Certain practices of the church still serve to unite believers across traditions.
d. The existence of multiple denominations has utterly destroyed the unity of the church.

Understanding the Reading

Put a check by the sentences that express a central idea from the reading and that would be included in a summary of it. Put an "X" by the sentences that express a detail from the reading and would not be included in a summary.

_____ 1. The church is constantly changing, but the apostles were thinking of this fluid, realistic church and not a perfect, fixed one.

_____ 2. Every day, older Christians die and new Christians come to faith.

_____ 3. The unity of the church is a spiritual unity that comes from the unity of the Trinity.

_____ 4. The early church faced a threat to its unity in the inclusion of Jewish and Gentile Christians, but remained unified.

_____ 5. Paul rebuked Peter at Antioch.

_____ 6. Unity in the church remains today, despite the church's appearance of being broken into many theological divisions.

Collocations from the Passage

Match the words on the left to their collocates on the right. Make sure you can verify your choices with examples in the reading passage.

ascribe	change
constant	enemy
various	characteristics
common	abilities
particular	members

Provide collocations from the reading passage for the words in the center bubbles below. These collocations may precede or follow these words. There are enough collocations so that all of the bubbles should be filled.

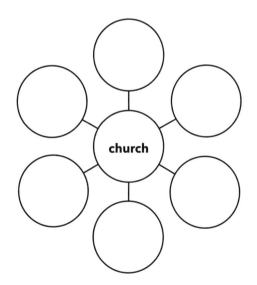

Fig. 26.1. Collocation Diagram 8
(see also next column)

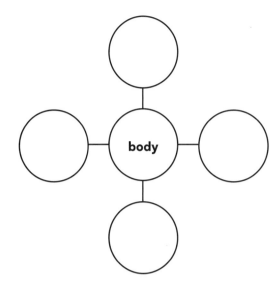

(1) Using some of the collocations above, write two to three sentences about how you are united to other believers.

(2) Using some of the collocations above, discuss with a partner how we can say that the church is one body. You can choose to focus your discussion more on how many members are united in one body or how many denominations are all considered part of the universal church.

Grammar Focus: Matching Subject and Predicate

In this lesson, we will continue to discuss important areas for editing structure and word choice, but we will take a step back to look at a more basic issue. We have looked at participles and *that* clauses, which both form part of a sentence, but what about the main subject and verb (predicate) of the sentence itself? How can we ensure that we have chosen the "right" subject and the "right" verb? This question is so basic that we might not even consider it. But if we do not, we may end up miscommunicating, or simply failing to communicate, with our readers.

So how do we go about "matching" our subject and predicate? In English, it all comes down to whether or not our subjects can perform the actions of their verbs. Note some of the simple **subjects** and <u>predicates</u> in the passage below.

All the same **the church** by reason of the various backgrounds and customs of the Christians who stemmed from Jews and those who stemmed from the Gentiles <u>encountered</u> a big impediment to this unity; often **the two groups** <u>stood</u> sharply opposed to each other in the frequently mixed churches, and sometimes, often, in fact, there was outright conflict between the two. Even **Peter** <u>proved</u> himself weak at a given moment in that conflict at Antioch and <u>brought down</u> Paul's reprimand upon his head (Gal. 2:11–14). But **the apostle of the Gentiles** who was a Jew to the Jews and became all to all <u>kept</u> the great goal of unity steadily before his eyes and in all the church <u>admonished</u> to love and peace. They were all, he said, one body, they all had one Spirit, one Lord, one baptism, one faith, one God and Father above all and in all (Eph. 4:4–6). Nor did they all have to be precisely alike, for **a body** <u>assumes</u> difference of members, and each was to serve the whole with his particular abilities (1 Cor. 12:4ff) and they had to honor each other's liberty (Rom. 14). By the death of Christ **the middle wall of partition** <u>was broken</u>, and those two, **the Jews and the Gentiles**, <u>were reconciled</u> with each other, and made to be a new man (Eph. 2:14ff).

In each of the examples above, the subject can do the action of the verb. Ordinarily, we would not say that the church can "greet"; nor can two groups "walk opposed to each other." The verb "stand" can be used with reference to these two groups only because, in this context, "stand" means "to maintain a position."

Subject		Verb
the church		greet encounter
two groups	can	walk stand
the apostle of the Gentiles		contain keep and admonish
a body		consider assume
the middle wall		be dismembered be broken

Activity 1

Choose five subjects and predicates from the following passage and fill out the chart below.

With the rise of nationalism in Europe another facet of catholicity gained attention. Describing the catholicity of the church under the gospel, the Westminster Confession notes that it is "not confined to one nation, as before under the law . . ." The international and cross-cultural extension of the church has given urgency to our understanding of catholicity. The history of Christian missions illustrates the conflict between colonialist exploitation of non-European peoples and continuing missionary advocacy of their place in Christ's universal church. When Spanish *conquistadores* in the New World exploited and enslaved the Indian people, Bartolomé de Las Casas, a Dominican missionary, denounced their atrocities, and labored for the conversion and welfare of the Indians. He secured from the Emperor Charles V the "New Laws" of 1542, favoring the rights of the Indians, but this legislation could not be enforced against the colonists. De Las Casas himself failed when he sought to block the enslavement of Indians by substituting the importation of black slaves from Africa.

Commitment to mission has driven Christ's church to deal with the issues of globalization. As the church catholic, it is called to set before the world a new humanity that joins together in loving fellowship the races and peoples of planet earth.[3]

Subject	can	Verb

Activity 2

Complete the following sentences by writing an appropriate word or phrase in the blank. More than one answer is possible.

(1) The church _____ many problems as it attempted to account for its diversity.

(2) _____ was restored when, in Christ, the Jew and the Gentile were united.

(3) Only when we embrace the spiritual unity of the church can we _____ the disunity that we see in the church today.

(4) Christ's union with the Father by the Spirit is the _____ upon which the unity of the church rests.

(5) _____ is called to be one, even though it _____ many members.

Activity 3

The following paragraph contains five errors with subjects matching predicates. Identify and correct each of these errors. Remember that you may need to remove or change the prepositions, depending on how you change the verbs.

In the body of Christ, God's Spirit binds believers to one another in faith. People from every tribe, tongue, and nation have been planned by God, and they are connected to each other because of their faith in Christ. This is important to remember today, when Christianity dwells with so much variety, for even though the gospel has traveled to all the nations, the individual people in those nations continue to misunderstand each other. That is what Paul is demonstrated in passages such as Ephesians 4, which writes that we must "maintain the unity of the Spirit in the bond of peace" (Eph. 4:3).

3. Clowney, *The Church*, 92.

27

The End of the Church

"The Church is the guardian of the truth, the citadel of the truth, and the defender of the truth over against all the enemies of the kingdom of God."
—Louis Berkhof, *Systematic Theology*

Lesson Goals

Theology–To understand the purpose and goal of the church
Reading–To make a detailed outline; to identify key words of a paragraph
Vocabulary–To learn and use additional collocations from the passage
Grammar–To learn additional verb/noun + preposition patterns

Introduction

The unity of the church is certainly important in a time when the phrase "global church" has become part of our standard vocabulary. The church is wonderfully diverse in our day, stretching across the globe, but that makes unity all the more critical. We can have a renewed appreciation for Jesus' prayer in John 17:1, where he asks the Father "that they [all believers] may all be one, just as you, Father, are in me, and I in you, that they also may be in us, so that the world may believe that you have sent me."

Part of what gives us unity in the body of Christ is our shared goal or end. What do you think our ultimate purpose is in the church? Revelation 21:1–5 offers us a picture of where we are headed.

Then I saw a new heaven and a new earth, for the first heaven and the first earth had passed away, and the sea was no more. And I saw the holy city, new Jerusalem, coming down out of heaven from God, prepared as a bride adorned for her husband. And I heard a loud voice from the throne saying, "Behold, the dwelling place of God is with man. He will dwell with them, and they will be his people, and God himself will be with them as their God. He will wipe away every tear from their eyes, and death shall be no more, neither shall there be mourning, nor crying, nor pain anymore, for the former things have passed away."

And he who was seated on the throne said, "Behold, I am making all things new."

Note that there is both continuity and discontinuity between the old and the new heaven and earth. The new heaven and earth are drastically different from the old (no death, crying, or pain). Yet, "despite the discontinuities, the new cosmos will be an identifiable counterpart to the old cosmos and a renewal of it."[1] While there is what Poythress calls a "comprehensive renovation," he also notes that "the result is the redemption of the old, not its abolition."[2]

If the new heaven and earth are a renovation and restoration of the old heaven and earth, then we might expect our role right now, as men and women in Christ, to be moving us toward that end. In the reading passage for this chapter, the author explores the mission of the church as we move ever closer to Christ's second coming, a time when he will make all things new (Rev. 21:5).

Background for the Reading

We might be tempted to think that the time of the Christian church is a "new" era in redemptive history. Certainly, the church of the New Testament ushers in a new era of God's plan to redeem fallen creation, but the church has, in one form or another, always existed. The temple of the Old Testament was a form of the church, as was the Garden of Eden. In this sense, the church is simply comprised of God's people, and redemptive history is the story of God's continual judgment, mercy, and grace toward that people. This "story does not begin at Bethlehem's manger: it begins in the Garden of Eden."[3] Just as Adam, the patriarchs, and Israel had the purpose of establishing and expanding God's temple, his church, so do we in the twenty-first century.

Reading Skill: Outlining

By this point in your academic career, you have probably made many outlines: organizing your ideas before writing a paper, taking notes when listening to a lecture, or perhaps jotting down your thoughts as you read. As the material you read becomes more complex, outlining a text becomes more helpful in understanding the author's argument and the structure of that argument. When a text is complex or when you need to have a clear and thorough understanding of it, making an outline can be very helpful. What follow are some basic instructions on how you might outline a complex reading passage.

Tips for Outlining

- If you are making your outline on paper, leave an empty line before each new point in case you need to make changes later.
- Think about how the information is organized and try to represent its organization visually.
- Clearly label your document with the title

How to Outline a Complex Reading Passage

1. Skim or read the entire passage to identify the thesis and overall structure of the argument.
2. Write the author's main claim (thesis) at the top of your outline.
3. You may need to infer some of the information (such as supporting reasons) that may not be clearly stated in a single sentence.
4. Use indentation to represent the supporting points and details visually.
5. Use clear abbreviations to write more quickly.
6. Your purpose in outlining will determine how much detail to include.

   - Are you outlining a passage to help you study from it later? You may only need a few details in your outline to help you remember the author's support.

   - Are you outlining a passage to summarize it or present on it? You may need a more detailed, thorough outline to be able to explain the author's argument clearly.

1. G. K. Beale, *The Book of Revelation*, New International Greek Testament Commentary (Grand Rapids, MI: Eerdmans, 1999), 1040.
2. Vern S. Poythress, *The Returning King: A Guide to the Book of Revelation* (Phillipsburg, NJ: P&R, 2000), 185.
3. Edmund P. Clowney, *The Church*, Contours of Christian Theology (Downers Grove, IL: InterVarsity, 1995), 27.

of the reading passage, its source, and the date on which you read it.

- Decide before you start whether you will use the author's exact words or paraphrase the ideas. Note this at the top of your outline in case you later need to summarize or cite it.

As you work through the reading passage in this lesson, underline or mark the main claim and important supporting ideas. After reading, you will be asked to complete a detailed outline of the passage.

Pre-Reading

Is there a sense in which our purpose is the same as that of Adam in the Garden of Eden or of the Levitical priests in the Old Testament? Explain.

Reading

In the following passage, G. K. Beale explains our role as priests in the new covenant.

[¶1] How does the vision of the worldwide temple in Revelation 21–22 relate to Christians and their role in fulfilling the mission of the church? We, as God's people, have already begun to be God's end-time temple where his presence is manifested[a] to the world, and we are to extend the boundaries of the new garden-temple until Christ returns, when, finally, they will be expanded worldwide.

[¶2] This is just what Ephesians 2:20–22 asserts: the church has "been built upon the foundation of the apostles and prophets, Christ Jesus Himself being the cornerstone, in whom the whole building, being fitted together is growing into a holy temple in the Lord; in whom you are also being built together into a dwelling of God in the Spirit." The church is growing and expanding in Christ throughout the present age (cf. also Eph. 4:13–16) in order that God's saving presence and "the manifold wisdom of God might now be made known" even "in the heavenly places" (Eph. 3:10). Likewise, quite comparably to Ephesians, after referring to Christ as a "living stone" (1 Peter 2:4), Peter alludes to[b] Christians as "living stones . . . being built up as a spiritual house for a holy priesthood" (1 Peter 2:5) in order to "proclaim the excellencies" of God (1 Peter 2:9). In both Ephesians and 1 Peter the church is an expanding, living temple of witness to God's saving presence.

> **Remember?**
> What verb goes with the subject "the church"? What subject goes with the verbs "is growing and expanding"?

[¶3] How do we first experience God's presence? By believing in Christ: that he died for our sin, rose from the dead, and reigns as the Lord God. Then God's Spirit comes into us and dwells in us, in a similar manner as God dwelt in the temple of Eden and Israel's temple.

[¶4] How do we increase the presence of God in our lives and our churches? How did Adam maintain God's presence in his life before the fall? Certainly, remembering, believing and obeying God's word was crucial[c] to a healthy relationship with God. Remember that after God put him into the Garden in Genesis 2:15 "for serving [cultivating] and guarding," he gave Adam a threefold statement to remember by which he would be helped to "serve and guard" the Garden-temple: in Genesis 2:16–17, God says, "From any tree of the garden (1) you may eat freely; but (2) from the tree of the knowledge of good and evil you shall not eat, (3) for in the day that you eat from it you shall surely die." When confronted[d] by the satanic serpent, Eve either failed to remember God's word accurately or intentionally changed it for her own purposes. First, she minimized their privileges by saying merely "we may eat," whereas God had said "you may eat *freely*." Second, Eve minimized the judgment by saying, "lest you die," whereas God said, "you shall *surely* die." Third, she maximized the prohibition by affirming, "you shall not . . . touch it," becoming the first legalist in history (for God had originally said only that they "shall not eat . . . it"). Adam and Eve did not remember God's word, and they "fell," and failed to extend the boundaries of God's Edenic temple.

[¶5] Jesus Christ, the last Adam and true Israel, however, knew the word and, by obeying it, established himself as God's temple. Remember when the devil tried to tempt Christ, in Matthew 4? With each temptation Jesus responded to Satan by quoting from the Old Testament, from passages in Deuteronomy where Moses rebuked Israel for failing in their task. Christ succeeded in just those temptations where Adam and Israel failed because he remembered God's word and obeyed it. Therefore, Christ is the last Adam and true Israel who rules by his word as King over evil in the way that Adam and corporate Adam, Israel, should have ruled.

[¶6] Do we come by faith to God's word daily, as did Jesus, in order that we may be strengthened increasingly with God's presence in order to fulfill our task of spreading that presence to others who don't know Christ? Believers express their identification with Christ's kingship when they spread the presence of God by living for Christ and speaking his word and unbelievers accept it, and Satan's victorious hold on their heart is broken.

[¶7] From one perspective, all believers are priests and they function as priests by offering up prayers in the sphere of the spiritual temple. But saints are also true Israelites who are in exile because they still exist in the exile of this old, fallen world. At the end, this old world will be destroyed, and a new world will be created in which God's people will be resurrected, completely restored to God, and consummately delivered from exile. They will take their place as the crown of the eschatological creation in Christ, the Last Adam. They will all be high priests, dwelling eternally in the new creational holy of holies and in the midst of God's full latter-day presence. Until then, however, we pray as new covenant priests in the New Testament equivalent of the holy place, which is a spiritual sphere of our ministry and witness as a lampstand in the world. We also pray as exiled new Israelites, as we live as pilgrims[e] on the old, fallen earth. In both cases, our prayer is directed towards God in his heavenly holy of holies, until it descends to fill and encompass[f] the new earth. Prayer as an activity inextricably[g] linked to the temple is what is behind Jesus' words in Matt. 18:19–20: "Again I say to you, that if two of you agree on earth about anything that they may ask, it shall be done for them by My Father who is in heaven. For where two or three have gathered together in My name, there I am in their midst."

[¶8] In summary, all Christians are now spiritual Levitical priests (in fulfillment of Isa. 66:21). Our ongoing task is to serve God in his temple in which we always dwell and of which we are a part. Our continual priestly tasks are what the first Adam's were to be: to keep the order and peace of the spiritual sanctuary by learning and teaching God's word, by praying always, and by being vigilant[h] in keeping out unclean moral and spiritual things.[4]

a. Manifest (v.): to show plainly
b. Allude to (v. phrase): to make indirect reference
c. Crucial (adj.): important or essential as decisive
d. Confront (v.): to stand facing or opposing especially in challenge, defiance, or accusation

e. Pilgrim (n.): one who journeys especially in alien lands
f. Encompass (v.): to form a circle around; to envelop
g. Inextricably (adv.): in a manner not permitting separation or disunion
h. Vigilant (adj.): alert or watchfully awake

Post-Reading

According to Beale, how do we fulfill our role as priests in the new temple of Christ?

Understanding the Reading

I. Detailed Outline

Use the statements in the "Notes for the Outline" section below to fill in the boxes of this outline. (The statements in the "Notes for the Outline" section are paraphrases from the text and can be found below the outline.) Cross out each statement as you use it.

Outline of Beale on the Role of Believers as Priests in the New Covenant

I.   What is the relationship between the temple (Rev. 21–22), Christians, and the church?
　　1.
　　　　a. We have God's presence.
　　　　b.
　　　　c.

II.
　　1. If you believe in Christ,
　　2. Then God's spirit lives in you.

III.
　　1. We look to Adam's example before the fall.
　　　　a.
　　　　b.
　　　　　　i.
　　　　　　ii.

4. G. K. Beale, *The Temple and the Church's Mission: A Biblical Theology of the Dwelling Place of God*, New Studies in Biblical Theology (Downers Grove, IL: InterVarsity, 2004), 395–98. Reproduced with permission of Inter-Varsity Press through PLSclear.

   iii. If you eat of that tree, you will die.

  c. However, Eve . . .

   i.

   ii.

   iii.

  d. Adam and Eve failed to spread God's presence.

 2.

  a. Jesus remembered and obeyed God's word.

  b.

  c.

IV. How do Christians today remember and obey God's word?

 1.

 2.

V. What is the role of believers today?

 1.

 2.

 3. In the new world, God will restore his creation and restore his people from exile.

 4.

VI.

 1.

 2.

  a. "Learning and teaching God's word,"

  b. "praying always,"

  c. "being vigilant to keep out unclean moral and spiritual things."

Notes for the Outline

- We are already the spiritual temple of God.
- We are to spread God's presence in this world.
- Christians are now spiritual priests.
- Increased what they were not allowed to do.
- How do Christians have God's presence?
- Eph. 2:20–22 and 1 Peter 2:4 provide support that the church is God's temple and witness of his salvation.
- God called Adam to remember and obey his word.
- He could eat freely.
- Lessened God's punishment.
- How do Christians enlarge God's presence personally and in the church?
- They serve God in his spiritual temple by:
- In these days before the new world, Christians are to pray like "new covenant priests" and exiles on earth.
- They recognize that this is the means for spreading God's word and presence.
- But not of the tree of knowledge.
- They meditate on God's word daily.
- The temptation in Matt. 4 demonstrates how Christ remembered God's word.
- Lessened what they were allowed to do.
- They fulfill the command God gave Adam.
- Jesus fulfilled God's command to Adam, just as Adam and Israel failed at it.
- In Gen. 2:16–17, Adam was told:
- Believers are like priests who pray to God.
- We look to Jesus' example.
- Believers are like the "true Israelites living in exile."

Activity: Identity and Responsibility

The author often links our *identity* to our *responsibility*. *Who we are* defines *what we do*. For each of the sentences that follow, write an "I" in the blank if the sentence is serving to identify someone. Write an "R" if the sentence is serving to describe our responsibilities. If both identity and responsibilities are in view, then write "IR."

_____ We, as God's people, have already begun to be God's end-time temple where his presence is manifested to the world.

_____ We are to extend the boundaries of the new garden-temple until Christ returns.

_____ All believers are priests and they function as priests by offering up prayers in the sphere of the spiritual temple.

_____ Saints are also true Israelites who are in exile because they still exist in the exile of this old, fallen world.

_____ Believers express their identification with Christ's kingship when they spread the presence of God by living for Christ and speaking his word and unbelievers accept it.

_____ Certainly, remembering, believing and obeying God's word was crucial to a healthy relationship with God.

_____ We also pray as exiled new Israelites, as we live as pilgrims on the old, fallen earth.

_____ All Christians are now spiritual Levitical priests (in fulfillment of Isa. 66:21).

_____ Our continual priestly tasks are what the first Adam's were to be: to keep the order and peace of the spiritual sanctuary by learning and teaching God's word, by praying always, and by being vigilant in keeping out unclean moral and spiritual things.

Main Ideas and Details

(1) Which of the following sentences summarizes the main idea of the passage?
   a. Ever since the time of Eden, we have been pilgrims in a fallen world.
   b. Adam failed in his task to follow God's Word in the Garden of Eden.
   c. A new world will be created in which God's resurrected people dwell.
   d. We are part of God's end-time temple and continue to serve as spiritual priests.

(2) In paragraph 2, the author cites Eph. 2:20–22. What is his purpose in doing this?
   a. Only to link to the previous paragraph.
   b. To establish that Christ is the cornerstone of the church.
   c. To support the claim that we are part of God's end-time temple.
   d. To support the idea that Paul speaks of God's saving presence.

(3) Why are believers being "built up as a spiritual house"? (Refer to paragraph 2.)

(4) What is the purpose of paragraph 2 in this passage?

(5) A **key word** is a repeated word that emphasizes the topic of the paragraph. Which of the following is a key word for paragraph 4?
   a. Tree.
   b. Guard.
   c. Judgment.
   d Remember.

(6) In the highlighted sentence in paragraph 4, what does the author do?
   a. Critiques Eve for being non-legalistic.
   b. Confirms that Eve has listened to God's Word.
   c. Critiques Eve for exaggerating God's prohibition.
   d. Suggests that Eve was right in maximizing God's prohibition.

(7) According to paragraph 5, why does Christ succeed in overcoming the devil's temptations?

(8) Which of the following sentences expresses the essential information in the highlighted sentence from paragraph 5?
   a. Christ is the King and ruler of his church.
   b. Corporate Israel also undertook Adam's role.
   c. Adam failed in his task to rule by God's word.
   d. Christ fulfills the Adamic task of ruling by God's word.

(9) Which of the following is a key word for paragraph 6?

a. Faith.

b. Heart.

c. Christ.

d. Presence.

(10) In paragraph 7, the word "sphere" could best be understood to mean _____.

a. Area.

b. Point.

c. Circle.

d. Perspective.

on the right. Make sure you can verify your choices with examples in the reading passage.

fulfill	the boundaries
extend	a mission
heavenly	restored
similar	relationship
healthy	places
completely	manner

Using some of the collocations above, answer the following question: In what ways are we like Levitical priests in the line of the second Adam?

Collocations from the Passage

Match the words on the left to their collocates

Grammar Focus: Preposition Patterns

Not matching the subject and predicate of your sentences will certainly make your meaning less clear. But less noticeable grammatical issues can obscure your meaning as well. In this lesson, we revisit patterns of preposition use, which we looked at in Lessons 14 and 22.

Even as you try to use patterns of prepositions with verbs and nouns, you may continue to make mistakes, so it is important to keep an eye on them when you edit your writing. Have a look at the prepositions in the following paragraph, along with the nouns and verbs that go with them.

How do we increase the **presence of** God in our lives and our churches? How did Adam maintain God's presence **in his life** before the fall? Certainly, remembering, believing and obeying God's word was crucial to a healthy **relationship with** God. Remember that after God **put him into** the Garden **in Genesis 2:15** "for serving [cultivating] and guarding," he gave Adam a threefold statement to remember by which he would be helped to "serve and guard" the Garden-temple: **in Genesis 2:16–17**, God says, "From any tree **of the garden** (1) you may eat freely; but (2) **from the tree** of **the knowledge of** good and evil you shall not eat, (3) for in the day that you **eat from** it you shall surely die." When **confronted by** the satanic serpent, Eve either failed to remember God's word accurately or intentionally changed it **for her own purposes**. First, she minimized their privileges **by saying** merely "we may eat," whereas God had said "you may eat *freely*." Second, Eve minimized the judgment **by saying**, "lest you die," whereas God said, "you shall *surely* die." Third, she maximized the prohibition **by affirming**, "you shall not . . . touch it," becoming the first legalist **in history** (for God had originally said only that they "shall not eat . . . it"). Adam and Eve did not remember God's word, and they "fell," and failed to extend the **boundaries of** God's Edenic temple.

Activity 1

Underline the prepositions and the nouns or verbs that accompany them in the following paragraph.

The nature of our sacrifices as obedient Adamic-like priests is vitally linked to the idea of expanding the sacred sphere of God's presence in order that others would experience it and come into the sacred temple themselves. Believers are priests in that they serve as mediators between God and the unbelieving world. When unbelievers accept the church's mediating witness, they not only come into God's presence, but they begin to participate themselves as mediating priests who witness. As priests, we should make sure that we ourselves are growing in the experience of the divine presence. When we do not compromise our faith and relationship in God's presence and, consequently, suffer for our unswerving commitment, we are sacrificing ourselves. It is this very sacrifice that God has designed in the new temple to be the means to move unbelievers to believe the church's testimony and to begin to experience God's presence themselves. The "two witnesses" in Revelation 11 offer themselves as sacrifices by suffering for their faith *as they go throughout the world* and are rejected because of their testimony to Christ.[5]

Activity 2

Do this activity without looking back at the reading. In each blank, write the most appropriate preposition. (More than one answer may be possible.) Then compare your answers with the prepositions used in paragraph 7 of the reading.

_____ one perspective, all believers are priests and they function as priests _____ offering up prayers _____ the sphere of the spiritual temple. But saints are also true Israelites who are in exile because they still exist in the exile of this old, fallen world. _____ the end, this old world will be destroyed, and a new world will be created _____ which God's people will be resurrected, completely restored _____ God, and consummately delivered _____ exile. They will take their place as the crown of the eschatological creation _____ Christ, the Last Adam. They will all be high priests, dwelling eternally in the new creational holy of holies and in the midst _____ God's full latter-day presence. Until then, however, we pray as new covenant priests in the New Testament equivalent of the holy place, which is a spiritual sphere of our ministry and witness as a lampstand _____ the world. We also pray as exiled new Israelites, as we live as pilgrims _____ the old, fallen earth. In both cases, our prayer is directed _____ God in his heavenly holy of holies, until it descends to fill and encompass the new earth. Prayer as an activity inextricably linked to the temple is what is behind Jesus' words in Matt. 18:19–20: "Again I say to you, that if two of you agree on earth about anything that they may ask, it shall be done _____ them by My Father who is in heaven. For where two or three have gathered together in My name, there I am _____ their midst."

Activity 3

Choose a preposition to link the sets of words below. An example is provided for you.

(1) Live   God's presence —live *in* God's presence

(2) Testimony   Christ—

5. Ibid., 399–400.

(3) Suffer   our faith —

(4) The idea   salvation —

(5) Prayer directed   God —

(6) The experience   God's presence —

(7) Prayer   an activity —

(8) Linked   the temple —

(9) Delivered   sin and death —

(10) New creation   Christ —

Summary of Theological Concepts for Unit 9

- The church is both militant and triumphant, visible and invisible, an organism and an institution.
- Despite its many divisions, the church is spiritually one, each member and individual church partaking of the same spiritual blessings of Christ.
- As members of the church, we are part of God's end-time temple, as we expand the church and continue to serve God by following his Word, until Christ comes again to make all things new (Rev. 21:5).

Activity 4

Paraphrase each of the concepts above in your own words.

(1)

(2)

(3)

Broken and United (ST Task 4)

To many skeptics and nonbelievers, the church seems to be fragmented and divided. Yet we have just read of how Bavinck defends the spiritual unity of the church. In light of this reading, consider the following scenario.

While serving as an associate pastor for a church in your area, you meet a young and enthusiastic convert to the Christian faith. His name is Peter. Peter has just come to faith and has been reading through the book of Acts. He writes you an email inquiring as to why the church seems to have been so unified in the time of the New Testament but now seems to be broken apart into countless denominations. Respond to Peter's email with a one-paragraph explanation, encouraging him with what you have learned about the spiritual unity of the church.

UNIT 10

HOW THEN SHALL WE LIVE?
(PRACTICAL THEOLOGY)

28

Connecting Scripture to Life

"God's Word is meant to inform and transform God's people."
—Michael R. Emlet, *Crosstalk*

Lesson Goals

Theology-To understand some of the difficulties and dangers in applying Scripture
Reading-To identify main ideas and relevant details, and to draw inferences
Vocabulary-To learn and use additional collocations from the passage
Grammar-To learn how to turn statements into questions

Introduction

In the final unit for this book, we will explore the genre of practical theology (including counseling), and we will complete our final genre study.

"Practical theology" might seem to be an odd phrase. While John Frame defines practical theology as "the science of *communicating* the Word of God," he quickly adds that *"all* theology is practical—at least *good* theology is!"[1] Typically, however, we think of practical theology more narrowly as involving the tasks of preaching, teaching, counseling, missions, evangelism, and worship.[2]

Practical theology can easily be misunderstood and undervalued, especially by theology students. We may tend to think of theology more broadly as "knowledge about God" or "knowledge about Scripture." But theology is not ultimately concerned with ideas; it is ultimately concerned with *people.* When we study theology, we aim to learn all that we can about God from his revelation and from our experience so that we can faithfully proclaim his gospel. And that gospel, as a friend once put it, is "a person, given for people."[3]

Where does this study begin? As you might imagine, it begins with Scripture. Among the many tasks with which practical theology is concerned, applying Scripture to our everyday lives is critical. Consider the following questions before we get to the reading passage for this lesson:

---

1. John M. Frame, *The Doctrine of the Knowledge of God*, A Theology of Lordship (Phillipsburg, NJ: P&R, 1987), 214.

2. Ibid. George Fuller suggests that the phrase "practical theology" brings to mind "all the things that a minister does: preach, pray, meditate, moderate, console, challenge, relate, repair." George C. Fuller, "Practical Theology: The State of the Art," in *Practical Theology and the Ministry of the Church: 1952–1984*, ed. Harvie M. Conn (Phillipsburg, NJ: P&R, 1990), 109.

3. Chris Carter used this expression in a joint presentation that he and I (Pierce) did on writing for counseling in the fall of 2013. I am still grateful for and appreciative of this eloquently expressed truth.

(1) What kinds of passages from Scripture seem to be easy to apply to your life?

(2) What kinds of passages seem to be difficult to apply to your life? Why?

Background for the Reading

Learning biblical theology—what Scripture teaches about who God is, who we are, and what our purpose is in the world—is not the end of the Christian life. The end of the Christian life is "to glorify God, and to enjoy Him forever" (WSC Q. 1). Part of glorifying God is following his word and living out that word in the world. That means that we must take abstract theological truths and *apply* them to real problems in our own lives and in the lives of others—practical theology. But working out practical theology can be quite difficult. As David Powlison sometimes tells his students, "It's easy to do poor practical theology."

What might help us to do effective practical theology? One of the keys to effective practical theology is knowing how to apply passages of Scripture to concrete situations, linking the past to the present and the present to the past.

Pre-Reading

What is a passage of Scripture that seems too removed from our everyday experience to be of any practical use?

Reading

In the following passage, Michael Emlet discusses the application of Scripture to real-life situations.

[¶1] Is it easy or difficult to connect the Bible and life? It depends, doesn't it? [The gap between passages that seem easy to apply and passages that seem difficult to apply I will call] the "Ditch[a] vs. Canyon[b] Phenomenon."

Remember?
Can you find any preposition patterns in paragraph 2?

[¶2] What I mean is this: sometimes use of Scripture in ministry has the feel of stepping across a ditch (easy!), and sometimes it has the feel of stepping across a canyon (impossible!). The challenge, really, is how to bridge[c] the gap between an ancient biblical text and a present-day life situation. How do we attempt to bridge that divide? Most of the time we assume that a direct line of connection must exist between the situation then (in the text) and the situation now. Or at the very least we think we can extract[d] some "timeless principle" from the text and bring it to the present. This mind-set, where we assume some kind of one-to-one correspondence[e] between a text then and a situation now, is admirable in its goal to "make" the Scriptures relevant[f] for the believer today.

[¶3] And, in fact, it often works when the passage speaks specifically about a situation or experience we're facing. Here are some examples of "ditch" passages. If you're not familiar with these passages, look them up as you go and see if you agree.

- Psalm 23 for fear.
- Psalm 51 for repentance.
- Proverbs 22:15 for discipling a child.

- Matthew 5:27–30 for understanding the depth and breadth of adultery/sexual lust.
- Ephesians 5:2–33 for marriage roles[g] and relationships.
- Philippians 4:6 for anxiety[h] along with Ephesians, James, and Proverbs passages on anger.

[¶4] Other passages seem to fit in this category, but they stretch the width of the ditch a bit more. What I mean is, these passages might not speak as specifically and explicitly about a particular struggle or situation, but they seem "close enough" to allow for[i] a relatively quick connection. Sometimes it's because of the positive or negative example the passage provides, and sometimes it's because of a general principle derived from the text. All in all, the path to application still feels relatively direct. For example:

- Philippians 4:8 for training your mind against sexually lustful thoughts.
- Joshua 1:9 as encouragement as you begin an evangelistic crusade in your church.
- The story of Joseph as an encouragement amid harassment[j] or persecution from others.

[¶5] But looking for the more direct connection ends up backfiring when we encounter passages that seem far removed from our day-to-day experiences. For example, when was the last time we demolished a house because of a mildew problem (Lev. 14:33–57)? Or used Numbers 5:11–31 as a test for adultery for couples in our congregations? When have we used the regulations for the building of the tabernacle (Ex. 25–31; 35–40) to encourage someone? What life-changing application have we made lately from the first nine chapters of 1 Chronicles, which is essentially a list of names? What should we do with Obadiah (a prophecy against Edom)? When have we used Revelation 17 (the woman and the beast) in a counseling session? What should we do with very specifically directed passages, as noted earlier with Alexander the metalworker in 2 Timothy? Suddenly we find ourselves facing a canyon! Now what?

[¶6] Our tendency, of course, is to gravitate[k] toward the "ditch" passages because they seem easier to apply; it's easier to make a connection between then and now. Ditch passages resonate[l] more quickly with our experiences. They have a greater immediacy, so we hang out in these tried-and-true passages and we skim—or avoid altogether—those pesky canyon passages. But what is the result?

[¶7] In practical terms, we end up ministering with an embarrassingly thinner but supposedly[m] more relevant Bible. Did you ever wonder why publishers sell the New Testament packaged together with Psalms and Proverbs? Why not sell the New Testament with Leviticus and Esther? Or the New Testament with 1 and 2 Kings and the Minor Prophets? A value judgement is being made. The New Testament, Psalms, and Proverbs are deemed[n] more relevant for contemporary life. The New Testament is included because it's about Jesus and the church. Proverbs makes the grade because of all that pithy, helpful, concrete advice. And the Psalms are important because of the emotions they evoke and because of their use in worship. (Of course, one must overlook the difficulties of using, for example, Psalm 3:7 in a ministry situation: "Arise O Lord! Deliver me, O my God! Strike all my enemies on the jaw; break the teeth of the wicked.")

[¶8] Have you succumbed° to this mind-set even if you don't frequently use an "abridged" Bible? Take a look at the Bible you regularly use—which pages are the dirtiest and most dog-eared? Hmm. The hard reality is this: genealogies, dietary laws, battle records, and prophecies against ancient nations all take a backseat to parts of the Bible that connect more easily and naturally to our modern lives. And this is true despite believing that *all* of Scripture is "God-breathed" and "useful for teaching, rebuking, correcting and training in righteousness" (2 Tim. 3:16). We confess that all of Scripture is helpful for all of life, but that's not the way the Bible actually functions in our lives and ministries.

[¶9] *Should* ditch passages be so easy to apply? . . . [Though you might think that Phil. 4:6–7 is easy to apply,] has it ever hit you that there is about a two-thousand-year gap between the Philippians who received Paul's letter and your friend who is struggling with anxiety? How much overlap is there between the people, the social-cultural context, and situation(s) in that first-century church and suburban America two millenia later?

[¶10] Similarly, life problems aren't as easy to assign to the ditch category. The fact is, people's lives are a complex maze of thoughts, emotions, actions, motives, circumstances, and experiences. . . . My intent is not to open a Pandora's box° of difficulties that limit your application of Scripture. Rather, I hope you will sense increasing freedom in your ministry as you engage the Bible and people more deeply.

[¶11] Let me give further encouragement: canyon passages aren't so impossible and canyon problems aren't so impossible! What makes canyon passages such as the building of the tabernacle, the book of Obadiah, or 1 Chronicles 1–9 potentially meaningful for believers today is that they are all part of an unfolding story of God's redemption, a redemption that finds its climax in Jesus Christ and into which we've been caught up by God's magnificent grace. We are those "on whom the fulfillment of the ages has come" (1 Cor. 10:11). Because we are united with the One who fulfills (completes) Israel's story, we share some measure of continuity with the Old Testament people of God, on whose behalf Exodus or Obadiah or Chronicles was written. Similarly, we stand after the cross, resurrection, and the pouring out of the Spirit, in continuity with the New Testament writers and their audiences. What sets up Philemon or the most perplexing⁹ parts of Revelation (or any part of the New Testament) to be relevant for us today is that we share the same Savior, the same redemption, and the renewed kingdom brought by Jesus Christ.⁴

---

4. Michael R. Emlet, *Crosstalk: Where Life & Scripture Meet* (Greensboro, NC: New Growth, 2009), 14–17, 19–21. *Crosstalk: Where Life and Scripture Meet* © 2009 by Michael R. Emlet. Used by permission of New Growth Press.

a. Ditch (n.): a shallow trench

b. Canyon (n.): a deep and narrow valley

c. Bridge (v.): to span or make a way across

d. Extract (v.): to derive or deduce from a specified source

e. Correspondence (n.): an instance or point of agreement, similarity, or analogy

f. Relevant (adj.): bearing upon or properly applying to the matter at hand

g. Role (n.): a function performed by someone or something in a particular situation, process, or operation

h. Anxiety (n.): mentally distressing concern; a state of being worried

i. Allow for (v. phrase): to give consideration; to make allowance

j. Harassment (n.): the act or an instance of vexing, troubling, or annoying continually or chronically

k. Gravitate (v.): to tend in a direction or toward an object

l. Resonate (v.): to vibrate sympathetically with (used metaphorically to mean "identify with")

m. Supposedly (adv.): in a manner believed to be or accepted as such usually on slight grounds or in error

n. Deem (v.): to come to view, judge, or classify after some reflection; to consider

o. Succumb (v.): to yield and cease to resist before a superior strength, overpowering appeal or desire, or inexorable force

p. Pandora's Box (n. phrase): something that produces many unforeseen difficulties (in Greek mytholody, a box containing all the ills of mankind and given by Zeus to Pandora, who opened it against the command of Zeus)

q. Perplexing (adj.): causing agitation or confusion due to a disturbing or puzzling situation or state of affairs

Post-Reading

Is the "difficult" passage you selected for the Pre-Reading question a "canyon" passage or a "ditch" passage? Why?

Main Ideas and Details

(1) What is the author's purpose in this passage?

   a. To encourage us to let pastors apply Scripture to our lives.

   b. To highlight and discuss the difficulty of applying Scripture.

   c. To discourage those without theological training from applying Scripture.

   d. To suggest that "ditch" passages are easier to apply than "canyon" passages.

(2) Which of the following can we say about "ditch" passages?

   a. They are represented by passages such as 1 Chronicles 1–9.

   b. They are not strictly part of the unfolding story of redemption.

   c. They are difficult to apply because they are usually longer and more complex.

   d. They seem easy to apply but can easily be misapplied or applied in a shallow manner.

(3) According to paragraph 2, what is the challenge of connecting the Bible to life?

(4) Which of the following can be inferred from the information in paragraph 2?

   a. Biblical texts do not contain "timeless principles."

   b. We cannot bridge the gap between an ancient biblical text and a present-day life situation.

   c. Assuming that there is any relationship between an ancient text and a present situation is naïve.

   d. We should not expect that there will always be a direct connection between an ancient text and a present situation.

(5) What is the referent for the phrase "this category" in the first sentence of paragraph 4?

(6) What is the referent for the pronoun "they" in paragraph 4?

(7) What is the purpose of paragraph 5 in this reading (what does it signal)?

(8) What is the purpose of the questions that the author provides in paragraph 5?

   a. To cause us to doubt the relevance of certain Old Testament passages.

   b. To suggest that asking questions is an effective way to learn more about an ancient text.

   c. To show that making connections between Scripture and present-day situations usually fails.

d. To illustrate the difficulty of making direct connections between certain Old Testament passages and present situations.

(9) Which of the following can we infer from paragraph 5 about "canyon" passages?
   a. They are far-removed from our daily context and are often exciting.
   b. They are far-removed from our daily context and are thus intimidating.
   c. They are more valuable than "ditch" passages because they are more complex.
   d. They present many difficulties and should be ignored unless absolutely necessary.

(10) In paragraph 7, the word "relevant" could be replaced by the word _____.
   a. Clear.
   b. Useful.
   c. Relative.
   d. Traditional.

(11) In paragraph 7, the word "overlook" means _____.
   a. Delete.
   b. Ignore.
   c. Oversee.
   d. Closely examine.

(12) In paragraph 10, the author makes the following statement:

The fact is, people's lives are a complex maze of thoughts, emotions, actions, motives, circumstances, and experiences.

   Why does he say this?
   a. To dissuade readers from applying biblical texts.
   b. To warn that "ditch" passages are far more complex than "canyon" passages.
   c. To contrast the simplicity of "ditch" passages with the complexity of life.
   d. None of the above.

(13) What is the referent for the pronoun "they" in paragraph 11?

(14) In paragraph 11, the word "finds" could be replaced by _____ .
   a. Reaches.

b. Explores.
c. Deciphers.
d. Investigates.

Understanding the Reading

Label each of the following passages as either a "ditch" passage (D) or a "canyon" passage (C).

_____   "Even though I walk through the valley of the shadow of death, I will fear no evil, for you are with me" (Ps. 23:4).

_____   "If his gift for a burnt offering is from the flock, from the sheep or goats, he shall bring a male without blemish, and he shall kill it on the north side of the altar before the LORD, and Aaron's sons the priests shall throw its blood against the sides of the altar" (Lev. 1:10–11).

_____   "Do not lay up for yourselves treasures on earth, where moth and rust destroy and where thieves break in and steal" (Matt. 6:19).

_____   "It is not the hearers of the law who are righteous before God, but the doers of the law who will be justified" (Rom. 2:13).

_____   "If you come across a bird's nest in any tree or on the ground, with young ones or eggs and the mother sitting on the young or on the eggs, you shall not take the mother with the young. You shall let the mother go, but the young you may take for yourself, that it may go well with you, and that you may live long" (Deut. 22:6–7).

_____   "With what shall I come before the LORD, and bow myself before God on high? Shall I come before him with burnt offerings, with calves a year old?" (Mic. 6:6).

_____   "Flee from sexual immorality. Every other sin a person commits is outside the body, but the sexually immoral person sins against his own body" (1 Cor. 6:18).

_____   "You shall season all your grain offerings with salt. You shall not let the salt of the covenant with your God be missing from your grain offering; with all your offerings you shall offer salt" (Lev. 2:13).

CONNECTING SCRIPTURE TO LIFE

_____ "No one shall be able to stand against you. The Lord your God will lay the fear of you and the dread of you on all the land that you shall tread, as he promised you" (Deut. 11:25).

Collocations from the Passage

Select the most appropriate word from the choices in the parentheses. All of these examples of collocations have been taken directly from the reading.

The difficulty in applying Scripture is that we must bridge the (*hole/divide/area*) between the past and the present. A biblical (*text/language/word*) is situated in history, and while we might think that we can simply draw general and timeless (*customs/principles/conventions*) from it, this is not always so easy. While many of us could offer positive (*instances/events/examples*) of when we applied a passage to a particular situation or life event, we could just as easily offer negative examples. Perhaps we encounter difficulty because we try to make a(n) (*instant/direct/primary*) connection from the biblical passage to our own lives, hoping to glean concrete (*advice/intelligence/apprehension*) from Scripture. But sometimes the connections between Scripture and life are more indirect, and we must be careful not to force a passage to say what we would like it to say.

Using some of the collocations above, discuss a time when you tried (successfully or unsuccessfully) to apply a biblical passage to your own life.

Grammar Focus: Forming Questions

We have now gone over several elements of grammar that you can check for when you edit your own writing: participles, *that* clauses, matching subject and predicate, and verb/noun + preposition patterns. In this lesson, we will consider a more basic structural problem: forming questions.

Incorrect question formation is a common problem in terms of sentence structure. See if you can recognize the errors in the following examples:

Why God did that to the Canaanites?
What we should do in this situation?
How God addressed the sin of his people in the Old Testament?

Each of these examples has a basic problem: In questions, the linking or helping verb needs to be placed *before* the subject, and the main verb takes the bare infinitive form (recall this change from Lesson 12, in which we studied modal verbs). We might call this the *principle of inversion*.[5]

Why did God did do that to the Canaanites?
What we should we do in this situation?
How did God addressed the sin of his people in the Old Testament?

For each of the questions in the passage below, underline the linking verb ("to be") or helping verb ("to have").

But looking for the more direct connection ends up backfiring when we encounter passages that seem far removed from our day-to-day experiences. For example, when was the last time we demolished a house because of a mildew problem (Lev. 14:33–57)? Or used Numbers 5:11–31 as a test for adultery for couples in our congregations? When have we used the regulations for the building of the tabernacle (Ex. 25–31; 35–40) to encourage someone? What life-changing application have we made lately from the first nine chapters of 1 Chronicles, which is essentially a list of names? What should we do with Obadiah (a prophecy against Edom)? When have we used Revelation 17 (the woman and the beast) in a counseling session? What should we do with very specifically directed passages, as noted earlier with Alexander the metalworker in 2 Timothy? Suddenly we find ourselves facing a canyon! Now what?

---

5. Traditionally, this is known as "subject-auxiliary inversion," but "the principle of inversion" is less technical and clearer for our purposes. See Ron Cowan, *The Teacher's Grammar of English: A Course Book and Reference Guide* (New York: Cambridge University Press, 2008), 71; and Michael Swan, *Practical English Usage*, 4th ed. (Oxford: Oxford University Press, 2016), entry 216.

Notice that the subject and the linking or helping verb switch places in questions as compared to statements. For "yes/no" questions, a form of the verb "do" is added in the helping verb position if there is not already a helping or linking verb for the statement form. See the example in the final row of the following table.

Statement	Question
<u>We</u> have used Revelation 17 in a counseling session.	When have <u>we</u> used Revelation 17 in a counseling session?
<u>We</u> should do X with very specifically directed passages.	What should <u>we</u> do with very specifically directed passages?
<u>Scripture</u> contains many applications for our lives today. ⬇ <u>Scripture</u> does contain many applications for our lives today.	Does <u>Scripture</u> contain many applications for our lives today?

Activity 1

Provide either a question form or a statement form of the information in each row of the table. (Hint: You may need to add the verb "do" to create some of the questions.)

Question	Statement
How should we apply Scripture to life in the twenty-first century?	
	There are many different ways to apply the same passage.
	Passages from Leviticus can be applied to us today.
Are the cleanliness laws of Leviticus relevant for our understanding of sin?	
	The Old Testament contains some passages that are difficult to interpret.
	Emlet distinguishes between "canyon" and "ditch" passages.

Activity 2

Working with a partner, turn the following statements into questions. More than one answer may be possible.

(1) We should examine the context of a passage of Scripture before we apply it.

(2) "Ditch" passages are always easy to apply to our lives.

(3) The regulations for the building of the tabernacle have been used to encourage others.

(4) We apply God's Word in concrete contexts.

Collocation Review

Fill in the missing collocations in the table below. While these collocations have been taken directly from Lessons 23–25, more than one answer may be correct. The important thing is to identify collocations that you can memorize and use in your own writing. Try to fill out the table below without looking at the reading. See what you can remember.

ascribe		healthy	
	a foundation		restored
constant			a divide
various			text
	enemy	timeless general	
particular		positive negative	
	a mission		connection
extend		contemporary	
	places	concrete	
similar			

Genealogies? (PT Task 1)

Introduction

Perhaps the most commonly avoided parts of Scripture are genealogies. Who wants to read a long list of names, and what good could it possibly do? We would be better off just imagining that they are not there, right?

No! All parts of Scripture are valuable, even the genealogies. The following commentator suggests what we might learn from the genealogy that begins Matthew's Gospel.

Learn from this list of names that *God always keeps His word*. He had promised that in Abraham's seed all the nations of the earth should be blessed. He had promised to raise up a Savior of the family of David. These sixteen verses prove that Jesus was the son of David and the son of Abraham, and that God's promise was fulfilled. Thoughtless and ungodly people should remember this lesson, and be afraid. Whatever they may think, God will keep His word.[6]

Task

While riding the train to a university campus, two high school boys who attend a private school take the seat in front of you. The one tells the other that his parents are forcing him to follow a year-long Bible reading plan, and that he even has to read the genealogies. His friend says, "Why? They don't even tell you anything."

Enter into conversation with the two high school boys by suggesting how genealogies can, in fact, tell us something important. Present your response to a partner. Once you have finished your response, your partner should try to summarize what you have said in a single sentence.

Learning the Genre: Practical Theology

As mentioned in the previous lesson, under the genre practical theology (PT), we treat both pastoral writing and counseling writing. Practical theology, when we view it more narrowly, is quite unique when compared to apologetics, biblical studies, church history, and systematic theology. All of the theological genres are interconnected, so there may be elements of each of these genres in a piece of PT writing, but there are certainly differences. As we did with the other theological genres, we can first come up with a rough definition for practical theology and then try to understand some of its communicative functions.

Practical Theology

There is certainly a sense in which all theology is "practical," since theology "is the application of the Word to all areas of life."[7] Practical theology, more narrowly defined, however, is "concerned to relate theology to the practice of ministry."[8] Traditionally, it involves preaching, worship, education, and pastoral

care.[9] But it can also include church administration and growth, in addition to ethics.[10]

With so many areas involved, how can we decide which *communicative functions* to focus on? It might be best to understand two larger communicative functions of practical theology more broadly, rather than trying to list many separate ones. Essentially, the communicative goals of practical theology are to (1) apply what Scripture teaches to all of life and (2) help people practically absorb and benefit from the richness of biblical truth. The achievement of these goals, as with the achievement of the goals in all of the other genres we have looked at, is properly the work of God himself. It is only the Spirit of God who can truly apply Scripture to life and help people absorb its teaching. But God certainly uses us as his instruments in that process, as preachers, teachers, and counselors.

Traits

In light of these communicative goals, we can choose a few of the *traits* of writing in this genre and see how authors use them. In what follows, we will consider how authors of the practical theology genre (1) ask and answer practical questions, (2) offer personal illustrations, and (3) use relevant details to engage with their readers. We might summarize these traits with the phrase **personal engagement**. Have a look at the passage below in which Tim Keller discusses gospel application and how such application can be carried out by leaders in the church.

How do we bring the gospel home to people so they see its power and implications? This can take place in a church in several ways. First, a church recovers the gospel through preaching. Preaching is the single venue of information and teaching to which the greatest number of church people are exposed. Are some parts of the Bible "better" for gospel preaching than others? No, not at all. Any time you preach

---

6. J. C. Ryle, *Expository Thoughts on the Gospels*, vol. 1, *Matthew–Mark* (Grand Rapids, MI: Zondervan, 1956), 3.

7. John M. Frame, *The Doctrine of the Christian Life*, A Theology of Lordship (Phillipsburg, NJ: P&R, 2008), 9.

8. D. J. Tidball, "Practical Theology," in *The New Dictionary of Theology*, ed. Sinclair B. Ferguson and David F. Wright (Downers Grove, IL: InterVarsity, 1988), 525.

9. Ibid.

10. Ibid., 526.

Christ and his salvation as the meaning of the text rather than simply expounding biblical principles for life, you are preaching toward renewal. Preaching this way is not at all easy, however. Even those who commit to Christ-centered preaching tend toward inspirational sermons about Jesus, with little application. . . .

The second way for a pastor or leader to recover the gospel in the church is through the training of lay leaders who minister the gospel to others. It is critical to arrange a regular and fairly intense time of processing these gospel renewal dynamics with the lay leaders of a church. The components of this training include both content and life contact. By "content," I propose studying elementary material such as D. Martyn Lloyd-Jones's chapter "The True Foundation" in *Spiritual Depression* or working through my book *The Prodigal God* along with the discussion guide. More advanced materials would include books by Richard Lovelace and Jonathan Edwards.[11]

Keller asks and answers a practical question: How can pastors and leaders in the church "bring the gospel home" to people? In other words, how can they help people implement the truth of Scripture in their individual lives? As he answers this question, he focuses on concrete solutions: (1) preaching Christ and his salvation, and (2) training church leaders in what he calls "content and life contact." He even suggests specific resources for "content": the books *Spiritual Depression* and *The Prodigal God*. See if you can locate the other traits of PT (offering personal illustrations and using relevant details) in the following passages.

Activity 3

In the passage below, Tim Witmer discusses how important it is for a pastor, a shepherd leader, to invest in his children.

> When children are small, it is difficult to imagine that a time is coming when they won't be there anymore. As a dad who is now an empty nester, I have seen how quickly those years flew by. You only have a limited amount of time to get to know your children, to be with them, and to influence them before they leave the nest. Time with children must be seen as time *invested*, not merely time *spent*. George Barna observes:
>
>> Those that warn that parents don't spend enough time inculcating values and sharing time with their families are often written off as ignorant fundamentalists, out-of-touch conservatives, or pontificating moralists. But their perspective, alarming, and uncomfortable as it may be for some, cannot be easily dismissed, given the weight of the evidence that confirms their contention. For instance, a number of scholarly studies have noted kids draw most of their information from the television, spending an average of more than 10,000 hours watching it by the time they reach age eighteen. (That, by the way, represents more than one entire year—twenty-four-hour days, seven days a Unit—absorbed in the messages broadcast by television producers).
>
> You have a lot of work to do if you are to be the primary influence in the lives of your children. It doesn't just happen. You have to make it happen.
>
> As with your wife, it starts with *daily* time. A good place to start is to commit the family to gather for dinner every day. This should be an "all hands on deck" rallying point to which everyone is committed.[12]

11. Timothy Keller, *Center Church: Doing Balanced, Gospel-Centered Ministry in Your City* (Grand Rapids, MI: Zondervan, 2012), 74.

12. Timothy Z. Witmer, *The Shepherd Leader at Home: Knowing, Leading, Protecting, and Providing for Your Family* (Wheaton, IL: Crossway, 2012), 48–49.

What traits of the PT genre do you see illustrated in this passage?

Tim Witmer uses a personal illustration to express how valuable time with children is. His children no longer live in his house, and so the time he had with them, now in the past, seems to have "flown by."

Notice that the author uses *idioms* to connect with the audience on a conversational level ("flown by," "empty nester," and "all hands on deck"). An **idiom** is "an expression which functions as a single unit and whose meaning cannot be worked out from its separate parts."[13] Witmer does not mean that time literally flies, or that he is literally perched high in a tree on a bird's nest. When we say that time "flies," we mean "it moves quickly." "Empty nester" is an idiomatic expression, meaning "a parent whose children have moved out of the house." And "all hands on deck" means "everyone is involved." The use of idioms is another potential mark of personal engagement.[14]

What about the next passage, by Ed Welch? Can you see traits of the PT genre there?

Shame and guilt are close companions but not identical. Shame is the more common and broader of the two. In Scripture you will find shame (nakedness, dishonor, disgrace, defilement) about ten times more often than you find guilt.

Guilt lives in the courtroom where you stand alone before the judge. It says, "You are responsible for wrongdoing and legally answerable." "You are wrong." "You have sinned." The guilty person expects punishment and needs forgiveness.

Shame lives in the community, though the community can feel like a courtroom. It says, "You don't belong—you are unacceptable, unclean, and disgraced" because "You are wrong, you have sinned" (guilt), *or* "Wrong has been done to you" *or* "You are associated with those who are disgraced or outcast." The shamed person feels worthless, expects rejection, and needs cleansing, fellowship, love, and acceptance.

Guilt and shame intersect when a particular sin is regarded, by yourself or others, to be worse than most sins. For example, get caught with child pornography and you will experience both guilt and shame. Same-sex attraction finds itself here too. But what if your anger briefly flares at a reckless driver? You might feel a little guilt but, most likely, no shame because everyone else has done similar things.

Don't forget that your sensors for guilt and shame are fallible. They can be silent when they should say something, and they can also sound false alarms. But, false alarm or not, when we hear them we must do something. They don't turn off automatically.[15]

What traits of the PT genre do you see illustrated in this passage?

Not only does Welch reference relevant details through examples (child pornography, anger at a reckless driver, etc.), but he also uses the *second person* quite frequently:

13. Jack C. Richards and Richard Schmidt, *Longman Dictionary of Language Teaching and Applied Linguistics*, 3rd ed. (New York: Longman, 2002), 246.

14. My thanks to Spencer Ewing, who pointed this out during a class discussion of the PT genre.

15. Edward T. Welch, *Shame Interrupted: How God Lifts the Pain of Worthlessness and Rejection* (Greensboro, NC: New Growth, 2012), 11. *Shame Interrupted: How God Lifts the Pain of Worthlessness and Rejection* © 2012 by Edward T. Welch. Used by permission of New Growth Press.

- You stand alone.
- You are responsible.
- You are wrong.
- You have sinned.
- You don't belong.
- You are unacceptable, unclean, and disgraced
- Wrong has been done to you.
- You are associated with those who are disgraced or outcast.
- Your anger.
- You might feel.
- Don't (you) forget.

At the end of his discussion, he uses the *first person plural* as if to say, "We're in this together." This, again, is a potential mark of personal engagement, and is common to the practical theology genre.

In summary, PT writers prominently display *personal engagement* by, among other things, (1) asking and answering practical questions, (2) offering personal illustrations, and (3) using relevant details to engage with their readers We can now update our table of genres to include what we have found.

Summary of Genres

Genre	Communicative Goals	Selected Traits
Apologetics	critiquing non-Christian thought defending biblical truth	Logical coherence: *internal* organization of ideas signaled *externally* by words and phrases
Biblical Studies	understanding (through explanation and description) what Scripture teaches building an argument in support of what Scripture teaches	Textual awareness: using details from the text to build an argument, and relating one text to another in support of a main idea
Church History	learning from and understanding figures and movements in church history answering a *how* or *why* question	Signals of time and context: pointing out the historical, social, economic, political, and other circumstances surrounding a figure or movement
Systematic Theology	presenting the gathered teachings of Scripture on a particular topic showing how abstract claims are rooted in Scripture showing the biblical contradictions or inconsistencies in other approaches to a specific topic	Appeals to authority: gathering Scriptural teaching to address a topical question, engaging with other figures in church history, and appealing to confessional documents
Practical Theology	applying what Scripture teaches to all of life helping people practically absorb and benefit from the richness of biblical truth	Personal engagement: asking and answering practical questions; offering personal illustrations; and using relevant details Other Potential Marks: the use of idioms, the second person, and the first person plural

29

As for the Lord

"Whatever you do, work heartily, as for the Lord and not for men,
knowing that from the Lord you will receive the inheritance as your reward.
You are serving the Lord Christ."
—Colossians 3:23–24

Lesson Goals

Theology–To understand the importance of working "as for the Lord"
Reading–To understand logical arguments within a text
Vocabulary–To learn and use additional collocations from the passage
Grammar–To practice writing sentences with multiple clauses

Introduction

The application of Scripture to all of life is a primary concern of practical theology, and it is so because "the Scriptures *are* practical theology."[1] When we read the Bible, we witness God working in the everyday lives of his people throughout history. And God is still working! For this reason, "wise practical theology not only studies the Bible; it also studies the here and now. . . . Done well, practical theology is both faithful to God's revelation and timely to us and our context."[2]

Just as we learned in the previous lesson, we should be striving to apply Scripture to our everyday lives, despite the difficulties and the challenges that presents. We should also make a consistent effort to let the truth of Scripture change what we do every day and how we do it. This is part of the power of the gospel.

The gospel worldview will have all kinds of influence—profound and mundane, strategic and tactical—on how you actually do your work. Every field of work is to some degree influenced by alternate worldviews and their attendant idols, each assigning ultimate value to some idol—that doesn't fully take into consideration our sin or God's grace. The particulars of how the gospel works out in each field are endlessly rich.[3]

In this chapter, you will have an opportunity to explore some of those particulars. Here are some questions that will help get us started.

---

1. David Powlison, "The Practical Theology of Counseling," *Journal of Biblical Counseling* 25, no. 2 (Spring 2007): 2.
2. Ibid.
3. Timothy Keller, *Every Good Endeavor: Connecting Your Work to God's Work* (New York: Dutton: 2012), 165.

(1) What does working "as for the Lord" look like for the owner of a restaurant?

(2) What does it look like for a restaurant owner not to work "as for the Lord"?

(3) What are some other jobs in which a Christian approach makes an obvious difference?

Background for the Reading

Our Christian faith is central to who we are. In Christ we are new creatures (2 Cor. 5:17), and we have been set free from the bonds of sin (Gal. 5:1). It can be easy to let this truth affect our thoughts and behaviors when we are in the context of ministry, but what about Christians whose occupations are outside of the church? Should they also do their work "as for the Lord"? Why does it matter?

Reading Skill: Logical Arguments

In constructing an argument, writers have *premises* and *conclusions*. A **premise** is a statement—true or false—that is used to support a conclusion. A **conclusion** is the claim or thesis being supported. In writing, it is important to structure your argument so that the premises logically lead to the conclusion and the conclusion is well supported. In reading, it is important to be able to understand how the author is constructing his or her argument.

In some arguments, each body paragraph is a premise that supports the thesis (the conclusion). Writers can also relate ideas within a paragraph or even a sentence using a logical premise and conclusion relationship. Good readers are equipped to recognize this relationship and determine the premise and the conclusion.

In some texts, the writer uses signal words to signal this relationship:

Words and Phrases that Signal Premises	Words and Phrases that Signal Conclusions
because *since* *owing to* *for (the reason that)* *as indicated by* *assuming that* *in that* *given that* *if*	*therefore* *thus* *as a result* *so* *suggests that* *consequently* *implies that* *accordingly* *then* [when part of an *"if…then"* statement]

In other texts, you need to read the sentence(s) carefully to understand the relationship. Ask yourself:

- What is being assumed as true? *This is likely the premise.*
- What is the result of that assumption? This is likely the conclusion.
- Does my answer make sense, given what I know of the subject and of the world? If not, either you have incorrectly understood the logical argument or there is a logical flaw in the argument.

Practice

Read the following statements, all taken from the reading passage for this lesson. Write "P" by the premise and "C" by the conclusion. Use the question to help you decide which is the premise and which is the conclusion.

Examples:

A. Which word or phrase in these sentences signals the conclusion?

P The reclamation of work in a fallen world begins where the Protestant ethic began—by declaring the sanctity of all legitimate work in the world, no matter how common.

C This means that no vocation, including church work, is regarded as more "spiritual" or more pleasing to God than other types of work.

Answer: We can use the phrase "this means that" to help us identify the logical order of relationships here.

B. What is being assumed as true? What is the result of that assumption?

P Here we find no hierarchy of occupations in the sight of God;

C Tending sheep or a nation both have the same validity.

Answer: The assumption here is that there is "no hierarchy of occupations in the sight of God." This is made clearer if you read paragraph 3 of the text and see that the Bible records many occupations and treats them all with equal respect. If there is no hierarchy, then "tending sheep or a nation" are of equal importance.

1. Which word or phrase in these sentences signals the premise?

_____ If work in this broader sense is to be redeemed in our thinking and doing,
_____ we obviously need a view of the goodness of mundane work.

2. What is being assumed as true? What is the result of that assumption?

_____ To believe that all of life is God's
_____ opens the door for all types of work to be glorifying to God.

3. What is being assumed as true? What is the result of that assumption?

_____ The dignity of common work is established in the Bible
_____ not so much by specific proof texts as by the general picture of life that emerges.

Pre-Reading

What does it mean for you to do your work "as for the Lord"?

Reading

In the passage below, Leland Ryken discusses our work from a Christian perspective.

[¶1] The reclamation[a] of work in a fallen world begins where the Protestant ethic began—by declaring the sanctity of all legitimate work in the world, no matter how common. This means that no vocation, including church work, is regarded as more "spiritual" or more pleasing to God than other types of work. We must remember too, that work is much broader than simply one's job. If work in this broader sense is to be redeemed in our thinking and doing, we obviously need a view of the goodness of mundane[b] work.

[¶2] To believe that all of life is God's opens the door for all types of work to be glorifying to God. This is how the Bible portrays work. Paul urged Titus to remind Christians, "to be ready for any honest work" (Titus 3:1). He also practiced what he preached. Paul was called to be an apostle, yet even in that calling he remained a tentmaker as a way of earning his livelihood.[c] One could not ask for a better justification[d] for the Protestant

Remember?
Try to turn the first complete thought of this passage into a question, using "begin" as your main verb.

rejection of the sacred-secular dichotomy.[e] Paul could have become a professional cleric but he refused to do so (cf. 1 Cor. 9:3–18; 2 Thess 3:7–9). Furthermore, as Alan Richardson notes, "It is assumed throughout the New Testament that daily work, so far from being a hindrance to Christian living, is a necessary ingredient of it."

[¶3] The dignity[f] of common work is established in the Bible not so much by specific proof texts as by the general picture of life that emerges. As we read the Bible we find a veritable[g] gallery of people engaged in the ordinary work of life. Many biblical characters are known to us by their occupations. There are soldiers, chariot drivers, garment makers, farmers, merchants, and judges. We see King Saul not only as a king but also as a farmer plowing with his oxen in the field (1 Sam. 11:5). His successor David was a shepherd:

> [God] chose David his servant,
> and took him from the sheepfolds;
> from tending the ewes that had young he brought him
> to be the shepherd of Jacob his people,
> Of Israel his inheritance.
> With upright heart he tended them,
> and guided them with skillful hand (Ps. 78:70–72).

Here we find no hierarchy of occupations in the sight of God; tending sheep or a nation both have the same validity.[h]

[¶4] The list of God-ordained occupations keeps expanding as we read the Bible. God called Abraham to be a wandering pilgrim, which at the same time entailed being a nomadic[i] shepherd. God called Bezalel to be an artist (Ex. 31:1–5) and Moses to be a national leader (Ex. 3:1–10). We find lists of people who mixed the spices and made the flat cakes for worship in the temple (1 Chron. 9). Ruth was a farmer's wife and mother, greatly blessed by God in her common work.

[¶5] This doctrine of the sanctity of common labor has immense implications for our daily work, beginning with our jobs. Anxiety among Christians about their jobs does not affect only people with menial[j] jobs, though it certainly includes them. I have known wealthy, successful Christians with financially prestigious jobs who felt guilty because their work seemed far removed from "kingdom service." There are, of course, jobs about which one should feel guilty (such as those that provide immoral services or involve immoral actions), but any job that serves humanity and in which one can glorify God is a kingdom job.

[¶6] The Christian glorification of common labor also obliterates[k] the social distinctions that society puts on occupations. In general, occupations that pay well or involve power are high on the ladder of prestige; menial or poor paying jobs are stigmatized.[l] This hierarchy of value with regard to work has an insidious way of infiltrating[m] churches and boards of

Christian organizations. Some church boards consist wholly of successful professional people whose professional accomplishments are flaunted at election time. The biblical view of the worthiness of all legitimate occupations shows that such an attitude is wrong. In God's sight, a banker or businessperson is not engaged in more important work than a carpenter or homemaker.

[¶7] Finally, the Christian attitude toward common work comes as good news regarding the work we do off the job. Here, in fact, is where we tend to have particularly negative attitudes toward work because it is unpaid and usually unglamorous work. God is interested in our washing of the clothes and painting of the house. In the words of Luther, "What you do in your house is worth as much as if you did it up in heaven for our Lord God."

[¶8] The Christian doctrines that all of life is God's and that God calls people to their work are two mighty assaults[n] against the curse of work. A third follows naturally from these two: the worker is a steward who serves God.

[¶9] A steward is one who is entrusted with a master's property. When applied to work this means that the work we perform in the world is given to us by God. To accomplish our work is to serve God with what he has entrusted, including strength, time, and ability.

[¶10] Several important ideas emerge from the principle that work is essentially a form of stewardship in which the worker serves God. One is that work is a gift. God gives the materials for the worker and the very ability of the worker to perform the work. Gratitude for work is the natural response. To complain about a gift we have received has always been near the top of the list of ignominious[o] behavior. Complaining about the gift of work is no exception.

[¶11] The perspective of stewardship also affects our attitude toward the "ownership" of work. When work began to be viewed in primarily economic terms with the arrival of the industrial revolution, it became customary[p] to look upon work as something the worker owns and sells to the highest bidder. Alternatively, capitalism often operates on the premise that society owns work. The Christian view of the worker as steward suggests something truly revolutionary: God is the rightful owner of human work. There is a sense in which workers offer their work back to God.[4]

a. Reclamation (n.): the act or process of reforming or restoring to use
b. Mundane (adj.): ordinary or common
c. Livelihood (n.): means of support; income
d. Justification (n.): something that proves the validity or usefulness of something else
e. Dichotomy (n.): a splitting into two parts or groups
f. Dignity (n.): the quality or state of being worthy or honored
g. Veritable (adj.): being actually that which is named
h. Validity (n.): the quality or state of being well-grounded or justifiable
i. Nomadic (adj.): roaming about from place to place without a fixed pattern of movement

4. Leland Ryken, *Redeeming the Time: A Christian Approach to Work & Leisure* (Grand Rapids, MI: Baker, 1995), 214–15, 218–20. Excerpt from *Redeeming the Time* by Leland Ryken, copyright © 1995. Used by permission of Baker Academic, a division of Baker Publishing Group.

j. Menial (adj.): of, relating to, or being work not requiring special skill and often regarded as lacking status

k. Obliterate (v.): to destroy utterly all traces of

l. Stigmatize (v.): to regard with contempt

m. Infiltrate (v.): to enter or become established in gradually or unobtrusively

n. Assault (n.): a violent attack with nonphysical weapons (such as words, arguments, or appeals)

o. Ignominious (adj.): characterized by disgrace or shame

p. Customary (adj.): commonly practiced, used, or observed

Post-Reading

Name one reason why, according to Ryken, it is important for us to do our work "as for the Lord."

Main Ideas and Details

(1) Which of the following is the main idea of the passage?
   a. Menial work is the best kind of work we can do.
   b. Those who look down upon menial work will be judged by God.
   c. Work of any kind is sacred and ultimately done in service to God.
   d. Though work in the church is more important, everyday tasks are important too.

(2) Which of the following can we infer based on paragraph 2?
   a. All of our work either glorifies or dishonors God.
   b. Paul preferred to be a tentmaker rather than an apostle.
   c. Most of those whom Paul knew were dishonest workers.
   d. Professional clerics should have other jobs to support themselves.

(3) In paragraph 3, the word "occupations" could best be replaced by _____.
   a. Arts.
   b. Jobs.
   c. Works.
   d. Missions.

(4) Which of the following is the purpose of the highlighted sentence in paragraph 4?
   a. To introduce a new idea to the paragraph.
   b. To suggest that Abraham followed God's call.
   c. To prove that shepherding can be an occupation.
   d. To provide an example of a God-ordained occupation.

(5) In paragraph 5, the word "immense" means _____.
   a. Vast.
   b. Good.
   c. Infinite.
   d. Overstated.

(6) Which of the sentences below best expresses the essential information of the highlighted sentence in paragraph 6?
   a. Social distinctions set by our work are unjust.
   b. A Christian approach to work leads to clear social distinctions.
   c. A Christian approach to work affirms all people equally in their tasks.
   d. The Christian glorification of social distinctions can bring peace to society.

(7) In paragraph 6, the word "insidious" could best be replaced by _____.
   a. Subtle.
   b. Obvious.
   c. Innocent.
   d. Insincere.

(8) Which of the following can we infer from paragraph 7?
   a. Work done in God's house is more valuable than earthly work.
   b. A Christian approach to work treats ordinary tasks as most important.
   c. We have negative attitudes toward work that is glamorous but unpaid.
   d. Without a Christian approach to work, we might undervalue common tasks.

(9) In your own words, what is the purpose of paragraph 9?

(10) Which of the following is the main idea of paragraph 11?
  a. God owns all human work.
  b. Capitalism operates on false premises.
  c. The Christian view of work is revolutionary.
  d. We cannot view our work in terms of economic gain.

Understanding the Reading

I. Contrast how the jobs below would be done differently by a non-Christian as opposed to a Christian worker. After you have contrasted the Christian and the non-Christian approach to these jobs, choose one of the examples and write a sentence summarizing how the Christian approach to that job is different.

Job	Non-Christian Approach	Christian Approach
Waiter/Waitress		
Landscaper		
School Teacher		

Sentence

II. *Role-Play*. Read about the situation below. Working with a partner, spend a few seconds deciding who will take each role and who will go first. Then speak until both individuals have fulfilled their tasks.

Lay person: You are an active member in your church, and you believe that God has given some people a special call to go into the ministry. This has led you to believe that those who are employed full-time in a ministry position have holier jobs than lay people. You see a young seminary student in your church and you want to congratulate and encourage that student for following God's call.

Task: Encourage the seminary student for following God's call and express that it is a holier calling than your own.

Seminary student: You are studying at a seminary and have just been reading and discussing Ryken's ideas about work. You want to acknowledge that you do feel called to the ministry, but that the ministry is no more or less important than any other job. You know that the lay person is a sincere Christian who wants to be encouraging, but you also want to help that person have a correct view of work.

Task

Graciously accept the layperson's encouragement but share the ideas about work that you have been learning.

Collocations from the Passage

Select the most appropriate word from the choices in the parentheses. All of these examples of collocations have been taken directly from the reading.

The way in which we view our work has (*implications/reasons/inferences*) for how we carry out that work. Various ideas have (*emerged/grown/happened*) with regard to how we should view work done outside the church, but perhaps Luther's notion of Christian work in his *On the Freedom of a Christian* is most helpful to us in a (*rotten/fallen/departed*) world. According to Luther, in a broader (*impression/way/sense*), all (*honest/direct/proper*) work is equally valuable, for it is all done for the sake of the Lord—the expansion of his kingdom and the glory of his name. Having this view of work encourages us to work passionately and diligently. However, the world encourages us to hold onto social (*changes/distinctions/separations*) and negative (*positions/attitudes/sensations*) that accompany our perception of certain kinds of work, such as manual labor. If we have this view of work, we are more likely to work for the wrong reasons—pride, self-fulfillment, materialism, and so forth. The (*natural/hereditary/accidental*) Christian response should be to see all work in God's world as being done for his glory and name's sake. Keeping this in mind can push us to carry out even the simplest tasks with sincerity.

Using some of the collocations above, write three to five sentences about how a particular job can be done "as for the Lord."

Grammar Focus: Multi-Clause Sentences (Embedded Clauses)

As we near the end of the textbook and our discussion about editing for structure and word choice, we revisit a point brought up in the very first lesson: sentences in TE can be very complex! In fact, sometimes they need to be complex in order to convey certain ideas clearly. This complexity is often the result of having multiple clauses within a sentence, which are sometimes called "embedded clauses." See if you can find the embedded clause in the sentence below.

while the traditional topics of theology as formulated by the clergy need not necessarily be abandoned	Dependent clause
they need to be applied to the context	Independent clause
in which people actually live their daily lives	Relative clause–embedded

While the traditional topics of theology as formulated by the clergy need not necessarily be abandoned, they need to be applied to the context in which people actually live their daily lives.[5]

The relative clause is included or "embedded" within the independent clause.

Look at the embedded clauses in the paragraph below. (Remember that a clause is a subject + finite verb.)

The perspective of stewardship also affects our attitude toward the "ownership" of work. When work began to be viewed in primarily economic terms with the arrival of the industrial revolution, it became customary to look upon work as something <u>the worker owns and sells</u> to the highest bidder. Altenatively, capitalism often operates on the premise that <u>society owns work</u>. The Christian view of the worker as steward suggests something truly revolutionary: God is the rightful owner of human work. There is a sense in which <u>workers offer their work</u> back to God.

Notice that certain clauses are *embedded* within a main clause. "It became customary to look upon work as something **the worker owns and sells to the highest bidder**." Why would an author do this? Why not

5. Ibid., 227.

just have all of his sentences be simple clauses? Embedding clauses helps you further describe and develop ideas. Sometimes this is done out of necessity, and other times the author does it by choice. In the example above, we do not know exactly what the noun "something" means, so the author *needs* to add a relative clause ("that" has been omitted as the object of the compound verb phrase "owns and sells").

Activity 1

Underline only the embedded clauses (not the main clauses) in the excerpt below. Then answer the questions that follow.

> [Work] should be looked upon—not as a necessary drudgery to be undergone for the purpose of making money, but as a way of life in which the nature of man should find its proper exercise and delight and so fulfill itself to the glory of God. . . .
>
> What is the Christian understanding of work? . . . I should like to put before you two or three propositions arising out of the doctrinal position which I stated at the beginning: namely, that work is the natural exercise and function of man—the creature who is made in the image of his Creator. . . .
>
> The first, stated briefly, is that work is not, primarily, a thing one does to live, but the thing one lives to do. It is, or it should be, the full expression of the worker's faculties, the thing in which he finds spiritual, mental, and bodily satisfaction, and the medium in which he offers himself to God.
>
> Now the consequences of this are not merely that the work should be performed under decent living and working conditions. That is a point we have begun to grasp, and it is a perfectly sound point. But we have tended to concentrate on it to the exclusion of other considerations far more revolutionary.[6]

(1) List two nouns (or noun phrases) that the author further describes with embedded (relative) clauses.

(2) The author writes that "work" is "the thing in which [the worker] finds spiritual, mental, and bodily satisfaction." Was it necessary to follow "thing" with a relative clause?

Notice how Dorothy Sayers "plays" with words to produce an eloquent and memorable statement: "Work is not, primarily, a thing one does to live, but the thing one lives to do." She uses the same words in a reverse order to convey the opposite meaning. In both clauses we have subject + verb + infinitive ("one does to live"; "one lives to do"). She simply switches the verb and infinitive in the second clause to produce her intended meaning

6. Dorothy Sayers, "Why Work?," in *Leading Lives That Matter: What We Should Do and Who We Should Be*, ed. Mark R. Schwehn and Dorothy C. Bass (Grand Rapids, MI: Eerdmans, 2006), 192.

(grammar). This leads to a unique pronunciation pattern (phonology), in which the verb "lives" takes on special stress the second time it is pronounced: "a thing one does to live, but the thing one LIVES to do." This pronunciation helps the hearer (or reader) better understand her meaning (reference): work should be our passion, not our punishment.

Activity 2

For each number below, use embedded clauses to combine the sentences into a single sentence.

(1) All work is done in service of God. God alone is the owner of all work.

(2) All honest work is biblical. This means that all of our work should be done in the light of Scripture.

(3) Our work is valuable. Our work sometimes seems unimportant. God judges all work.

30

Godly Counsel

"Godly counseling will not be forthcoming if we incorporate the world's failures into the church, baptizing them as Christian when, in fact, they are not."
—Jay E. Adams, *Competent to Counsel*

Lesson Goals

Theology–To understand the need for biblical counseling
Reading–To identify main ideas and details from the reading, and to draw inferences
Vocabulary–To learn and use additional collocations from the passage
Grammar–To learn how to use adjectives effectively

Introduction

We come at last to the final chapter of the book. We began with God's creation; we end with godly counsel.

Counseling is an important part of practical theology, and we are living in the midst of a revolution in Christian counseling that has been going on since the late 1960s: the biblical counseling movement. Why is such a revolution necessary?

David Powlison suggests that there was an absence of Christian counseling several decades ago. Secular counseling and psychology were all that were available at that time. He writes,

The counseling vacuum among evangelicals was inversely proportional to the counseling plenum in the surrounding culture. The twentieth century had witnessed the birth and proliferation of the modern secular psychologies, and of those mental health professions that mediated such theories into lives. Secular institutions teamed with the mainline churches, the latter being part product and part co-author of the emerging therapeutic culture.[1]

The result, for Powlison and others, was not acceptable, since the theories and practices it produced were not purely biblical. Instead, they argued "that the church needs above all else a comprehensive and case-wise pastoral theology, something worthy of the name *systematic biblical counseling.*"[2] What do you think such an approach would look like? Consider these questions before going to the reading passage for this chapter:

---

1. David Powlison, "Cure of Souls (and the Modern Psychotherapies) Part 1: The Counseling Revolution," *Journal of Biblical Counseling* 25, no. 2 (Spring 2007): 6.
2. Ibid., 7.

Have you ever given someone counsel before? Did you feel as if your counsel was "biblical"?

What might be the dangers of borrowing counseling theories from non-Christians?

Background Information

As noted above, biblical counseling is a relatively new movement in the church.[3] As the name suggests, the Bible is the foundation of the approach: in Scripture we find the basic diagnosis for all of the world's evil (sin) and also the only lasting answer to our suffering (Christ).

At the heart of biblical counseling is the truth that sin is the root cause of all evil, that not *all* of the social problems we encounter are issues with the mind that can and should be addressed through psychotherapy and medication. Many, if not most, are issues of the heart.[4] For Jay Adams, "the gamut of problems in living found their cause—remote, proximate, and immediate—in human sin."[5]

Biblical counseling also takes into account that we are body-spirit image bearers of God. By this, we mean that we are not just spiritual creatures; we have bodies, and those bodies are related to our spiritual lives, as marred and in need of renewal as our souls. Therefore, we must resist the tendency to treat bodily problems as divorced from our spiritual lives and vice versa.

Pre-Reading

What do you think might be the greatest challenges to a counseling method founded upon Scripture?

Reading

In the following passage, David Powlison outlines important issues for the biblical counseling movement.

[¶1] I have identified six crucial[a] issues facing contemporary biblical counseling. These six are not the only issues. They are, however, the issues I believe merit the adjective "crucial." If we address them, we will grow in wisdom. If we neglect them, we will stagnate[b] or even distort the counsel of God.

Remember? Can you find the three embedded clauses at the end of this paragraph?

[¶2] 1. *The "same old issues" still face us.* The first issue is an old one. The problems that animated[c] biblical counseling at its start remain live problems today. Counseling in the Christian church continues to be signficantly compromised by the secular assumptions and practices of our culture's reigning psychologies and psychiatries. Biblical-nouthetic counseling[d] was initiated to provide two things: a cogent[e] critique of secularism and a distinctly biblical alternative. The traditional insights, strengths, and commitments of nouthetic counseling must be maintained. Biblical counseling operates within the worldview of the Bible, with the Bible in hand. It is centered on God even (especially!) when it thinks about man. It is centered on Jesus Christ, who became man in

---

3. It traces back to Jay E. Adams and his work opposing common psychiatric practices and assumptions in the late 1960s. Adams's book, *Competent to Counsel*, was published in 1970, which is considered the start of the "biblical counseling movement." David Powlison, *The Biblical Counseling Movement: History and Context* (Greensboro, NC: New Growth, 2010), 51.

4. See Powlison, *The Biblical Counseling Movement*, 101.

5. Ibid., 102.

order to save us. It is centered in the midst of Christ's people, who are called to pray for one another and to counsel one another in love.

[¶3] Secular pyschologies remain major competitors with the church. We face a zoo of systems united by only one thing. At best, "god" is a comforting auxiliary[f] to the human psychic drama. At worst, he/she/it is a delusion. Lacking God, the human problem (and the power to understand and to solve that problem) is perceived to lie somewhere within or between human beings. Christ died for nothing.

[¶4] The enemy was not only out there somewhere. "We have met the enemy . . . and they are us," Pogo once remarked. Secular psychological modes of thinking continue to inhabit the church of the living God. Witness the rampant[g] self-esteem and need psychologies that bypass the man-God relationship in order to make the human psyche the place "where the action is." The living God is shriveled[h] into an actor within an all-important psychic drama.

[¶5] *2. The questions touching on human motivation must be explored and integrated more firmly within both our theory and practice.* Nouthetic counseling has uniquely comprehended that the goal of counseling should be nothing less than visible obedience to the Lord. No other counseling system perceives that this is the central issue facing troubled, sinful, and suffering human beings. The counseling world around us (Christian and non-Christian alike) is agog[i] with speculations about human motivation. Biblical counseling has rightly stressed behavior—love and good works—as the simple and accessible evidence of true change.

[¶6] Biblical counseling must walk a fine line, however. There is patent[j] "danger to the left of us." Speculative psychological systems pretend[k] to an analytic insight into the motivations of the human heart. Biblical counseling has been rightfully suspicious of psychodynamic[l] explanations. Purely mythical constructions like id, ego, and super ego are reified.[m] Self-esteem or "needs" become the magic crucible[n] from which all human life flows. My "self-talk" is invested with supreme power to determine the course of my life. Our wariness at such pseudo-explanations perhaps carries over (illegitimately) into a wariness toward the whole subject of motivation.

[¶7] But we who are sensitive to danger on the left, to rank speculation about the motives and motivational structure of the human heart, often forget there is "danger to the right of us" as well. We depart from the Bible if we ignore motives and drift toward an externalistic view of man. The caricature[o] that we are behavioristic may indeed be true more often than we would like to admit. The Bible itself tells us that behavior has reasons.

[¶8] *3. The relationship between human responsibility and human suffering needs a great deal of clarification.* Crucial issue 1 established our foundation for faith and practice. Crucial issue 2 made us rethink the nature of biblical change. Crucial issue 3 now challenges us to rethink our vision of the counselee and the counselee's situation. How do we see and understand the people whom we counsel? What kind of attention do we pay to the kind of world the counselee inhabits? How important are the counselee's past and present circumstances?

[¶9] One of the most refreshing characteristics of nouthetic counseling has been its affirmation of human responsibility. The counseling world, Christian and non-Christian alike, concocts elaborate systems that rationalize sin by making people fundamentally victims determined by forces outside their control. . . . Biblical counseling has resisted seeing people as determined—whether by heredity, the sins of others, organic imbalances, poor models, unmet needs, mental forces imposing on us as "illness," or demonic inhabitants.

[¶10] Our treatment of the victim side of the biblical portrayal of man has been anecdotal and occasional, not systematic. Under issue 2 we noted that rampant speculations about human motivation should not keep us from tackling the motivation questions biblically. Equally, rampant and systematized blameshifting should not deter[p] us from developing the biblical view of how the things we suffer affect us.

[¶11] *4. We need to press much further in understanding the biblical data about the counselor-counselee relationship.* Crucial issue 1 reaffirmed our epistemological and practical foundation. Issue 2 probed the nature of change. Issue 3 reexamined our understanding of the counselee and his situation. Issue 4 asks, "What is the nature of the relationship between the counselor and the counselee?"

[¶12] Biblical counseling has always contained the seeds of two complementary[q] visions of counseling: one relatively more authoritative and the other relatively more mutual. The former has been articulated in detail [we are all subject to the authority of God's Word]. The latter has always been more implicit, more the logical implication of the competency[r] of wise people to help one another. These other dimensions in the counselor-counselee relationship must be articulated explicitly.

[¶13] *5. Biblical counseling must be contextualized to new audiences.* To date we have reached thousands of Christian people with the message of biblical counseling. We need to continue to reach these same people as our primary focus. The local church people are the salt of the earth, the light of the world. But we also need to analyze a different audience and expend some legitimate effort in reaching the educational wing[s] of Christendom. Is addressing academia simply a nice idea, to be attended to someday? I think it is a crucial issue now. The future of the *local church* is involved! Where are the church leaders and counselors of tomorrow being trained today? They are being trained in institutions where biblical counseling is dismissed with a wave of the hand.

[¶14] *6. The relationship of biblical counseling to secular psychology needs to be publicly clarified.* We need to clarify the nuances in our view of secular psychology. Our rejection of secularism has been in the headlines. The subtleties[t] of the biblical response to secular knowledge have been in the fine print. Both halves of our view need to be developed if we are not only going to squeeze error out of the church but also going to speak cogently and persuasively to a psychologized culture.

[¶15] Each of the crucial issues facing contemporary biblical counseling is a test, illuminating where we are. Each delivers a challenge, calling us to where we must go. Each holds a promise, inviting us to the fresh wisdom that will come as we explore the riches of Scripture and life, and as we pursue new friendships within the body of Christ. Biblical truth is balanced, elegant, and potent[u] to transform lives. Our exploration of neglected riches will bring biblical counseling practice into greater conformity with such truth.[6]

a. Crucial (adj.): important or essential as decisive or as resolving a crisis

b. Stagnate (v.): to fail to advance or develop (Note: This verb is intransitive, but the author is using it creatively as a transitive verb.)

c. Animate (v.): to permeate deeply in such a way as to stimulate and enliven

d. Nouthetic counseling (n. phrase): biblical counseling or Christian counseling ("nouthetic" comes from a Greek word meaning "admonish)

e. Cogent (adj.): appealing persuasively to the mind or reason

f. Auxiliary (n.): one that functions or serves in a supplementary often subordinate position

g. Rampant (adj.): marked by the absence of check or restraint; unbridled

h. Shrivel (v.): to become reduced to helplessness or inefficiency

i. Agog (adj.): full of intense interest, ardent anticipation, or extreme excitement

j. Patent (adj.): open to view; readily visible or intelligible; evident

k. Pretend (v.): to put in a claim; to lay claim; to allege a title

l. Psychodynamic (adj.): relating to mental or emotional forces or processes developing especially in early childhood and their effects on behavior and mental states

m. Reify (v.): to convert mentally to something concrete or objective; to materialize

n. Crucible (n.): a place in which concentrated forces interact to cause or influence change or development

o. Caricature (n.): an exaggeration by means of deliberate simplification

p. Deter (v.): to turn aside, discourage, or prevent from acting

q. Complementary (adj.): mutually supplying each other's lack

r. Competency (n.): the quality of being adequate or sufficient in knowledge, judgment, skill, or strength

s. Wing (n.): any section of a building (here used metaphorically)

t. Subtlety (n.): a fine-drawn or delicate distinction

u. Potent (adj.): having or wielding strength, force, or authority; powerful, strong

Post-Reading

Based on what you have learned from the reading, what do you think might be a popular critique of biblical counseling?

Main Ideas and Details

(1) Which of the following can we infer based on paragraph 2, concerning the first issue that faces the biblical counseling movement?

a. We must continue to grow in wisdom.

b. Christ became man in order to save us.

c. We are called to pray for and counsel one another.

d. Secular practices still compromise Christian counseling.

(2) In paragraph 2, by the word "reigning," the author means _____.

a. Helpful.

b. Wicked.

c. Dominant.

d. Sovereign.

(3) According to paragraph 2, what two things was biblical-nouthetic counseling meant to offer?

(4) In paragraph 3, the author writes that, for secular psychologies, "At best, 'god' is a comforting

6. Powlison, *The Biblical Counseling Movement*, selections from 241–58. *The Biblical Counseling Movement: History and Context* © 2010 by David Powlison. Used by permission of New Growth Press.

auxiliary to the human psychic drama." What does the author intend to convey about secular psychologies?

a. They value God as an unnecessary comfort.

b. They consider Christianity to be a valid religion.

c. They significantly understate the importance of God to psychological studies.

d. They openly proclaim that God does not exist and so should not be worshipped.

(5) Which of the following can we infer based on paragraph 3?

a. Secular approaches to psychology are entirely unhelpful.

b. The human psychic drama is crucial to Christian counseling.

c. Secular psychologies assume God cannot help with the human problem.

d. There are some secular approaches that are minor competitors with the church.

(6) What is the purpose of the final sentence in paragraph 3?

(7) True (T) or False (F)_____: The second issue that faces the biblical counseling movement is that secular counseling has many speculations about the motivation of human behavior.

(8) In paragraph 6, when the author says that biblical counseling must "walk a fine line," he means that biblical counseling must_____.

a. Be careful.

b. Be anxious.

c. Be aggressive.

d. Be sure of itself.

(9) Which of the following statements is not implied by the first sentence of paragraph 9?

a. Nouthetic counseling affirms human responsibility.

b. There are many characteristics of nouthetic counseling.

c. Secular counseling properly accounts for a person's responsibility.

d. Secular approaches to counseling downplay personal responsibility.

(10) In paragraph 9, the word "rationalize" could best be replaced by _____.

a. Clarify.

b. Justify.

c. Support.

d. Condemn.

(11) Each of the elements in the list at the end of paragraph 9 is an example of what?

(12) In paragraph 14, the author makes the following statements: "Our rejection of secularism has been in the headlines. The subtleties of the biblical response to secular knowledge have been in the fine print." By this, he means that the biblical response to secular knowledge is

_____.

a. Clear.

b. Not well known.

c. Fully developed.

d. Frequently referenced.

(13) What three things does the author say about each of the crucial issues facing contemporary biblical counseling? (Refer to paragraph 15.)

Understanding the Reading

Try to complete this activity without looking back at the reading. The author lists six crucial issues facing the biblical counseling movement. (If necessary, you can glance at the reading to remember what the six issues are.) Place a number (1–6) next to each sentence below based on which issue it supports.

_____   Our rejection of secularism has been in the headlines. The subtleties of the biblical response to secular knowledge have been in the fine print.

_____   Biblical counseling has resisted seeing people as determined—whether by heredity, the sins of others, organic imbalances, poor models, unmet needs, mental forces imposing on us as "illness," or demonic inhabitants.

_____   But we also need to analyze a different audience and expend some legitimate effort in reaching the educational wing of Christendom.

_____   Biblical counseling operates within the worldview of the Bible, with the Bible in hand.

_____   Biblical counseling has rightly stressed behavior—love and good works—as the simple and accessible evidence of true change.

_____   We depart from the Bible if we ignore motives and drift toward an externalistic view of man.

_____   Secular pyschologies remain major competitors with the church.

Collocations from the Passage

Select the most appropriate word from the choices in the parentheses. All of these examples of collocations have been taken directly from the reading.

If we are to address the crucial (*issue/outcome/ trouble*) of how we can approach the cure of souls biblically, we must begin by finding out how secular (*premises/assumptions/precepts*) have been embraced and practiced by the church. Building a cogent, biblical (*review/ examination/critique*) of these assumptions is a good starting point for re-envisioning our practice of counseling in the body of Christ. Of course, taking up a biblical (*portrayal/ picture/rendering*) of humanity as made in God's image will introduce several (*logical/ rational/coherent*) implications and ensuing questions: How much can we retain from secular theories of psychology? What notions of secular restoration need to be exchanged for the biblical (*truth/fact/case*) of regeneration in the Spirit? These are pressing questions.

Provide collocations from the reading passage for the words in the center bubbles below.

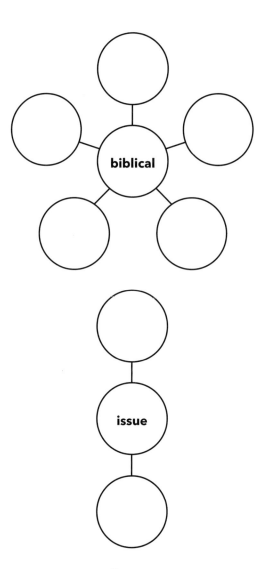

Fig. 30.1. Collocation Diagram 9

Grammar Focus: Effective Use of Adjectives

In our final lesson, we discuss a kind of word choice that might seem less critical in our editing process. Some students have had English teachers tell them to avoid using adjectives and adverbs because they over-complicate or cloud the message. Yet, when used carefully, adjectives can add a great deal of meaning to your sentences, and they may even be necessary to your message. Have a look at some of the adjectives in one of the paragraphs from the reading.

1. The "**same old** issues" still face us. The first issue is an **old** one. The problems that

animated **biblical** counseling at its start remain **live** problems today. Counseling in the **Christian** church continues to be signficantly **compromised** by the **secular** assumptions and practices of our culture's **reigning** psychologies and psychiatries. **Biblical-nouthetic** counseling was initiated to provide two things: a **cogent** critique of secularism and a distinctly **biblical** alternative. The **traditional** insights, strengths, and commitments of **nouthetic** counseling must be maintained. **Biblical** counseling operates within the worldview of the Bible, with the Bible in hand. It is centered on God even (especially!) when it thinks about man. It is centered on Jesus Christ, who became man in order to save us. It is centered in the midst of Christ's people, who are called to pray for one another and to counsel one another in love.

Sometimes using adjectives is unavoidable; you may need them to focus your reader on particular things (e.g., Powlison refers not merely to counseling, but to *biblical* or *nouthetic* counseling). At other times, using adjectives at key places can improve the effectiveness of your message by clarifying your meaning. "Reigning," for example, tells us that the secular psychologies and psychiatries "rule" in the broader counseling field.

There are two kinds of adjective errors that you should consider when editing your own writing.

1. **Incorrect word form**

We have already studied the forms of adjectives (Lessons 3 and 21), so you are familiar with the adjective endings. But sometimes English language learners use a noun form instead of the adjective form.

- Jesus is a history person. . . . Jesus is a *historical* person.
- David was righteousness before God. . . . David was *righteous* . . .

2. **Incorrect word choice**

Choosing the wrong adjective can also be a problem for students. This surfaces with regard to (1) collocation (the adjective does not go with the noun in question) and (2) word choice. Collocation errors occur when the adjective seems as if it would fit the context, but we simply do not use that adjective with a particular noun. Word choice errors occur when the adjective cannot modify a particular noun.

The biblical counseling movement is mighty strong in parts of North America. (Collocation)

Biblical counseling is condensed in focused on Christ. (Word choice)

Activity 1

Underline the adjectives in the following passage. Which adjectives seem to be communicating something important to the author's message (list two)? Be prepared to explain your answers.

In a thoughtful and thought-provoking personal letter, John Carter of Rosemead Graduate School, one of the leading critics of nouthetic counseling, commented that nouthetic counseling could only speak to audiences "who already shared Jay Adams's perspective." There was little that could be done creatively within the "radically biblical perspective" because everything such a limited perspective could say had been said already either explicitly or implicitly. As a movement we were likely to stagnate into rehashing among ourselves the thoughts of one man.

Carter's words are sobering and challenging. If he is right, we are less than biblical. For the Bible portrays itself as a fountain of life, granting fresh wisdom to all who ask and dig, producing ministry that changes lives significantly. If he is right, then this article has been wrong, and it is a pathetic dream for me to lift up my eyes and see the whole world waiting. But I think Carter is wrong. Our vision has always far outstripped our attainment because it is a biblical vision. If we are indeed *biblical*, then the foundational presupposition—radically biblical counseling—will generate a dynamic of life, growth, and expansion, not stagnation. It will liberate, not limit.[7]

Activity 2

Below is an example of biblical counseling in practice. In three to four sentences, describe the counsel being offered, comparing it with that of a non-Christian to the same event (the car accident).

My daughter had a car accident that was her fault. She wasn't hurt, but it was going to cost us money. Before she arrived home, we heard the news from a friend who had seen my daughter and her friend walking away from the damaged car.

My daughter was most concerned about how her mother and I would respond. She dreaded the thought of explaining it to us. When she came in the house, we could see her trepidation, so we spared her the storytelling.

"We know what happened with the car. It's okay."

In an instant she realized we didn't look mad. We weren't going to send her to prison or do whatever worst-case scenario she was anticipating. We still loved her just as we did before the accident. It had to be a high point in her life.

You, like the Samaritan woman and my daughter, don't have to go into the details of your life's shameful events either. Before you can construct a strategy to cover them up, Jesus says, "I know what happened to you," or "I know what you have done." Immediately, you can tell he doesn't reject you, expose you, or pull back to avoid being contaminated by you. He just says, "Be sure to come back."

But old habits die hard. You don't trust people messing with the fine china of your past, so you move the topic off you and onto religion. It's an age-old diversion.

"With so many denominations and religions, who is to know what's true?" It's a silly thing to say, but this entire conversation [of Jesus and the Samaritan woman] has been shocking from start to finish, so an odd response here and there is understandable. Maybe you anticipate that Jesus is going to tell you to go to church more, so you mention something about hypocrites. Either way, you still don't get who Jesus is. You are just scrambling to avoid your shame.

"What is most important is that you look away from yourself to the true God. No matter who you are or where you are from, you will be able to know him and worship him. And when you worship him, it means you are accepted into his presence."

When in doubt, look at the Lord. Life up your eyes (Numbers 21:4–9). That will be something it will take all your life to master, but what better time to start than now? Still, you can't imagine being an invited worshiper of God.

Someday. Maybe. Hope rises, but it is so foreign you don't know what to do with it. You *certainly* don't want to get too excited and be disappointed yet again.

"Yes, Jesus, someday."

"I—the one speaking with you right now—am the true God."

This is the last word. Jesus always has the last word, and it is always a good last word. It is always about him and it always takes you by surprise with his love and acceptance. What is your response?[8]

---

7. Ibid., 258.

8. Edward T. Welch, *Shame Interrupted: How God Lifts the Pain of Worthlessness & Rejection* (Greensboro, NC: New Growth, 2012), 123–24. *Shame Interrupted: How God Lifts the Pain of Worthlessness and Rejection* © 2012 by Edward T. Welch. Used by permission of New Growth Press.

Collocation Review

Fill in the missing collocations in the table below. While these collocations have been taken directly from Lessons 26–27, more than one answer may be correct. The important thing is to identify collocations that you can memorize and use in your own writing.

bridge	
biblical	
timeless general	
positive negative	
	connection
contemporary	

	advice
address	
	issue
secular	
	critique
	alternative portrayal
logical	

In a Christlike Manner (PT Task 2)

Introduction

As Christians, we know that Christ is Lord over all areas of our lives, not just our "spiritual" or "ministerial" lives. Even tasks that seem unrelated to the gospel can and should be done in a Christ-like manner, as a service to God and our neighbors.

Can you drive a bus in a Christ-like manner? According to Col. 3:23, yes, you can. What might that look like? For an example of what this could look like, watch the video clip posted at http://www.dump.com/drivershoes/.

Is there anything lacking in the man's response about why he did what he did? In what sense do you see his action as Christ-like?

Task

On your everyday commute to work, you have met a person who works as a manager of a local clothing store. You have recently learned that this person, Thomas, is a new Christian, but he is frustrated by what he calls the "menial nature of his work." He tells you that he does not see a way for his Christian faith to have any impact on what he does every day. He asks you if you have any ideas for him. You tell him that you will think about it and email him that night with your ideas as to how he can bring his faith to bear on his everyday tasks.

Draft an email to Thomas outlining your thoughts. Your email should be between 200 and 300 words. Try to be as concrete as you can in your suggestions.

ANSWER KEY

Unit 1: Lesson 2

Main Idea Practice

1.
   a. S
   b. G
   c. √

2.
   a. G
   b. √
   c. S

4.
   a. S
   b. G
   c. √

5.
   a. √
   b. G
   c. S

6.
   a. G
   b. √
   c. S

Main Ideas and Details

1. c

2. a

3. d

4. God's authoritative revelation in nature and Scripture

5. Goodness

Understanding the Reading

1. False

2. True

3. False

4. False

5. True

6. False

Collocations

Theologians in the Reformed tradition make a clear (*point/value/distinction*) between the Creator and his creatures. This Creator-creature distinction assumes that there are two different (*positions/levels/standings*) of being: that of the independent Triune God and that of the dependent creature. In that sense, there are two (*strange/unique/different*) kinds of being. Yet, while these kinds of being are (*opposed/different/diverse*) in character, they are still related, because God's creatures are made in his image (Gen. 1:26). In all areas of theology, this Creator-creature distinction is an important (*feature/character/nature*) of orthodox Christian belief.

Grammar Focus: Activity 1

There are levels of reality.

There is no continuum between God's knowledge and ours.

There is a standard that guides a creature's knowledge.

There are two different kinds of goodness, justice, wisdom, and knowledge.

There are two circles in Van Til's diagram of the Creator-creature distinction.

Grammar Focus: Activity 2

1. There are
2. There is
3. There is
4. There is
5. There are
6. There are
7. There is

Unit 1: Lesson 3

Main Ideas and Details

1. d
2. b
3. b
4. a
5. c
6. d

Understanding the Reading

1. It would be problematic to say that revelation only provides us with "information" about God because revelation draws us into a *personal relationship* with God. Through revelation, we know God himself, not just information about God.

2. The authors might say several things to those who claim that revelation is not necessary for knowledge of God. (1) They might say that we are surrounded by revelation, so it is impossible for revelation to *not* be necessary (since it is all we have); (2) they might say that we can know about God from general revelation (the natural world), but we cannot understand even that general revelation correctly or have any hope of salvation and redemption apart from special revelation; (3) they might say that the triune

God simply *is* the one who reveals himself, so if we have "knowledge" of a being apart from revelation, that being is not God, but an idol.

Collocations

There was nothing that compelled God to reveal himself. His love and glory could have been kept a (*mystery/secret/puzzle*). But he chose to reveal himself in what could only ever be a pure (*act/doing/statute*) of God. And once God chose to reveal himself, this revelation took a (*big/sovereign/central*) place in the Creator-creature relationship, for at the same (*time/minute/stretch*) that God revealed himself, he bound us in covenant with himself. That is why covenant is a key (*idea/thinking/plan*) in Scripture, from Genesis to Revelation.

Grammar Focus: Activity 1

See paragraph 2 of the reading for Lesson 3.

Grammar Focus: Activity 2

Answers will vary for this exercise.

Learning the Genre (AP) Activity

The internal structure of the passage below is a back-and-forth movement from (A) humanity and mortality to (B) divinity and immortality, as shown below. This back-and-forth movement is signaled by the underlined words and phrases, which point to the reasoning that supports the author's argument.

The Word perceived that corruption could not be got rid of otherwise than through death (A); yet He Himself, as the Word, being immortal and the Father's Son, was such as could not die (B). For this reason, therefore, He assumed a body capable of death (A), in order that it, through belonging to the Word Who is above all (B), might become in dying a sufficient exchange for all (A), and, itself remaining incorruptible through His indwelling (B), might thereafter put an end to corruption for all others as well (AB), by the grace of the resurrection (B).

Unit 2: Lesson 4

Main Ideas and Details

1. a

2. b

3. He means that our mind reveals something about the character or nature of God.

4. c

5. b

Collocations

Van Til was always conscious of the Creator-creature distinction when it came to (*person/human/mankind*) knowledge. While there might be many ways to describe his understanding of our knowledge, perhaps the most (*appropriate/necessary/positive*) word is *analogical*, which is the word Van Til himself adopted. For him, there was an important (*divergence/disagreement/difference*) between knowing the (*reason/truth/validity*) in a limited but true sense, and knowing the truth exhaustively. It seemed (*appropriate/fitting/suitable*) to him to explain this difference with the terms analogical, equivocal, and univocal. [[NOTE: in the final sentence, *any* of the words could fit.]]

Grammar Focus: Activity 1

Van Til realized that the epistemological disagreements between believers and unbelievers could not be resolved in a neutral fashion, and though the issue of God's existence and character (and man's relationship to Him) could be treated as secondary—and thus temporarily set aside without any commitment one way or another—while abstract philosophical issues were debated and settled. It is often, but vainly, imagined that once we come to agreement on our epistemology, we can apply those epistemological standards to the questions of whether God exists, whether miracles occur, whether the Bible is true, etc. By contrast, Van Til taught that abstract epistemological neutrality is an illusion and that, given the kind of God revealed in the Bible, imagined neutrality is actually prejudicial against God.

Grammar Focus: Activity 2

Active	Passive
Man knows God through his revelation.	*God is known by man through his revelation.* *Through his revelation, God is known by man.*
God's thought transcends human thought.	*Human thought is transcended by God's thought.*
Van Til presented the idea of analogical thinking.	*The idea of analogical thinking was presented by Van Til.*
Mankind imitates God on a creaturely level.	*God is imitated by man on a creaturely level.* *On a creaturely level, God is imitated by man.*
Creatures follow their Creator.	*The Creator is followed by his creatures.*

Grammar Focus: Activity 3

Answers to this question will vary.

Grammar Focus Activity 4

Answers to this question will vary.

Unit 2: Lesson 5

Main Ideas and Details

1. d
2. b
3. c
4. d
5. b
6. c

Understanding the Reading

1. I (Irrationalist)
2. R (Rationalist)
3. B (Biblical)
4. I (Irrationalist)
5. I (Irrationalist)

Collocations

Though it is true that all words have a (*area/scope/range*) of meaning, it does not follow that words have no stable meaning. In fact, words have ultimately stable meaning because God is stable and immovable. In light of this, we (*own/possess/have*) a responsibility to respect the stable meanings of the words people speak. If we do not, we violate the moral (*standards/criteria/measures*) that God has set in place by his creation of human language.

Grammar Focus: Activity 1

Answers for this exercise will vary, but here are some possibilities.

1. *Theological*—Negative Comparison

   His approach is less theological than others.

2. *Research* (n.)—Intensified Comparison

   He has done much more research on this than others in the field.

3. *Faith* (n.)—Comparison of Equality

   For some people, it takes as much faith to believe in the gospel as it does to believe in God.

4. *Emphasize*—Comparison

   Calvin emphasizes the teaching of total depravity more than many other theologians.

5. *Disciplined*—Intensified Comparison

   Luther was much more disciplined in his prayer life than many of us are today.

6. *Consistent*—Comparison

   Van Til is more consistent in his apologetic methodology than other theologians.

7. *Reasonable*—Negative Comparison

   His position is less reasonable than that of Van Til.

8. *Recent*—Comparison

   His work on the doctrine of the Trinity is more recent than Smith's.

Grammar Focus: Activity 2

Answers for this exercise will vary.

Grammar Focus: Activity 3

Answers for this exercise will vary.

Unit 2: Lesson 6

Using Context to Understand Unknown Words

1. c

2. a

3. a

Main Ideas and Details

1. b

2. b

3. c

4. d

5. Scripture

6. c

Understanding the Reading

1. T

2. T

3. F, "doing things backwards"

4. F, "in our hearts"

5. F, "we should seek"

6. F, "brought to obey him"

Collocations

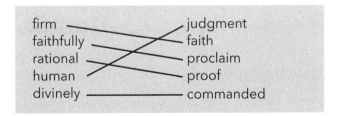

Grammar Focus: Activity 1

Let this point therefore stand: that those <u>whom the Holy Spirit has inwardly taught</u> truly rest upon Scripture, and that Scripture indeed is self-authenticated; hence, it is not right to subject it to proof and reasoning. And the certainty <u>it deserves</u> [[Reduced relative]] with us, it attains by the testimony of the Spirit. . . . We seek no proofs, no marks of genuineness <u>upon which our judgment may lean</u>; but we subject our judgment and wit to it as to a thing <u>far beyond any guesswork</u> [[Reduced relative]]! This we do, not as persons <u>accustomed to seize upon some unknown thing</u> [[Reduced relative]], <u>which, under closer scrutiny, displeases them</u>, but fully conscious that we hold the unassailable truth!

Grammar Focus: Activity 2 (possible answers)

1. Scripture, which is the Word of God, is not subject to proof or reasoning.

2. The Spirit must persuade us that the prophets, who were God's servants, spoke what God commanded.

3. We subject our judgment, which is fallen, to Scripture.

4. Many Christians who are passionate about their faith may think that they have to prove the truth of Scripture.

5. We trust God's Word because we trust God himself, who is the giver of all blessings.

Grammar Focus: Activity 3 (possible answers)

Noun/Noun Phrase	Appositive Phrase
The Son	*the Word of the Father*
The Holy Spirit	*the second person of the Trinity*
Scripture	*the word of God revealed to man*
Isaiah	*a great prophet of the Old Testament*
language	*a gift of the Trinitarian God*

Grammar Focus: Activity 4

Answers for this exercise will vary.

Unit 3: Lesson 7

Main Ideas and Details

1. Answers will vary, but your sentence should include some key words such as *inerrancy, infallibility, Scripture, evidence, truth,* and *modernism.*

2. (1) MI; (2) D; (3) MI; (4) D; (5) D; (6) MI; (7) D; (8) D

3. a

4. d

5. a

6. He uses the word "interesting" to begin his critique of Wright's approach. However, if you include something about "irony," that would be acceptable as well.

7. b

Understanding the Reading (possible answers)

John Frame challenges us to examine our method when it comes to supporting the truth of Scripture. While Wright uses evidence/scholarship to support the historical validity of Christianity, he seems to put too much weight on this, which amounts to trust in humanity/academia. In doing so, he also fails to account for the presupposition that everyone has in interpreting history. As Christians, we must make sure that our method is biblical and not submit the truth of Scripture to a human standard, even if that standard or tool provides us with helpful information that can support our faith.

Collocations

When it comes to the truth of Scripture, some theologians might suggest that we should go first to history in order to settle historical (*things/matters/events*). Rather than take God at his word, we should look for some way to make sure that God is, in fact, telling the truth in Scripture, or at least make sure that God's instruments (the human authors) did not make mistakes in transmitting God's revelation. Indeed, there is a strand of biblical (*knowledge/literacy/scholarship*) that encourages this approach. But more (*conservative/safe/old*)

scholars take a different approach and uphold the self-authenticating nature of Scripture. This, they claim, is what all Christian (*scholars/authorities/apprentices*) should do, because it is consistent with their belief in the ultimate authority of God's revelation.

Grammar Focus: Activity 1

See paragraphs 5 and 6 from the theological reading.

Grammar Focus: Activity 2

In Scripture, God's covenant lordship has three major connotations: (1) God, by his almighty power, is fully in *control* of the creation. (2) What God says is ultimately *authoritative*, in the sense we have discussed previously. (3) As covenant Lord, he takes the creation (and parts of the creation, such as Israel, or the church) into special relationships with him, relationships that lead to blessing or cursing. So he is always *present* with them. He was literally present with Israel in the tabernacle and the temple. He became definitively present to us in the incarnation of Jesus Christ. And his Spirit indwells NT believers, making them his temple. Truly God is "God with us," Immanuel.

Grammar Focus: Activity 3

Answers for this exercise will vary.

Unit 3: Lesson 8

Main Ideas and Details

1. A: Accurate; B: Not accurate, "an empty set"; C: Not accurate, "what God forbids"; D: Accurate; E: Not accurate, "relative ways"

2. d

3. a

4. c

5. d

6. d

7. The author italicizes these words to emphasize them (to draw our attention to them). If you were reading this paragraph out loud, you would place extra stress on these two words.

Understanding the Reading

Answers for this exercise will vary.

Collocations

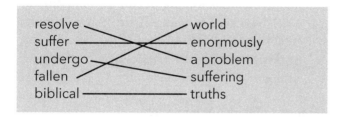

resolve — a problem
suffer — enormously
undergo — suffering
fallen — world
biblical — truths

Grammar Focus: Activity 1

Meanwhile, <u>the</u> consequences of [[X]] human sin infest many of our experiences with some measure of pain. Such afflictions may be splashed onto <u>the</u> canvas of human history with <u>a</u> very broad brush. Thus [[X]] God says to Jerusalem, "I am against you. I will draw my sword from its sheath and cut off from you both <u>the</u> righteous and <u>the</u> wicked" (Ezek. 21:3). In one sense, of course, no one is [[X]] righteous (Rom. 3:10ff); but that is not what <u>the</u> prophet means here. He means that when devastation descends on Jerusalem, the people who will suffer will include both those whose immediate sins have brought <u>the</u> city to this horrible punishment, and those who have not participated in <u>the</u> sins that have brought about <u>the</u> destruction of <u>the</u> nation.

Grammar Focus: Activity 2

Transfigured Hermeneutics 4–Jesus as God's Glory Face in John's Gospel [[Correct]] Buckets and Burning Churches: Luther, <u>the</u> Church, and Catholicity Meet <u>the</u> New American Dream Infant Baptism and <u>the</u> Promise of Grace WHAT IF: Duns Scotus had not been a Theologian? [[Correct]] Conformity to Jesus as <u>the</u> Paradigm for Christian Ethics The Incarnation of God [[Correct]]
The End of Christmas [[Correct]] The Fruit of <u>the</u> Spirit 5: Patience Swimming in <u>the</u> Glorious Deep Blue Sea Baptist Foundations [[Correct]] Halloween: A Distinctively Christian Holiday [[Correct]] Defending Substitution [[Correct]] The World in <u>the</u> Church: A Distracted World, <u>a</u> Distracted Church? The Allure of Gentleness [[Correct]]

Grammar Focus: Activity 3

Answers for this exercise will vary.

Unit 3: Lesson 9

Main Ideas and Details

1. Answers will vary, but the author defines this as "the view that human beings have the right to seek knowledge of God's world without being subject to God's revelation."

2. (1) D; (2) D; (3) D; (4) MI; (5) MI; (6) MI; (7) MI; (8) D

3. d

4. "[Sin] assumes that God does not exist, or that he has not given us a personal word."

5. b

Word Forms (possible answers)

Noun Form	Other Forms of the Word in the Passage
Ex. Intellect	Intellectual
Autonomy	Autonomously
Rationality	Rationalism, rationalistically
Satan	Satanic

Collocations

In an important (*level/degree/sense*), Adam and Eve's experience in some way parallels our experience in a sinful world. Adam and Eve made a (*option/decision/conclusion*) in the face of God's clear and present revelation, just as we do each day. We repress the (*knowledge/data/information*) we possess as covenantal creatures made in God's image, just as they did. We have the opportunity to make wise (*decisions/challenges/opinions*) according to the (*clear/crystal/transparent*) knowledge we have from God and his Spirit's work in us. The ultimate (*essence/meaning/scheme*) of those decisions is provided by God's plan for redemptive history.

Rhetorical Focus: Activity 1

See paragraph 4 of the reading.

Rhetorical Focus: Activity 2

Alright, so now Paul is into the suppression aspect of what <u>we</u> do with the knowledge that <u>we</u> have. Now again, <u>he's</u> talking about people as <u>they</u> are in Adam. Remember, Paul's going to get to what it means to be in Christ—<u>he's</u> getting to <u>that</u> later. But before <u>you</u> understand <u>that</u>, <u>you</u> need to know what it means to be in Adam; and to be in Adam is to be a covenant breaker—it's to be before the face of God, knowing God, but being disobedient to <u>him</u> and suppressing—trying to hold down—that knowledge that God has given. <u>I</u>'ve used the illustration before that somebody said to <u>me</u> one time: it's sort of like having a beach ball that <u>you</u> sort of try to hold under water—it's a big beach ball full of air and <u>you</u>'re trying—<u>you</u>'re pushing <u>it</u> down, pushing <u>it</u> down. But what's <u>it</u> doing? <u>It</u> keeps trying to pop up! And so <u>you</u>'re working all the time to keep <u>it</u> under, to keep <u>it</u> under, see, and <u>that</u>'s what Paul's saying here—<u>you</u>'re trying to keep <u>that</u> down, but <u>it</u>'ll bounce up, and then <u>you</u>'re trying to keep <u>it</u> down again. <u>You</u> don't want to have God in <u>your</u> thoughts. Like Adam and Eve, <u>you</u>'re trying to hide, but there's no place to go, because God's presence is everywhere, and as <u>he</u> makes <u>himself</u> known, <u>you</u> and <u>I</u> continue to know <u>him</u>.

Rhetorical Focus: Activity 3

Answers for this exercise will vary.

Rhetorical Focus: Activity 4

Answers for this exercise will vary.

Unit 4: Lesson 10

Main Ideas and Details

1. Answers will vary, but you should have something like "the way God provided a plan for redemption throughout history."

2. __6__ On this basis, we may be confident of their salvation.

   __3__ Adam believes God's promise that she will bring forth living children and that one of those will bring redemption from death altogether.

   __2__ But instead Adam called her Eve, "life-giver."

   __1__ Adam might have named his wife "death," because her decision brought death into the world.

   __4__ Similarly, when Eve bears Cain in Gen. 4:1, she says, "I have gotten a man with the help of the Lord."

   __5__ So both Adam and Eve express faith in God's promise.

3. (a) the ground; (b) the promise of enmity between the serpent's offspring and man; (c) man; (d) the man and the woman's; (e) Adam and Eve expressing faith in the promise; (f) the time of Seth and Enosh

4. Adam names her "Eve" or "life-giver" because he "believes God's promise that she will bring forth living children and that one of those will bring redemption from death altogether."

Collocations

At the fall, God certainly pronounced (*order/judgment/conviction*) on the serpent, Adam, and Eve, but he also delivered a promise. In his promise, God told Eve that someone in her line would (*bear/produce/generate*) a child who would crush the head of the serpent. Until that day came, Adam and Eve, along with their offspring, would have to (*instruct/teach/tell*) their children on the necessity of sacrifice.

Grammar Focus: Activity 1

Verb	Noun	Adjective	Adverb
Create	Creation	Creative	Creatively
Promise	Promise	Promising	Promisingly
Deceive	Deception	Deceptive	Deceptively
Redeem	Redemption	Redemptive	Redemptively
Will	Will	Willing	Willingly
Rebel	Rebellion	Rebellious	Rebelliously
Sacrifice	Sacrifice	Sacrificial	Sacrificially
Save	Salvation	Salvific/Saving	Savingly
Inquire	Inquiry	Inquisitive	Inquisitively

Grammar Focus: Activity 2

One particularly instructive example of Jesus' temptation occurred when he was driven out into the <u>wilderness</u> after his <u>baptism</u>, but before his earthly ministry (Matt. 4; Luke 4). These passages record (in slightly different order) three <u>temptations</u> from Satan: (1) to turn stones into bread, (2) to throw himself down from the temple, testing God's promise of angelic <u>protection</u>, and (3) to worship Satan in order to gain all the kingdoms of the world. . .

We can be thankful that Jesus rejected these <u>temptations</u>. He refuted Satan's false <u>application</u> of Scripture with right uses of it, turning Satan away by the sword of the Spirit. But these are the same <u>temptations</u> that we continue to face each day. Satan continually seeks to make us embrace his <u>lordship</u> in place of God's.

Grammar Focus: Activity 3

Answers for this exercise will vary.

Unit 4: Lesson 11

Main Ideas and Details

1. (1) MI; (2) MI; (3) MI; (4) D; (5) MI; (6) MI; (7) D; (8) D

2. a

3. The author uses the word "still" to emphasize that the sacrifice continued in Jesus' day.

4. The New Testament (NT)

5. c

6. c

7. d

8. b

Grammar Focus: Activity 1

People might question whether the <u>sacrificial</u> system of the Old Testament was <u>necessary</u> if God knew that it would be replaced by the perfect <u>sacrifice</u> of Christ in the New Testament. Yet, here it is <u>important</u> to remember that <u>revelation</u> unfolds in <u>history</u>, and God has his own <u>reasons</u> for doing this. Some of these reasons we might be able to discern, but others we cannot, for they have not been <u>revealed</u> to us. For example, if we say that God should have "skipped" the Old Testament sacrificial system, we are in danger of downplaying the <u>importance</u> of history. What, then, is keeping us from saying that God should have sent his Son at the beginning of history? For that matter, what is keeping us from saying that God should have solved the problem of sin before it even started by killing the serpent in the Garden of Eden, thus avoiding the historical problem altogether? Our desire to make history completely <u>reasonable</u> can lead us to set up an idol of reason, a standard to which God must submit.

God values history, and our choices within our <u>historical</u> context are <u>meaningful</u>. We cannot always discern that <u>meaning</u>, but we know it exists. The faithfulness of God's revelation <u>necessitates</u> that meaning is omnipresent, because God is omnipresent. In this vein, we do not know exactly why the Old Testament sacrificial system was <u>introduced</u>, but we do know that its <u>introduction</u> cannot be detached from the meaning of Jesus' sacrifice. The law delivered at Sinai and the following sacrificial atonement regulations were "part of the program of grace whereby God works to fulfill his promises to Abraham." Those promises were <u>sufficient</u> at one stage of history and yet fulfilled by Christ in another stage. Their inadequacy from our perspective serves to show the eternal <u>sufficiency</u> of Christ's death and resurrection. Christ is utterly and exclusively sufficient for our salvation. So, perhaps God instituted the Old Testament sacrificial system with the future <u>glory</u> of Christ in mind. This would make perfect sense when we read the evangelist's words in John 12:28, "'Father, <u>glorify</u> your name.' Then a voice came from heaven: 'I have glorified it, and I will glorify it again.'" The Father had in mind the glory of the Son even in instituting a sacrificial system that he would fulfill hundreds of years after its installation.

Grammar Focus: Activity 2

The sacrifices we find offered in the Old Testament (OT) are differently *different* from the sacrifice of Christ in the New Testament (NT), in many ways. First, Christ's sacrifice in the NT was prophesy *prophesied* about by the Bible *biblical* authors, whereas the OT sacrificed *sacrificial* system was delivered by God to Moses at the time it was to be practiced. Second, although both the OT sacrifices and Christ's sacrifice in the NT were meant to atonement *atone* for sin, only Christ's sacrifice in the NT definitive *definitively* atoned for sin, "for it is impossibility *impossible* for the blood of bulls and goats to take away sins" (Heb. 10:4). Third, a person was never offered as a sacrificial *sacrifice* in the OT, but the person of Christ was offered for us in the NT. Thus, the NT sacrifice of Christ has far more valuable *value* to Christians than the OT sacrifices, even though the latter are still important in redemptive history and foreshadow the work of Christ.

Collocations

1. d
2. a
3. c
4. b

Unit 4: Lesson 12

Main Ideas and Details

1. *A screen* (to contain the holy threat of the Lord's presence) and *a way* (of approach).

2. The tabernacle.

3. d

4. c

5. d

6. The phrase "the Isaac God has provided" refers to the ultimate sacrifice that would take the place of man, just as the ram was offered in place of Isaac, the son of promise, in Gen. 22:13.

7. The promises of the Seed of the woman and the Seed of Abraham.

8. The theme of blessing upon the remnant of the nations with the remnant of Israel.

9. Answers will vary.

10. The author says this because the Old Testament is ultimately all about the fulfillment of God's promises in Christ.

Understanding the Reading

Answers for this exercise will vary.

Collocations

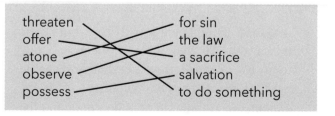

Grammar Focus: Activity 1

Edmund Clowney notes that "David foreshadows the longsuffering restraint of Christ's humiliation." We <u>can</u> confirm this if we reflect on the traumatic stage of David's life, when he was fleeing from Saul. As a devout follower of the Lord, David knew that he <u>should/could</u> not raise his hand against the Lord's anointed (1 Sam. 24:6; 26:9). But what happens when the Lord's anointed is seeking to take your life, as Saul was?! Here, we <u>might</u> think that David would be permitted to make an exception. But he refused to do this; he simply <u>would</u> not harm one whom God had put in charge of his people. <u>Could</u> you do that in David's situation? Could I? Surely, this is one of the ways in which David was longsuffering and restrained himself in obedience to God.

Grammar Focus: Activity 2 (possible answers)

1. We *would* have never been saved. We *would* still be lost in our sin. We *would* not be reconciled with God.

2. A person *must* believe in what God has done in Christ by the power of the Spirit. A person *must* put his or her trust in Christ alone.

3. God *can* comfort his people with his promises. God *can* rescue his people from sin and corruption.

Learning the Genre (Biblical Studies) Activity

In the following paragraph, the author relates Daniel 7 to Luke 7.

In contrast to Dan. 7, which portrays the Son of Man surrounded by <u>an angelic royal host</u> (cf. <u>vv. 9–10</u>) as he approaches the heavenly divine throne to receive a kingdom, Luke 7:34 depicts Jesus as beginning to fulfill the Daniel prophecy in an apparently different way than prophesied. The wording <u>"the Son of Man has come"</u> is sufficient to recognize an allusion to Daniel, and, as with <u>Mark 10:45</u>, it is best to assume that Luke has in view incipient fulfillment rather than a mere analogy to Daniel's Son of Man. Strikingly, those who surround the coming of the son of Man are <u>not angels</u>, as in Dan. 7, but rather Jesus's retinue is <u>tax collectors and sinners</u>. Again, this appears to be part of his incognito victorious coming to receive authority over a kingdom, which begins even before his death and resurrection. Although explicit suffering is not mentioned here, his seeming <u>ignoble appearance</u> receives ridicule and condemnation from the religious leaders. Although a number of scholars have thought that <u>the "wisdom" saying</u> in Luke 7:35 was a floating piece of tradition inserted willy-nilly here, it actually fits well: <u>"Yet wisdom is vindicated by all her children."</u> Jesus is one of God's wise children (he is the "Son"), and God's wisdom of turning the world's values on their head is illustrated with him. The wisdom of the world judged him to be an ignoble figure, but in reality he was a faithful son who persevered through suffering and insults while at the same time inaugurating his own kingdom. God's wise way of <u>ironically introducing the kingdom</u> through Jesus was vindicated at Jesus's resurrection and will be at the end of the age by the resurrection of all the saints who have followed in his ironic footsteps.

Unit 5: Lesson 13

Main Ideas and Details

1. Answers will vary, but your sentence should say something about how the author of Hebrews gives equal attention to Jesus' divinity and humanity.

2. (1) T; (2) F, "that he might die"; (3) F, "an infinite distance"; (4) T; (5) F, "could not die"; (6) F, "the truth of the humanity of Christ"; (7) T; (8) F, "it is not meant that death was desired by him . . ."

3. c

4. d

5. d

6. d

7. Answers will vary, but your summary should
    include how Christ was fully man and at the
    same time remained the Son of God.

Understanding the Reading

1. H (but DH is also acceptable)

2. H

3. D

4. D

5. H

6. D

7. D

Collocations

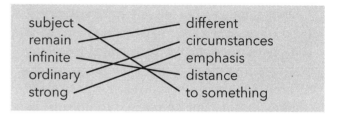

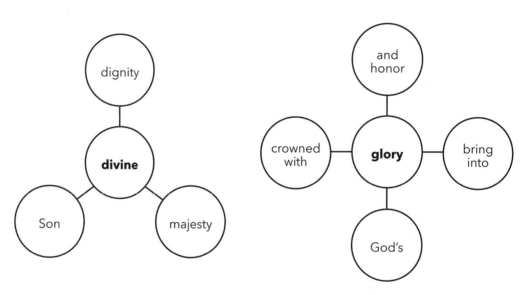

Fig. AK.1. Collocation Diagram 3 Completed

Grammar Focus: Activity 1

Two verb tenses used in this paragraph are the
simple present and simple past. The author
follows the principle of using the simple past
to refer to Jesus' historical life and the simple
present to comment on Scripture or make truth
claims.

Grammar Focus: Activity 2

Answers for this exercise will vary.

Grammar Focus: Activity 3

Answers for this exercise will vary.

Unit 5: Lesson 14

Reading Skill: Making Inferences (Practice)

1. b

2. b

Main Ideas and Details

1. c

2. Answers will vary, but you should say something about the unbreakable connection between Christ's resurrection and our own.

3. c

4. d

5. Answers will vary.

6. The concept of organic union.

7. The author uses the phrase "initial enjoyment" because while we presently possess the Spirit of life, we will possess all of the blessings of salvation only after the resurrection of the dead.

8. You should have at least underlined the following expressions: "the reason," "the force," and "grounds the statement."

9. b

Collocations

1. b

2. d

3. a

4. a

5. a

6. d

Grammar Focus: Activity 1

Rather he stands out in Paul's mind as the beginning of the manifold yield produced <u>by</u> the preaching of the gospel (cf. 1 Cor. 16:15). The broader significance of "the firstfruits of the Spirit" in Romans 8:23 will occupy us below. For the present, however, we can note that, regardless whether the genitive is partitive or appositional, the thought is plainly that the Spirit presently possessed <u>by</u> believers is a token, an initial enjoyment of the adoption (cf. v. 15) which hereafter will be fully and openly received <u>at</u> the resurrection of the body.

Grammar Focus: Activity 2

While we often praise God for sending Jesus to <u>die for</u> our sins, we might not as quickly praise God for raising him from the dead. But this is critical! Our world is <u>governed by</u> death and decay. We <u>belong to</u> a realm that is utterly fallen, and we need to be constantly <u>reminded of</u> the truth that death has lost its sting (1 Cor. 15:55). Even though we daily <u>fight against</u> the destructive forces of evil and the discouragement of our own sin, we know that Christ has overcome the world (John 16:33) and that our sins—past, present, and future—have been <u>atoned for</u> by the blood of Christ (Col. 2:13). But all of this—the loss of death's sting, the restoration of a decayed physical and moral world, the victory we have in Christ over sin— has been <u>sealed by</u> the resurrection of Christ. When the tomb opened and our Lord walked in the light of day, everything wicked and ruinous was definitively <u>overcome by</u> the God of grace and love. If Christ were not <u>raised from</u> the dead, then, as Paul said, "we are of all people most to be pitied" (1 Cor. 15:19). But he *has* been raised. As new creatures in Christ we are being redeemed and <u>sanctified by</u> the Spirit every day, we are of all people most to be envied. Our praise should thus be <u>offered to</u> the risen Lamb of God, not just to the crucified Son. We are united with the one who was born, suffered, died, rose, and <u>ascended to</u> the right hand of the Father.

Grammar Focus: Activity 3

Answers for this exercise will vary.

Unit 5: Lesson 15

Main Ideas and Details

1. a
2. c
3. a
4. b

Collocations

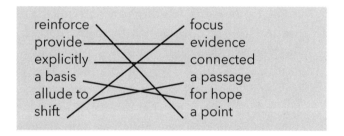

reinforce   focus
provide   evidence
explicitly   connected
a basis   a passage
allude to   for hope
shift   a point

Grammar Focus: Activity 1

1. God's being "for us" is seen climactically in his giving of his beloved Son.

2. But the way Paul puts it here suggests a comparison between Christ and Isaac.

3. Older Greek manuscripts of the New Testament

5. Answers will vary.

6. The author uses the modal verb "may" because he is not certain of the conclusion.

7. The author says that it is "not clear why Paul disrupts his neat parallelism" to show humility and limitation. Rhetorically, this may help the reader to put more trust in the author.

contain no punctuation at all, so editors of modern Bibles have to decide how to do it.

4. The quotation of Psalm 44:22 in verse 36 is a bit of a detour in the logic of Paul's argument.

5. This felicitous rendering of the Greek verb *hypernikao* (to more than triumph over) goes all the way back to the sixteenth-century Geneva Bible.

Grammar Focus: Activity 2

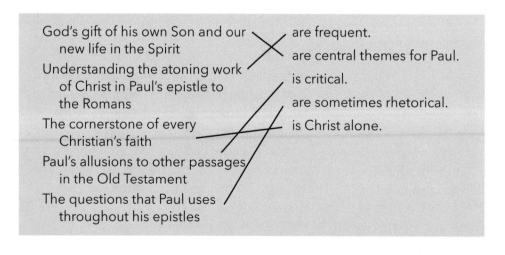

God's gift of his own Son and our new life in the Spirit — are frequent.

Understanding the atoning work of Christ in Paul's epistle to the Romans — are central themes for Paul.

The cornerstone of every Christian's faith — is critical.

Paul's allusions to other passages in the Old Testament — are sometimes rhetorical.

The questions that Paul uses throughout his epistles — is Christ alone.

Grammar Focus: Activity 3

Answers for this exercise will vary.

Unit 6: Lesson 16

Main Ideas and Details

1. Answers will vary, but you should include something about how the giving of the law was an act of grace.

2. False.

3. b

4. The exodus and the covenant with Abraham.

5. "Grace." The author repeats this because his goal is to link the giving of the law to God's grace.

6. The author believes that the law "is part of the program of grace whereby God works to fulfill his promises to Abraham."

7. a

8. c

9. The fact that breaking the law carries penalties.

Cause, Effect, and Logical Relationships

Part 1	Part 2	Marker
The mighty acts of God in Egypt were performed	because of the promise to Abraham (Ex. 2:23-25).	*Because*
What follows then cannot be a program aimed to achieve salvation by works	since they have already received it by grace.	*since*
Israel as a nation is expected to be faithful to the law	if it is also to enjoy the blessings of God.	*if*

Collocations

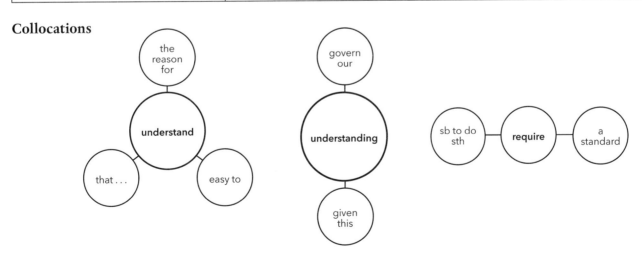

Fig. AK.2. Collocation Diagram 4 Completed

Grammar Focus: Activity 1

The book of numbers relates the incidents between Sinai and the entry [into the promised land]. In so doing it presents a rather gloomy picture. Israel . . . is shown (**adj.**) <u>to be</u> rebellious and ungrateful. . . . After the Sinai encounter the nation asserts its independence of God by refusing the opportunity (**n.**) to take possession of the promised land (Numbers 13–14). The forty years wandering in the wilderness disposes of the generation of adults who came out of Egypt, leaving their children (**n.**) to go in and possess the land.

Grammar Focus: Activity 2

1. Inability *to achieve.*
2. Careful *to examine.*
3. Works (v.) *to fulfill.*
4. Decides *to do something.*
5. Choice *to save his people.*
6. Dangerous *to rebel against him.*

Grammar Focus: Activity 3

Answers for this exercise will vary.

Unit 6: Lesson 17

Main Ideas and Details

1. In this passage, Beale argues that Exodus 32 is an example of the kind of idolatry that the writer has in mind in Deut. 29, and that the people become like the golden calf that they worship, whereas Moses becomes like the one true God.

2. The author says this to acknowledge that a certain kind of textual evidence is not present.

3. Deuteronomy 28–32.

4. The author uses words and phrases from another portion of Scripture (Deut. 9).

5. Answers will vary, but Beale notes that "the golden calf idolatry was seen to be paradigmatic of Israel's future idolatry."

6. a

7. d

8. God's wrath against the people.

9. He infers that the Israelites are being divinely mocked.

Understanding the Reading

Claim	Scriptural Support
The people became spiritually like the calf they worshiped.	Deut. 29:4
That the golden calf episode is significantly referred to in this section of Deuteronomy.	Deut. 9:6–21; 31:27–29
Moses describes Israel in a manner that sounds like they are being portrayed as wild calves.	Ex. 32:8, 9, 25, 26, 34; 33:3, 5; 34:9

Claim	Scriptural Support
Israel's stubbornness like a rebellious calf or sheep is idol worship, which in Hosea is often calf worship, and is punished by God through leaving them without a shepherd.	Hosea 4:16–17
The only reality of a calf-like divine presence that they would experience was through Moses.	Ex. 34:29–35
Veiling would appear to be an act of some degree of mercy in the midst of judgment.	Ex. 34:29–35

Collocations

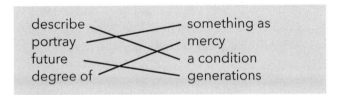

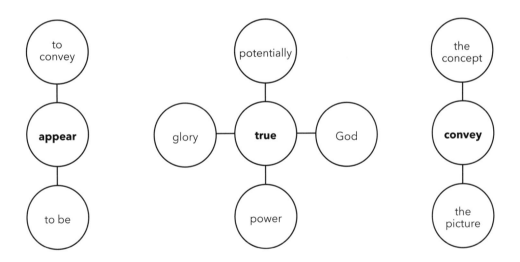

Fig. AK.3. Collocation Diagram 5 Completed

Grammar Focus: Activity 1

The first generation of Israelites did not <u>literally</u> become petrified golden calves like the one that they worshiped, but they are depicted <u>as</u> acting like out-of-control and headstrong calves, <u>apparently</u> because they were being mocked <u>as</u> having become like the image that represented a <u>spiritually</u> rebellious and ornery calf that they had worshiped.

Grammar Focus: Activity 2 (possible answers)

1. There are many idols today that we worship and serve *thoughtlessly/faithfully*.

2. Materialism is one idol that *often* steals our

attention and *subtly* suggests that our present comfort is most important.

3. However, we are never *completely* fulfilled by material possessions because they offer *only* momentary satisfaction.

4. True satisfaction is found *solely* in Christ, and in Him God has *graciously* provided for all of our deepest needs.

Grammar Focus: Activity 3

Answers for this exercise will vary.

Unit 6: Lesson 18

Reading Skill: Understanding the Author's Purpose (Practice)

1. c

2. b

3. a

Main Ideas and Details

1. God's making Adam in his image and likeness is what enables Adam to carry out the commission.

2. The essence of the commission is subduing and ruling over the earth and filling it with God's glory; especially through glorious image-bearing progeny.

3. "The seed" would finally fulfill the commission on behalf of humanity.

4. a

5. False.

6. b

7. c

8. a

9. The escalated blessing of incorruptibility.

10. That Christ himself ruled, subdued, multiplied spiritual progeny and filled the earth with God's glory.

11. a

12. Justification.

Collocations

In order to (*receive/take/give*) the eschatological (*joys/blessings/ideas*) that were offered to Adam and Eve, they would have had to obey God's Word. Adam and Eve, after all, were (*commissioned/nominated/requested*) to rule over and subdue creation. God had given them everything but the fruit of a single tree. But instead of taking God at his Word, they took the serpent at his.

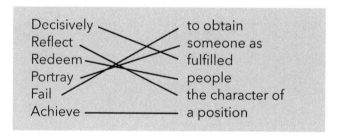

Grammar Focus: Activity 1

I argued in an earlier work that in Revelation a "mark" on the forehead and hand identifies one with commitment to the beast, and a different mark also distinguishes the followers of the Lamb (see Rev. 13:16–14:1). These marks connote that the followers of Christ and the followers of the beast are stamped with the image (= character) of their respective leader. Each group also bears the "name" of its respective leader (whether of the beast or of the Lamb and God). We also saw that to bear or reflect the name of someone is to reflect that person's character. I argued that this is likely the conceptual way . . . that Revelation conveys the idea of fallen humans bearing the image of Christ and the Father (see Rev. 14:1).

Thus, one resembles what one reveres, either for ruin or for restoration.

What often begins the noun clauses in this paragraph? "that"

Grammar Focus: Activity 2 (possible answers)

Subject and Verb	Noun Clause	Sentence
The Last Adam; *succeed*	that the Last Adam succeeded in obeying God's Word . . .	*That the Last Adam succeeded in obeying God's Word* is clearly implied in 1 Cor. 15.
Christ; *rise (from the dead)*	that Christ rose from the dead	Christians believe *that Christ rose from the dead*.
The covenant; *entail*	what the covenant entailed	The Israelites knew *what the covenant entailed*.
We; *resemble*	whatever we resemble	*Whatever we resemble* is what we have been worshiping.
Sin; *defeat*	that sin has been defeated	We rejoice in the knowledge *that sin has been defeated*.

Grammar Focus: Activity 3

Answers for this exercise will vary.

Unit 7: Lesson 19

Main Ideas and Details

1. Answers will vary, but you should include something about "a selected number of Luther's more famous works, taken from early in his career."

2. False.

3. d

4. c

5. a

6. Negative—it suggests a careless use of Luther's work, one that does not account for historical complexities.

7. b

8. "New questions."

9. Nuance or change his statements.

10. a

11. c

Understanding the Passage

1. D
2. A
3. D
4. A
5. A

Collocations

When investigating a historical figure, we should consider how that figure's work affects us in practical (*words/terms/sayings*). Does the person's thought shed light on our own ethical (*doings/behavior/acting*), or does it leave our moral development entirely (*unaffected/unused/ignored*)? Do we come away from our study of the figure noticing that we have obvious (*problems/hurts/pains*) with our own approach to a given topic? Does the figure's thought have a positive or negative (*role/act/job*) when it comes to our assessment of contemporary life? These are questions that will help us to benefit practically from a study of history.

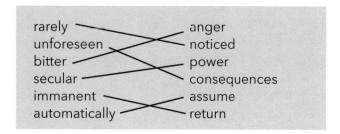

Grammar Focus: Activity 1

Head nouns are **bolded**. (Note: we have underlined only noun *phrases*, not all nouns.)

Luther's basic **position** on righteousness is set forth in his 1519 **sermon** "Two **Kinds** of Righteousness." There he distinguishes between alien and proper **righteousness**. *Alien righteousness* is that which the **Christian** obtains when he receives Christ by faith. This is an infinite **righteousness** that swallows up all **sins** and renders the **believer** perfect before God. There is progression in this **righteousness**, but it is **progression** gauged by **growth** in faith and **knowledge** of Christ, and thus should not be confused with **growth** in what we might term actual **righteousness**. *Proper righteousness* involves the **slaying** of the flesh and the **crucifying** of wicked desires, coupled with the **performance** of good works for our neighbors. This is akin to what we might typically call the **work** of sanctification, and it has an outward **manifestation**.

Grammar Focus: Activity 2 (possible answers)

Head Noun	Noun Phrase
Position	Luther's position on eschatology
Righteousness	The righteousness that comes by faith
Eschatology	An already-not-yet eschatology
Perspective	The Reformed perspective
Decision	Paul's decision to appeal to Rome
Power	The power to overcome the grave

Grammar Focus: Activity 3

Answers for this exercise will vary.

Learning the Genre (CH) Activity

Passage 1

1. Answers will vary, but Chadwick is centrally concerned with *how* Augustine was influenced by Cicero's dialogues.

2. There are many signals of time and context in this passage, but here are three: "the young Augustine," "as a nineteen-year-old student at Carthage," and "as a skeptical teenager."

3. Answers will vary.

Passage 2

1. Answers will vary, but Pelikan seems to focus on *how* or *why* Christian apologetics developed in response to pagan allegorization.

2. Again, there are many signals of time and context in this passage. Here are a few: "pagan criticism of the stories in the Bible," "the Greek myths," "sophisticated pagans," and "As the apologists came to grips with the defenders of paganism."

3. The author hopes to convince readers that allegorizing texts is not exclusive to Christianity, and the early Christian apologists used allegorical interpretation to defend their faith.

Unit 7: Lesson 20

Reading Skill: Identifying an Author's Stance

Yet increasingly he was <u>dissatisfied</u> by Manichaean belief, and as he pursued academic success in Rome and Milan he was <u>haunted by doubts and anxieties</u> about the nature of truth, reality and wisdom. As he ceased to find Manichaeism of use, he turned to Neoplatonist belief, but in Milan he also became fascinated by Bishop Ambrose. Here, for the first time, he met a Christian whose self-confident culture he could respect and whose sermons, sonorous and rich in their language, made up for the <u>crudity and vulgarity</u> of the Bible which had <u>distressed</u> the young Augustine. Even though he remained <u>embarrassed</u> by his mother's <u>demonstrative piety</u> (she had followed him to Milan), he now contemplated a faith which united the imperious nobleman in the pulpit with the elderly woman from a <u>provincial backwater.</u> The <u>contradictory</u> influences of career and Christian renunciation came to <u>tear him apart</u> and <u>made him disgusted</u> with his ambitions.

Main Ideas and Details

1. d
2. The Greek Church.
3. a
4. b
5. d
6. Augustine's experience of reading Romans 13:13–14.
7. Augustine's plan to found a monastery bringing the best of the culture of old Rome into a Christian context.

Understanding the Reading

1. D
2. D
3. D
4. A
5. D
6. D
7. D
8. A

Collocations

Though some people today might have (*little/few/small*) interest in an early church figure such as Augustine, we can learn much from him. Like all of us, Augustine struggled with his own (*inside/internal*) conflicts: How could he live a truly "good" life? How does Christian faith engage with a person's contemporary culture? While Augustine originally sought a promising (*job/career/life*) as a teacher of rhetoric, he realized that academic (*success/victory /winning*) would not ultimately fulfill him. The only "good" life that any of us can hope to live is a life that remains (*faithful/trusting/constant*) to God. All of us, like Augustine, must eventually abandon our (*plans/actions/thoughts*) and surrender to God's will as revealed in Scripture. While in modern (*years/eras/times*) Augustine may seem outdated, studying his life and work can be particularly relevant to us in our own Christian (*setting/context/place*).

Grammar Focus: Activity 1

From 387 the Donatists suddenly gained the advantage of political support from a <u>local rebel ruler</u>, Gildo, <u>who established a regime semi-independent of the emperor</u>. In 391 Augustine happened to visit <u>the struggling Catholic congregation</u> in the city of Hippo Regius (now Annaba in Algeria), <u>the most important port of the province after Carthage</u>. The bishop, <u>an idiosyncratic but shrewd old Greek named Valerius</u>, encouraged his flock to bully <u>this brilliant stranger</u> into being ordained priest and soon Augustine was coadjutor (assistant) bishop in the town. From Valerius's death until his own in 430, he remained Bishop of Hippo. All his theological writing was now done against a background <u>of busy pastoral work and preaching for a Church in a world in collapse</u>; much of it was in the form of sermons.

Grammar Focus: Activity 2

1. Prepositional phrase.
2. Adjective phrase.
3. Relative clause.
4. Adjective phrase.
5. Prepositional phrase.
6. Adjective phrase (but the whole structure is a noun phrase).
7. Prepositional phrase.
8. Prepositional phrase.

Grammar Focus: Activity 3

Answers for this exercise will vary.

Grammar Focus: Activity 4

Answers for this exercise will vary.

Unit 7: Lesson 21

Main Ideas and Details

1. c
2. c
3. d
4. b
5. b
6. b
7. c
8. Question.
9. d
10. The author likely repeats "particular" because this word is what accounts for the "offense" of evangelicalism.
11. b

Understanding the Passage

Paragraph	Main Idea
1	Modern evangelicalism has often been offensive and confusing theologically.
2	The great evangelical hymns clearly portray the central theme [redemption through Christ] of evangelicalism.
3	Toplady's popular hymn, "Rock of Ages," was influential in its centering evangelical hymns around the saving death of Christ.
4	The classic evangelical hymns do not contain theologically, doctrinally, or politically offensive material.
5	Many of the offenses committed by evangelical churches result from promoting divisive beliefs or practices.
6	The hymns have remained offensive by focusing on the message, 'Jesus Christ Saves Sinners.'
7	The great evangelical hymns highlight redemption through Christ, and this is evangelicalism's strength.

Collocations

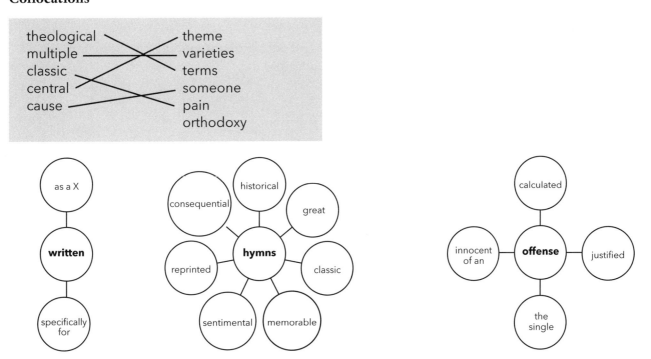

Fig. AK.4. Collocation Diagram 6 Completed

Grammar Focus: Activity 1

Evangelicals, in point of <u>historical</u> fact, may have never been factious, fissiparous, and sectarian as is commonly thought. To be sure, leaders of <u>evangelical</u> groups have indulged in their fair share of back-stabbing, power-mongering, petty minded polemicizing, <u>gratuitous</u> boundary-marking, and <u>schismatical</u> devilment. Although I am convinced that lay evangelicals have done better than their leaders in preserving the unity of the Body of Christ, there is enough fragmentation in the evangelical world to go around for all. I have often heard said in my circles what is no doubt said about <u>different</u> issues in other communions as well: the presence of three <u>confessional</u> Presbyterians guarentees at least four potentially schismatic options on the doctrine of predestination.

NOTE: "schismatic" would also be acceptable for the second sentence.

Grammar Focus: Activity 2 (possible answers)

1. Traditional hymns.

2. Contemporary debates.

3. Central message.

4. Basic requirement.

5. Biblical doctrines.

Grammar Focus: Activity 3

Answers for this exercise will vary.

Grammar Focus: Activity 4

Rock of Ages / cleft for me / let me hide / myself in thee

Let the water / and the blood / from thy riven side / which flowed

Be of sin / the double cure / cleanse me from its guilt / and power.

Not the labours / of my hands / can fulfill / thy law's demands.

Could my zeal / no respite know / could my tears / for ever flow

All for sin / could not atone / thou must save / and thou alone.

Nothing in my hand / I bring / simply to thy cross / I cling

Naked / come to Thee / for dress; / helpless, / look to thee / for grace;

Foul I / to the fountain fly; / wash me saviour / or I die.

Unit 8: Lesson 22

Main Ideas and Details

1. Answers will vary, but you should have something about (1) how faith unites us to Christ and (2) how union with the person of Christ is central to Paul's soteriology.

2. We are dead in trespasses and sins.

3. Sin (and all its consequences).

4. b

5. Individual and communal.

6. Personal and corporate/cosmic salvation are equally important for Paul.

7. c

8. d

9. c

Understanding the Passage

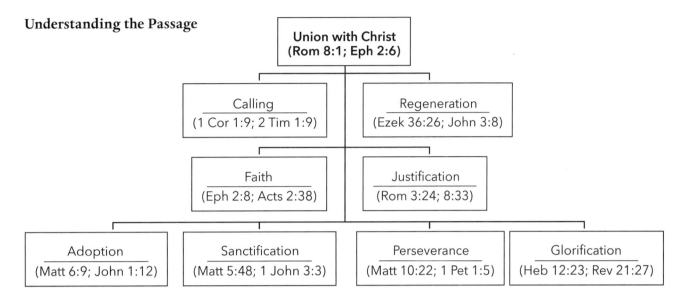

Fig. AK.5. Benefits of Union with Christ Completed

Collocations

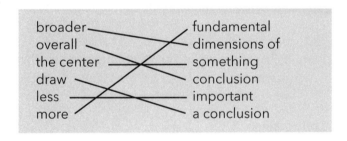

Grammar Focus: Activity 1

Prepositions preceding or following nouns are underlined.

At the opening of Book 3 of his *Institutes of the Christian Religion* and controlling all that he has to say about "the way" of salvation— that is, its personal, individual appropriation, including what he will eventually say about justification—Calvin writes, "First, we must understand that as long as Christ remains outside of us, and we are separated from him, all that he has suffered and done for the salvation of the human race remains useless and of no value for us." This is eminently faithful to Paul and is quoted here because it captures the essence of his soteriology.

Grammar Focus: Activity 2

Several Reformed theologians have argued that, for Paul, union with Christ is a central theme. Our union with the person of Christ is at the center of our understanding of salvation. If we are, in Calvin's words, "separated from him," then what he has done cannot benefit us. To be united with the person of Christ, to be "in Christ," is "all-encompassing, extending in fact from eternity to eternity." And this everlasting union that we have with Christ is both *mystical* and *spiritual*. It is mystical "in the sense of involving 'a great mystery' that for Paul apparently has its closest analogy in the relationship between husband and wife (Eph. 5:32)." It is spiritual "because of the activity and indwelling of the Holy Spirit."

Grammar Focus: Activity 3 (possible answers)

Phrase from the Text	Your Example
center of	The *center of* Reformed theology is Scripture.
the question of	The question of where a person's salvation lies is critical.
for the Reformers	For the Reformers, faith with the person of Christ is central.
emphasis on	Paul's emphasis on faith cannot be overlooked.
for guilty sinners	Christ is the only answer for guilty sinners.

Grammar Focus: Activity 4

Answers for this exercise will vary.

Unit 8: Lesson 23

Main Ideas and Details

1. b

2. c

3. d

4. a

5. Richard B. Gaffin Jr., the Westminster Standards, and John Calvin.

6. Answers will vary, but you should say something about "the twin truths" that the author introduces in the topic sentence.

7. c

Understanding the Passage

1. F, Before ~~union with Christ~~ particular benefits are presented in the Westminster Larger Catechism, union with Christ is discussed ~~particular benefits are presented~~.

2. T

3. F, Justification ~~Union with Christ~~ is an attendant benefit of ~~justification~~ union with Christ.

4. T

5. T

6. F, In reflecting on Gal. 2:16, Murray notes that ~~justification~~ union with Christ is antecedent to our ~~union with Christ~~ justification.

Collocations

Both union with Christ and justification come to us by faith (*only/alone/solely*). It is by Spirit-wrought faith that we are joined to Christ, and it is through that same faith that the benefits of salvation are (*applied/associated/engaged*). While we could be more (*sophisticated/elaborate/simple*) here, we can say concisely that faith plays the (*central/middle/innermost*) role in our redemption. On this point, the creeds of the church, the majority of Reformed theologians, and, most importantly, the biblical (*confirmation/testimony/conjecture*) are in agreement. It is in the larger (*place/climate/context*) of union with Christ that we receive all of the spiritual blessings mentioned in Eph. 1:3.

Grammar Focus: Activity 1

1. b

2. c

3. c

4. a

5. b

6. b

Grammar Focus: Activity 2

Moving now in a positive direction, we need to note first and foremost that no aspect of forensic justification comes to [[X]] believers (logically or temporally) prior to union with Christ by faith, so that [[X]] *justification sola fide depends on union with Christ sola fide.* This statement has significant implications that we need to spell out more clearly.

The declaration of righteousness depends on and brings into view the righteousness of Christ that is imputed *by faith alone* to the believer. The declaration of justification brings into the tribunal of God (objective aspect) the concrete reality of union with Christ by Spirit-wrought faith, and the imputation of his righteousness received by faith alone (subjective aspect), as that reality to which the declaration is addressed. It is only when the sinner, by faith, is united to Christ in effectual calling, and when the sinner receives by faith alone the imputed righteousness of Christ, that the sinner is declared righteous before God.

Grammar Focus: Activity 3

Answers for this exercise will vary.

Unit 8: Lesson 24

Main Ideas and Details

1. b

2. The author uses "seem" to suggest that the inference is wrong.

3. The perversity of the inference.

4. Answers will vary slightly, but paragraph 2 provides background on the concept of death so that in paragraph 3 the author can explain what Paul meant with the statement "we died to sin."

5. d

6. The condition of the believer.

7. c

8. This is tricky, but Murray seems to mean that the church needs to account for the personal growth and maturity of believers. It would be unnatural (a monstrosity) for a child to act as a man, so we should not expect new Christians to be immediately mature in their faith. Likewise, it would be unnatural for a man (a mature believer) to act as a child, so we should hold mature Christians accountable for their conduct.

9. Each of the passages focuses on the concept of growth.

10. Answers will vary, but the author's main point is that progressiveness and growth apply *both* to the individual and to the body of Christ.

11. d

Understanding the Reading

1. P

2. F

3. F

4. P

5. F and P

6. P

Collocations

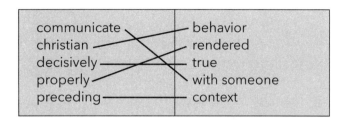

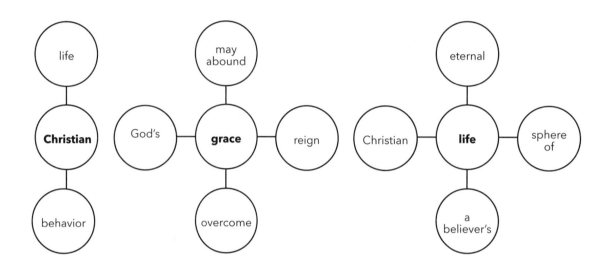

Fig. AK.6. Collocation Diagram 7 Completed

Grammar Focus: Activity 1

What is this sanctification? No passage in the New Testament is more instructive than Rom. 6:1–7:6. The teaching here is oriented against the question with which Paul begins: "Shall we continue in sin that grace may abound?," a question <u>provoked</u> by the exordium <u>accorded</u> to grace in the <u>preceding</u> context. "Where sin abounded, grace superabounded, that as sin hath reigned in death, even so might grace reign through righteousness unto eternal life through Jesus Christ our Lord" (Rom. 5:20, 21). If the grace of God, and therefore his glory, are magnified the more according as grace overcomes sin, the inference would seem to be: let us continue to sin in order that God's grace may be the more <u>extolled</u>. It is this inference the apostle rejects with the most emphatic negative at his disposal, properly <u>rendered</u> in the <u>corresponding</u> Hebrew idiom,

"God forbid!" The perversity of the inference he lays bare by <u>asking</u> another question: "How shall we who are such as have died to sin live any longer therein?" (Rom. 6:2). The pivot of the refutation is: "we died to sin." What does Paul mean?

Grammar Focus: Activity 2

For Murray, sanctification as a "<u>mortifying</u> and <u>cleansing</u> process is concerned with sin and defilement still adhering to the believer, and it contemplates as its aim the removal of all defilement of flesh and spirit." <u>Examining</u> our own spiritual lives, we find many concrete ways in which we are still "defiled." We awake each morning <u>knowing</u> that we will be faced with material temptations as well as opportunities to display our pride. All throughout the day, the devil uses the "principalities and powers" around us (Eph. 6:12), <u>encouraging</u> us to profane God's name. And by the time night comes, we often forget the <u>liberating</u> truth of the gospel. We may even bring glory to someone other than Christ. But thank God that we are not left to ourselves! The Spirit of the <u>living</u> God always "works in the interests of glorifying Christ, and of bringing to perfection the goal of the redemptive process." <u>Sheltered</u> and <u>protected</u> by the power of the Spirit, we are progressively refined and purified, <u>conforming</u> more closely each day to the image of Christ.

Grammar Focus: Activity 3

Answers for this exercise will vary.

Learning the Genre (ST) Activity

1. The author is answering the question of what comprises a "good" work, and he suggests that a good work involves three components: (1) a heart purified by faith, (2) obedience to God's Word, and (3) the right end, the glory of God.

2. The author appeals to the tradition of Reformed theology, the WCF, and Scripture.

Unit 9: Lesson 25

Main Ideas and Details

1. Militant/triumphant; visible/invisible; organism/institution.

2. The author means that the church cannot "take it easy" and rest, even though she has done much work.

3. If the Church on earth is the militant Church, the Church in heaven is the triumphant Church.

4. The Reformers were sometimes accused of claiming that there were two separate churches.

5. "It" has no referent. This word simply stands in for the subject (cf. the grammar focus in Lesson 2).

6. c

7. b

8. c

9. d

Understanding the Reading

1. Answers for this question will vary.

2. __2__ The union of believers with Christ is a mystical union; the Spirit that unites them constitutes an invisible tie.
   __1__ The church is duty bound to carry on an incessant warfare against the hostile world in every form in which it reveals itself.
   __1__ The Church reflects the humiliation and exaltation of her heavenly Lord.
   __3__ This is a distinction that applies to the *visible* Church and that directs attention to two different aspects of the Church considered as a visible body.
   __2__ This church is essentially spiritual and in her spiritual essence cannot be discerned by the physical eye.
   __1__ The church must be engaged with all her might in the battles of her Lord, fighting in a war that is both offensive and defensive.
   __2__ There may be unregenerated children and adults who, while professing Christ, have no true faith in Him.
   __2__ The opponents of the Reformers often accused them of teaching that there are two separate Churches.

Collocations

The church (*engages in/fights for/combats*) spiritual (*fighting /warfare /quarrels*), and for Berkhof, it is both militant and triumphant. We recognize this (*value/separation/distinction*) because we know that, on the one hand, we are still fighting against the powers of evil, and, on the other hand, Christ is ultimately victorious. While we spend all of our (*seconds/time/moments*) fighting against the destructive powers of sin, we know that the battle has been (*won/waged/succeeded*). We live in a hostile (*world/planet/place*), but Christ has overcome it (John 16:33).

Grammar Focus: Activity 1

This means <u>that the Church of God is on the one hand visible, and on the other invisible</u>. It is said <u>that Luther was the first to make this distinction</u>, but the other Reformers recognized and also applied it to the Church. This distinction has not always been properly understood. The opponents of the Reformers often accused them of teaching <u>that there are two separate Churches</u>. Luther perhaps gave some occasion for this charge by speaking of an invisible *ecclesiola* within the visible *ecclesia*. But both he and Calvin stress the fact <u>that, when they speak of a visible and an invisible Church, they do not refer to two different Churches, but to two aspects of the one Church of Jesus Christ</u>. . . . Now it is undoubtedly true <u>that the triumphant Church is invisible to those who are on earth</u>, and <u>that Calvin in his *Institutes*</u> <u>also conceives of this as included in the invisible Church</u>, but the distinction was undoubtedly primarily intended to apply to the militant Church. As a rule it is so applied in Reformed theology. It stresses the fact <u>that the Church as it exists on earth is both visible and invisible</u>. This Church is said to be invisible, because she is essentially spiritual and in her spiritual essence cannot be discerned by the physical eye; and because it is impossible to determine infallibly who do and who do not belong to her.

Grammar Focus: Activity 2 (possible answers)

1. Berkhof suggests that we should understand the church as both militant and triumphant.

2. That the church is not always visible might seem odd to people today.

3. The author's argument is that we should keep these distinctions in mind.

4. It is critical that the church continue to wage war against the devil and his spiritual armies.

Grammar Focus: Activity 3
Answers for this exercise will vary.

Grammar Focus: Activity 4
Answers for this exercise will vary.

Unit 9: Lesson 26

Main Ideas and Details

1. c

2. The militant/triumphant church.

3. c

4. b

5. Repeating the word "same" emphasizes the unity of the body of Christ.

6. c

7. c

8. d

9. The Jews and Gentiles.

10. d

Understanding the Reading

1. √

2. X

3. √

4. √

5. X

6. √

Collocations

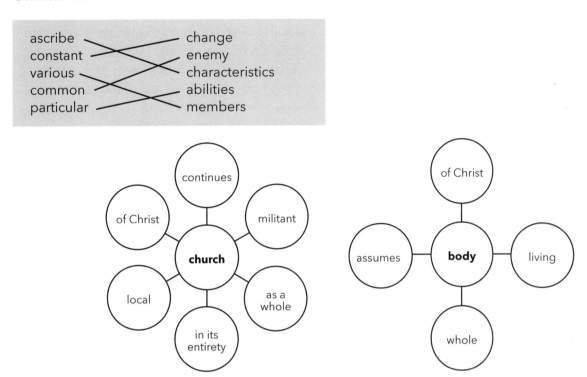

Fig. AK.7. Collocation Diagram 8 Completed

Grammar Focus: Activity 1

Subject		Verb
Facet		gain attention
The Westminster Confession	can	note
The history of Christian missions		illustrate
Spanish conquistadores		exploit and enslave
Bartolomé de Las Casas		denounce and labor

Grammar Focus: Activity 2 (possible answers)

1. The church encountered many problems as it attempted to account for its diversity.

2. Unity was restored when, in Christ, the Jew and the Gentile were united.

3. Only when we embrace the spiritual unity of the church can we address the disunity that we see in the church today.

4. Christ's union with the Father by the Spirit is the foundation upon which the unity of the church rests.

5. The church is called to be one, even though it has many members.

Grammar Focus: Activity 3 (possible answers)

In the body of Christ, God's Spirit binds believers to one another in faith. People from every tribe, tongue, and nation have been ~~planned~~ chosen by God, and they are connected to each other because of their faith in Christ. This is important to remember today, when Christianity ~~dwells with~~ has so much variety, for even though the gospel has ~~traveled~~ spread to all the nations, the individual people in those nations continue to misunderstand each other. That is what Paul ~~is demonstrated~~ argues in passages such as Ephesians 4, which ~~writes~~ says that we must "maintain the unity of the Spirit in the bond of peace" (Eph. 4:3).

Unit 9: Lesson 27

Understanding the Reading

Part 1: Detailed Outline

I. What is the relationship between the temple (Rev. 21–22), Christians and the church?
    1. We are already the spiritual temple of God.
       a. We have God's presence.
       b. We are to spread God's presence in this world.
       c. Eph. 2:20–22 and 1 Peter 2:4 provide support that the church is God's temple and witness of his salvation.

II. How do Christians have God's presence?
    1. If you believe in Christ,
    2. Then God's Spirit lives in you.

III. How do Christians enlarge God's presence personally and in the church?
    1. We look to Adam's example before the Fall.
       a. God called Adam to remember and obey his word.
       b. In Gen. 2:16–17, Adam was told:
          i. He could eat freely,
          ii. But not of the tree of knowledge.
          iii. If you eat of that tree, you will die.
       c. However, Eve . . .
          i. Lessened what they were allowed to do;
          ii. Lessened God's punishment;
          iii. Increased what they were not allowed to do.

d. Adam and Eve failed to spread God's presence.
    2. We look to Jesus' example.
       a. Jesus remembered and obeyed God's word.
       b. The temptation in Matt. 4 demonstrates how Christ remembered God's word.
       c. Jesus fulfilled God's command to Adam, just as Adam and Israel failed at it.

IV. How do Christians today remember and obey God's word?
    1. They meditate on God's word daily.
    2. They recognize that this is the means for spreading God's word and presence.

V. What is the role of believers today?
    1. Believers are like priests who pray to God.
    2. Believers are like the "true Israelites living in exile."
    3. In the new world, God will restore his creation and restore his people from exile.
    4. In these days before the new world, Christians are to pray like "new covenant priests" and exiles on earth.

VI. Christians are now spiritual priests.
    1. They fulfill the command God gave Adam.
    2. They serve God in his spiritual temple by . . .
       a. "Learning and teaching God's word";

b. "Praying always";

c. "Being vigilant to keep out unclean moral and spiritual things."

Part 2

___I___ We, as God's people, have already begun to be God's end-time temple where his presence is manifested to the world.

___R___ We are to extend the boundaries of the new garden-temple until Christ returns.

___IR___ All believers are priests and they function as priests by offering up prayers in the sphere of the spiritual temple.

___I___ Saints are also true Israelites who are in exile because they still exist in the exile of this old, fallen world.

___IR___ Believers express their identification with Christ's kingship when they spread the presence of God by living for Christ and speaking his word and unbelievers accept it.

___R___ Certainly, remembering, believing and obeying God's word was crucial to a healthy relationship with God.

___IR___ We also pray as exiled new Israelites, as we live as pilgrims on the old, fallen earth.

___I___ All Christians are now spiritual Levitical priests (in fulfillment of Isa. 66:21).

___R___ Our continual priestly tasks are what the first Adam's were to be: to keep the order and peace of the spiritual sanctuary by learning and teaching God's word, by praying always, and by being vigilant in keeping out unclean moral and spiritual things.

Main Ideas and Details

1. d

2. c

3. "In order to 'proclaim the excellencies' of God (1 Peter 2:9)."

4. Answers will vary, but the central purpose is to provide biblical support for the author's claim in paragraph 1.

5. d

6. c

7. Christ succeeds because he remembers God's Word and obeys it.

8. d

9. d

10. a

Collocations

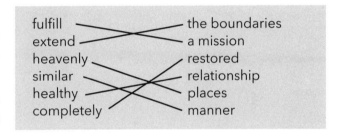

Grammar Focus: Activity 1

The <u>nature of</u> our sacrifices as obedient Adamic-like priests <u>is</u> vitally <u>linked to</u> the <u>idea of</u> expanding the sacred <u>sphere of</u> God's presence in order that others would experience it and <u>come into</u> the sacred temple themselves. Believers are priests in that they <u>serve as</u> <u>mediators between</u> God and the unbelieving world. When unbelievers accept the church's mediating witness, they not only <u>come into</u> God's presence, but they begin to participate themselves as mediating priests who witness. As priests, we should make sure that we ourselves are <u>growing in</u> the <u>experience of</u> the divine presence. When we do not compromise our faith and relationship <u>in God's presence</u> and, consequently, <u>suffer for</u> our unswerving commitment, we are sacrificing ourselves. It is this very sacrifice that God has <u>designed</u> <u>in</u> the new temple to be the means to move unbelievers to believe the church's testimony and to begin to experience God's presence themselves. The "two witnesses" <u>in Revelation</u> 11 <u>offer</u> themselves <u>as</u> sacrifices by <u>suffering</u>

for their faith *as they go throughout the world* and are rejected because of their <u>testimony to</u> Christ.

Grammar Focus: Activity 2

See paragraph 7 of the reading.

Grammar Focus: Activity 3 (possible answers)

(1)	Live	God's presence . . . live *in* God's presence
(2)	Testimony	Christ . . . testimony *of* Christ
(3)	Suffer	our faith . . . suffer *for* our faith
(4)	The idea	salvation . . . the idea *of* salvation
(5)	Prayer directed	God . . . prayer directed *toward* God
(6)	The experience	God's presence . . . the experience *of* God's presence
(7)	Prayer	an activity . . . prayer *as* an activity
(8)	Linked	the temple . . . linked *to* the temple
(9)	Delivered	sin and death . . . delivered *from* sin and death
(10)	New creation	Christ . . . a new creation *in* Christ

Unit 10: Lesson 28

Main Ideas and Details

1. b
2. a
3. The challenge of connecting the Bible to life is bridging the gap between an ancient text and present-day situation.
4. d
5. The category of "ditch" passages.
6. Other passages that "stretch the width of the ditch a bit more."
7. The purpose of paragraph 5 is to introduce the difficulty of applying "canyon" passages.
8. d
9. b
10. b
11. b
12. c
13. Canyon passages.
14. a

Understanding the Reading

_D_ "Even though I walk through the valley of the shadow of death, I will fear no evil, for you are with me" (Ps. 23:4).

_C_ "If his gift for a burnt offering is from the flock, from the sheep or goats, he shall bring a male without blemish, and he shall kill it on the north side of the altar before the LORD, and Aaron's sons the priests shall throw its blood against the sides of the altar" (Lev. 1:10–11).

_D_ "Do not lay up for yourselves treasures on earth, where moth and rust destroy and where thieves break in and steal" (Matt. 6:19).

_D_ "It is not the hearers of the law who are righteous before God, but the doers of the law who will be justified" (Rom. 2:13).

_C_ "If you come across a bird's nest in any tree or on the ground, with young ones or eggs and the mother sitting on the young or on the eggs, you shall not take the mother with the young. You shall let the mother go, but the young you may take for yourself, that it may go well with you, and that you may live long" (Deut. 22:6–7).

_C_ "With what shall I come before the LORD, and bow myself before God on high? Shall I come before him with burnt offerings, with calves a year old?" (Mic. 6:6)

_D_ "Flee from sexual immorality. Every other sin a person commits is outside the body, but the sexually immoral person sins against his own body" (1 Cor. 6:18).

_C_ "You shall season all your grain offerings with salt. You shall not let the salt of the covenant with your God be missing from your grain offering; with all your offerings you shall offer salt" (Lev. 2:13).

_DC_ "No one shall be able to stand against you. The LORD your God will lay the fear of you and the dread of you on all the land that you shall tread, as he promised you" (Deut. 11:25).

Collocations

The difficulty in applying Scripture is that we must bridge the (*hole/divide/area*) between the past and the present. A biblical (*text/language/word*) is situated in history, and while we might think that we can simply draw general and timeless (*customs/principles/conventions*) from it, this is not always so easy. While many of us could offer positive (*instances/events/examples*) of when we applied a passage to a particular situation or life event, we could just as easily offer native examples. Perhaps we encounter difficulty because we try to make a (*instant/direct/primary*) connection from the biblical passage to our own life, hoping to glean concrete (*advice/intelligence/apprehension*) from Scripture. But sometimes the connections between Scripture and life are more indirect, and we must be careful not to force a passage to say what we would like it so say.

Grammar Focus: Activity 1

Question	Statement
How should we apply Scripture to life in the 21st century?	We should apply Scripture to life in the 21st century.
Are there many different ways to apply the same passage?	There are many different ways to apply the same passage.
Can passages from Leviticus be applied to us today?	Passages from Leviticus can be applied to us today.
Are the cleanliness laws of Leviticus relevant for our understanding of sin?	The cleanliness laws of Leviticus are relevant for our understanding of sin.
Does the Old Testament contain some passages that are difficult to interpret?	The Old Testament contains some passages that are difficult to interpret.
Does Emlet distinguish between "canyon" and "ditch" passages?	Emlet distinguishes between "canyon" and "ditch" passages.

Grammar Focus: Activity 2 (possible answers)

1. Should we examine the context of a passage of Scripture before we apply it?

2. Are "ditch" passages always easy to apply to our lives?

3. Have the regulations for the building of the tabernacle been used to encourage others?

4. Can we apply God's Word in concrete contexts?

Learning the Genre (PT) Activity

See the explanations following each of the questions.

Unit 10: Lesson 29

Reading Skill: Logical Arguments

__P__ If work in this broader sense is to be redeemed in our thinking and doing,

__C__ we obviously need a view of the goodness of mundane work.

__P__ To believe that all of life is God's

__C__ opens the door for all types of work to be glorifying to God.

__C__ The dignity of common work is established in the Bible

__P__ not so much by specific proof texts as by the general picture of life that emerges.

Main Ideas and Details

1. c

2. a

3. b

4. d

5. a

6. c

7. a

8. d

9. Answers will vary, but the central purpose of paragraph 9 is to define and describe the role of a "steward."

10. a

Understanding the Reading

Answers for these exercises will vary.

Collocations

The way in which we view our work has (*implications/reasons/inferences*) for how we carry out that work. Various ideas have (*emerged/grown/happened*) with regard to how we should view work done outside the church, but perhaps Luther's notion of Christian work in his *Liberty of the Christian Man* is most helpful to us in a (*rotten/fallen/departed*) world. According to Luther, in a broader (*impression/ way/sense*), all (*honest/direct/proper*) work is equally valuable, for it is all done for the sake of the Lord—the expansion of his kingdom and the glory of his name. Having this view of work encourages us to work passionately and diligently. However, the world encourages us to hold onto social (*changes/distinctions/ separations*) and negative (*positions/attitudes/ sensations*) that accompany our perception of certain kinds of work, such as manual labor. If we have this view of work, we are more likely to work for the wrong reasons—pride, self-fulfillment, materialism, etc. The (*natural/ hereditary/accidental*) Christian response should be to see all work in God's world as being done for his glory and name's sake. Keeping this in mind can push us to carry out even the simplest tasks with sincerity.

Grammar Focus: Activity 1

[Work] should be looked upon—not as a necessary drudgery to be undergone for the purpose of making money, but as a way of life <u>in which the nature of man should find its proper exercise and delight and so fulfill itself to the glory of God</u>. . . .

What is the Christian understanding of work? . . . I should like to put before you two or three propositions arising out of the doctrinal position <u>which I stated at the beginning</u>: namely, <u>that work is the natural exercise and function of man</u>—the creature <u>who is made in the image of his Creator</u>. . . .

The first, stated briefly, is <u>that work is not, primarily, a thing</u> <u>one does to live</u>, but the thing <u>one lives to do</u>. It is, or it should be, the full expression of the worker's faculties, the thing <u>in which he finds spiritual, mental, and bodily satisfaction</u>, and the medium <u>in which he offers himself to God</u>.

Now the consequences of this are not merely <u>that the work should be performed</u> <u>under decent living and working conditions</u>. That is a point <u>we have begun to grasp</u>, and it is a perfectly sound point. But we have tended to concentrate on it to the exclusion of other considerations <u>far more revolutionary</u>.

1. "A way of life," "the doctrinal position," "the creature," "a thing," "the medium," "a point," and "considerations."

2. Yes, it was necessary to follow "the thing" with a relative clause because we do not know what "the thing" means. The relative clause gives specific content to that noun phrase.

Grammar Focus: Activity 2 (possible answers)

1. All work is done in service of God, who alone is the owner of all work.

2. All honest work is biblical, which means that all of our work should be done in the light of Scripture.

3. Our work, which sometimes seems unimportant and yet is judged by God, is valuable.

Unit 10: Lesson 30

Main Ideas and Details

1. d

2. c

3. A cogent critique of secularism and a distinctly biblical alternative.

4. a

5. c

6. The purpose of the final sentence is to show the logical outworking of the secular claim that God is not necessary for solving "the human problem."

7. False: the second issue that faces the biblical counseling movement is the need to address questions touching on human motivation, in both theory and practice.

8. a

9. c

10. b

11. Each of the elements in the list at the end of paragraph 9 is an example of something that allegedly "determines" a person.

12. b

13. He says that each of the issues is a test, a challenge, and a promise.

Understanding the Reading

__6__ Our rejection of secularism has been in the headlines. The subtleties of the biblical response to secular knowledge have been in the fine print.

__3__ Biblical counseling has resisted seeing people as determined—whether by heredity, the sins of others, organic imbalances, poor models, unmet needs, mental forces imposing on us as "illness," or demonic inhabitants.

__5__ But we also need to analyze a different audience and expend some legitimate effort in reaching the educational wing of Christendom.

__1__ Biblical counseling operates within the worldview of the Bible, with the Bible in hand.

__2__ Biblical counseling has rightly stressed behavior—love and good works—as the simple and accessible evidence of true change.

__2__ We depart from the Bible if we ignore motives and drift toward an externalistic view of man.

__1__ Secular pyschologies remain major competitors with the church.

Collocations

If we are to address the crucial (*issue/outcome/ trouble*) of how we can approach the "cure of souls" biblically, we must begin by finding out how secular (*premises/assumptions/precepts*) have been embraced and practiced by the church. Building a cogent, biblical (*review/ examination/critique*) of these assumptions is a good starting point for re-envisioning our practice of counseling in the body of Christ. Of course, taking up a biblical (*portrayal/ picture/rendering*) of humanity as made in God's image will introduce several (*logical/ rational/coherent*) implications and ensuing questions: how much can we retain from secular theories of psychology? What notions of secular restoration need to be exchanged for the biblical (*truth/fact/case*) of regeneration in the Spirit? These are pressing questions.

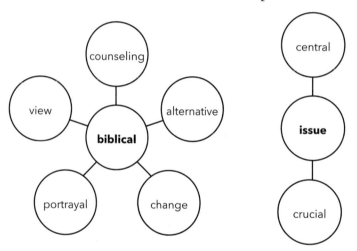

Fig. AK.8. Collocation Diagram 9 Completed

Grammar Focus: Activity 1

In a <u>thoughtful</u> and <u>thought-provoking</u> <u>personal</u> letter, John Carter of Rosemead Graduate School, one of the <u>leading</u> critics of <u>nouthetic</u> counseling, commented that <u>nouthetic</u> counseling could only speak to audiences "who already shared Jay Adams's perspective." There was little that could be done creatively within the "radically <u>biblical</u> perspective" because everything such a <u>limited</u> perspective could say had been said already either explicitly or implicitly. As a movement we were likely to stagnate into rehashing among ourselves the thoughts of one man.

Carter's words are <u>sobering</u> and <u>challenging</u>. If he is <u>right</u>, we are less than <u>biblical</u>. For the Bible portrays itself as a fountain of life, granting <u>fresh</u> wisdom to all who ask and dig, producing ministry that changes lives significantly. If he is <u>right</u>, then this article has been <u>wrong</u>, and it is a <u>pathetic</u> dream for me to lift up my eyes and see the whole world waiting. But I think Carter is <u>wrong</u>. Our vision has always far <u>outstripped</u> our attainment because it is a <u>biblical</u> vision. If we are indeed <u>*biblical*</u>, then the <u>foundational</u> presupposition—radically <u>biblical</u> counseling—will generate a dynamic of life, growth, and expansion, not stagnation. It will liberate, not limit.

Two adjectives that seem to communicate something important to the author's message are "sobering" and "challenging." These adjectives convey that Carter's critique should be taken seriously.

Grammar Focus: Activity 2

Answers for this exercise will vary.

APPENDIX 1

Theological Chart for TE Units

Who are we?

Creatures made in the image of the triune, speaking God

What is truth?

The speech of God: the revelation of God in his Word (special revelation)

What is wrong?

Sin, which has corrupted the whole world, including our minds

How is it made right?

Through the atoning sacrifice of Christ, who fulfills all of God's promises

How are we saved?

By union with the person of Christ through the power of the Holy Spirit

Where have we been?

Many places in the last two thousand years, but always with the core of our faith: God's grace in Christ Jesus

Do we still need the OT?

Yes, since the OT is about Christ and is part of the unified message of God's redemptive plan

Who is Jesus?

The fully human and fully divine, resurrected Son of God

Where does the church fit?

We are all, as one people, the body of Christ, united in faith

How then shall we live?

As if Christ's lordship changes everything, because it *has*

APPENDIX 2

Punctuation

While we did not cover punctuation in this textbook, it is very important in clarifying sentence structure and even affects meaning. Below we have summarized the rules of the most common marks of punctuation, and illustrated these rules with theological examples.

Commas

- RULE 1: Use a comma before a conjunction that joins main clauses.[1]
  - » Many of the Israelites perished in the wilderness, but God always preserved a remnant in order to uphold His promise to Abraham.
  - » We must always take prayer seriously, for Jesus told his disciples not only *that* they should pray but also *how* they should pray.
- RULE 2: Use a comma after an introductory phrase.
  - » In search of eternal life, the rich young ruler asked Jesus what he had to do in order to achieve his goal (Matt. 19:23).
  - » Without exception, Jesus' teaching never fails to cause the rise and fall of many people in every generation (Luke 2:34).
  - » In spite of all his learning, Paul persecuted the church.

- RULE 3: Use a comma before and after non-restrictive clauses.
  - » In a *nonrestrictive clause*, the meaning of a noun is not fundamentally changed, or "restricted," by the relative clause that follows it. The clause simply adds information:
    - It was the task of Martin Luther, who is the most notable figure of the Reformation, to challenge the tradition of the established church.
    - Special <u>revelation, which God revealed through Scripture, is</u> necessary for salvation.
  - » When the relative clause following a noun provides information that restricts the meaning of the noun, then we *do not* use commas. This is a restrictive clause. We must read what follows that word in order to understand its meaning:
    - "Hypotheses or interpretations <u>that on careful analysis are found to contradict Scripture</u> can have no standing in Christian thought."[2]
- RULE 4: Use a comma before and after a transitional phrase.
  - » We must remember, then, that Scripture is trustworthy because it is the revelation of a trustworthy God.

---

1. Rules on comma use are taken from H. Ramsey Fowler and Jane E. Aaron's *The Little, Brown Handbook*, 11ᵗʰ ed. (New York: Longman, 2010), 422–43. Only the main rules are covered here. For details, see the pages referenced.

2. John M. Frame, *The Doctrine of the Knowledge of God*, A Theology of Lordship (Phillipsburg, NJ: P&R, 1987), 65–66. We are not talking about any hypothesis or interpretation, only those ones that are found to contradict Scripture.

» The apostles knew that Scripture, after all, is the only trustworthy interpretation of reality.

- RULE 5: Use commas between items in a series.
  » Many New Testament scholars debate the origin, author, and validity of apocryphal gospel accounts.[3]
  » There were three choices presented to David: his people could suffer from famine for three years, flee from their enemies for three months, or suffer from pestilence for three days (2 Sam. 24:10–14).

- RULE 6: Use a comma to separate coordinated adjectives.[4]
  » Martin Luther spent many long, difficult years in hiding from papal authorities.
  » Calvin was always careful to remind his readers that humans are sinful, depraved creatures.

- RULE 7: Use a comma after introducing a quotation.
  » In Gen. 1:26, God says, "Let us make man in our image, after our likeness."
  » Oliver Crisp notes, "For the most part, Calvin was not a fan of speculative theology, which he often rails against."[5]

- RULE 8: Use a comma to prevent misreading.
  » UNCLEAR: Soon after the seminary was founded by J. G. Machen.
  » CLEAR: Soon after, the seminary was founded by J. G. Machen.

Do Not Use Commas...

- To separate a subject from its verb
  » Incorrect: Many theologians, returned from the synod with hopes for change.

- To separate a pair of elements joined by a coordinating conjunction

» Incorrect: Many theologians questioned if, and when Luther would return.

Semicolons

- RULE 1: Use semicolons between two highly related independent clauses.[6] Conjunctive adverbs or transitional expressions are often used after the semicolon.
  » The fear present in the Israelites as they fled from Egypt is often underrated; after all, they were being chased by one of the mightiest armies that history has witnessed.
  » Jesus and his disciples wasted no time; they gathered into the boat and pushed off from the shore.

- RULE 2: Use semicolons to separate complex items in a series, especially when commas are used within items.
  » There are many things to consider when planning a Bible study: what day and time to meet; how many people will attend, and at what level of maturity they are in the faith; which book or passage of the Bible to study; and whether breakout sessions are necessary.
  » God's revelation comes in various forms: in speech, particularly from God to His prophets and apostles; in writing, through the inscription of the Ten Commandments and, later, of the whole canon of the Old and New Testaments; and in proclamation and preaching by His servants.

Colons

- RULE 1: Use a colon after an independent clause to introduce a list, an example, or a quotation.
  » There are several elements to the Christian life: prayer, Christian fellowship, repentance, and service.
  » Martin Luther is reported to have said

---

3. The comma after the final element in the list is optional, but it is good to use a comma if it more clearly distinguishes the elements in the list from other elements in the sentence.

4. Coordinate adjectives are present when two or more adjectives "modify the same word equally," and when their order can be switched without altering the meaning (for example, a *driven, dedicated* student). See Fowler and Aaron, *The Little, Brown Handbook*, 433.

5. Oliver D. Crisp, *Retrieving Doctrine: Essays in Reformed Theology* (Downers Grove, IL: IVP, 2010), 6.

6. Rules on semicolon use are also taken from Fowler and Aaron, *The Little, Brown Handbook*, 443–51.

many things concerning the necessity of the church: "Anyone who is to find Christ must first find the church. How could anyone know where Christ is and what faith is in him unless he knew where his believers are?"[7]

- RULE 2: Use a colon to introduce an answer to an implied question.
  - » There is only one thing required for salvation: faith in the son of God.
  - » Every person is ultimately searching for one thing: reconciliation with God.

Apostrophes

We use apostrophes to indicate possession and to show a contraction. If you have a plural noun that you wish to make possessive, place the apostrophe after the final "s."

- RULE 1: Use an apostrophe to show possession for a noun.
  - » Paul's understanding of justification is heavily debated.
  - » The Pharisees' pride was often condemned in Jesus' parables.

- RULE 2: Use an apostrophe to show that you have contracted two words.
  - » It's difficult to begin explaining eschatology.
  - » There's little chance that the West will restrain its use of visual media.
  - » He didn't have a reason for coming to class late.

NOTE: DO NOT use an apostrophe to show possession for a noun that is not animate (see the use of "its" in reference to "the West" above).

Hyphens

Hyphens have various uses, but the one most common to graduate level writing is linking parts of a compound adjective.[8]

- RULE 1: Use hyphens to link words of a compound adjective before a noun.
  - » The synod-supported decrees usually carried weight throughout the Roman Empire.
  - » The church-generated funds were enthusiastically supported by Pope Nicholas V.

- RULE 2: Use a hyphen to stand in for a repeated word.
  - » Throughout his term, the Roman Emperor both under- and overestimated the power of the early church.
  - » The church was to have a circular-, cross-, or rectangular-patterned layout.

En Dashes

- RULE 1: Use en dashes to link verses in a Scripture quotation.[9]
  - » The calling of Matthew is an interesting pericope in the first gospel (Matt. 9:9–13).
  - » Paul is clear about non-believers having no excuse for disbelief (Rom. 2:1–6).

- RULE 2: Use en dashes to link page numbers (even in footnotes) or dates.
  - » On pages 61–84 of *The Unfolding Mystery*, Clowney discusses the heir of the promise.
  - » In the time span of about twenty-five years (1984–2011), several kinds of the New International Version of the Bible were published.

Em Dashes

- RULE: Use an em dash to set off interrupting elements or to show a change in the flow of ideas.[10]
  - » We studied five books of the Bible—the most difficult ones—and then presented our findings to the class.
  - » Suffering—the idea of which is never comfortable and always disturbing—is presented in Scripture as one of the tools that God uses to strengthen our faith.

---

7. *Sermons of Martin Luther*, ed. John Nicholas Lenker, trans. John Nicholas Lenker et al. (Grand Rapids, MI: Baker, 1995), 1:169–70.

8. This can be inserted by pressing the button for the minus sign on the number pad. Rules for hyphen use are taken from Anne Stilman's *Grammatically Correct*, 2nd ed. (Cincinnati, OH: Writer's Digest Books, 2010), 137–40.

9. An en dash can be inserted by pressing Ctrl + the minus sign on the number pad.

10. An em dash can be inserted by pressing Ctrl + Alt + the minus sign on the number pad.

Punctuation with Quotation Marks

- RULE 1: When a quotation is followed by parentheses, ending punctuation goes OUTSIDE the quotation marks.
  - » Bavinck writes that "mystery is the lifeblood of dogmatics" (29).

- RULE 2: When a quotation is followed by a footnote, ending punctuation goes INSIDE the quotation marks.
  - » Bavinck writes that "mystery is the lifeblood of dogmatics."[11]

- RULE 3: Semicolons and colons *that you insert* always go OUTSIDE the quotation marks.
  - » Bavinck wrote that "mystery is the lifeblood of dogmatics"; it is mystery that keeps dogmatics alive.[12]

Parentheses

- RULE 1: Use parentheses to enclose phrases or clauses that add important, but not essential, information.[13]
  - » The enormous size of St. Peter's (over 160,000 sq. ft.) draws a huge crowd of tourists every day.

- RULE 2: Though it is optional, you can use parentheses to enclose numbers in a list that occurs in the middle of text.
  - » There are several things to consider when studying Scripture: (1) your understanding of language; (2) the goal of your studies; and (3) the method you will use to discover meaning, your hermeneutic.

Brackets

- RULE: Use brackets to indicate comments or changes you have made to a quotation.[14]
  - » "The dogmatic difference between these views [i.e., that the earth was created out of nothing, or was created out of chaos] turns on what is entailed by the divine fiat in the act of creation, not whether God has, in some sense, created the temporal world."[15]
  - » ORIGINAL: "This idea that God orders all things that come to pass, such that no event occurs without his concurrently bringing it about in conjunction with mundane creaturely causes, is usually referred to as *meticulous providence*."[16]
    - The "idea that [He] orders all things that come to pass …"
    - "Without his concurrently bringing [every event] about," God, as the Reformed tradition suggests, would cease to be omnipotent.

---

11. Herman Bavinck, *Reformed Dogmatics*, vol. 2, *God and Creation*, ed. John Bolt, trans. John Vriend (Grand Rapids, MI: Baker, 2004), 29.

12. Bavinck, *God and Creation*, 29.

13. See Fowler and Aaron, *The Little, Brown Handbook*, 472–73. Parenthetical material includes "explanations, digressions, and examples that may be helpful or interesting but are not essential to meaning."

14. Ibid., 474–75.

15. Crisp, *Retrieving Doctrine*, 10.

16. Ibid., 13.

APPENDIX 3

Introductory Theological Texts

What follows is a list of introductory level theological texts that would be a good starting point for building your theological reading skills and vocabulary. Each book is marked for the theological genre in which it fits.

Beale, G. K. *The Morality of God in the Old Testament.* Christian Answers to Hard Questions. Philadelphia: Westminster Seminary Press, 2013. (Biblical Studies)

Bray, Gerald. *Augustine on the Christian Life: Transformed by the Power of God.* Theologians on the Christian Life. Wheaton, IL: Crossway, 2015. (Church History)

Clowney, Edmund P. *The Unfolding Mystery: Discovering Christ in the Old Testament.* 2nd ed. Phillipsburg, NJ: P&R, 2013. (Biblical Studies)

Duguid, Iain M. *Is Jesus in the Old Testament?* Christian Answers to Hard Questions. Philadelphia: Westminster Seminary Press, 2013. (Biblical Studies)

Edgar, William. *Schaeffer on the Christian Life: Countercultural Spirituality.* Theologians on the Christian Life. Wheaton, IL: Crossway, 2013. (Church History)

Frame, John M. *Systematic Theology: An Introduction to Christian Belief.* Phillipsburg, NJ: P&R, 2013. (Systematic Theology)

Grudem, Wayne. *Systematic Theology: An Introduction to Biblical Doctrine.* Grand Rapids, MI: Zondervan, 2000. (Systematic Theology)

Hughes, R. Kent. *The Pastor's Book: A Comprehensive and Practical Guide to Pastoral Ministry.* Wheaton, IL: Crossway, 2015. (Practical Theology)

Oliphint, K. Scott. *Should You Believe in God?* Christian Answers to Hard Questions. Philadelphia: Westminster Seminary Press, 2013. (Apologetics)

———. *Covenantal Apologetics: Principles and Practice in Defense of Our Faith.* Wheaton, IL: Crossway, 2013. (Apologetics)

Powlison, David. *Seeing with New Eyes: Counseling and the Human Condition through the Lens of Scripture.* Phillipsburg, NJ: P&R, 2003. (Practical Theology—Counseling)

Poythress, Vern S. *Christian Interpretations of Genesis 1.* Christian Answers to Hard Questions. Philadelphia: Westminster Seminary Press, 2013. (Biblical Studies)

———. *God-Centered Biblical Interpretation.* Phillipsburg, NJ: P&R, 1991. (Biblical Studies)

———. *What Are Spiritual Gifts?* Basics of the Faith. Phillipsburg, NJ: P&R, 2010. (Biblical Studies)

Tripp, Paul David. *Instruments in the Redeemer's Hands: People in Need of Change Helping People in Need of Change.* Phillipsburg, NJ: P&R, 2002. (Practical Theology—Counseling)

Wilken, Robert Louis. *The Spirit of Early Christian Thought: Seeking the Face of God.* New Haven, CT: Yale University Press, 2003. (Church History)

Index of Subjects and Names

Adams, Jay E., 303, 309, 352

adjectives, 3, 6–7, 18, 25–26, 39, 50, 78–79, 101, 108, 158, 167–68, 177–78, 190, 204, 213–14, 308–9, 322, 336, 353, 358–59

adverbs, 6, 18, 50, 101, 108, 167–68, 187, 199, 223, 308, 322, 358

analogical thinking, 36, 38–41, 44, 47, 224, 283, 315–16, 325, 339

apologetics, vii, ix, 1, 4, 7–9, 11, 22, 31–32, 46, 72, 83, 119, 191, 216, 219, 244, 247, 288, 291, 314, 335, 361

appositives, 6, 57–58, 318

articles, 6–7, 77–79, 102, 198

Augustine, x, 78, 105, 198–99, 202–3, 206, 245–46, 335–36, 361

autonomy, 84–87

Bavinck, Herman, 21–23, 26, 45, 233, 260–62, 360

Beale, G. K., 64, 121–22, 154, 160, 163, 165, 168–69, 171, 173–74, 178, 267–68, 270, 274, 330, 361

Berkhof, Louis, 142–43, 244–45, 252, 254, 343–44

biblical studies, vii–ix, 4–5, 7, 83, 118–19, 126, 166, 191, 219, 244–45, 248, 288, 291, 325, 361

Calvin, John, 21, 54–57, 73, 78, 177, 206, 223–24, 245–46, 317, 339–40, 344, 358

Carson, D. A., 45, 74–76, 79

Chadwick, Henry, 198, 335

church history, viii–x, 5, 7, 83, 183–84, 191–92, 197–98, 202, 219, 244–48, 288, 291, 361

Clowney, Edmund P., 83, 111–12, 114, 117–19, 154, 162, 252, 257, 259–60, 265, 267, 325, 359, 361

comparative structures, 50–51, 147

complex sentences, 18, 25, 39, 50, 68, 77, 100, 147

Creator-creature distinction, 13–18, 25, 35, 39, 44, 73, 245, 313–15

ecclesiology, viii, 343–44

Emlet, Michael R., 280, 282, 286, 349

Frame, John M., x, 4, 8, 13–15, 17, 35, 44, 64–71, 81, 84–85, 95, 97, 99, 101, 244, 247, 251, 279, 288, 319, 357, 361

Gaffin, Richard B., Jr., 45, 53, 55, 114, 119, 137, 154, 219, 220–24, 340

genres, 4, 7, 83, 119, 121, 126, 191–92, 197, 244–47, 279, 288, 290–91, 314, 325, 335, 343, 350, 361

genre traits, 119, 121, 192, 244, 247, 291

Goldsworthy, Graeme, 109, 154, 156–59

inference, 327

infinitives, 6, 39, 57, 116, 158–59, 167, 177, 223, 241, 285

interrogative form, 285

justification, viii, 4, 144, 191–92, 220, 223, 225–26, 228, 237, 243–44, 296, 332, 339–40, 341, 359

Keller, Timothy, 163, 288–89, 292

logical arguments, 293, 350

logical coherence, 119

MacCulloch, Diarmaid, 12, 83, 197–99, 201–2, 204

Machen, J. G., 57, 78, 358

main idea, xi, 5, 7, 13, 15–17, 23, 25, 38, 48, 56, 67, 76, 83–85, 87–88, 107, 115, 119, 121, 128–29, 135–36, 138, 156, 166, 187, 210–11, 240, 244, 248, 262, 272, 291, 293, 297–98

modal verbs, 6, 116–18, 130, 147, 168, 199, 285, 328

Moo, Douglas, 83, 144

multi-clause sentences, 7, 299

Murray, John, 220, 222, 234, 237, 239–40, 243, 252, 340–42

Noll, Mark, 207

noun clauses, 6, 148, 177–78, 189, 203, 223, 333

noun modification, 6, 77, 203–4

noun phrases, 6, 25–26, 39, 50, 57, 68, 99, 108, 148, 177, 189–91, 203–4, 223, 334, 336, 351

Oliphint, K. Scott, 4, 8, 11, 22, 31–32, 46, 64, 81, 90–91, 216, 361
outlining, 5, 267, 311

paragraph coherence, 85–86, 235, 244, 247, 291
paragraph development, xi, 18, 24, 83, 86, 165, 188, 191, 244, 252, 306, 334
paragraph unity, viii, 86–87, 251, 263, 345
parallelism, 210, 328
paraphrasing, 27, 84, 268
participles, 7, 26, 39, 57, 131, 213, 241–43, 263, 285
passive voice, 6, 39–41
Pelikan, Jaroslav, 335
Piper, John, 27
Powlison, David, 280, 292, 302–3, 306, 309, 361
Poythress, Vern, x–xi, 3, 8–9, 11, 39, 44–45, 48, 53, 65, 103, 160, 267, 361
practical theology, viii–ix, 5, 7, 279–80, 287–92, 302, 311, 350, 361
prepositions, 6–7, 15, 25, 39, 78, 139, 147–48, 158, 190, 204, 223–24, 285, 336, 339
pronouns, 5–6, 17, 39, 56–57, 86, 97, 99, 107, 114–15, 129, 166, 177, 198, 202–3, 283–84

redemptive history, 86, 97, 99, 102–4, 108, 111, 321, 324
relative clauses, 6, 57–58, 147–48, 177, 204, 299, 336, 351, 357
revelation, vii, 14, 18, 22–26, 35–37, 40, 44, 47, 56, 58, 68, 73, 84–86, 108, 111, 119, 153–54, 178, 183, 189, 196, 216, 245–46, 267, 279, 285–86, 292, 313–14, 316, 319–21, 323, 332, 347, 357–58
rhetoric, 7, 86, 203–4, 336
Ryken, Leland, 294, 296–98

sanctification, viii, 111, 187–88, 190, 213, 220, 223, 237, 239–40, 242–44, 334, 342

stance, 5, 168, 198–99, 335
subject and predicate agreement, x–xi, 3– 4, 6–7, 14, 17–19, 25, 35, 38, 50, 54, 68, 72–73, 76, 78, 81, 85, 87, 98–100, 120, 138, 143, 162, 168, 174, 183–84, 198, 211, 214, 223, 225, 247, 259–60, 263–64, 283, 285– 86, 288, 293–94, 310, 313, 319, 335, 338, 343–44
suffixes, 6, 100–102
summarizing, 5, 236
systematic theology, viii–x, 5, 7, 21, 36–37, 64, 83, 95, 99, 101, 126, 142–43, 162, 196, 234, 244–48, 251, 254, 288, 291, 343, 361

that clauses, 148, 177, 263, 285
theological English, iii, vii–ix, xi, 3–4, 6–7, 18, 25, 39, 50, 57, 68, 77, 100, 147, 157, 299, 355
Tipton, Lane G., 83, 216, 226, 228, 231–32
topic, 5, 7, 15–16, 48, 76, 83, 87–88, 99, 130, 146–47, 188, 244–48, 272, 291, 310, 334, 340
Trinity, the, ix–xi, 8, 11, 18, 35–36, 39, 53, 57, 73, 163, 196, 262, 313, 317–18
Trueman, Carl R., 4, 83, 125, 183–84, 186–87, 191–92, 196–98, 206
Turretin, Francis, 95, 234

Van Til, Cornelius, 14, 16, 18, 29, 35–40, 57, 64, 81, 91, 196, 314–17
verb tense, 6, 68–71, 77, 102, 130–32, 147, 168, 326
Vos, Geerhardus, 64, 96, 119, 154, 244

Waltke, Bruce K., 105, 163, 180
Welch, Edward, 290, 310
Westminster Confession of Faith, 53, 64, 226, 228, 231–32, 247, 264, 340, 345
Witmer, Timothy, 289–90
word families, 108
Wright, N. T., 64–71, 288, 318–19